ST. CYRIL OF ALEXANDRIA

THE CHRISTOLOGICAL CONTROVERSY

OF ALEXANDRIA

M. CAREY

St. Cyril of Alexandria

THE CHRISTOLOGICAL CONTROVERSY

Its History, Theology, and Texts

by

JOHN A. McGUCKIN

ST VLADIMIR'S SEMINARY PRESS
CRESTWOOD, NEW YORK 10707
2004

Library of Congress Cataloging-in-Publication Data

McGuckin, John Anthony.
St. Cyril of Alexandria : the Christological controversy : its history, theology, and texts / by John A. McGuckin.
p. cm.
Originally published: Leiden ; New York : E.J. Brill, 1994, in series: Supplements to Vigiliae Christianae ; v. 23.
Includes bibliographical references and index.
ISBN 0–88141–259–7 (alk. paper)
1. Jesus Christ—History of doctrines—Early church, ca. 30–600. 2. Cyril, Saint, Patriarch of Alexandria, ca. 370–444. I. Title: Saint Cyril of Alexandria. II. Cyril, Saint, Patriarch of Alexandria, ca. 370–444. Selections. English. 2004. III. Title.
BT198.M3994 2004
273'.5—dc22

2004004375

ST VLADIMIR'S SEMINARY PRESS
575 Scarsdale Road, Crestwood, NY 10707
1–800–204–2665

ISBN 0–88141–259–7

PRINTED IN THE UNITED STATES OF AMERICA

Ἀφιεροῦται
Εἰς τὴν προσφιλεστάτην σύζυγόν μου
Εἰρήνην

Let us keep the title 'Pharoah', for it conveys well both the power of the bishop of Alexandria and that imperious and vehement character we see in Cyril himself, although all this energy is tempered, one must say, by a christian grandeur of spirit and channelled by a mind of genius. In the history of dogma Cyril's role can only be compared with that of Athanasius, and St. Augustine is the only other figure in the history of theology who is his equal in terms of the authority afforded to his teachings. Standing against Origenism, and against the Antiochenes, he represents a definitive theology, even more so than the Cappadocian Fathers.

—P. Battifol, *La Littérature Grecque*

Let Your Holiness be assured that we follow the opinions of the holy Fathers in all things, especially our blessed and all-renowned Father Athanasius. We refuse to differ from them in any respect. Let no one doubt this.

—Cyril of Alexandria, *Letter to John of Antioch*

It is one and the same Holy Spirit, which the Fathers at Nicaea had within them as they defined the faith, which was in the soul and voice of our most holy and venerable Father the Archbishop Cyril when he dictated this for the correction of the errors that the reverend Nestorius introduced to the church.

—Bishop Hermogenes of Rhinocourouros,
Acclamation at the Council of Ephesus

CONTENTS

PREFACE

In the ten years since I first wrote *St. Cyril of Alexandria and the Christological Controversy*, there has been a considerable renewal of interest in the teachings of this giant of patristic theology. Several closely argued word studies and doctoral dissertations have been added to the ever-accumulating evidence of his masterly command of biblical, christological, soteriological, and sacramental theology. New collections of translated texts have also appeared (Russell, 2000), amplifying those of Wickham (1983), McEnerney (1987), and myself (1994), thus allowing the English-speaking reader to access more of his *opus*.

What had been the constant belief of the Eastern Churches—namely that St. Cyril represented a "seal" over all the other Fathers (that is the *sphragis*, or authoritative stamp that capped them)—has come to be a perspective shared more widely in European theological scholarship, which had unquestionably been hostile to him, both doctrinally and historically, in most commonly available treatments throughout the late nineteenth and twentieth centuries. I have reflected this extending interest in Cyril's achievements by updating the list of Cyrilline studies in the bibliography.

I am delighted that St. Vladimir's Press is offering a new printing of this book. My work was designed from the outset as a student-friendly introduction to the fascinating events surrounding the Council of Ephesus (431), as well as a serious theological reassessment of Cyrilline theology. Brill of Leiden first produced my text in a very fine cased library edition, but this paperback version suits my initial vision for it as a popular textbook. It was meant to be usable and useful: not a definitive "last word," but more an argument for what patristic theology looked like in full swing, as well as a major gathering of the primary texts to allow readers to research material and form their own opinions. Besides being an introduction to major events in christology and church history of the fifth century, it is (and was by design meant to be) an introduction to the contextual exegesis of patristic writings.

I hope that a new range of readers will be attracted to the story and find this book illuminating—discovering in the process the inner vitality of Orthodox christology and patristic thought. Theology in the hands of the great masters exceeds a desiccated "quest for accuracies"; it becomes a spiritual quest after the divine truth that liberates and transfigures, and thereby validates its own authenticity. Cyril himself understood this with great clarity, and the issue certainly retains its importance in the contemporary scholarly environment.

Fr. John A. McGuckin
January 2004, New York
Feast of Saints Athanasius
and Cyril of Alexandria

ABBREVIATIONS

AB	Analecta Bollandiana.
ACO	Acta Conciliorum Oecumenicorum, Ed. E. Schwartz, Berlin, Leipzig, 1927f.
BiNJ	Bijdragen van de Philosophische en Theologische Faculteiten der NederlandscheJezuiten. Roermond & Maastricht. 1938f.
BLE	Bulletin de Littérature Écclesiastique. Toulouse.
CHR	The Catholic Historical Review, Washington, 1915f.
CSCO	Corpus Scriptorum Christianorum Orientalium. Paris, Louvain.
DCB	Dictionary of Christian Biography, London, 1877.
DHGE	Dictionnaire d'Histoire et de Géographie Écclesiastique. Paris 1912f.
Dom Stud.	Dominican Studies. Oxford.
DOP	Dumbarton Oaks Papers. Cambridge, Mass.
DTC	Dictionnaire de Théologie Catholique. Paris 1909f.
EE	Estudios Ecclesiasticos. Madrid. 1922f.
EO	Echos D'Orient. Paris, 1897–1942.
E Ph	Ekklesiastikos Pharos. Alexandria.
Eph Th Louv.	Ephemerides Theologicae Lovaniensis. Louvain.
E.T.	English Translation.
GOTR	Greek Orthodox Theological Review. Brookline, Mass.
HCO	Histoire des Conciles Oecuméniques. Ed. G. Dumerque. Paris.
Hefele.	C.J. Hefele (with annotations by Dom. Leclercq, Histoire des Conciles, Vol.2. pt.1. (Council of Ephesus), Paris, 1908.
ITQ	Irish Theological Quarterly, Maynooth.
JEH	Journal of Ecclesiastical History, Cambridge.
JTS	Journal of Theological Studies. Oxford.
Kopt. Akt.	Koptische Akten zum ephesinischen Konzil vom Jahre 431. Transl. W. Kraatz. TU 26.2.

LXX	Septuagintal version. (LXX after a biblical reference does not signify Cyril's use of the Septuagint, which is his habitual text, rather those instances where the LXX version departs substantively from the Masoretic text of the OT).
MSR	Mélanges de Science Religieuse. Lille.
MTZ	Munchener Theologische Zeitschrift. Munich.
MUS	Le Muséon. Louvain.
NRT	Nouvelle Revue Théologique. Tournai.
OC	Orientalia Christiana. Rome.
OCA	Orientalia Christiana Analecta. Rome.
OCP	Orientalia Christiana Periodica, Rome.
OECT	Oxford Early Christian Texts.
Or Chr.	Oriens Christianus. Leipzig 1901–1941, Wiesbaden 1953f.
PBR	Patristic and Byzantine Review. New York.
PL	Patrologiae Cursus Completus. Ed. J.P. Migne, Series Latina, Paris, 1844–1855.
PG	Ibid. Series Graeca, Paris 1857–1866.
PO	Patrologia Orientalis.
RAC	Reallexicon für Antike und Christentum.
REB	Revue des Études Byzantines. Paris.
RES	Revista Espanola de Teologia. Madrid 1941f.
Rev Et Aug.	Revue des Études Augustiniennes. Paris.
Rev SR	Revue des Sciences Religieuses. Strasbourg, Paris.
Rev Thom.	Revue Thomiste. Paris.
RHE	Revue d'Histoire Écclesiastique.
RIT	Revue Internationale de Théologie.
ROC	Revue de L'Orient Chrétien. Paris.
RSPT	Revue des Sciences Philosophiques et Théologiques. Paris.
RSR	Recherches de Science Religieuse. Paris.
SC	Sources Chrétiennes. Paris.
SCA	Studies in Christian Antiquity. Washington,1941f.
SCH	Studies in Church History. Cambridge.
Schol.	Scholastik. Freiburg.
SJT	Scottish Journal of Theology.
ST	Studi e Testi. Rome.
StC	Studia Catholica. Roermond & Nijmegen, 1924f.
Stud. Pat.	Studia Patristica. (TU 63–64,78–81, Berlin, 1957–

	62) & Oxford 1987f. (Proceedings of the Oxford Internat. Conferences on Patristic Studies, 1987f).
TU	Texte und Untersuchungen zur Geschichte der altchristlichen Literatur. Leipzig, Berlin, Oxford.
ZKG	Zeitschrift für Kirchengeschichte. Gotha-Stuttgart.
ZNW	Zeitschrift für die Neutestamentliche Wissenschaft und die Kunde der alteren Kirche, Berlin.

CHAPTER ONE

THE CONTEXT OF THE EPHESUS CRISIS

1. THE EARLY LIFE AND WRITINGS OF CYRIL, 378–428

Cyril of Alexandria was not only one of the finest christian theologians of his day, he also stands out in the ranks of the greatest patristic writers of all generations as perhaps the most powerful exponent of christology the church has known and, after Athanasius, the writer who has had the greatest historical influence on the articulation of this most central and seminal aspect of christian doctrine. When one adds to this the political aspects of his life, the fact that he occupied the throne of one of the most important sees of the Byzantine Oecumene and was, by virtue of that office, in the select ranks of the most powerful men in the world of his time, then the extraordinary range of his life and work stands out all the more vividly and in relief. Cyril is, without doubt, a profound and controversial figure.

For the Eastern church he is the father of Orthodox christology par excellence; a great exegete as well as a spiritual guide, a saint in the full range of his doctrine and his life's energy and focus, the two aspects being inseparable in the Orthodox understanding of the nature of theology and sanctity. Much modern work on christology and church history is, however, loud in his criticism, yet frequently that criticism only lightly masks the theological contentions from which it springs. Much the same can be observed even in his own lifetime. He was regarded by some of his episcopal colleagues, though a minority it must be added, as a great heretical manipulator of the church. By most others he was regarded as the greatest theologian living, and by many as a living saint and defender of the truth in a time of crisis in the manner of a new Athanasius or Gregory Nazianzen. He was capable, both in terms of his political manoeuvres as well as his theology, of stirring up violent feelings for and against him, wherever he went. In itself this is a testimony to the extraordinary vigour of his mind and his character. Small men do not create such large effects. No less than his enemies admitted that his intellectual work could not be disregarded, and even bitter opponents such as Theodoret of

Cyr came in the end to adopt much of the argument for which Cyril had been pressing, even expressing it in Cyrilline terms which they had earlier denounced.[1] Because of this, since he represents the central Eastern tradition of christological sprituality, and because he is a conciliar symbol, like Athanasius, over whom theological and historical disagreement endures in modern thinking, then his life and doctrine have a canonical and contemporary relevance of no small proportions.

The records of the great christological controversy, in which Cyril was a leading protagonist after 429, and the voluminous correspondence it stimulated, have left the historian with an abundance of detailed sources for the reconstruction of Cyril's activities after this date. His earlier life is less well documented, indeed the dates only tend to become clear after 403.

According to the 7th century Coptic bishop and historian John of Nikiu[2] Cyril was born in the obscure Egyptian town of Theodosios close to, if not identical with, the present village of Mahalla el Kobra.[3] Later tradition, especially in Greek sources, has tended to locate his birth in Alexandria, which of course is the locus around which all the important aspects of his life certainly revolved. We could posit a date for his birth some time near 378. His mother seems to have originated from Memphis, and in her younger years spent some time as a refugee in a monastic house in Alexandria, moving about 120 kms. from the capital in order to be married. Her elder brother, Cyril's uncle the priest Theophilus, remained in the city, eventually becoming one its most powerful bishops in 385, when Cyril was about seven or eight years of age. Cyril's mother evidently kept in close contact with her brother after his ecclesiastical advancement[4] and it cannot be doubted that Theophilus would have guided his nephew's education and advanced his ecclesiastical career from the outset.

Cyril's mature writings show quite clearly the depth and rigour of his educational training, and bear clear witness to its christian

---

[1] In his later writing, especially the Eranistes, Theodoret applied the Cyrilline usage of 'hypostatic christology' for which in his earlier writings he had loudly criticised Cyril. cf. Richard (1936).

[2] The Chronicle of John of Nikiu; Ed. & tr.(from the Coptic) by Zotenberg, Paris, 1883; E.T. R.H. Charles, The Chronicle of John Bishop of Nikiu, London, 1916. q.v. p. 76.

[3] cf. Munier (1947).

[4] In a hostile account in his Life of Chrysostom, the historian Palladius says that Theophilus arranged for her to give false witness against a certain priest he wanted to depose.

inspiration. He was evidently schooled in rhetoric, but the substance of his learning is built upon the twin pillars of biblical theology and the prior patristic tradition, mainly the writers of the Alexandrian church. R.M. Grant has demonstrated that when he criticised pagan culture in his Contra Julianum, a work of his last years, he gained his knowledge for most of his learned allusions to pagan literature, by following up the references suggested in the writings of previous christian apologists, particularly Eusebius of Caesarea.[5]

Chief among his sources is Athanasius the Great, but he is also aware of the exegetical work of Origen, Didymus, and even Chrysostom, whom on occasion he paraphrases extensively.[6] He also knows some of Jerome's exegetical writing,[7] who for a time had allied himself with Theophilus in the early attack on Origenism the archbishop conducted in the Egyptian monasteries. The exact relationship Cyril had with Isidore of Pelusium, eighteen years his senior and a notable leader in the monastic circles of Egypt, is one that still needs clarification. Isidore wrote to Cyril with great frankness, and although his letters are frequently critical, there is no sign that they were resented, even though Isidore was a provincial cleric within Cyril's jurisdiction. Isidore enjoyed a freedom of speech with the archbishop that apparently belonged to a trusted counsellor and perhaps mentor from his past. Among Isidore's 'letters to Cyril'[8] there is a complaint that Cyril is a little too fond of worldly interests when he should be busying himself with the pursuits of solitude. Some have taken this to suggest that Cyril was himself a monk, perhaps for something like five years in the desert at Nitria, but if this was the case it is surprising that he himself does not make any reference to it despite numerous communications with the Egyptian monks when he subsequently became archbishop of Alexandria. Severus of Antioch, one of the great Cyrilline disciples of the 6th century knew this tradition but was doubtful of it.[9] It seems to have been sustained largely through the later work

---

[5] see Grant (1964) and Malley (1978).

[6] McGuckin (1987).

[7] Abel (1941); Kerrigan (1952). Wickham (1983, xvi, fn.15) notes that he probably knew Jerome by means of the Greek translation made by Sophronius. Several parallels can be explained by mutual dependence on Origen who was a massive source (frequently undisclosed) for Jerome too.

[8] Not all Isidore's 'letters to Cyril' ought to be presumed, however, to be addressed to the patriarch Cyril. See: PG 78.361; 78.369; 78.373; 78.392.

[9] CSCO 101, p. 252f.

of Ibn Al Muqaffa[10] but he goes on to say that Cyril's monastic father was not Isidore of Pelusium, but Serapion the Wise. Wickham has drawn attention to the dubious reliability of this late source.[11] Perhaps we may safely surmise that Theophilus patronised his nephew's preparation for an ecclesiastical career, and that this would have included the solid basis of a formal education in Alexandria as well as long term christian studies which would not rule out periods of staying in the monasteries, which then, as now, were the bastions of Egyptian christianity.

Cyril's written style has an abundance of rare forms and stylisations which are typically Alexandrian. Nestorius criticised him for being stuffy and difficult to read, but that was a classic example of the pot calling the kettle black. Cyril's Greek is certainly dense and difficult, but the difficulty is as often related to the subtlety and compactness of his thought as it is to the heavy loads he frequently places on his syntax, and his preference for Atticising forms.

Cyril is unusual among the Greek Fathers for having even a little knowledge of the Latin tradition, and if he was not bi-lingual himself he certainly saw to it, as a scholarly archbishop, that the important materials he sent for Pope Celestine's perusal at Rome were quickly and accurately translated into Latin before they left Alexandria. When he assembled lists of patristic Testimonia before and after the council of Ephesus he was able to cite Cyprian and Ambrose as authorities.

His period of formal education, following Abel,[12] would probably have covered grammatical studies between 390 and 392 at the usual ages of 12–14, followed by Rhetoric and Humanities between the ages of 15 and 20, in the period 393–397. After this we should locate a specific time of christian theological and biblical studies beginning probably in 398 (the year that the great Alexandrian theologian and exegete Didymus the Blind died) and ending sometime around 402. Already from this period, when Cyril was in his early twenties, begins his familiarity with the scriptural text that bore fruit in his monumental works of exegesis. Today Cyril is largely regarded as a major theologian of the Person of Christ because of his involvement in the Nestorian crisis. In his own time, however, he probably thought that it would be his great biblical commentaries that would earn him his immortality

[10] History of the Patriarchs of the Coptic Church of Alexandria. Ed. & Tr. by B. Evetts, Patrologia Orientalis. 1.427f.

[11] Wickham (1983) pp. xi–xii, fn. 3.

[12] Abel (1947) p. 230.

as a christian thinker. Most of these works of commentary are produced in this early period, before the christological controversy diverted his energies to other pressing matters.

At the end of his years of study, in 403, when he was about 25 years of age, Cyril was ordained Lector of the church of Alexandria by Theophilus, and he began his ecclesiastical career at his uncle's side. We may presume that in the years following he advanced to higher clerical offices, but from this time onwards he was intimately attached to the chancery of the Alexandrian church. By the time of the Nestorian crisis, when Nestorius himself had been occupying the throne of the imperial city for merely a year, Cyril was already endowed with twenty five years' experience of church politics at the highest level. The difference in political acumen between the two men is obvious from the outset.

In that same year of 403 Cyril attended his uncle at the Synod of the Oak in Constantinople, which deposed John Chrysostom an event which Cyril recalls in a later letter to the aged Acacius of Beroea who was also present and survived long enough to become an important broker in the delicate negotiations that were conducted after the council of Ephesus.[13] Having been involved in this trial of the great Chrysostom, Cyril stood firm with his uncle in the opinion that John had been rightly deposed, even to the extent of allowing the issue to cause a cloud to descend on relations between the Alexandrian church and Rome, which demanded John's rehabilitation. Relations between Rome and Alexandria remained poor until the early years of Cyril's administration.

When Atticus, John's second successor in the see of Constantinople, wrote to inform Cyril of the decision to restore John's name in the liturgical commemorations (the diptychs) of the churches at Constantinople and Antioch he received, as first response, a rebuff from Alexandria.[14] John's eventual rehabilitation (traceable at Egypt from about 417) seems to have been a gradual and a diplomatic one as Cyril moved from the policy of Theophilus to his own understanding of present ecclesiastical exigencies. In the time of the Nestorian controversy he wrote to the imperial court signalling his partial acceptance of the policy to restore John's memory, by contrasting Nestorius' unorthodoxy with John's purity of doctrine. This was a subtle manoeuvre on Cyril's

[13] Cyril, Ep. 33. PG.77.159; ACO 1.1.7.p.148. See the translations following.
[14] Cyril, Ep.76. PG.77.351–360.

part in so far as John's deposition had been secured by Theophilus at the Synod of the Oak on disciplinary, not theological, grounds. But even in 432, in his letter to Acacius of Beroea, Cyril has no qualms about standing up for the legitimacy of John's deposition.

It is not necessary to presume that Cyril ever actually restored John's name to the diptychs of the church of Alexandria either in 417 or at any later date. There was no standard practice at that period which would require him to do so. It was enough, to regain communion with the Roman see and to find favour with the royal court, to signal his tacit assent to the policy. Cyril's willingness to use John's works, and speak of him as a standard of orthodoxy, suggests that he progressively abandoned the previous public policy of his church in a slow process of readjustment, in which he was ever careful not to lose face.The truth of the matter, in terms of John's rehabilitation in the eyes of Cyril and the Alexandrians, probably lies somewhere between John of Nikiu's eager statement that Cyril was 'filled with great joy' at the prospect of restoring John's honour 'because he loved and honoured him as a great teacher'[15] and the caustic comment of the deposed Nestorius who listed the Constantinopolitan hierarchs whom he accused the Alexandrians of destroying and then said to Cyril: 'I will pass over John in silence, whose relics you have now come to venerate, however unwillingly.'[16]

In his period assisting Theophilus, Cyril saw at close hand how powerful the office of archbishop could be in the hands of a determined man. The Byzantine administration was clearly not looking for the family tradition to continue, given the controversies that had never seemed to be absent in Theophilus' days. When Theophilus died on Tuesday October 15th, 412, they had already made moves to secure the election of the incumbent archdeacon Timothy. Theophilus still had numerous followers, however, and Cyril's support was buoyant. It was evident that the nephew had been groomed for office and in his nine years of service he had already secured his position in the church on his own merits. The two factions in the Alexandrian church immediately clashed, causing no small political and civil disturbance which the contemporary historian Socrates records.[17] It is indicative of the extent of Cyril's ecclesiastical and popular support

[15] Charles (1916) pp. 95–96.
[16] Loofs, Nestoriana (1905) p. 300.
[17] Socrates Hist.Eccl. 7.7. ET. Nicene and Post Nicene Fathers, Oxford, 1891.

at this period that despite the direct opposition of Abundantius, the Byzantine commander of the Egyptian garrisons, who sided with Timothy's faction, it was Cyril who was consecrated archbishop on the Friday of the same week, October 18th 412. He was about 34 years of age and his episcopal career was born among the kind of riot which showed all too clearly how volatile were the city and church politics of Alexandria.

Socrates paints a turbulent picture of Cyril's early administration, recounting his confiscation and seizure of the Novatianist churches in the city, progressive friction with the Urban Prefect Orestes, and mob violence involving attacks on Jewish elements, as well as the infamous assassination of the pagan philosopher Hypatia by a Christian mob in 415. Socrates telescopes the issues together in what becomes generally a gloomy picture, but his account is far from unbiased. He has two axes to grind against Cyril, for he is himself both a Novatianist sympathiser, and a Constantinopolitan in outlook. Both attitudes prejudice him somewhat in his assessment of Cyril's actions.

The position of the Archbishop of Alexandria had consolidated from the time of Athanasius, when even then it was considerable enough for the imperial court to have good reason to respect it, and in the hands of Theophilus and Cyril it was to reach the zenith of its influence. The leader of the church there was one of the chief powers of Byzantine Egypt, rivalling the importance of the city Prefect, with access to a large, vociferous, and mobile source of support in the form of the monks, as well as a standing bodyguard of Parabalani[18] of considerable size. Socrates[19] says that 'Cyril came into possession of the episcopate with greater power than Theophilus had ever exercised. For from that time the bishopric of Alexandria went beyond the limits of its sacerdotal functions and assumed the administration of secular matters.' This seems to have in mind particularly Cyril's legal moves against the Jews and Novatianists.

Cyril's early actions as archbishop reveal him as a reformer, trying to bring order into the ecclesiastical administration, but not entirely able to control the popular forces on which his power base depended. His early actions attempted to repress the vestiges of the heretical

---

[18] Originally able-bodied men who attended and ministered to the sick in a form of early Christian 'guild'. They came to be a force of attendants at the service, and under the direction, of the Archbishop. cf. W. Schubart. Parabalani. Journal of Egyptian Archaeology, 40, 1954, 97–101; Philipsborn (1950).

[19] Hist. Eccl. 7.7; 7.13.

groups in the city, in line with imperial religious policy of the period as supervised by the Augusta Pulcheria, Theodosius The Younger's elder sister. Cyril's writings that predate 429 are full of references to the continuing fight against heresy, but those he turns his attention to are the famous and classic varieties—Sabellians, Arians, Manicheans, and Adoptionists. Until the Nestorian controversy he never refers, for example, to the Pelagians or the Apollinarists.[20]

One of his first acts in this campaign against dissidents was to move by law against the Novatianist sect, to dispossess their church and their bishop Theopemptus. In this policy he was responding to the current political climate. From Theodosius the Great (346–395) onwards, Roman legislation had increasingly disabled heretical meetings, threatening confiscation of goods. Cyril's application of the law signalled a renewal of the campaign, just as Nestorius received the same commission at Constantinople on his appointment there. The law penalising heretical meetings was explicitly reaffirmed in May 428.[21]

The Novatianists, however, despite Socrates' propulsion of them to centre stage, were already a thing of the past. After his suppression of their church Cyril turned to face the two real ideological and political opponents of the christian church in Alexandria, that is the common people who still actively maintained the 'old religion' of the pagan cults (especially strong in the rural regions), and the Jews, whose presence in Alexandria for centuries had made the city a veritable centre of Jewish learning as well as commerce.

The modern contexts of toleration and religious pluralism may well generate a very negative view of the repressive measures Cyril can be seen to have taken against his opponents, and this applies both to those outside the church as well as to his christian antagonists of later years. It is necessary, however, to locate this activity of Cyril's in its ancient context rather than in any modern perspective, and in this regard two background considerations are important.

In the first place the early church instinctively shared the exclusivity of Judaism. No common agreement or toleration was felt to be possible for moral or religious pluralism. By the fifth century Paganism and Judaism were perceived as the contrary enemies of the christian religious system—a view which is exactly parallel, of course, to Judaism's own view of both christianity and paganism. The monks of Egypt in this

[20] cf. Durand (1964) p. 15.
[21] Codex Theodosianum 16.5.165.

period are frequently found destroying the ancient pagan shrines and idols, at least wherever they could get away with it, where local pagan opposition was ineffective. This is desecration of the holy places of other religions, or active evangelisation depending on the viewpoint of the modern beholder, but for the christians of Cyril's age the destruction of pagan shrines, to take an extreme physical encapsulation of the wider movement of the fifth century christian predominance over paganism, was not only an important element in evangelisation, it was seen as the purification of a nesting-place of demonic forces in that area. The early church did not regard the pagan temples as barren conventicles of false superstition, rather as the active centres of demonic enmity and malice to local christians. Cyril's instinctive beliefs in this regard can be seen in the illuminating episode of his translation of the relics of Alexandrian martyr saints to the Isis cult centre at Menouthis, an event which shall be noticed later.

Secondly, in terms of the clash with Judaism, the implacable opposition between the two religions was the result of two large political and corporate bodies of a mixed population in Alexandria, who by race and religion would not be assimilated to each other. The opposition was focused by religion but flowed out in all other areas of life, and was an indication of the great power that both religious systems could hold over their respective peoples. Like the Jews, the christians' religion constituted them as a 'Genos', a particular people, and in the Theodosian renewal that race of the Greeks (the christians) was felt to have come into its full inheritance of the earth.

Liberal ecumenism, even in the contemporary world, is taken aback when it finds its principles of toleration and accommodation wholly ineffective in the face of such powerful religio-political currents and, in consequence, may judge Cyril harshly for his attitudes, but the contexts and agendas of liberal ecumenism do not accurately convey the realities of fifth century Alexandria. It is a matter of some debate whether, in the face of innumerable examples ranging from Israel to Northern Ireland, Yugoslavia, Sri Lanka, Russia, Cambodia, (the list is endless) whether those contexts can even be said accurately to describe the realities of religion and politics in the late twentieth century either.

The church in Cyril's day had already sensed its victory over paganism. For over a century, since the time of Theodosius I, the christian religion had been enshrined as the imperial religion of the Romans. It had an energy and political environment that empowered its sense of mission and establishment. Paganism still lingered on, sometimes as a vital force, in the hearts and affections of the simple country people, and pagan philosophy was still an important intellectual critic of Christianity, as evidenced by the scholarly elite of the city. Nonetheless the church sensed that the tide had already turned against the old religion, even in its heartlands of Rome, Asia Minor and Egypt. The edict of Honorius and Theodosius II suppressing pagans and heretics, dated to 407, captures the mood of the time, and in its final prescriptions also explains Theophilus', and Cyril's, legal base of operations in their assaults on paganism.[22]

That the tide had turned against them could not be said, however, of Judaism. Despite the innumerable hardships and political disasters that had befallen the Jewish nation, the Alexandrian community of Jews was still immensely vigorous in the fifth century. Theologically, morally, and in terms of communal cohesion, the church found in the synagogue its most serious opponent. The conflict between the two peoples was perhaps more acute at Alexandria than anywhere else in the Late Antique Roman world, given the great size and importance of the respective communities of that city. At that time Alexandria was still the veritable capital of world Judaism.

The early Paschal Homilies of Cyril demonstrate his concern over the assimilation of christians to Jewish customs, a problem that can be found in patristic apologetic two hundred years previously.[23] In Cyril's time relationships between the christian and Jewish inhabitants were full of friction, and that friction in the volatile city environment was able soon enough to ignite dangerous fires of longstanding differences. The first three political crises which embroil Cyril as a young bishop typify his problems; the first was a major incident with the Jewish community, the second a clash with the Urban Prefect, the third a murder scandal involving the pagan intelligentsia.

It was a longstanding custom for the congregation to applaud in church, or to shout out signs of their disapproval, when bishops preached to them. There are several indications in the fifth century patristic homilies of the bishops sometimes struggling for control over their audience. In the Alexandrian cathedral one of Cyril's avid followers,

---

[22] 'Pagan altars in all places should be destroyed and all temples on our (imperial) estates should be transferred to suitable uses......to bishops of the local regions we grant the faculty of ecclesiastical power to prohibit the said practices.' Codex Theodosianum 16.10.19.

[23] cf. McGuckin (1992); Ibid. (1985); Wilken (1971).

the lay professor Hierax, had the function of leading the applause during Cyril's sermons. Hierax was a well-known figure; a prominent christian, and a highly visible member of Cyril's entourage.

Shortly after Cyril's consecration as archbishop the Urban Prefect Orestes was delivering a series of official edicts in the Alexandrian Theatre, primarily addressed to the Jewish community, and regulating entertainments that could be held on their sabbath day. A group of Cyril's supporters, including Hierax, turned up for the occasion to find out what was being allowed or prohibited, and their presence so inflamed the crowd that they beat up the unfortunate man, whom they recognised immediately, and denounced him to Orestes as a spy of Cyril's. The Prefect arrested him and used him to demonstrate his malice towards the archbishop by having him questioned in prison under torture. Socrates says that: 'Orestes had long regarded with jealousy the growing power of the bishops because they encroached on the jurisdiction of the authorities appointed by the Emperor.'[24] Cyril responded to this by sending the Jewish authorities a formal warning not to engage in further molestation of christians. He did so secure in his own mind that he had the tendency of the law behind him, which under Theodosius II had increasingly enacted measures disabling Jewish rights.[25]

Hard on the heels of this episode a local riot in one of the city quarters where relations between Jews and christians had reached breaking point, led to a major incident. A Jewish group living beside the 'church of Alexander' sent runners through the streets late one night crying out that there had been a fire in the church building. This brought local christians in numbers to the site where they were set upon in pre-arranged attacks, adding to the confusion, and some were killed.[26] The incident could not be contained and may have been interpreted as the beginning of a dangerous concerted movement. Whatever the case there was a mass gathering of christians at the cathedral the following morning demanding redress, and under Cyril's leadership, acting as judicial magistrate and ethnic Archon, this moved

---

[24] Hist. Eccl.7.13.

[25] e.g the punishment of Jewish proselytizers of Christians in 415 (Cod. Theod. 16.8.22) which involved even the degradation of the Jewish patriarch Gamaliel. There were also edicts in 409, 412, 415 417 & 423. The last edict was designed to prohibit any 'future burning of synagogues' yet it does so almost as a concession to "the wretched requests" of the Jewish communities.

[26] Socrates. Hist. Eccl. 7.13

as a column to the synagogues of the chief suspects. The crowd seized the buildings and devastated them, with the action soon degenerating into widespread looting.

Socrates, in this connection, speaks of Cyril instigating a mass expulsion of Jews from the city, but this is surely an exaggeration. Cyril's administration certainly marks a stage in the increasing christian domination of fifth century Alexandria but the Jewish presence there would remain strong and influential for a long time to come. The expulsions of Jews he instigated should rather be seen as particularised and related to the incident of the Alexander church murders; an aspect of Cyril's claims to exercise independent judicial power in matters relating to religion, in the face of Orestes' civil jurisdiction. Far from being the whole Jewish population the exiles probably constituted the group around the Alexander church. It was, nonetheless, a strong signal to the Jewish population as a whole.

The bad relations between Cyril and Orestes degenerated further when a large group of monks from Nitria came to the city 'to fight on Cyril's behalf'.[27] They came up to Orestes in his chariot and surrounded the vehicle, jostling it, and denouncing the Augustal Prefect as a pagan, presumably because his enmity of the archbishop was public knowledge by this time, and because his social contacts included notable pagan litterateurs and philosophers. His answer to them was that he was indeed a christian, but one (he was glad to say) that had been baptized by the archbishop of Constantinople. In his answer he not only distanced himself from Cyril, but also gives an indication of an important factor in the subsequent controversy with Nestorius, and that is the innate rivalry that existed between the two christian cities.

Alexandria looked back to its ancient pedigree as a rich source of patriarchs and martyrs. Constantinople regarded itself as the epitome of christian civilisation and culture, and particularly disdained the Egyptian provincials. Mockery of the Alexandrian accent was a longstanding joke in Byzantium. Orestes' evident outrage and disdain for the monks inflamed matters further and stones began to fly, one of which hit the Prefect on the head, drawing blood. Most of the attendant troops, according to Socrates, 'plunged into the crowd to escape' but local citizens felt that the monks had gone too far and intervened to break up the fracas. The monk who threw the stone, by name of Ammonius, was arrested and brutally tortured by Orestes,

---

[27] Socrates. Hist. Eccl.7.14.

doubtless in an attempt to uncover a link with Cyril and provide an excuse for his arraignment. Ammonius died from injuries sustained while in Orestes' custody, and in reply Cyril pointedly gave the unfortunate man a triumphant funeral, even speaking of him as a new martyr for the faith. Harassment of paganism by the monks, even to the extent of physically demolishing the shrines was by then an established custom of the Alexandrian church, and Cyril's eulogising remarks on Ammonius can possibly be contextualised in this light. In other words, Cyril did not disabuse his monastic supporters as to Orestes' supposedly pagan inclinations and sustained the notion that the monk had died at the hands of infidel torturers on account of his protests against idolatry.

The particularly pugnacious nature of the monks' attack on paganism was a notable factor in Egypt, but the repressive policy in general is not a peculiarity of Cyril's. It was, in the main, a shared perspective of several christian hierarchs of the time. Theodoret, in his history, makes a special point of commending Theophilus[28] for his root and branch extirpation of pagan cults in Alexandria, citing with evident approval and admiration the famous attack on the Serapeum in Alexandria when the monks sawed up the cult statue of the god. Such a frontal and public assault on the main centre of pagan civic and religious life speaks volumes about the power of the archbishop of Alexandria in the early fifth century, and Cyril, in this episode of Ammonius' funeral, is clearly warning off the civil Byzantine power from an encroachment onto that area of public influence his see had already established.

The third notable episode of this early period of Cyril's administration is perhaps the most infamous—the murder of the pagan Neo-Platonic philosopher Hypatia by a christian mob. At the time, as indeed they have since, his enemies tried to lay responsibilty for this personally at Cyril's door. This crime was committed shortly after the clash with Orestes when a crowd, possibly composed of many of Cyril's parabalani since they were led by someone who held the office of lector in the church, met with Hypatia's carriage in the city streets. She was the leading light of the city's philosophical schools, an eminent teacher and a social figure who counted in the ranks of her most ardent disciples the philosopher Synesius, whom Theophilus had subsequently consecrated as bishop of Ptolemais in 410. As far as the mob were concerned

[28] Hist. Eccl.5.22.

this cultured woman represented a focus of unyielding opposition to Christianity. They appear to have connected her in some way with Orestes' continuing hatred of their archbishop Cyril, and when they stopped her carriage they dragged her from it and pulled her into the Great Church, formerly the Caesareum, of Alexandria.

This incident occurred during Lent, in March 415, the time of the preparation of catechumens. Was it an attempt to force her to acknowledge the Gospel? The mob stripped her in the church before stoning her to death with tiles. Perhaps it was a grim parody of the baptismal rite which degenerated into a frenzy of hate and destruction that resulted in the literal tearing apart of her body and the burning of the sections of her corpse.[29] Whatever light one puts upon the crime the fact was that here was a grotesque murder within the very church building, and it was a scandal that reverberated round all parts of the city, Jewish, pagan, and christian factions alike, and even further afield. Socrates says that this event, 'brought no small reproach on Cyril and the church of the Alexandrians'.[30] Some, most famously Gibbon who calls the murder 'an exploit of Cyril's,' blatantly misinterpret this remark when they consider the murder as an act in which he was personally involved. Socrates' point is that the behaviour of this mob at their own church spread disgrace upon the whole christian community, including its archbishop, and called out for closer control of the volatile popular factions in Alexandria.

The pagan philosopher Damascius also recounted the incident specifically attributing personal blame and complicity to Cyril, but he was writing 130 years after the events, and his whole account is evidently prejudiced from the start and suffused with a bitter hatred of the way in which Christianity had suppressed his profession and way of life. Following Gibbon, Charles Kingsley, with more regard for romance than fact in his novel 'Hypatia', lost no opportunity to paint Cyril as the evil villain of the piece, and the mythic caricature he provided became fashionable. More recently, Wickham is more just to Cyril, and certainly on the grounds of deeper scholarly judgement, when he summarises the early crises of his administration as follows: 'The facts are not to be denied. The picture they yield is not one of a fanatical priest, hungry for power, heading a howling

---

[29] cf. F. Schaefer. 'Cyril of Alexandria and the Murder of Hypatia.' Catholic University Bulletin, 8, (Washington) 1902, 441–453.

[30] Hist. Eccl. 7.15.

mob, but of an untried leader attempting, and initially failing, to master popular forces'.[31]

As a result of the violence the Urban Prefect denounced Cyril to the imperial court at Byzantium. Theodosius II was only fourteen years of age at the time, and already under the sway of his dominant sister Pulcheria, the regent Augusta from 414. Cyril wrote to justify his actions in expelling the Jews, and claimed that he was defending christian interests in the city in the face of concerted attacks. If Orestes was hoping to have the archbishop deposed his plans did not come to fruition. There was one concrete result, however, which demonstrates a degree of official disapproval of Cyril's political role, and that was the initiation by Pulcheria of a formal commission of enquiry.

In 416 Aedesius the imperial commissioner who had been sent from Constantinople concluded that the guild of parabalani was a threat to public order, and in September of that year their numbers were restricted by imperial edict to less than 500, and they were brought under the legal inspection of Orestes as the city Prefect. The decree seemed to have reined in Cyril's growing influence: 'It pleases our Clemency that clerics should have nothing in common with public affairs or matters pertaining to a municipal Senate'.[32] And yet, within two years of this decree Cyril's reputation had risen so high at court that the law was again altered in his favour. On February 3rd 418[33] the number of the parabalani was increased to 600, and once more they were placed under Cyril's jurisdiction: 'to obey the most reverend bishop's orders and directions.' It is a remarkable witness to Cyril's ability to spring back from adversity, something that characterises all his life's story, but also to his capacity to command considerable influence at the imperial court, frequently far more than even provincial governors could summon up.

Cyril's literary work[34] before the Nestorian controversy is largely concerned with books of exegesis. If they had not been subsequently overshadowed by his own brilliant apologetic works of christology, the Commentaries on the Old Testament which he produced could well have come to be regarded as his crowning glories. He composed at this period his Thesaurus, which is largely a digest of St. Athanasius'

---

[31] Wickham. (1983.) p. xvi.

[32] Cod. Theod.16.2.42.

[33] Cod. Theod. 16.2.43.

[34] For a fuller listing, chronological location, and brief outline of the contents of Cyril's works see J. Quasten, (1975), 119–135.

Discourses Against the Arians, his Commentary on St. John's Gospel, and the Dialogues On The Trinity. Even in the midst of pressing concerns he never allowed his scholarly work to falter. It was a workload that prepared him for the controversies to come, when in the years after 429 he was able to produce a phenomenal outpouring of writing at a rate his opponents could not match.

The external problems that faced him as a christian theologian at this period are largely provided by the continuing intellectual opposition of Judaism, and the more practical opposition of popular pagan religion. One other episode of Cyril's activity relating to this latter aspect of life in fifth century Egypt is known to us and can probably be located in this earlier period, indeed as perhaps the last known incident before he became embroiled in the Nestorian issue. It consists in his formal translation of the relics of the martyr saints Cyrus and John[35] from Alexandria to Menouthis in an attempt to suppress the cult of Isis which was still flourishing there to the detriment of the church.[36]

The episode is preserved for us by Sophronius[37] who has also retained fragments of Cyril's festal homilies given on the same occasion.[38] The translation of the relics shows, in miniature, the great attractive power of popular religion, the old Egyptian cults, and Cyril's christian policy which meets the old ways head on providing a new set of focal holy places and rites to draw away and redirect popular allegiance.

Along the eastern littoral from Alexandria was the town of Menouthis. The christian community was represented there by the small church of the holy evangelists built in Theophilus' day, but the religious centre of the town's life, and to which it attracted a wide traffic, was the great shrine of Isis. After Theophilus' successful policy of destroying the pagan temples in Alexandria, the countryside continued much longer, with more successful resistance, in its accustomed ways. The Isis cult, with its great statue of the goddess, flourished at Menouthis and oracles were still given there. It had also become a healing centre, replacing the functions of the destroyed Serapeum, and thus a

[35] The 'Holy Unmercenaries'.

[36] A fuller discussion of the events is given in my paper: 'The Influence of the Isis cult on St. Cyril of Alexandria's Christology.' Studia Patristica, 24, Leuven, 1992, 191–199. Here the christological implications of Cyril's actions are highlighted as a most consistent encapsulation of interests which he sustained throughout all his christological thought.

[37] Laudes in Ss. Cyrum et Joannem. PG.87.3380–3424 (q.v. 3412f).

[38] Homiliae Diversae.18. PG.77.1100–1106.

pilgrimage locus. The temple priests served the petitioners with some medical benefits for which offerings were made, and there seems to have been some form of incubation ritual in the temple precincts whereby sufferers would sleep in the shrine overnight and receive healings in dream-intimations, as at Aesculapean shrines.

Sophronius describes the cult in a way that gives the instinctive christian understanding of its significance:

> A foul demon appeared in the desert, in the form of a woman, which caused many phantasms and seemed to give forth numerous oracles, though they were utterly false. They purported to concern the specifics of healing remedies, though they were of no use at all except to bring to destruction all those who trusted in them. Many people were caught in the hidden snare of this evil spirit and thought they should honour the demon with sacrifice and fat-offerings. In its name they made many offerings to the shrine. . . . . . When Cyril heard of the phenomena at Menouthis he prayed for a way from God to overthrow the demon.[39]

In Cyril's second homily on the occasion when he went to Menouthis, he himself suggests that the Isis phenomena had even weakened the local church:

> We wished to bring assistance to all the local regions and especially the district around the church of the holy evangelists because many people had gone off into other various parts seeking out testimonies, and even christians were being led astray.[40]

Like his uncle before him, Cyril attacked the pagan practice of oracular divination, but the principle of spiritual communications and influences, far from being rejected, is here taken with the utmost seriousness. To the threat of a maleficent demonic presence in the area he applies the remedy of the beneficial presence of the more powerful christian martyrs, now localised by bringing their relics to the place where their efforts were needed. In response to the Isis shrine's appeal to the validation of oracular guidance from the deity we see the christian 'counter' with an account from Sophronius of Cyril's own vision given to him as hierarch of the great Church of Alexandria. Sophronius' account appears to be partly based on records of Cyril's, otherwise lost, and it tells us that, 'After Cyril's long prayers an angel appeared to him by night'[41] instructing him to translate the relics of St. Cyrus

[39] PG 87.3693.
[40] PG.77. 1101.
[41] PG.87.3688–3689, 3693.

the martyr from Alexandria to Menouthis. The tomb was opened in the church at the place which had been signified,[42] and indeed relics were found, but not of one but two people. Cyril set up a commission to inquire into the provenance of the relics[43] which identified them as the Diocletianic martyrs the monk Cyrus and the soldier John. Cyril declared both saints to be virgin-martyrs and in his sermon at Menouthis he confesses that not knowing which one was the Cyrus he had been instructed to take, he had simply brought both. He placed their relics under the protection of the monks of the old Pachomian monastery at Tabennisi who sent a delegation to Menouthis to take charge of the devotions there.

After his discovery of the saints Cyril inaugurated an octave of solemn celebrations. There was a great liturgical ritual culminating in the anointing of the relics in myrrh and perfumed balms, and then they were wrapped in linen and deposited in a heavily jewelled gold casket. Cyril carried the reliquary to Menouthis in a chariot at the head of a massive procession of the Alexandrian church.[44] The three fragments of Cyril's homilies that survive from this occasion are dated over the period of a week from July 26th to August 1st (possibly 427/8).

Cyril's intent was that the relics of the martyrs would immediately serve as a christian focus of opposition to the allurements of the Isis cult. To this end his own apologetic centres on two aspects. In the first place he argues that by their superior spiritual power, as virgin martyrs, the two ascetics would ruin the psychic force behind the sexually explicit temple rites of Isis, and expose them as morally dubious. For this reason he constantly characterises the martyrs as virginal ascetic warriors and, as such, a fitting inspiration for the celibate monks who would guard their tomb and whose very presence in the area would serve to subdue, in a very concrete way, any unbounded pagan enthusiasms. In the second place Cyril hopes to provide an alternative pilgrimage centre for popular hopes of healing which, as his final words suggest, will henceforth be free of charge:

---

[42] For a similar epiphany of hidden relics cf: Augusta Pulcheria's dream in which St. Thyrsos, in the time of Archbishop Proclus (434–446), appeared to the Empress to reveal the whereabouts of the relics of the Forty Martyrs of Sebaste. The events are well connected by Holum (1982), p. 137 and passim, with the claim to sacral Basileia.

[43] PG.77.1101.

[44] PG.87.3696.

> The holy martyrs Saints Cyrus and John came out ready to do battle for the christian religion.... As their reward for their love of Christ they received the power to trample on Satan and expel the force of evil demons. Now that those who once were going astray have turned to the true and unmercenary healer, none of us need make up dreams, none of us cries out to the pilgrims: "The Mistress has spoken, and commands you to do this or that." For how can one be a Mistress and also a god expecting worship? Among the demons there is neither male nor female. What kind of character can they have when they want to be called by girls' names?[45] Now the people trample on these brainless myths and worn-out deceptions of divination, and instead are coming to the true and heavenly healers, those to whom the all-powerful God gave the authority to be able to effect cures when he said: Go and heal the sick. You received without charge, give without charge[46] (*Mt.10.8.*).

Cyril's strategy for evangelisation, more subtle than that of his uncle, seems to have worked. The name of Abba Kyros the martyr has been preserved down through the centuries, even under Islamic domination, to the present village of Aboukir.[47]

Such events, controversies, and literary engagements were the concerns, then, of the early years of Cyril's episcopate up to 428. What transpired afterwards is far better documented because it worked itself out on an international stage at a high academic and political level. Nonetheless the controversy that was now to begin to unfold springs from the same concerns that Cyril had so far consistently witnessed as an active pastor in his diocese, that is his desire to apply the christian religion in all its implications to the people at the most direct and engaging level he could. He was determined to draw water from the deep wells of popular christian piety, wishing to communicate a sense of the immediacy of the presence and power of his divine Lord, whose presence, as for example in the eucharistic mysteries, or in the healing virtues of the sacred relics of the martyrs, depended first and foremost on the immediacy and validity of the divine presence in the Incarnate One.

For Cyril, the elevated intellectual argument about christology and the validity and security of a simple christian life were ultimately one

---

[45] A mocking allusion to the Navigium, or ship-carrying, one of the main festivals of the Isis cult when it was the custom for male devotees to masquerade as women.

[46] PG.77.1105.

[47] Present feast day of Ss. Cyrus and John, the 'Holy Unmercenaries', is in the eastern calendar on January 31st.

and the same thing. This insight goes a long way to explain the passion and profundity of his systematic theological opposition to Nestorius of Constantinople. It is an issue of oecumenical significance for christian theology, spirituality, and worship, that cannot be reduced merely to the level of political antagonisms, however much these forces did play a part in creating the overall climate of dissent.

2. The Nestorian Controversy: The Prelude to an Oecumenical Crisis, 428–431

In 428 the throne of Constantinople was vacant, following the death of Sisinnius, and the ecclesiastical politics of the great city were once again in ferment. Sisinnius himself had been consecrated as a compromise candidate, and on his death after a very short time in office, the factional rivalry had reopened. One of the contenders for the earlier appointment had been Proclus, a bishop consecrated for the see of Cyzicos who had been unable to take up his office because the local clergy had disregarded the canonical rights of Constantinople and consecrated their own candidate.[48] In consequence, he became a significant figure in Constantinopolitan affairs, allied with leading monastic figures such as the famous recluse the archimandrite Dalmatius who had refused the Emperor's personal appeal to be elevated to the episcopal throne,[49] and the lay lawyer Eusebius (later to become Bishop of Dorylaeum) a leading actor in this crisis as well as in the controversies that preceded the councils of 449 and 451. Proclus' power base was not inconsiderable for he was closely associated with the Augusta Pulcheria, but the imperial court finally decided to circumvent the factions yet again by calling in an external candidate, a rank outsider by the name of Nestorius, who enjoyed in his own region of the Syrian church a high reputation for preaching and the ascetical rigour of his monastic life.

Nestorius had been a childhood friend of the recently appointed archbishop John of Antioch and presumably had some experience in the affairs of that church from the base of his own monastery of Euprepios, near Antioch itself. It cannot be doubted that Nestorius owed his appointment to the personal recommendation of John. Nestorius was also a close friend of Bishop Theodoret of Cyr, and together with Andrew of Samosata these three represented a scholarly

[48] Socrates. Hist. Eccl. 7.28.

[49] cf. Nestorius' account of the electioneering in his Book of Heraclides. Nau (1910), 242–243.

triumvirate of Antiochene theologians rooted in the tradition of the earlier Syrian teachers such as Mar Diodore (of Tarsus) and Mar Theodore (of Mopsuestia) who were then regarded as the great teacher-saints of Syria, having the status and venerability there that such as St. Athanasius had in Alexandria, though with less of an international following in the church at large. Nestorius, Theodoret, and Andrew were to be the main theological opponents of Cyril.

In the great conflict that was now to unfold, the issues cannot be reduced merely to the level of personality clashes, or even to the complex issue of the precedence of sees, or the involved political machinations of the imperial court (however important all three factors might be as constituent elements of the scene) for what was about to clash was no less than two great schools of ecclesiastical reflection, piety, and discourse. It would be no exaggeration to say that the theological disruption this caused, and the need for theological re-articulation it summoned forth, was of no less import than the Arian crisis of the preceding century and, as in that great dispute, the central issues of the faith were sensed to be threatened to such an extent that the argument ran on through numerous synods over more than one generation. Indeed the resolution of centrally important theological questions such as the unity and diversity of God, in the Logos doctrine of the Anti-Arians from 325–362, and the Trinity doctrine of the Council of 381, had itself created the conditions that demanded a clearer resolution of christological doctrine. This task fell to the generation of Cyril in the mid fifth century.

Nestorius was enthroned as archbishop on April 10th 428, and set to work immediately. He brought with him a delegation from his monastery including the priest theologian and zealot Anastasius, who would lead him to his ruin. Nestorius has tended to be romanticised by several mid-twentieth century accounts just as Cyril has been cast in the role of éminence grise. The facts are clear, however, that Nestorius was no less 'dogmatic', uncompromising, and ready to use the full extent of his powers, both political and canonical, than Cyril or any of the other leading hierarchs of this period. This entirely fits the context of fifth century Byzantine life. To cast the ancient hierarchs in the mould of twentieth century western european gentlemanly churchmanship is a peculiarly misinformed canon of judgement.

The contemporary historian Socrates[50] called Nestorius a proud and ignorant man whose innate and undisputed oratorical power masked

[50] Hist. Eccl. 7.29, 32.

a weakness of incisive thought. There is a lot in this that is true, but Nestorius was certainly no fool. Socrates' accusation that Nestorius was 'disgracefully illiterate' is partly his own type of Constantinopolitan prejudice against foreigners and partly based on Nestorius' claim that the earlier patristic tradition did not support or validate the title Theotokos (Mother of God) for Mary, whereas Socrates (doubtless using the florilegia that Cyril subsequently produced on the theme)[51] was able to demonstrate his own superior erudition by listing the Fathers who did in fact use the term.[52] At this period, however, Nestorius' failure to apply the title Theotokos is not a sign of theological incompetence[53] rather it demonstrates his thesis that the christological use of the word (which was now to come into the central arena of the argument) had never before been elaborated properly. Indeed the list of Fathers who had used the title, excepting the Cappadocians who depended on Origen, did little more, in Nestorius' estimation, than confirm his suspicion that here was a peculiarly Egyptian theologoumenon which he did not wish to see imposed on the church universally.

In fact, in all his doctrinal statements Nestorius shows himself to be a consistent, if none too clear, exponent of the longstanding Antiochene dogmatic tradition. He is no creative genius; most of what he says being a re-statement of his teacher Theodore of Mopsuestia's viewpoint, but he is an able enough repetiteur of an old tradition, though tragically not one whose genius could extend to remodelling it creatively in the light of a new and pressing need to redraft its understanding of Christ's personal integrity. It surprised him greatly that he should stir up so much controversy in Constantinople for merely saying what he had always taught about Christ, with no troubles whatsoever, at home in Antioch.

---

[51] His treatises addressed to the Royal Princesses, and to Theodosius, cf. De Recta Fide, (Pusey) 1877.

[52] Origen, Commentary on Deuteronomy, PG.12.813; Ibid. In Ps. 21.21; Ibid. Hom.7 In Lucam 7; and Ibid, as Socrates narrates 'in the first volume of his commentary on Romans' (Socrates. Hist. Eccl.7.32); Peter of Alexandria, PG 18.517; Alexander of Alexandria, Ep. Ad Alexandrum 12, PG. 18.568; Eusebius of Caesarea, Vita Constantini 3.43, PG. 20.1104; Athanasius, Con. Arianos 3.14, PG.26.349; Ibid. Vita Antonii 36, PG. 26. 897; Gregory Nazianzen Ep. 101. PG. 37.177; and of particular interest Gregory Nyssa Ep.3. PG.46.1024, where he pairs the term Theotokos with the corresponding Anthropotokos (Mother of the man) in which Nestorius followed him.

[53] Socrates himself admits that apart from his views on the Theotokos title, he did not think Nestorius was really heretical at all (Hist. Eccl. 7.32).

His importance actually lies in this fact of his representativeness, although at the same time it must be remembered to what extent the other representatives of the Antiochene tradition, such as John of Antioch, Theodoret, and Andrew of Samosata, could all in their own ways recognise, more readily than he, the point of the argument for Christ's integrity, and admit the ill-advised nature of Nestorius' immoveability. Whatever the respective merits of the personal qualities Nestorius brought to bear in this period, he is undoubtedly the man who brings two great and disparate traditions of christian theology into conflict in an open forum, and this was to demand that christians clarified longstanding presuppositions they had held since the close of the biblical era about the person of Christ. The synthesis that was called for in the light of this clash, one that was subsequently worked out across no less than the next four oecumenical synods, formed the tide mark of orthodoxy in Christianity for subsequent centuries.

On assuming office Nestorius set to work, in much the same way as had Cyril sixteen years earlier, by attempting to bring his episcopal city to a common religious view and practice. His hold over Constantinople, however, was by no means as secure as Cyril's over Alexandria, and Nestorius' early reformist efforts brought him a harvest of discontent, at home as well as abroad. He immediately alienated the monks of the city by recalling them to their monasteries, and forbidding their involvement in the numerous 'unofficial' ministries they had instituted around Constantinople. The monks had long been a focus for opposition forces both to court and episcopal palace. Before Nestorius' arrival there had been severe tension between the local hierarchs and the monks, and Pulcheria had intervened in the arguments to take some of the monastic groups under her protection, especially those led by notable ascetics in the suburbs of the imperial city such as Dalmatius, Alexander, and Hypatius. This was a move that greatly pleased the common people, whereby she extended her own sphere of influence while disarming the potential dangers to the dynasty of an unaligned source of popular power.[54] Nestorius was to make little headway in his efforts to bring the monks into line. The disaffection he caused

[54] The popular violence that the monks could rouse at synodical meetings, is often taken as a scandalous example of social decline—this judgement is frequently found in assessments of Cyril and Memnon's behaviour at Ephesus. The judgement neglects the realities of Byzantine politics in the fifth century. For a fuller context see Dagron (1970) and Gregory (1979).

in his own see was a major weakness when he was later to launch into international controversy.

He also dismayed many members of the aristocracy when he began to apply legal proscriptions against the heretics with little regard for the political ramifications. He possibly composed, as his own initiative, the harsh terms of anti-heretical legislation we find issued from the court of Theodosius at this time (428).[55] One of his first acts in fleshing out the legal policy was to order a demolition squad against the last remaining Arian chapel in Constantinople. This was pre-empted by the desperate congregation who themselves set the torch to the building which was subsequently burned to the ground. This was symbolically a dangerous act indeed considering how the barbarian tribes were flooding over the northern borders of the Eastern empire to infiltrate and conquer the provinces of the West, and how the Byzantine armies at this period still relied on Arian German mercenaries whose religious sensitivity it would be foolish to offend.[56] The destruction of the Arian chapel was seen as an unnecessarily dramatic and tactless way of proceeding. The unfailing wits of the city thereafter tagged Nestorius with the nickname of 'Torchie' as a sardonic comment on how he was heating up ecclesiastical life in so short a time after his appointment.

He certainly warmed the temper of the Augusta Aelia Pulcheria who wielded immense power in the Palace, manipulating her vacillating brother Theodosius II. Hers was a power base that cannot be underestimated throughout this theological conflict. Through Proclus she came down, eventually, on the side of Cyril. It was a theological preference for the Theotokos doctrine in which she was partly helped by her decided personal antipathy to Nestorius, and partly because she sensed in the dispute a whole reflection on the role and importance of woman's power—a direct parallel to the political role she had created for herself within the Basileia of her brother, and yet independent of it (to an extent)[57] by virtue of her very public repudiation for herself and for the younger princesses, of any possibility of dynastic marriage. The altar proclaiming her perpetually dedicated virginity stood prominently in Nestorius' cathedral. The Virgin Mary was a patroness

[55] cf. Holum (1982) p. 150.

[56] cf. Barhadbeshabba, Hist. Eccl. 21, P.O. 9. 528.

[57] The Basilissai did not, for example, have a power base like the Emperor's that was rooted in the command of magistracies. Deprived of this legal supremacy they developed a far more wide-ranging nexus of political influences.

for her, fruitful and powerful in her virginity.[58] This virginal status, and the great wealth which had been bequeathed to her and amassed during her time as Regent in her brother's minority, lay at the heart of the great sway Pulcheria commanded. It was a mistake of phenomenal importance for Nestorius to cross her on this very matter. But he did so nonetheless, possibly in all innocence at first, even on the occasion of the first state liturgy he conducted.

In the liturgy of the Great Church at Constantinople Pulcheria had claimed, and apparently been granted by Nestorius' predecessors, the privileges traditionally associated with the reigning Emperor. He alone of all laymen was allowed to receive the Eucharistic mysteries within the sanctuary. Pulcheria had customarily been at her brother's side to do so, and possibly regarded her virginal status allied with her Augustal rank as two important sacral reasons why she should continue in this privilege.[59] Nestorius was taken aback when she processed into the sanctuary on his first celebration and he refused to administer the sacraments. Sharp words were exchanged and he subsequently compounded his mistake by casting aspersions on the kind of virginity Pulcheria practised. In his own later writings, and certainly in the writings of the later Nestorian historians, nothing was too bad to attribute to Pulcheria. She became regarded as the Jezebel of the whole story, the evil woman who cast down the saintly archbishop. But in the same way she became the ascetic Saint Pulcheria for the Chalcedonians.

The later accounts Nestorius gives in his Book of Heraclides are particularly bitter and ought to be read with caution. There[60] he accuses her directly of being an adulteress, but more interestingly also calls her 'an aggressive female'. He liked independent women no more than he relished the unaligned monastic factions. In his attempts at this same period to stop women coming to Vespers in the cathedral (since no decent woman, he said, would want to be out at night in the city) he was certainly trying to undermine the status of female ascetics and the aristocratic women in the capital. One wife of a leading

---

[58] See Holum (1982) esp. ch. 5.

[59] Sources in the Nestorian text: Letter to Cosmas, para.8, Patrologia Orientalis, 13. 279; Book of Heraclides, Nau (1910) pp. 361–362; Abramowski (1963) pp. 15–20, has doubts about the tradition but still assigns to it the status of local gossip and dates the text to 436. Holum (1982) treats the source positively as an important indicator.

[60] Nau (1910) p. 89.

Senator shouted out from the women's gallery of his church exactly what she thought of him[61] as he was passing by in a procession one day.

At the time of his refusal of Pulcheria's right to communicate alongside the Emperor, Nestorius probably had no more in mind than the public statement that women ought to be subservient in church, and that if the Augusta wanted to be a consecrated virgin she ought to lead a retired life in a convent, not the spectacular social calendar she presided over in the palace. This could only have been seen by Pulcheria as a direct assault against her political power, and as a particularly bitter personal insult to her honour, for a public refusal by the bishop of her claim to consecrated virginity needed only a little elaboration in the bazaars of the city to become no less than a public slur against her chastity. In a similar show of his disapproval of Pulcheria's pretensions he removed a costly robe she had given as an altar covering in the sanctuary. This could only have been a studied insult against her, and a repudiation of her claims to any sacral standing within the church. A virgin's robe was a fitting gift to the Virgin's Son, but a matron's dress would have no place in the holy of holies. Nestorius' removal of the covering seems to have been a further and deliberate step in his moves against Pulcheria, and again it must inevitably have been seen as a rejection of her claims to an independent female basileia. The incident probably ought to be located later in 430 when Nestorius had persuaded the Emperor to support him, and his confidence ran high that he would be able to summon a general council to Constantinople and despatch his enemies without difficulty. Pulcheria's undoubted intervention then was still able to ruin his plans as we shall see.[62]

On Nestorius' part we must interpret his actions as proceeding either from bare-faced ambition, or crass ineptitude. Whatever was the case it was to cost him dearly, as he later had cause to ponder in the long years of his exile. It might have been that Nestorius was trying to intrude himself between the weak Emperor and the dominant sister, as the palace eunuch Chrysaphius successfully managed to do (for a short time) somewhat later.[63] Theodosius had depended utterly on

---

[61] Accounts in Barhadbeshabba, Hist. Eccl. 21. P.O. 9, 528; & John Rufus Plerophoria, 36, P.O. 8. 81–82.

[62] It was doubtless her influence that relocated the proposed general synod from Constantinople to Ephesus: the site, with its great shrine of Mary and its powerful bishop who was antagonistic to Nestorius could not have been better chosen to disadvantage the archbishop of Constantinople.

[63] Pulcheria's first act on seizing supreme power after the accidental death of her

Pulcheria throughout the early years of his reign. She had even chosen a bespoke bride for him in the person of the Empress Athenais—Eudoxia. He itched to break free of her dominion, yet time and again could not bring himself to do so. Cyril too sensed the weakness of this fracture-line in the imperial household and later took advantage of it by appealing to the Theodosian royal women independently of the Emperor. The touchy rebuke this drew down on his head from the Emperor, despite Theodosius' claims that all were unanimous in the royal court, demonstrates that Cyril's reading of the relative worth of the power bases was perhaps more accurate than that of Nestorius.

On top of all this Nestorius had to deal with the problem of the unsettled factions within the church which he had inherited on his consecration. His announcement early in the summer of 428 that he intended to bring a strong hand to ordering the theological affairs of the Great Church opened up a local dispute that soon was to grow into an international crisis whose dimensions he could never have imagined.

The monastic party under the archimandrite and deacon Basil, (with Bishop Proclus behind them), with the support of the lawyer Eusebius and several other aristocratic patrons in the wings (not least the Augusta Pulcheria by this stage) came to Nestorius with a theological test-case for him to settle. They wanted him to make a statement affirming the orthodoxy of the veneration of Mary as Mother of God. They had clashed with a group, possibly that of Nestorius' own chaplain Anastasius, who were propagating the old Antiochene christology, arguing that the Theotokos title evidenced a defective theological understanding that could only be put right by the application to Mary of the title Anthropotokos (Mother of the Man). The Constantinopolitan monks were obviously wanting to draw Nestorius out into the open. When he later wrote to John of Antioch Nestorius described this as a local theological problem he found within his church.[64] He was not being entirely open about the fact that his own campaign of propagating Antiochene theology heavily at Constantinople had served to initiate the argument.

In a private audience in his palace Nestorius attempted an eirenic compromise by proposing a moderated form of Antiochenism to the local monks. He admitted that the terms God-Mother and Man-Mother, as they were being used by both contending parties, were capable

---

brother was to have Chrysaphius decapitated and impaled as a public enemy.

[64] Loofs, Nestoriana (1905) p. 185.

of orthodox interpretation, and ruled that each party's demand that the other should be proscribed as heretical was inadmissible.[65] His own solution to the dispute was to be followed by all. He pronounced that the argument had arisen because strictly speaking[66] both titles were inaccurate and capable of leading to foolish or heretical views about the person of Christ, or at the very least susceptible of serious misinterpretation, as had clearly proved to be the case. Theotokos, he argued, did not do justice to the fact that, strictly speaking, Mary was not the mother of God but rather the mother of the man whom christian faith recognizes as divine and thus calls God. On the other hand, the term Anthropotokos acknowledges that Mary is the mother of this man but can itself be taken to suggest that he is merely a man, which again is offensive to orthodox christian faith in the deity of Christ. One notices how the phrase 'strictly speaking' features prominently in his analysis. Throughout all his work Nestorius stressed the need for semantic exactness in this difficult theological area, to such an extent that the approach became the hallmark of his style.

In the end he sent both parties away having vetoed the use of their respective catch-phrases, and suggesting their reconciliation in his more accurate proposal that they should adopt the biblical notion of Mary as the Christ-mother (Christotokos). To describe Mary as the mother of the Christ was entirely accurate, he said, and capable of no heretical misinterpretation. By the use of this title it was clearly affirmed that it was the Christ who was God and Man. Mary was neither Mother of God nor merely Mother of the man. How he thought this would please anyone, even his own party, is difficult to comprehend.

His solution, far from ending the dispute with common agreement as to the archbishop's superior theological skills, convinced the monastic party that they had good grounds for their unease. Nestorius' refusal to allow the validity of the Theotokos title convinced them that, despite his avowals, his own christology was that of a 'mere man' (psilanthropism) in the manner of the ancient heresy of Paul of Samosata.[67] They arrived at this view on the basis of the following syllogism which was evidently a mockery of Nestorius' own pedantry: 'If Mary is not, strictly speaking, the Mother of God, then her son is not, strictly speaking, God.' The syllogism became a rallying standard for the whole opposition move-

[65] Nestorius, Ep. to John of Antioch. Loofs (1905) Nestoriana, p. 185.

[66] Akribos; a very common term in Nestorius.

[67] A form of Adoptionism whereby the Logos visited a human person, Jesus, to 'indwell him' with divine inspiration. The deity was quite distinct from this human

ment to Nestorius henceforth. The Mother of God title was seen as an absolute marker of the faith—now not only defending the honour of the Virgin Mother (whose cult had risen to newly important proportions in the fifth century), but more significantly in this argument fulfilling the role of a cardinal defence of belief in the personal deity of the Saviour. The idea that the Theotokos title is a bulwark of this christological confession, serves as the key argument in Cyril's first letter on the controversy 'To the Monks of Egypt'. He wrote this early in the following year, and clearly incorporated at the beginning of his discourse the arguments that his allies in the imperial city had already been using against their archbishop.

The failure of Nestorius' attempt to reach a satisfactory compromise on this deep-seated disagreement led to the rapid and more complete disaffection of the monastic party and, through the international network of monastic travel, news of the argument began to seep out far and wide. It is without question that Cyril had intelligence of the controversial debate from its inception. The monastic party looked to him from the earliest days as a protector, but his own ecclesiastical representatives, or agents, at the imperial court were highly skilled and already long experienced in negotiating a way through the complex factions of the corridors of power, far more so than Nestorius' Antiochene clergy at this period. Cyril's excellent intelligence network, the wealth of his church, and his powerful ability to represent himself at court became important factors in the subsequent dispute. At this period, however, in the late summer and Autumn of 428, he seems to have kept only a watching brief.

Matters began to move more quickly in the early part of 429 when Nestorius decided to pursue the theological controversy more systematically by initiating a series of public lectures in the cathedral on the nature of proper faith in Christ. His chaplain Anastasius gave the opening address and chose to begin, provocatively, with a thesis on the error of using the Theotokos title. His words repeated the longstanding argument: 'Let no man call Mary Mother of God for she was but a woman, and it is impossible for God to be born of a woman.'[68] He meant to exclude all notion of Mary as some form

---

person, the man Jesus. It was a case of two subjects alongside another (allos kai allos). The doctrine was condemned at the Synod of Antioch in 268, and Paul's name was associated with all similar schemes thereafter.

[68] In the sense that the very term 'God' means 'to have no birth in time'. He is arguing that the incarnation did not change the unchangeable God, relativize the

of 'goddess' producing a divine offspring whose humanity was questionable, but the effect was to bring a very complicated issue into the public domain, for he had made his remarks in the cathedral church itself. Socrates tells us that his sermon 'created a great sensation, and troubled many both of the clergy and the laity who had previously been taught to acknowledge Christ as God.'[69] He is being somewhat disingenuous at this point in his narrative in suggesting that Anastasius had any intention of denying that Christ was God, but he intends to bring out the sense of scandal that this refined Antiochene christological approach gave to simple believers who confessed Jesus as God, or Christ as God, synonymously, and troubled to make no distinctions or qualifications at all in their language about the incarnate deity.

Bishop Proclus soon made a counter-attack with a famous sermon on the Virgin Mother of God, preached in the presence of Nestorius himself, on the Sunday before Christmas 428.[70] The sermon was greeted with loud applause, to the great annoyance of the archbishop. He felt his pulpit had been subverted by an enemy within the camp, and as soon as Proclus was finished he seems to have stood up to answer his points in a critical way.[71] It is possible, given the truncated ending of the present state of Nestorius' reply, that he was not listened to by the congregation.[72] Several of the ascetics already regarded themselves as separate from Nestorius' communion at this stage, including one of the most famous, St. Hypatius the archimandrite at Chalcedon, a spiritual teacher of Pulcheria and the royal princesses.

Nestorius would not let the matter rest with this. He decided to back up Anastasius' lead lecture with a series of his own sermons. These he delivered in the cathedral throughout the early months of 429. He intended them for publication and circulation in the neighbouring churches. Cyril's agents sent copies of these to him in Alexandria, and Marius Mercator, a Latin layman living in Constantinople at the time, also seems to have gathered information and translated at least five of the christological sermons among other works of the

---

absolute, or make historical the eternal. Cyril would have agreed entirely with the first two arguments, and found the whole point of his Christological disagreement with Nestorius in the third, which for him was not a statement to be avoided in Christology, rather the entire goal and glory of a belief in Christ.

[69] Socrates, Hist. Eccl. 7.32.

[70] ACO 1.1.1.103–107.

[71] fragments in Loofs, Nestoriana (1905) 337–338.

[72] So Bauer (1919) p. 31.

archbishop's.[73] It is quite possible that Mercator was one of the Papal agents in the city who from this time kept Pope Celestine's archdeacon Leo (later to be Pope Leo the Great) abreast of developments. Mercator is particularly interested to note how the christological issues relate to the current Western policy of the suppression of Pelagianism. It is highly doubtful whether anyone else in the East, at this period, saw any connection whatsoever.

In Nestorius' sermons the Theotokos title was one of the chief targets of attack. Socrates suggests that he became obsessed with it in a quite unreasonable way—but perhaps not so unreasonably when one considers that he identified the Theotokos camp as the locus of all opposition to his episcopal reforms in his own city. A large part of the vehemence of his moves against the theological tradition was probably directed against what he saw as the unpardonable disobedience of his episcopal power; nonetheless the rancour of the start of the campaign carried it far afield in the international domain and Cyril was surprised to see here such a stark Antiochenism, almost as if it were resuscitated from a previous generation, and apparently attempting to move itself to the centre stage by seizing the imperial capital.

After hearing Nestorius' sermons in the cathedral, his monastic opponents labelled him a new Paul of Samosata reviving the ancient heresy that Jesus was not 'strictly speaking' God, only a God-inspired man, and by implication not uniquely different from a whole series of other prophets and saints. The best interpretation that they were willing to give of his doctrine was that because of his insistence on precise qualifications of language in christology he foolishly taught some kind of split personality in Christ, a man Jesus alongside the divine Logos in some form of bi-polar relationship. Both interpretations were, of course, the caricatures of enemies rather than sympathetic scholarly attempts to give him a hearing. But although much recent scholarship has argued (accurately enough) that Nestorius was badly understood in his own day, it must be remembered that in ancient controversies the implications of a doctrine were as much part of the debate as the actual statements made, and in theological argumentation precedents were always sought from the nearest parallel in history much as legal argument today looks to precedent for its authority. In this case Nestorius' teaching was related back immediately to the

[73] cf. Loofs, Nestoriana (1905) pp. 225–361; Bibliographical details on the sermons of Nestorius and their present locations in Quasten (1975) p. 518.

earlier Syrian tradition of Diodore of Tarsus. For this reason it began to be propagated that Nestorius was teaching there were 'Two Sons' whereas orthodox faith demanded the believer should acknowledge only one. These criticisms of his doctrine were to stick, and to this day the popular view of Nestorianism is that it propounded a double subject, or 'Two Sons' christology. Nestorius himself never exactly states this. Later in exile, he denied the legitimacy of such a doctrine explicitly. The fact remains, however, that people were looking more to the implication of his words than their exact context, and his reliance on semantic niceties in a series of preached sermons subsequently published shows a singularly bad choice of didactic method. Many at the time thought that he had implied the 'Two Sons' approach by attacking its apparent opposite, subsumed in the Theotokos title, without giving a sufficiently clear indication in his own theory as to why he should not be regarded as a disciple of Diodore's.

In the early months of 429 Cyril sat down to compose his Paschal Homily for that year, his seventeenth. In this encyclical letter to Egypt the patriarch announced the date of Easter and gave general exhortations to his churches. It is here that we see the first signs of a considered theological assessment of the current debate emerging, even though it is embryonic in form. In the text of the letter there is no direct reference to Constantinople or the Nestorian affair but it is undoubtedly in Cyril's mind for he uses the occasion to affirm the reality of the manhood of Christ but insists on the singleness of his divine personality—the classical and orthodox Alexandrian position from which he will not move an inch in all his subsequent theologising. In the Paschal Homily 17 he takes care to apply the title Meter Theou (a synonym of Theotokos) to demonstrate his point.

In the Spring of that same year matters reached a serious pitch at Constantinople when the lawyer Eusebius arranged for a public placard to be carried around the city openly accusing the archbishop of the heresy of the Samosatene.[74] The monastic leaders caused demonstrations in the cathedral to disrupt Nestorius' preaching. On one such occasion the Master of Offices came down with instructions from the archbishop to lay hands on one monk who was haranguing him from the body of the church. The official was going to flog the insubordinate and exile him from the capital but a crowd of supporters overwhelmed him and carried the ascetic off in triumph, shoulder

[74] ACO 1.1.101.

high, to the protection of the monastery of St. Euphemia which had barred its doors to Nestorius. There, with complete impunity, he carried on his campaign of insulting his archbishop.[75] On another occasion Nestorius answered his monastic hecklers, who kept raising objections and questions in the course of his sermons, to the effect that he would certainly give them a proper reply if they should care to call at his palace the following morning. Some innocents took him at face value; led by the archimandrite Basil they duly turned up at his residence the next day and received a good thrashing for their pains. This was heralded as Nestorius' inability to engage in rational exchange, and lost him some ground in the city. The monks composed a formal petition to the Emperor seeking Nestorius' trial for heresy and mismanagement of church affairs.[76] There are signs that the civic authorities became increasingly unwilling to intervene when he wished to pursue the dissidents with the force of law. One reason for this must have been the known fact that many of the aristocrats had lost sympathy with him, and that the Augusta Aelia Pulcheria had opened a church near her own quarters where the protesting ascetics could celebrate the sacraments apart from their archbishop's communion, safe under her protection. She had championed dissident ascetics against the hierarchy in the administration of Nestorius' predecessor, and it was public knowledge that she had emerged the victor in the contest of authorities then. Court officials were unwilling to cross her and accordingly not ready to support Nestorius' zeal with police force.

It was at this time that Cyril decided to move publicly himself. He had been circumspect up to the point that Nestorius' treatises began to circulate openly but by the time that the argument had become common knowledge in the monasteries of Egypt he regarded it as his canonical right to intervene, as the problem had now affected his own church. At this time he composed his important Letter to the Monks which he circulated through Egypt and ensured that copies were sent to Constantinople. It considerably annoyed Nestorius when he read it. From this point onwards Cyril began to make a serious patristic and biblical study of the issues involved. His background reading is quite evident in the large works he was shortly to send to the imperial court, replete as they are with patristic and biblical substantiations. This first venture into apologetic christological writing

[75] John Rufus, Plerophoria, P.O. 8, 78–81.
[76] ACO 1.5.7–10.

was soon to develop into a veritable avalanche of texts over the next two and a half years.

Nestorius meanwhile directed one of his colleagues, Photius, to draft an answer to the points Cyril raised in his Letter to the Monks. He also made significant moves on the wider political front which set off loud resonances in the Eastern and Western churches alike—particularly those of Rome, Alexandria, and Ephesus, whose common unity at a political as well as an ecclesiastical level was to prove disastrous for Nestorius at the later council. It seemed a small action, easily passing out of notice unless one realised the implications, but he began two commissions of enquiry in his ecclesiastical chancery: an examination of certain complaints from Alexandrian clerics, and a review of the claims of certain exiles from the West who had been condemned by Western synods. The first case was a veiled legal review of Cyril's administration. The second a review of Papal policy condemning the Pelagians.

The canonical right of the church of Constantinople to act as supreme court of appeal for the Eastern churches had been enshrined by the canons of the Council of Constantinople in 381.[77] From the outset, however, Rome had been unwilling to recognise the validity of these specific canons. It is not simply that Constantinople had assumed a secondary rank in the list of most important sees, for the various 'rankings' were not strictly hierarchical at any stage of the functioning of the Pentarchy of patriarchs—what was really at issue was the jurisdictional purview of the see of the imperial city. Its remit was already extending out over the territories of Asia Minor and its undisputed place as the capital of the civilised world was now pressing the church courts at Constantinople into the role of the leading christian tribunal of the entire oecumene, a role which until the end of the fourth century Rome had fulfilled without rival. Alexandria shared Rome's aversion to the rise of the new star in the ecclesiastical firmament, as did Ephesus, the metropolitan capital of the Asian Province whose bishops had seen their prestige wane as the imperial city waxed. The affair of the deposition of John Chrysostom, from Cyril's youth, showed how alive the whole issue still was. Chrysostom had applied the canons of Constantinople I rigorously in a campaign

[77] Canon 3: 'Let the bishop of Constantinople have the priorities of honour after the bishop of Rome, because of its being New Rome.' Pedalion. p. 210, New York, 1983.

designed to bring the churches of Asia Minor more directly under his control. In the course of his campaign he had even deposed bishops on canonical charges, thereby undermining the range of the authority of the bishops of Ephesus. What Nestorius was doing, by adjudicating in these two cases relating to Rome and Alexandria alike, was taking care to send clear signals to his episcopal colleagues that Constantinople was now ready to assume the role of the ultimate court of appeal in the christian world, on matters of discipline but also, implicitly, on doctrinal standards too. For these reasons it is not possible to regard Nestorius' decision to open these two commissions of enquiry as simply coincidental.

In the first instance Nestorius decided to hear the case of certain clerics and lay people who felt they had been too harshly treated by Cyril's judicial court at Alexandria. The review of the cases at Constantinople signalled a clear threat to Cyril, and was recognised as such from the start, for Cyril was careful to disarm it in his Second Letter to Nestorius where he gave his legal evidence against the convicted laymen,[78] and glossed over his quarrel with his dissident clergy (he was hastily patching up all differences with them behind the scenes).[79] If Nestorius found for the petitioners, the best that could result would be a public humiliation for Cyril, the worst could be no less than a legal call for his deposition from office.

In the second instance Nestorius was aware that several Western bishops had fled to the imperial court for redress after their synodical excommunication by Pope Celestine on charges of Pelagianism. They had been in the East for some while. Theodore of Mopsuestia had received them amicably in his own see several years earlier, and possibly Nestorius had made their acquaintance then. It was always useful to have dissidents at the Royal City, as a leverage point on others to be used when occasion should demand. Now it seemed their time had come.

The exiles were highly prominent figures including the main opponent of St. Augustine, Bishop Julian of Eclanum, along with Bishops Florus, Orontius, and Fabius. Together they commanded no little theological ability and would have been able to press their case both politically and theologically with a degree of persuasiveness. The East

---

[78] 'Having a reputation one would not wish upon one's worst enemy.'

[79] cf. Schwartz (1928); After Ephesus the dissident clerics are found back in the Alexandrian Church with Cyril.

did not really see the point of the Pelagian dispute at this period. Much of what Pelagius had said about the need for the human individual to 'work out his own salvation in fear and trembling' simply seemed to be a re-statement of centuries of traditional ascetical doctrine. Allied to this Augustine's central emphasis on predestination appeared to many in the East (as it still does) a particular theologoumenon of the African tradition which ought not to be imposed, in its stated form, on the church universally. Nestorius was much occupied how to use the presence of the exiles to the greatest effect and, without actually committing himself to a formal retrial, he did send to Rome a letter informing the Pope of the attendance of the exiles at the royal court and the nature of the charges they were making about the injustice of their treatment. The letter was peremptory in tone and carefully designed to raise the suspicion of a suggestion that he might open up the case again.

As far as the West was concerned the exile of the Pelagians was seen as a hoped-for end to the long drawn out controversy, and there was no desire to see it re-opened in the present climate of the great waves of barbarian incursions currently threatening to break over the Western provinces, especially Africa. Similarly, any canonical review of the case in Constantinople would have been an implicit assertion of the juridical superiority of New Rome over Old Rome, and this Pope Celestine refused to admit under any circumstances. The fact that Nestorius seemed to be sheltering these prominent exiles was brought to the attention of the Pope much quicker than Nestorius had presumed, by means of the papal agents in the capital. This was to lose him a lot of ground indeed.

After receiving a copy of Cyril's Letter to the Monks, Nestorius lost no time in informing Cyril that he regarded the work as a gratuitous and undeserved act of aggression. Cyril's reply, his First Letter to Nestorius,[80] made it clear that he regarded Nestorius, not himself, as the direct cause of the dispute, and that he saw it as his episcopal duty to safeguard the character of the faith which he felt had been unnecessarily compromised. In this letter Cyril suggested that he was not only acting on his own behalf, but answering queries put to him by others concerning the faith of Nestorius. The implication was very pointed here, to the effect that Rome was closely scrutinising the case, and that Cyril enjoyed Celestine's confidence. Cyril had in effect replied in kind to Nestorius' canonical threats.

[80] Ep.19.

Nestorius' response was to bluff it out, but this was a serious mistake which he proceeded to compound. After his first letter to Rome was duly ignored by the papal chancery Nestorius sent a second, even sharper, note requiring that Celestine should send him information on the Pelagians—presumably the dossiers of evidence from the earlier synodical processes, which indicated clearly that he intended to proceed with a formal review of their cases. Rome would never acknowledge this aspect of the controversy. It regarded the Pelagian condemnations as irreversible judgements, and filed this second letter, unanswered, along with its precursor as it turned to gather more evidence of its own on the new Archbishop and the nature of the reports that were emanating from his city to suggest that there was a theological crisis developing.

Cyril's implication in his first letter to Nestorius that Rome was interested in the theological controversy, was no idle threat. Indeed it was Cyril who had ensured that, apart from its own intelligence reports sent from Constantinople, the Roman chancery should have the advantage of all the evidence he himself had acquired. Throughout the winter of 429 and the early months of 430 he had worked through the published writings of the new Archbishop and digested sections of the sermons which he thought to be particularly objectionable. This dossier was assembled in parallel with a florilegium of unimpeachable patristic authorities to serve as a contrasting canon. It was a first draft, as it were, of the more substantial work, De Recta Fide, which he would later send to the Emperor. With a fine diplomatic gesture of having the complete work translated into Latin for the benefit of the Romans he sent this to the Pope by the hand of his own deacon Posidonius at Easter of the year 430. After receiving Cyril's dossier, Rome's suspicions were confirmed and the Archdeacon Leo set up a formal commission of enquiry, asking the easterner John Cassian, the abbot of Marseilles, to comment on the writings in preparation for a formal synodical hearing at Rome later in the year.

In the meantime Nestorius had been continuing his campaign unabashedly. In February of 430 news filtered back to Cyril in Alexandria of the latest scandal that had set the city talking. Nestorius had invited his friend Bishop Dorotheus of Marcianopolis, in the province of Moesia near the capital city, to preach in the cathedral during the course of one of his visits. He was a hardliner and took matters beyond their present level by actually asserting that anyone who 'dares to call Mary the Mother of God is anathema'.[81] When

[81] The story is preserved in Cyril's Letter to Celestine after the Council of Ephesus.

he had finished preaching, Nestorius went with him into the sanctuary where they communicated together and concluded the liturgy. It was now clear to all where Nestorius' real sympathies lay.

Cyril, hearing of this, sent his now famous Second Letter to Nestorius[82] which demonstrates the effect his own extensive study has had. This letter was destined to be given canonical standing at the councils of Ephesus and Chalcedon as a synopsis of the key theological issues at stake. In it, Cyril not only defends the title Theotokos against accusations that it was reviving the heresy of Apollinarism, but he denies the very legitimacy of using alternative christological schemes such as the 'association of personas' the Antiochene thinkers had spoken of. This was the mainstay of Nestorius' own way of thinking, and neither side was unaware that now the argument had polarised sharply. Cyril also composed, and began to circulate in this Spring of 430, his Five Books Against Nestorius.[83]

For his part Nestorius followed the signal given in the sermon of Dorotheus and began to treat his dissidents in Constantinople as recalcitrant heretics. He deposed several of the leading monastic agitators, who inevitably appealed to the Emperor against him, demanding that an oecumenical council should review their case. It was the first time the idea had been mooted, and it seems to have lodged in the Emperor's head as a possible way out of an increasingly intractable dispute. Nestorius also composed an irate reply to Cyril's Second Letter. In this text Nestorius argues that Cyril was right to teach the two natures were united in one person, and right to say that the divinity cannot suffer in itself, but that when he goes on to speak of the deity 'participating in suffering' he undoes all his good work. His conclusion is heavy with sardonic insult. Cyril, he suggests, is a little 'too zealous for the cause of God' and too interested in the affairs of the church of Constantinople. Nestorius tells him that he has been misinformed about the real state of affairs in the capital by clerics who have since been tried and condemned for the heresy of Manicheism. All is well in his church, and the Emperor professes an irreproachable faith. The last two points are, again, merely lightly veiled threats. What he means is that Cyril's monastic party have already been tried and deposed by his synodical court, and that the Emperor is fully on his side.

Throughout the summer of 430, however, the ascetics continued

---

[82] Ep. 4. PG. 77.44–50.
[83] ACO 1.6.13–106.

secure in their high moral standing at the capital, attracting much sympathy in the general knowledge that they had powerful patrons behind them. As for Theodosius being in support of the Archbishop, this did indeed seem to be the case, despite the problems Nestorius had caused. Knowing this to be so Cyril directed substantial works to the Palace directly. The De Recta Fide was sent to the Emperor personally, and separate treatises (Ad Reginas) to the Empresses Pulcheria and Eudoxia, and another to the Royal Princesses Arcadia and Marina. These were designed to give, in separate works, the basic issues of the dispute, the centrally important authorities, and some aspects of the higher level of argumentation that was going on.

In his De Recta Fide Cyril presents the Emperor with a long line of unimpeachable authorities, and then attempts to isolate a central argument to the effect that although Nestorius was not mistaken in his desire to distinguish natures in Christ this was not much more than a stating of the obvious—that deity is not flesh or vice versa. Cyril must have heard that it was already on the basis that the Alexandrian opposition heretically confused the natures that Nestorius had presented himself as a champion of orthodoxy to the Emperor and had thus gained his ear. Cyril wanted to disabuse Theodosius of that idea and thus pricked the bubble by going on to argue, in his apologia, that Nestorius moved from the statement of a truism of the difference of natures to a heretical and logical error in presuming that this differentiation must inevitably mean a separation of natures, and even worse a differentiation of subject centres in Christ.[84] The work is an important chapter in the developing argument. Its two great constitutive ideas are firstly that if it is not God who personally effects our salvation as the subject of the incarnation then salvation is rendered ineffectual and the whole point of Christianity is lost; and secondly that a double-subject christology which divorces the man from the God in Christ makes void the church's hope and experience of redemption in and through the Eucharist, since the Eucharist is a life-giving sacrament precisely because it is the very flesh of God himself.[85] The eucharistic aspect of the controversy was never afterwards far away from Cyril's mind, which is a demonstration of how practical and concrete[86] his theology always was, rising as much from liturgical and spiritual experience as from logical and traditional systematic prescripts.

---

[84] cf. De Recta Fide. ch.6.

[85] cf. Gebremedhin (1977); Mahe (1907); Michaud (1902); Chadwick (1951).

[86] Or in Cyril's terms 'Economic'; that is, to do with the 'Economy' of salvation

Cyril's attempt to hedge his political position by appealing separately to Theodosius and the royal women misfired on this occasion, for it was greatly resented by the Emperor. He had been touched on a nerve, and in his subsequent letter summoning Cyril to attend his council he rebuked him for his impudence in even suggesting that all were not unanimous within the Royal Household.

This backfire of Cyril's plans must have encouraged Nestorius greatly at this period in the late summer of 430, and made him feel secure in the patronage of the Emperor. By this time he had grave suspicions that Cyril was seeking synodical support from the West, and the silence with which Rome greeted his letters must have struck him as ominous. He decided, therefore, to adopt a similar strategy and pre-empt all moves against him. He wrote at this time to John of Antioch appealing for assistance and advice. He also seems to have petitioned Theodosius to order an international Synod to review the whole theological question, not least Cyril's part in it. He wanted a small gathering of theological experts from each ecclesiastical province. It was thus not so much a general council he had in mind[87] as a more representative version of his own local synod, and the way he described the agenda made it clear that it would be a trial of Cyril not simply a general theological colloquium. He clearly thought that this policy was a sure way out of all difficulties, and would unquestionably establish his hold over his own church as well as consolidating his international standing. The fatal presupposition was that the meeting would take place, naturally enough, in the Royal City itself.

Although this seems to have been part of Theodosius' initial agreement to the idea, which he eventually gave in the winter of 430, by the time the international synod became a reality, in the Spring of the following year, someone had changed the venue to the city of Ephesus, the great Marian shrine in Asia Minor. One can

---

which God was working in the act of Incarnation. The Incarnation is, thus, for the Alexandrian fathers, primarily an energy of transformation, a soteriological impulse designed to redeem and deify human beings. All Cyril's thought about Christology is characterised by these dynamic motives.

[87] Councils of the church had always included all bishops, however unlearned, for they were not seen so much as theological colloquia as inspired perceptions of the truth by sacred hierarchs. His brief experience of his own synods at Constantinople might have led him astray on this point, for they were more in the manner of consultative assemblies for the Archbishop of Constantinople when leading bishops came to visit the royal court. This 'Home Synod' of Constantinople, however, was not a commonly accepted archetype of what a 'council' meant in the fifth century church.

but suspect the hand of Pulcheria here. At a stroke she had deflected the tide that had hitherto been running in the Archbishop's favour. When Nestorius finally heard this bombshell he must have had cause to regret his own proposal of the idea of a synod, for the circumstances of using Ephesus could hardly have been less favourable for him. Other pieces of news as they came in to him in that end of year and early spring were to give him further cause for anxiety. John of Antioch, on whom he had been relying to offset any possible official censure from Rome or Alexandria, replied to him in a very lukewarm fashion, urging caution and compromise. Nonetheless, armed with the increasing confidence that he had secured Theodosius' agreement to an international meeting, he wrote his Third Letter to Celestine where he describes the Theotokos dispute as a ploy on Cyril's part to avoid his own trial and censure for canonical irregularities. The letter to Celestine suggests very heavily that a large synod is to adjudicate the issue in the Royal City, but it was a premature bluff. Theodosius' formal agreement was still not given, and Nestorius at that time only had in his hand the cards of the various complaints he had received from a few disreputable Alexandrians against Cyril's administration. He must have known that he was leaning on a fragile reed there. His letter is, therefore, quite misleading, and was possibly designed to forestall any synodical meeting held against him in Rome, which by now he had deduced was a real possibility. This third Roman letter, like its two earlier exemplars, was greeted by silence.

From Cyril's point of view, before he received the Emperor's acerbic letter at the end of the year, everything seemed to be running in his favour. The disaffected clergy at Constantinople, orchestrated by Cyril's own agents there, had drafted a petition which they wished to present to the Emperor, calling for Nestorius' deposition. Cyril's agents sent him a draft of this, hoping that he would be the sponsor for its passage through the royal court but he was not at all pleased with this development and ordered the move to be abandoned. He had already initiated a proper canonical procedure and had no wish to use the Emperor to short-circuit ecclesiastical law, particularly when Nestorius had a readier access to the court than he did, and when Theodosius was so notoriously a vacillator. He told his apocrisarii to await the results of the Roman commission of enquiry. This reply to his own agents, and through them to the dissident faction at Constantinople, proves the falsity of the oft-heard complaint that it was Cyril's great fault never to have really listened to what Nestorius was saying, for his letter is a succinct and cogent analysis of his opponent's argumentation. In it Cyril concludes that Nestorius' replies to his previous letters had centred only on the notion of the impassibility of the Godhead, and that this merely sidestepped the real point at issue, which was the personal integrity of the incarnate Lord. Both this, and his argument in the De Recta Fide, clearly show Cyril had his finger well and truly on the pulse of the issue. In comparison Nestorius' analyses of the argument and his sermons are circular and unfocused. The same can be said of the other Antiochene apologists.

In the summer of 430 Cyril's new books, the Five Tomes Against Nestorius, were beginning to circulate and have their desired effect. Rome was meeting to adjudicate the issue, and its verdict was already assured as far as Cyril was concerned. Everything must have seemed more than satisfactory. Indeed this point of summer and late autumn of 430 marks the pinnacle of his early successes. Things were to become increasingly difficult for him thereafter.

The Orientals seemed to Cyril to be an obviously problematic area and to approach them he wrote in the late summer of 430 directly to the 'Grand Old Man' of the Oriental churches, the centenarian bishop Acacius of Beroea. Cyril was hoping to influence wider Syrian opinion through him. He had an earlier acquaintance with Acacius from many year's previously when they were both present at the Synod of the Oak engaged in the trial of St. John Chrysostom. Acacius' reply to Cyril's overtures was, however, evidently non-committal. He refused to be drawn into the dispute. He answered that he could see no great problem with Nestorius' doctrine anyhow, and expressed his sorrow that such a scandalous argument should have arisen at all. Cyril was counselled to seek for a peaceful and edifying solution to the conflict.

Having made no progress in this quarter his spirits were certainly raised by the long-awaited news from Rome that arrived at the end of summer of that busy year of 430. Archdeacon Leo's consultation with Cassian had been concluded (rather poorly it must be admitted for he had only produced a rambling and unfocused critique of Nestorius' works) with Cassian's pronouncement against the orthodoxy of Nestorius. He connected it, and thus fatally doomed it as far as Rome was concerned, with the heresy of Pelagianism—something that had probably already been in his initial brief from Rome. A Synod was called at Rome on August 11th 430 and Nestorius' teaching was formally anathematised by Pope Celestine and the Italian Bishops.

The Pope demanded a recantation from Nestorius and a profession of orthodox faith. He did not specify what this should be, except that it should harmonise with the creed of the Roman and Alexandrian churches. In his letter to Alexandria, Celestine effectively made Cyril the representative and executive of the Roman synodical decree, and this nominal delegation strengthened Cyril's hand canonically to such an extent that he continued to regard himself acting and speaking for the two great sees even up to the following year, and even when Celestine had sent his own delegation to the council at Ephesus. The Roman synod also communicated its verdict directly to the East—to Nestorius, to John of Antioch, Juvenal of Jerusalem, and the chief bishops of Macedonia (which at that period looked canonically to the Roman see) bishops Rufus of Thessalonike and Flavian of Philippi.

The crisis had now gained an irreversible momentum. Antioch and Constantinople were busy with consultations, the latter involving the royal court which now began to realise that the dispute had moved into a much more serious international context. The rift with Rome threatened the internal spiritual unity of the Empire at the very time when barbarian incursions were threatening its political coherence, especially in the West.

In conveying his verdict to Constantinople Pope Celestine had vindicated Cyril's theology as in accordance with the Latin tradition of Hilary, Damasus, and Ambrose. In a clearly hostile letter he mentioned Nestorius' sheltering of Pelagian heretics, and nullified his canonical depositions of his opponents at Constantinople, giving him ten days in which to recant. The christological issue had not really been addressed, and the old problem of Rome's canonical right to intervene in the East had risen once more to the fore, clouding the issue rather than resolving it. Despite Rome's hope that its word would be enough,[88] this manner of resolving doctrinal disagreement had never been the canonical procedure of the Eastern churches, who from the earliest times had followed a synodical process, not allowing monarchical rights of governance to any supreme bishop.[89] Immediately on

---

[88] As Augustine had expressed it: Roma locuta est causa finita est. (Rome has spoken, the issue is resolved); many catholic church histories continue to approach the entire controversy as a demonstration of the principle of papal primacy. In the fifth century the only party who held that perspective on matters was the Roman Chancery itself.

[89] From the time of Constantine I the eastern bishops had applied synodical process, appeals to the great metropolitan sees, and direct petitions to the Emperors, all as

receipt of the Pope's letter in Constantinople the Emperor resolved on his course of action. His capital's see had to be saved from public humiliation, and so, in November 430, he signalled his final agreement to the proposals for an oecumenical synod to consider the whole issue from the beginning. In the eyes of the court, this oecumenical gathering would supercede, de iure, the Roman synodical decrees, or those of any other local church. At the moment, however, Cyril was not aware of these developments.

When the Roman verdict was communicated to Alexandria, it was the occasion for Cyril to convoke his own synod of Egyptian bishops. They formally repeated, in November of the same year, the condemnation of Nestorius' doctrine, and whereas the Roman synodical letter had not made a christological exposition, Cyril remedied the defect and ensured that his own church would supply one. This he did in two forms. The first amounts to his Third Letter to Nestorius, which is a general statement of the Alexandrian position to which Rome itself had given its assent. The second was to raise storms of controversy, for he appended to the letter a list of twelve propositions to be formally renounced by Nestorius (the Twelve Chapters, or Anathemas) if he wished to avoid the sentence of condemnation from the churches of Rome and Alexandria. Cyril made acceptance of the anathemas a condition of Nestorius' readmission to communion, and therefore designed the exposition of Alexandrian christology propositionally in the most direct fashion, in primary colours as it were, specifically determined to deny the major premises of Nestorius' thought, and to allow him no room for verbal manouevring.[90]

Rome's vague desire that Nestorius should recant his opposition to the Theotokos doctrine and profess a consonant faith, had left the

---

legitimate methods of securing religious policy. Especially from the time of Damasus onwards, Rome had developed its theologoumenon of the prime apostolicity of its see (because of its Petrine tradition). This had a great impact on the Western churches who looked to Rome as their metropolitan centre, because no other see in the West had any claim to having been founded by an apostle. This was hardly the case in the Eastern church. So many cities claimed the apostles as their original founders that the doctrine of apostolicity had developed along different lines: any church which preserved apostolic doctrine was regarded as an apostolic see. From the earliest times the difference of ecclesiology led to a different view between Rome and the Eastern churches over episcopal rights of intervention in other churches. The issue continues to the present day in the division between the Orthodox and Roman communions.

[90] He had already stated that he regarded Nestorius as 'crooked' in his use of words, and rightly sensed that the latter could easily make a confession of faith that was as ambivalent as his other statements if it was not specified for him in advance.

door open to a large measure of possible adjustment between the different theological positions, given that a broad agreement on single-subject christology had been secured. When John of Antioch received a copy of the Roman verdict he had in fact urged Nestorius to conform to its reasonable demands, adding that this was the advice of many of the other oriental bishops.[91] By adding the Anathemas to specify the nature of Nestorius' recantation, Cyril had shown his determination not to leave the central issue of the christology open to such a breadth of interpretation. He was determined to press the point of single-subject christology in the most vigorous manner he could, and this is why his Anathemas leave no room at all for manouevre. They are a bold and strong statement of the Alexandrian position, in the graphic language of paradox, especially the famous twelfth, or 'Theopaschite', anathema urging the full implication of incarnational theology—that God died in the flesh.

Up to the point of sending these Chapters attached as a necessary condition of Nestorius' rehabilitation, Cyril had found that the resolution of the controversy was moving more or less satisfactorily in his direction. The furore caused by the publication of the Anathemas in the oriental churches changed the picture considerably, and was to put him on the defensive for the next three years, for it was widely believed by the orientals of the great Antiochene patriarchate (a belief much fostered by Nestorius) that Cyril had greatly overstated his case. Several of the hardline opponents of Alexandria were certain that he had even lapsed into the heresy of Apollinaris. Before the end of his life Cyril had to provide no less than three full scale works of apologetic to defend his cause by explaining what he really meant by the Anathemas. The Explanation of the Twelve Chapters in the present collection of translated texts is one example of these, addressed to a wide circle of bishops and designed to regain support for himself as the spokesman of a properly oecumenical christology. The other two apologies were designed to refute the more detailed attacks on his position by able theologians of the Antiochene tradition—mainly Andrew of Samosata and Theodoret of Cyr. From 430 onwards these two were his main intellectual opponents.

On more than one occasion, particularly at the council in the following year, Cyril must have questioned the wisdom of summarising his careful and complex thought in that vulnerable propositional format,

[91] ACO 1.1. 93–95.

for it was to cost him such a large diversion of his energies. Nonetheless, when he attached them to the Egyptian synodical letter he must have felt greatly confident, still unaware that Nestorius had pre-empted him by persuading Theodosius to move for a general council. At first Nestorius gave no answer, but Cyril was determined to press home the canonical sentence and sent from Egypt a delegation of four of his bishops, Theopemptus, Daniel, Potamon, and Comaros, to deliver the synodical documents in person and to demand a response on the spot.

They arrived from Alexandria in the imperial city on Saturday December 6th 430. On the Sunday following they entered the cathedral at the most dramatic moment they could choose, during the course of a liturgy which was being attended by most of the members of the royal court. Entering the apse, where Nestorius was enthroned, they delivered their texts and decree to him personally. He was unable to make much of a response in the circumstances, and so arranged for them to attend at his palace the following morning. Subsequently, having read the texts, he refused them an interview when they arrived the next day. His feelings of outrage surfaced on the following Saturday December 13th when he arranged to speak to a packed cathedral on the matter.

'Isn't the Egyptian the eternal enemy of Constantinople and Asia?' he said, colouring the dispute as if it was another version of the attack on St. John Chrysostom, the great saint who symbolically united both cities. He suggested in this sermon that Cyril's political ambitions were at the root of the whole controversy which he felt had grown out of all proportion from a dispute over the honorific title of the virgin Theotokos. This he was now prepared to accept, 'for the sake of peace', as long as it was generally agreed that all Arian and Apollinarist readings of the term were ruled out. This, his first public gesture of compromise,[92] appeared on the occasion to be popular. When he repeated in the liturgy of the following Sunday that he was prepared to accept the legitimacy of the title Theotokos he was loudly applauded by his congregation. He still argued that the adoption of the title Christ-Mother would be a far better theological procedure, and so even after his compromise his opponents must have felt that there had been no movement whatsoever from his first arrival in the city when he adopted the same position. At the end of his Saturday sermon Nestorius had concluded on a buoyant note: if Cyril came to the imperial city,

[92] Following the advice given by John of Antioch.

where the Emperor's troops would ensure that no riotous machinations could take place, then everything could be sorted out very quickly indeed. Of course he did not specify whether this would be by theological exchange or merely the arrest of Cyril—and archimandrite Basil and his monks, still nursing their bruises, must have had cause to ponder his meaning. The remark, however, indicates his self-confidence was running high at the prospect of what he still thought at this stage was to be the order of the day—a council held in Constantinople under his presidency, and which would probably include a judicial review of Cyril's behaviour. His presumptions were to prove sadly unfounded.

The Augusta Pulcheria had not been idle in the meantime, and when the formal arrangements for the great council were begun Nestorius could only have been dismayed to find out that the venue had been determined for Ephesus, the metropolitan capital of Asia Minor. The site had ostensibly been recommended for its capacity to supply foodstuffs for the assembly from a greater agricultural hinterland than Constantinople; but in reality Ephesus was the greatest christian shrine dedicated to Mary then in existence. A place more likely to be antagonistic to Nestorius could not have been thought of. Nestorius must have been further dismayed when he found out that an insignificant detachment of troops had been allocated to superintend the proceedings. Nestorius clearly had a sharper sense of Cyril's political weight than Theodosius had been able to gain over a much longer time occupying the highest offices of state.

When the imperial Sacras were sent out to all the major christian hierarchs summmoning them to attend at Ephesus at Pentecost, the following year, both Nestorius and Cyril knew that matters had taken a turn that could be detrimental to both of them. The copy of the letter which Theodosius sent with Cyril's personal Sacra was hostile in tone. It probably served to warn Cyril that not only was the Emperor annoyed at his appeal to the Empresses, but that plans to move against him juridically might still be a real possibility. Indeed from the winter of 430 onwards Nestorius had seized on the Twelve Chapters as his life-line, depicting them to the court and the Antiochene patriarchate alike as a revival of Apollinarism.

Nestorius lost no time in communicating them to his most able colleagues in the oriental churches, Andrew of Samosata, and Theodoret of Cyr. They too were of the opinion that Cyril had wrongly overstated his case on the monosubjectivity of the divine person in the incarnation, and both of them independently set to work composing a detailed refutation and exposure of Cyril.[93] The quality of their work was more considered than that of Nestorius himself, and in the course of answering their more advanced theological criticisms Cyril was himself to gain a deeper understanding of the ramifications of the christological argument than ever he would have achieved having merely Nestorius as his intellectual foil.

Andrew of Samosata robustly accused Cyril (quite wrongly in terms of his reading of the evidence) of the profoundly Apollonarist belief that Christ's flesh was not of real, human, derivation. Theodoret's accusations were often more diffuse, but in the course of their attacks both orientals made substantial advances on the earlier Antiochene theology as represented by Theodore Mopsuestia (and now seemingly being restated by Nestorius). These changes in position were not immediately recognised at the time of the conflict, but they marked a significant concession on the part of the Antiochenes to some of the essential points Cyril was trying to secure. In the aftermath of the council of Ephesus, particularly in his letters to Eulogius, Cyril is able to state that he can now distinguish between the correct intention of the orientals in general to secure a single-subject Christology, and what he still sees as the heretical dubiousness of Nestorius on this point. Even after his recognition of the orientals' substantial orthodoxy he makes it clear to Eulogius that he would not use their language by preference, but cannot any longer agree to reject it on principle.[94] Andrew of Samostata, for example, when he turns from a misrepresentation of Cyril's version of the unity of subject in Christ and attempts to describe it on his own terms argues that we must discount the view that Jesus could be seen as a pre-eminent saint, and he speaks of the worship that is due to one single Son. Theodoret, in his turn, interprets the phrase 'God assumed man' as meaning God assumed manhood, the human state, rather than an individual man in any adoptionist sense. This is the neo-Antiochene position that resulted from, or was at least clarified by, the clash with Cyril, and it represents a considerable distancing of christological opinion from that of Diodore of Tarsus and Theodore Mopsuestia even though this was never publicly admitted. Such clarifications, which Cyril had been pressing to receive from Nestorius and had not, in the years after the council of Ephesus

[93] cf. Mahé (1906).

[94] In the Letter to Eulogius he puts it (para.3.) as follows: 'The Orientals confessed these things even if they were somewhat obscure in their terminology. . . . This is not what Nestorius does . . .'

were to form the basis of the rapprochement of the Alexandrian and Antiochene theological traditions that was to lead into the Chalcedonian council of 451 and beyond. But for the moment, as the storm clouds gathered in the late winter of 430, no-one was currently thinking of rapprochement.

Cyril buried himself in further writing between December 430 and May 431. He composed replies to both refutations of the orientals, once he had received them, that became his treatises, Response To The Orientals, and To Euoptus (Against Theodoret). In both works he denied and disproved the accusations of Apollinarism in his theology. Then, as now, many people cried 'Apollinarism' against him without quite understanding what this meant: some even to the point of thinking that one was Apollinarist if one believed in the singleness of subject in the incarnate Lord. So, as a first premise, Cyril tried to define the nature of the heresy being attributed to him. He described the Apollinarist error as resting upon two main tenets both of which he was determined to demonstrate he abhorred and had denied in his own work; the first was that the manhood of the Saviour was devoid of a soul, that is mindless (without Nous) or lacking its own rational life-principle and thus merely an automaton of the deity; the second was that the flesh of Christ was 'heavenly' that is not like other human bodies but, as it were, a different entity of 'divine flesh'.[95] Here Cyril knew that he was on safe ground for he had consistently denigrated such positions in his earlier work. His problem was how to demonstrate his own theological conception so as to differentiate it clearly from sounding like an Apollinarist theory.

He decided to turn the argument back to its positive aspect and in his reply to the orientals posed as the key theological issue that underlay the whole argument the question whether Jesus should be properly and distinctly (idikōs) viewed as a human individual (a Jewish man) or whether he was the divine Son in person (God). His apologetic riposte was not wholly satisfactory. He was to realize at Ephesus, six months later, that he still had not done enough to disarm his most vociferous critics, and that the problem lay in the clarity and consistency of his use of his own chosen technical terms to describe his christology.

Some key issues in the argument still needed several more years

---

[95] The appeal to the concept of 'heavenly flesh', generally alluding to 1 Cor.15.47 as a key proof text, was a graphic way of synopsising the Apollinarist understanding of the Krasis or fusion of the divine and human natures in Christ to form a new 'mixture' of a newly constituted single nature.

to reach a better resolution, in particular the way in which the manner or mode of union of the divine and human in Christ could fruitfully be articulated. The orientals accused Cyril either of having muddied it so much as to make the relative attribution of qualities break down into extreme, impossible, or unfitting paradoxes such as 'the death of God', or 'God's sorrowing tears' (which they felt to be tantamount to mythical paganism), or of having so absorbed the reality of Christ's manhood into the power of the active deity of the Logos that the manhood became merely a symbolic cipher involved in the divine act of redemption, rather than a primary instrument of that redemption. In trying to answer these two key criticisms Cyril's thought reached a new intensity of focus. In essence he rejected the first, but qualified the second. The 'unfitting paradoxes' which his opponents saw were for him the power and point of the incarnation, made comprehensible only as the wonderful humility of the God who abased himself for our sake. He would not give ground on this point at all. As to the second objection, he accepted that the humanity was not a cipher but a primary instrument of redemption, and tried to re-articulate why his understanding of the incarnation did not involve the annihilation of humanity in Christ, rather its enhancement. The process of this intellectual war will be further discussed when we subsequently consider Cyril's theology on its own terms.

Once Cyril felt that his central point of single-subjectivity in Christ had been secured, he showed himself willing to give ground, but in the Spring of 431 he certainly did not feel that such an admission had clearly been gained either from Nestorius or from the oriental theologians. Probably in a growing state of alarm he wrote to Pope Celestine, somewhat desperately, to raise the query whether their mutual synodical condemnation of Nestorius should stand, despite the imperial convocation of an oecumenical synod subsequent to it. If the Pope supported him, Cyril could have a canonical right to insist that Nestorius could not appear at the Ephesian synod except as a defendant. This would not only secure his own case, at least symbolically, in advance of the council, but it would also debar Nestorius from raising any canonical charges against Cyril himself. Someone being formally arraigned could not legally impeach his accuser or judges at the same trial. It was a clever manoeuvre, but one that he could not be sure would work. It was clear, in the face of the impending oecumenical synod, that the higher ecclesiastical court would, *de iure*, be able to review and reconsider all the issues afresh, however much Rome and Alexandria might protest that the issue had already been finally decided. Pope Celestine seems to have had no illusions on this score. While Cyril's letter to him has not survived, the Pope's response to it on May 7th 431 has, and in it he advises the necessity of moderation and discretion so that Nestorius may be won back.

Unknown to Cyril Celestine composed another letter on the following day addressed to the Emperor Theodosius, but only to be delivered in certain circumstances. He sealed this and proceeded to arrange, with the Archdeacon Leo, the delegation that would represent Rome at the forthcoming council. It was to consist of the bishops Arcadius and Projectus and the priest Philip who seems to have been a member of the Roman chancery.[96] The delegates were instructed to follow the line and tenor of Cyril's lead but on no account were they to become embroiled in the controversies between opposing parties. On the contrary they were to stand apart and adjudicate as befits judges. Since the only foreseeable controversy 'between parties' could be that between the Alexandrian and Antiochene camps, it is interesting to discern in the Pope's instructions a certain desire to distance himself now from the carte blanche he had given to the Alexandrian Patriarch in the preceding Autumn.

The sealed letter was another indication of Celestine's political distancing. If Cyril won the day at Ephesus, the papal legates were instructed to travel on with him to Constantinople and present the secret letter to the Emperor. In this the Pope insisted on the right of bishops to determine the true faith, and requested that the Emperor should sanction what the council had decided, and what he himself had already determined in advance of it. On the other hand, if Cyril lost the day, the papal legates were to stay with him at Ephesus and reconsider their position after consultation.

For all Celestine's careful planning he could not possibly have foreseen the actual diplomatic chaos that would ensue. His letters clearly presume that Nestorius' position will be rejected at Ephesus, but he had sufficient doubts as to the fate of Cyril to make him want to secure his own position independently.

Theodosius had set the council to begin at Ephesus on Pentecost

---

[96] In the early sessions of the council at which the Romans were present it is Philip who evidently carries the authority to speak, but as time wore on and the Pope's original directions became less relevant, the bishops reassert their independent judgement and he fades from the scene. Doubtless they were encouraged in this policy by Cyril as well as the sight of the eastern synodical process in full spate.

of 431, which was to fall that year on June 7th. He appointed Count Candidianus, head of his own Palace Guard, to supervise the synod and ensure that good order was kept in the city. It is difficult to determine whether Candidian was as neutral a figure from the outset as many have supposed, and only turned against Cyril after the proceedings had started. In retrospect (and it was certainly the complaint of the Cyrilline party at large), Candidian's actions showed a constant bias in favour of Nestorius and his rapid alliance with his friend and colleague Count Irenaeus (who was in personal attendance on Nestorius) makes his neutrality at least suspect. Perhaps Theodosius' choice of a sympathetic military presence was designed to offset his concession to those who had urged him to site the meeting in Asia Minor.

Candidian's primary instructions were to clear out monks and lay people coming to Ephesus out of curiosity, that is to ensure that the bishops engaged in dialogue and heard one another out, without resorting to popular or monastic factions to settle the arguments more robustly. He was ordered to stop any bishop leaving the council prematurely, trying to appeal personally to the Imperial court. Theodosius was determined that the bishops should be held together long enough until they had resolved the entire issue definitively.

Following the religious policy laid down by the founder of his house, Theodosius I,[97] he insisted that Candidian should not intervene or involve himself in the theological proceedings themselves, but keep a strict surveillance on the legal processes and see to the good order of the synod as a whole. This instruction not to be involved in the theological discussions was written explicitly into Candidian's personal Sacra, the very one that had to be read out publicly at the start of the whole legal processes. It was to prove the fatal flaw of the best laid plans of the Emperor. Dvornik has shown[98] how synodical procedure from the earliest days of the Byzantine Empire was based upon the Senatorial model, and this seems to have been Theodosius' image and expectation of his oecumenical council. The separation of state legal prescript, however, and ecclesiastical canonical precedents (issues such as which see had the right to precedence and chairmanship of the proceedings) were far too complicated to have been

[97] For interesting parallels between this and the policy of military supervision at the Council of Constantinople I in 381, convoked by Theodosius the Great, see Ep.136 of St. Gregory Nazianzen. PG 37. 232.

[98] (1934), (1966).

theoretically divided out in such a crude way as Theodosius does. Candidian's task had been made impossible even before he left the imperial city with his detachment of troops. Subsequent events were to prove this only too clearly.

Now, in the late Spring of 431, feverish activities were being made across the christian world, from Persia to Carthage, for the great journey to Asia Minor and all the hardships it would impose. More involved than anyone else were the Archbishops of Constantinople and Alexandria who presumed they would meet face to face, for the first time, after such hard exchanges of words.

3. A Year of Intrigues: The Council of Ephesus, 431

The Emperor had designed the Council, as outlined in his Sacra,[99] so that each metropolitan bishop throughout the provinces would attend and bring with him some of his more distinguished suffragans. The discussions he must have had with Nestorius over the issues at stake, and his subsequent receipt of Cyril's weighty treatises, including the De Recta Fide, had served to impress him with the complexity of the theological issues that needed resolution. His stated intention, to reserve personal matters of the judgement of bishops to the supreme court at Constantinople for the whole duration of the conciliar proceedings, was evidently designed as an attempt to focus the agenda of the bishops strictly on to the christological problem. It manifests his unwillingness at this stage to pursue Nestorius' policy of prosecuting Cyril on the basis of complaints received. Theodosius was also sufficiently impressed by the preliminary arguments he had so far heard as to give Count Candidian strict instructions not to get involved in the theological proceedings.

Theodosius' arguments in this case were, like much else he did, admirable in theory but easily subverted in practice. Like many other paper preparations for important and volatile meetings, the imperial design theory was to bear little relationship to the reality that was now to unfold. The first vague instruction in the Sacra, to bring only eminent suffragans, was interpreted with wide variations in the different provinces. John of Antioch's province of Syria was an incredibly vast ecclesiastical territory in geographical extent. The christian bishops of Persia and parts of Arabia even looked to him as their titular

[99] cf ACO 1.1.114–116.

spokesman, and the physical geography of the territory in question meant that delegations would have to be gathered by dromedary caravans from the deserts, and pack trains through and across the mountains. John began the lengthy process of alerting this great and diverse constituency, and of gathering in his delegates.

From the issue of the Sacra on November 19th 430, to the proposed opening of the council at Pentecost (June 7th 431), there was precious little time for the Syrians to get organised, especially (as John was later to complain) when the invitation itself was considerably delayed in its arrival from Constantinople. John's central party was to include Theodoret whom he would rely on to match Cyril in intellectual debate. Andrew of Samosata was not in attendance at Ephesus but the work of both he and Theodoret, in the previous year, had been explained to the oriental bishops when they assembled in synod at Antioch before setting out on their journey. For the rest, John restricted his representatives to his metropolitan archbishops alone who were each allowed to bring with them no more than two suffragan bishops. This ensured a wide representation of the Syrian churches while only requiring a relatively modest number to brave the hardships of the long overland journey from Antioch to Ephesus. When he subsequently held his separate meeting of delegates at Ephesus, even with the support of several of Nestorius' party, his voting list could only stretch to 43.[100]

Nestorius similarly followed the instructions of the Sacra fairly closely. Aware that the theological heavyweights would be arriving in the Syrian delegation he gathered a party from the immediate region of Constantinople of only sixteen bishops. Socrates describes him as arriving at Ephesus with 'a large number of armed guards',[101] but the remark needs to be treated with great caution. There can be little doubt that he arrived in Ephesus, as Archbishop of the imperial city, in the company of the detachment of troops sent out under the command of Count Candidian. These were not exactly his own bodyguard. As events subsequently unfolded they came to be closely associated with him as Candidian's neutrality was more and more abandoned, and this version of events, dating from many months after the council itself, must have become the standard perception which reached Socrates. From the first days Nestorius' personal bodyguard was provided by his friend Count Irenaeus. This was a determined

---

[100] cf. ACO 1.5.119–124.
[101] Hist. Eccl.7.34. PG.67.813.

and important military factor. No Byzantine aristocrat would have travelled across the provinces without a skilled military force at his disposal, but despite the fact that it would have included all the servants who were to look after the needs of the party in their time at Ephesus, its size cannot have been particularly large. Theodosius had allowed Irenaeus to attend on Nestorius, doubtless aware that this would ensure the personal safety of his Archbishop, but he was forbidden to involve himself in the conciliar proceedings. The subsequent alliance of Candidian's soldiery with the personal retinue of Irenaeus had a decided influence on events in Ephesus despite all Theodosius' pious, and somewhat naive, intentions expressed in his Sacra. On the day that Nestorius arrived in Ephesus, in the company of the complete imperial guard, along with his personal retinue, it must have seemed to the local church there that he had brought with him a small number of bishops who were insignificant in comparison to the numbers of troops. It was taken by some as a sign of his policy for the forthcoming council.

Memnon, the Metropolitan archbishop of Ephesus, drew in almost the full extent of his Asian[102] suffragans for what was, for them, a local council. He was thus able to summon a group of forty hierarchs and a further twelve from neighbouring Pamphylia. He was to be Cyril's closest ally, politically as well as theologically, at the forthcoming council. Memnon was also able to count on the fervent and unquestioned loyalty of the local people of the province, who looked to him as their leader with far more immediacy than the imperial troops who claimed a somewhat distant authority for their mandate. Memnon was a power to reckon with, and in the face of the imperial troops commanded a great reservoir of popular factions that was more than capable of balancing them out if it came to a test of strength. This remained so even after Candidian, in his alarm at the political climate of the city, had drafted in the emergency reinforcements of a local garrison.

As for Egypt, the imperial instruction to assemble mainly metropolitan bishops had little relevance there from the start. The great expanse of the Alexandrian patriarchate ecclesiastically mirrored the political reality of the country—that there was one great city alone, and that was Alexandria, with a vast hinterland of small, sometimes tiny, local churches with village bishops. Cyril accordingly assembled

[102] ie. The Roman Province of Asia Minor, largely covered by present day Turkey.

his delegation from among his suffragans in a similar way to Memnon. He brought together fifty Egyptian hierarchs, representing about one half of the Egyptian sees. There is no doubt that he was determined to be secure in the voting. Several commentators have accused Cyril of bringing with him a riotous assembly of sailors, parabalani, monks and assorted villains to threaten the peace of Ephesus. Frequently they have attributed to him all the civil disturbances that took place during the council, but there is little justification for this, and even less if we separate out Memnon's role from that of Cyril. The orientals are quite clear that it was Memnon whom they wanted to accuse of fomenting civil unrest. In a letter now only extant in Coptic[103] Cyril justifies himself by oath exactly on this point as he writes back home to Alexandria from his imprisonment at Ephesus: 'Since now, indeed, I know that some have written to Constantinople about my character, that I have brought with me from Alexandria a crowd of reckless fellows, and ships loaded with grain,[104] and they have brought forward many other slanders against me, for this reason it was necessary for me to inform your Piety also about this matter, to the effect that neither has any reckless fellow at all followed me, nor have we brought a single measure of grain. God is my witness . . . we are here each isolated with only two attendants and the necessary clerics who look after us in a fitting way.' The text slightly fudges the issue of how many monks were in attendance, refusing to call them 'reckless fellows' and insisting they were 'clerics', but the point still stands that there is no hard evidence to suggest Cyril brought with him the 'army' that he is often depicted as being able to call on in Ephesus. The relative ease with which Nestorius' lay adherents were able to cut off the supplies and communications of the much larger Cyrilline majority gives the lie to this version of relative political strengths.

Cyril's party of bishops came to Ephesus by sea, following the path of the established corn-route from Alexandria to Constantinople. This traversed the islands up the coast of Asia Minor. Cyril travelled in the same ship as the thaumaturg Shenoude, and his senior hierarchs. A severe storm seemingly made it a trying passage, and writing back to his church from Rhodes where they had taken shelter he describes the adventures.[105] When they finally arrived in Ephesus they assembled

---

[103] Ep. 108, ET. McEnerney. (1987) pp. 172–174.
[104] As bribes.
[105] Ep. 20. ACO.1.1.1. p. 116; E.T. McEnerney (1987) pp. 98–99.

into a triumphant procession including all the bishops, monks, and sailors who had navigated them, and made their way into the city to a warm welcome provided by Memnon. Nestorius must have had great cause for misgiving; from the moment of his arrival the local bishop had refused to communicate with him, and barred his churches to him, treating him like a canonical defendant (as he technically was since the Roman synod had found against him) who had to be heard in council before he could be rehabilitated. On Cyril's arrival this was the policy the latter also adopted. Not once did the two great rivals exchange a word face to face in all the time they were together in the city of Ephesus. By contrast Cyril was made welcome at Ephesus by the local clergy as a highly important visiting dignitary.

The representation of the Western church was to be minimal. Apart from the papal delegation of Bishops Arcadius and Projectus and the priest Philip, Italy was unrepresented. Even this delegation did not physically arrive until early July when the main drama of the council had been acted out. The ancient sees of Africa were in the throes of the Vandal invasion, and the Imperial military cause was not going at all well. Transport from town to town was dangerous, taking ship across the Mediterranean almost an impossibility. Only one messenger was sent, the deacon Bessula who came to represent Bishop Capreolus of Carthage, the primatial see of Africa. He brought news of Augustine's death along with a general letter that urged the assembled bishops to allow no innovation in the faith—a vague letter which Cyril was to interpret as Africa's endorsement of conciliar proceedings. Apart from the symbolic value of the papal support for Cyril, Western influence at this council was to count for very little indeed. Flavius of Philippi and the Macedonian delegation were the most westerly provinces represented in the actual conciliar debates. These were staunchly on Cyril's side.

The council had been called by Theodosius to open on Pentecost Sunday, June 7th. Nestorius and his sixteen bishops were the first party of visitors to arrive in Ephesus. They came in good time in advance of the date, and were followed by Cyril and the Alexandrians who arrived only a few days before Pentecost. There was no sign, however, of the Antiochene or Roman delegates. The bishops of Palestine, led by Juvenal of Jerusalem, amounted to sixteen in all, and when they arrived a week later on June 12th they immediately aligned themselves with the parties of Cyril and Memnon of Ephesus. Flavian of Philippi arrived at the same time. The latter took a leading role in the operation of the synodical proceedings and became a close ally of Cyril. The fact that Memnon had publicly closed the churches to Nestorius, refusing to allow him the right to celebrate any service of prayers or liturgy until his case had been reviewed by the council, must have brought home to Nestorius that his hopes to make the meeting a judicial review of Cyril were no longer a political reality. Memnon was undoubtedly hostile to all that Nestorius stood for, but his closure of the churches to him was in strict accordance with ecclesiastical protocol once the result of the Roman synod had been publicly notified, and the further one came away from Constantinople the more did ecclesiastical precedent weigh more heavily than current imperial policy. It was a lesson that was imposing itself ever more urgently on Nestorius. The growing weight of numbers of the assembled bishops, and the clear signs of an early alignment with Cyril, must also have given him cause for disquiet. Still there was no sign of the Syrian delegation.

John of Antioch had been preparing his delegates for the theological issues they would be required to adjudicate at Ephesus. The land journey from Antioch to Asia Minor would take thirty days under normal conditions, given that the bishops could use the facilities of the imperial post stations. But before they had even left Antioch a combination of circumstances conspired to delay them. Theodosius' announcement at Easter that the Council would open at the following Pentecost, by the time it was delivered to John at Antioch, left him insufficient time to organise the gathering of his delegates. John's letter summoning the Syrian bishops[106] allowed twelve days for them to assemble in the Syrian capital. Easter that year was on the 19th April, but in Antiochene custom the feast involved not merely the ceremonies of Holy Week itself, but a solemn octave of liturgical celebrations following. This 'Apodosis' of the feast meant that the Syrians did not set out until April 27th, leaving themselves hardly any margin of time for a feasible Pentecost rendezvous. The journey, once undertaken, proved to be far from the express thirty days passage they might have hoped for. The river Orontes burst its banks in the rains and cut off their intended route, imposing a considerable detour. Sickness among the entourage (and there was a number of aged bishops in the company) hampered their progress, and the death of some of the delegates en route delayed them further. All in all it seems to

[106] Evagrius. Hist. Eccl.1.1.3.

have been a miserable passage, and this goes a large part of the way to explaining John's undiplomatic and unconsidered actions as soon as he arrived in Ephesus only to discover the whole journey had been rendered pointless.

As the heat of June wore on, the general feelings and tensions at Ephesus were running higher and higher. Physically the conditions were uncomfortable for all the visitors. Ephesus had been selected partly as a provincial metropolis large enough to provide for the extraordinary influx of visitors in terms of food and accommodation. The city's agricultural hinterland, and the produce available through the port, were supposed to be able to cope with the great influx but the city's resources were clearly strained considerably by the synod: large numbers of important entourages could not be accommodated indiscriminately, in addition there were the band of accompanying servants, clerics, notaries, and soldiers. Even at the very beginning of the council the long delay caused by the Syrians was beginning to put a strain on all involved. By the end of the synod, several months later, the crisis (exacerbated by the embargo imposed by Cyril's opponents) had reduced many sections of the city to starvation point.

The delay of the Syrians gave the occasion for much lobbying among the bishops already in attendance. Cyril, in another letter home to Alexandria, complains of Nestorius prowling about like Satan sleeplessly 'plotting against the glory of Christ—though he makes no headway'.[107] Cyril lobbied extensively himself, but refused to communicate in any way with Nestorius, a public sign that he regarded the Roman verdict as having already settled the matter in hand. With Memnon and the Palestinian hierarchs he was now able to reckon on the support of at least one hundred and twenty bishops strongly committed to the anti-Nestorian cause.

Similarly Nestorius had gathered a firm group of adherents around him chief among them being the very outspoken Dorotheus of Marcianopolis whom he had earlier used to preach in the Great Church at Constantinople, anathematising all those who used the Theotokos title. The key factors in this immediate prelude to the council were the Syrian delegation (which had a policy, as Cyril already knew, designed to attack his own theology as outlined in the Twelve Chapters)

[107] Ep. 21. ACO. 1.1.1. p. 117; E.T. McEnerney (1987) p. 100. Cyril's reference is to 1 Peter 5.7–9, which very appositely gives an insight into his feelings on the eve of the opening of the council.

and the large number of undecided bishops, sixty or seventy in total[108] who felt, as yet, no need to commit themselves to any party in advance of hearing both sides of the argument. Of these some had no opinion because they had not fully understood the complexity of the issues, others were still trying to finalise their understanding of the controversy, and yet others were simply not prepared to grant Cyril the right to presidency of the council, given his involvement in the dispute, and were waiting for the arrival of John of Antioch to decide the matter of who should take the chair and finalise the agenda.

As there was still no sign of the Syrians, both Cyril's and Nestorius' parties concentrated on changing the minds of the neutrals. It did not take long, however, for the latter to be more and more identified as potentially hostile to Cyril and to Memnon the local hierarch, and this was taken with some umbrage by the Ephesian populace who, like all provincials in ancient cities, had little love for visitors who did not respect their local prestige, especially as it was epitomised in the wishes of their bishop, for them the authentic voice of 'Ephesian' Christianity. The vacillating brethren among the neutral group of bishops were certainly shaken by the hostility they soon began to encounter from the local people, for whom Memnon and Cyril were the heroes of the day. The popular celebrations following the announcement of the deposition of Nestorius after the council's first session cannot wholly be explained by the orchestration of the events by pro-Cyrilline clerics, for the citizens of Ephesus were wholeheartedly behind the propagation of the Theotokos title. For them the defence of the Mother of God was synonymous with upholding the honour of their own city whose christian identity and prestige was inextricably linked with her cult. The church of the Virgin and the tomb of John the Apostle were the chief glories of christian Ephesus, and an essential part of the city's redefinition of identity in the Byzantine period. The Mother of God as patroness would ensure that Ephesus had as glorious a future in the christian oecumene as once it had in its now overshadowed past when it was dedicated to the Mother Goddess, Ephesian Artemis, whose shrine was one of the chief wonders of the ancient world. The great basilica church of the city was dedicated to Mary. This was set aside for the very meetings of the council that was soon to assemble. Devotion to Mary at a popular level was a factor that Nestorius had underestimated in Constantinople. He again seems to

[108] The conciliar lists fluctuate slightly.

have underestimated its impact on the people of Ephesus. His customary style of proposing his arguments half jestingly, as he ridiculed what he saw as the excesses of devotional theology, served only to increase his isolation in the city. What was worse, his highly propositional style of argument not only bamboozled ordinary people, it left many of the bishops (some of whom were definitely illiterate)[109] equally confused and increasingly unfavourable to him.

When marks were daubed, threateningly, on their lodging houses one night, several of this central group of unaligned bishops were sufficiently alarmed as to throw in their lot with Cyril and Memnon's majority forthwith. As the tensions in the city rose, and frustrations increased because of the delay of the Syrians, without news, the growing number of clashes between the various camp-followers (and even some of the bishops themselves who almost came to blows on occasions if Nestorius' later account in the Book of Heraclides is to be accepted) alarmed Count Candidian so much that he drafted in military reinforcements from neighbouring provincial garrisons, to police the city and prevent the delegates from further mutual intimidation.

Two significant events in the theological lobbying occurred during this preliminary period, which can even be regarded as the decisive moment of Nestorius' downfall. They consisted in the public arguments, at Nestorius' lodging house, between himself and his former friend Acacius of Melitene,and another oriental bishop Theodotus of Ancyra. Acacius was a skilled Syrian theologian who had been in communication with Cyril, and was concerned to secure on the part of his oriental colleagues the clear rejection of a double-subject christology. The more he did this the more did tempers start to fray among the Nestorian circle.

Theodotus of Ancyra, another oriental bishop entertained by Nestorius, found the Archbishop's theological style an irritant, in the way he insisted on strict formality of intellectual discourse. Nestorius seems to have regarded Theodotus as a simpleton, and was instructing him,

---

[109] Theodore, the Bishop of Gadara in Palestine, when he came to sign the condemnation of Nestorius sent his Archdeacon up, who (rather unkindly) drew everyone's attention on the legal paper to the fact that the Bishop 'did not know his letters' (ACO.1.2.63. signature 190). The same bishop however, was one of those who stood up in the course of the debates to give his opinion, quite robustly, that Cyril's letters were undoubtedly pious, and in accordance with Nicene faith, and by implication that those of Nestorius were not ACO 1.2.20.(para.47). He was not one to be refused his say on the faith simply because he had no intellectual qualifications. There must have been many like him, even among those who could sign their names.

as he had done the people in Constantinople over the previous two years, on the necessity of making strict distinctions in language between the human and divine conditions apparent in the incarnation. In the course of this exchange he seems genuinely to have scandalised Theodotus. The incident led to the bishop indignantly abandoning his former colleague, soon to be followed by Acacius.

The public defection of Acacius and Theodotus from Nestorius' camp, and their evidence formally rehearsed in the council's first session, effectively secured Nestorius' condemnation. The latter was certainly loose in his talk, ironically so for one who was always arguing the point of strict logical propriety in theological discourse. When Acacius had pressed him to admit that the unity of subject in the incarnate Christ was secured by seeing the divine Logos as the immediate subject of the incarnate acts, Nestorius countered in his usual way that such a view endangered the sense of the impassibility of the Logos. However, he put his point in a very testy way, evidently an argument *ad hominem* in the heat of the moment, and said to Acacius: 'If it is God the Word, second Person of the Trinity, who is made flesh, then you must confess that the Holy Spirit, and God the Father himself, have equally been made flesh, because the Trinity is threefold but only one in substance'.[110] He obviously meant to ridicule Cyril's position. It is also highly probable that his remark rose out of the specific context of an argument over Cyril's conception of a natural union (mia physis, henosis physike) of the divine and human in Christ which Nestorius took to be nothing more than Apollinarism revisited. Nestorius rejected the possibility of using the category of nature/natural to signify the christological union on the grounds of a strict logical syllogism that will be elaborated more fully later, but can be stated briefly here for the sake of clarification. In his view if a 'natural union' was posited as the basis of Christ's personal integrity then it would be entirely appropriate to ask what was this integral nature that was so attributed? If it was a divine nature, then Christ could not be a man; if it was a human nature then Christ could not be God; and if it was a synthetically combined semi-divine and semi-human nature then such a hybrid could neither claim to be God nor man. In short by this trinitarian test case Nestorius was demanding that Cyril clarify his understanding of the manner of the christological union, accusing him in the process of a teaching that was heretical in its implications.

[110] ACO 1.2. p. 38. which gives Theodotus' and Acacius' evidence.

Nonetheless, whatever the sophistication of his intentions, his stark *reductio ad absurdum*, 'If God the Word became flesh then all the Trinity must have become flesh since the Trinity is bound together as one nature' sounded in the popular forum (both at street level and in the conciliar chamber where it was cited as evidence of his present state of mind since he would not attend to speak in his own defence) as capable of bearing only two possible interpretations. The first was that the Archbishop of Constantinople was theologically illiterate: did he, for example, really think that all the acts of the incarnation had to be referred to the eternal life of the Trinity? This would be a revival of the crassest form of pagan Hellenistic myth. The second possibility was that he knew this statement was an absurdity, and thus to avoid it was arguing simply that the one who became incarnate was not the Word of God, and therefore could only be a man. This was widely recognised as the heresy of Paul of Samosata condemned in the Third Century, and the very heresy which his own clergy had formally accused him of holding.

The high probability that Nestorius only meant to ridicule the Cyrilline thesis of the 'natural union' as a viable model for christology, not to deny the divinity of the Saviour which most christian parties in the fifth century held as axiomatic to the faith, should not blind us to the evident fact that Nestorius' language frequently betrayed him, as not having thought through the ramifications of all that he said. This was Cyril's own point in reply to Nestorius' accusations, that the implications of his opponent's teachings simply did not correspond to the oecumenically perceived faith of the church; that is the christian people at large. Cyril primarily understood this to be the Apostolic tradition, or 'paradosis', as can be exemplified by his constant reference to prior patristic argumentation, but there was a profound echo to his stance in the importance fifth century Byzantine political and religious life attached to the 'Voces Populi'. The popular acclaim (or disapproval) that greeted the policies of Emperors or other civic and religious leaders was not a factor that could be safely ignored. Much later, after the council, when Theodosius was vacillating over what position to take, such a popular demonstration in the imperial city when the crowds protested against Nestorius, more than decided the Emperor to abandon him to his fate, and sign a decree of exile. While he had been in office in the imperial city Nestorius had attempted to ride over the local opposition, here in Ephesus he found it much harder to do so.

Acacius of Melitene also gave witness on the same occasion in the Ephesian council that one or two days after the incident with Theodotus of Ancyra he was again engaged in the theological discussions held in Nestorius' lodgings when one of his accompanying bishops (he is not named but one suspects Dorotheus of Marcianopolis) gave a discourse that argued for Diodore of Tarsus' christology of Two Sons. Acacius told the assembled synod that at this point he walked out from Nestorius' lodging house and refused to attend any further meetings. Here was a question of guilt by association, and it was widely presumed that behind all the complexities and obscurities of Nestorius' teachings was a simple reversion to the position of Diodore which had been rebutted by no less an authority than Gregory of Nazianzen two generations earlier.

The remarks of Nestorius to Theodotus of Ancyra further illustrate how effectively he was alienating the middle ground of bishops at Ephesus by this series of meetings in advance of the council. When Theodotus was asked to explain the whole story of how he had been scandalised, a large number of the bishops assembled in council identified with him, and were indignant at Nestorius' arrogance. It appeared that on the 18th of June Nestorius lost patience with Theodotus in explaining his position on the basic rules of theological discourse as he understood them—on why the title of God ought to be reserved for the acts proper to the Logos, why the title of 'Jesus' ought to be reserved to the acts proper to the human being (such as Jesus eating, drinking, and so forth), and why the titles 'Christ', 'Lord', or 'Son', ought to be reserved to signify the sphere of concerted action. To what appears to have been Theodotus' appeal for a simpler answer as to what was wrong with the straightforward confession of Jesus as God, Nestorius replied impatiently: 'We must not call the one who became man for us, God'. He decided to press his point home, that language about the incarnate Lord had to observe strict rules if it was to avoid foolish incongruities,[111] and compounded his difficulties by telling the shocked Theodotus: 'I refuse to acknowledge as God, an infant of two or three months old.' Once again we can interpret Nestorius' primary intention here as the application of rhetoric to ridicule his opponent's theology, in so far as the Alexandrian tradition habitually applied paradoxes in incarnational discourse to heighten

[111] Cyril's description of this attitude, in his conciliar report to the Emperor, describes Nestorius' behaviour as 'the mockery of our august and divine mystery'. ACO 1.3.3–5. (Gesta Ephesina Doc.81. para.6.).

the sense of the divine condescension in the incarnation, paradoxes such as the 'swaddling bands of God', as had been traditionally used in theological discourse for a considerable time. However, his apparent meaning was all too starkly clear to Theodotus and the assembled bishops who later heard the account—the baby of two months old, Jesus of Nazareth, was not God. Although it was not his explicit intention to say so, Nestorius' peculiarly rigid scheme of permissible language about christology was popularly heard to be no less than a denial of the deity of Christ.

The out and out defection of Acacius and Theodotus brought about a swell of feeling in the Cyrilline majority that would tolerate no further delay. John of Antioch had been awaited for 11 days after Pentecost by this stage, but when he was more than a fortnight overdue Cyril began to suspect that his slowness might be a diplomatic one. The suspicion was, of course, in Cyril's favour, but there are grounds for not dismissing it entirely out of hand as simply the wishful thinking of a political manipulator. Cyril notes two main points in his justification to the Emperor of why he opened the proceedings without John. The first is the pressure placed upon him by bishops who were growing weary of being cooped up in Ephesus in high summer. 'Some of the holy bishops', he says, 'suffering from their advanced years could no longer bear to stay in this foreign place, others were seriously ill with diseases, others indeed ended their life in the metropolis of Ephesus'.[112] In short, he advances as his reasons for beginning the synod the selfsame reasons John had submitted[113] to explain why he should not have done so. The second gives a very strong hint (explicated more fully in the letter the council sent on the same occasion to Pope Celestine) as to his suspicions of John's motives in his delay. Cyril notes how other bishops coming from further afield than John had arrived in Ephesus on the morning of June 21st. Chief among them were the definitely anti-Cyrilline theologians Alexander of Apamea and Alexander of Hierapolis. His point seems to be that if John had sent these on ahead, then it only meant that if he himself had wished to be present he could have been. The deduction is perfectly accurate.

In the letter he sent ahead of him, in the hands of this Syrian advance party, John indicated that they were still five or six stages

[112] ACO 1.3.3–5. Doc. 81, para.2.

[113] The Syrian bishops were aged, weary, sick, and some had died, and thus the delay was legitimate. Cyril, by using the selfsame arguments, countered that just so was his commencement of the proceedings.

away,[114] at least a week's travel. He expressed his regret for the delay and assured Cyril that he had not taken a moment's break in the last thirty days of hard travelling. His letter is exceptionally warm and cordial in tone, even allowing for the usual rhetorical flourishes. It is by no means certain that John would have supported Nestorius vigorously if he had arrived in other circumstances, especially since in his pre-conciliar correspondence he had urged him to compromise and moderate his language. For John, as can be clearly discerned in the events of the two years following Ephesus, the substantial issues of the rejection of a Two Sons Christology and the admission of the validity of the Theotokos title were already accepted. John's letter to Nestorius, after he had received news of the Roman and Alexandrian synods' condemnations of 430, had even suggested the value of recantation, as Theodore of Mopsuestia, their common teacher, had once recanted on an occasion when he had been formally convicted of error.[115]

Cyril knew, however, that John's Syrian delegation would take its lead from Theodoret of Cyr, and he already had more than enough evidence to assure him that his own Twelve Chapters were going to be the prime object of the latter's attack. Theodoret had arrived in Ephesus in good time and was already making noises about the Chapters' orthodoxy. It was at this critical juncture that a highly controverted exchange took place.

Although there is no trace of it in the formal letter of John, Cyril maintained both in his synodical report to the Emperor, and in the formal report to Pope Celestine[116] that John of Antioch sent a verbal communication by Alexander of Apamea and Alexander of Hierapolis that Cyril ought to 'proceed with business if he were further delayed'. The fact that John took care to leave it out of his formal letter is interesting (it was a legal requirement imposed on all parties by the Emperor's Sacra to be in attendance by Pentecost and accordingly an illegal act to be seen to be intentionally avoiding this duty). There are no good grounds at all for doubting the authenticity of this message. Cyril would not have made this claim, twice, in formal reports, if he could not substantiate it in the presence of several witnesses, and he tells the Pope that the two Alexanders indicated not once, but

[114] ACO 1.1.119.
[115] ACO 1.1.93–95. paras.3–4.
[116] ACO 1.3.3–5 para.3; ACO 1.3.5–9. paras.3–4.

several times, that John had instructed them to inform Cyril that if he arrived 'late' he should delay the council no longer but proceed 'with what has to be done'.

Nonetheless, when Cyril and Memnon took them at face value and began the proceedings, both Alexanders were completely furious and protested at the action. It would seem, then, that while John certainly did send such a message what he probably meant was that Cyril should open the council if he was delayed any more than the extra week he could see that he would need to bring the Syrian entourage altogether into Ephesus. For Cyril, however, a crucial impasse had been resolved, and that was the lingering doubts over his canonical right to claim the presidency of the assembly. It was enough for him that John had indicated, in principle, that Alexandria had the right to preside—that he should do what had to be done.

John's instructions to his advance party were obscure on two key points; firstly on what constituted further delay, and then on what it was that 'had to be done'. It was certainly a strange message and Cyril's interpretation of it as a face-saving strategem on John's part (so that he would not have to be involved with the deposition of his erstwhile friend) cannot wholly be dismissed as an entirely mischievous exegesis. For Cyril, the verbal message and this lingering behind the advance party was a signal that John had not wished publicly to abandon Nestorius but was not as wholly committed to his defence as Theodoret, and in fact was willing to accede to the principle of his deposition if necessary. The behaviour of the Antiochene party when they subsequently arrived does not do much to dissipate this suspicion, for with the exception of a few hard-line supporters among them, Nestorius soon found that he was not greatly welcomed by the Syrian hierarchy as a whole. Similarly John's own statement at the opening of his separate council, once he had arrived in Ephesus, may give away more than he thought when he said: 'On my part I had hoped to avoid deposing anyone from the priesthood . . .'[117] Cyril put his finger on the reason for the suspected subterfuge in his letter to Celestine where he mentions John's problems in holding together his patriarchate which had widely differing views on the issues at stake. This was undoubtedly an accurate political assessment of John's unenviable difficulties on the home front.

Cyril's synodical letter to Pope Celestine puts his suspicions of John's

[117] ACO 1.5. 119–124, para.12.

delay much more openly than the script he wrote to the Emperor. This is partly because there was little point making this an explicit charge against John in the letter to be sent to the court when, by the necessities of imperial etiquette and law, John could in no possible sense admit that he had delayed for such motives, and partly because in the synodical letter to Celestine Cyril was aware that he had to justify his action in starting without John on grounds that were more in accord with ecclesiastical precedent and canon. Here he tells Celestine what he thought John was up to: 'The Very Reverend John of Antioch was in default [of the Emperor's command to be present for Pentecost] not by accident or only because the long distance of the voyage had hindered him, but because he concealed in his heart a plan and an intention that was not of God. This became clear soon after, when he arrived at Ephesus. . . . We waited for sixteen whole days while many bishops and clergy became ill, and greatly cast down. Some even died. John's behaviour, as Your Holiness can see, was interpreted as an act of Hubris against the holy council. His culpable delay was so great that other bishops who had even further to travel were arriving before him. Nonetheless, after the sixteenth day of waiting some of his accompanying bishops turned up, the two metropolitans Alexander of Apamea and another Alexander of Hierapolis. When we asked them about the long-delayed arrival of the very Reverend bishop John they told us, not once but several times—John has instructed us to inform Your Piety that if he is any further delayed you should not hold up the council, but rather do what has to be done. And when this was announced it seemed obvious to us that by his slowness and by these messages we were receiving from him he was trying to avoid being involved, either because of his friendship with Nestorius, or because Nestorius had been a cleric of his own church, or because he was under pressure from certain people who were lobbying on his behalf. This was why the council opened its session in the Great Church at Ephesus dedicated to Mary'.[118]

In this great international convocation two closely related, but nonetheless distinct, systems of law were governing procedure in the minds of all the clerical parties in attendance: imperial decree and canonical precedent. It is clear that by June 21st the difficulties of life in Ephesus had made further delays more and more resented by the great majority of bishops in the city. It is equally evident that

[118] ACO 1.3.5–9 paras.3–4, (Ep.ad Celestinum).

Nestorius had signally failed to impress many of the previously unaligned bishops. Cyril, with some justification, sensed that if he could only convoke the council matters could be resolved quickly to his satisfaction. In John's verbal message he had received sufficient moral indication that Syria acknowledged his right to precedence as chairman in the proceedings. Only one thing now stopped him from action.

In the universal understanding of the Byzantine church such a council could only be convoked by the Emperor himself and this was to be done symbolically only by the formal reading of the imperial Sacra to the assembled bishops; the letter of legal constitution in which he also set out his royal intentions and requirements for the meeting. Count Candidian held this, and he had increasingly become alienated from Cyril and Memnon as the days wore on after Pentecost and he sensed the troubling swell of popular power which they commanded even in the face of his troops. He was also annoyed at the way Nestorius had been excluded from the synod from his first arrival in Ephesus. In his interpretation of the Sacra he saw that the Emperor wanted a full and free discussion of all the issues with all the main characters involved. That this ran counter to the canons forbidding deposed clerics to fulfil their ecclesiastical duties until synodically tried did not appear to him to matter. He was made to give ground on the treatment of Nestorius before the council started, but was all the more determined to wait until the arrival of John before permitting the synod to begin.

By the 21st of June this aspect of the royal policy was well enough known. It was also deduced that, in line with the general Theodosian procedure in church affairs, the bishops would be left to decide the matters relating to faith without lay intervention. This deduction was to be proved right, for the Sacra contained explicit instructions to the royal officials not to become involved in the theological debates. The bishops, however, did not simply regard themselves as mere instruments of the imperial will. It is doubtful at any stage in Byzantine history whether the hierarchy as a whole could ever be characterised in such a supine way as this. They saw the definition of the church's faith and canons of good order as supremely their affair, with or without the leave of the Emperor. They also needed no one to remind them that Synodical process pre-dated the christianisation of the royal court by several centuries. In the fifth century it would not be a Constantine who took the presidential chair of a council, but as it had been in the days even before there was a christian Basileus, the senior bishop present.

Accordingly, in the light of the evidence afforded by Acacius of Melitene and Theodotus of Ancyra, and in the knowledge of the considerable episcopal resentment that had accumulated because of John's delay, Cyril decided to act after he had weighed the implications of the Syrian report. He would open the session of the council. It was midsummer's day, the late morning of June 21st 431.

Most of the criticism he has attracted for this action centres round a somewhat 'modern' sense of fair play in democratic process, or gentlemanly behaviour in intellectual argument. The case is often epitomised in highly anachronistic comments to the effect that if both parties (Cyril and Nestorius) had calmly heard one another out they could surely have come to a sensible resolution of their theological differences through compromise. But whether or not this is even an accurate description of how twentieth century university theologians behave with one another (and that is a debatable case) it certainly could not lay any claim to represent patristic procedure. Several contemporary perspectives on the conciliar fathers tend to represent them as 'seeking' the mind of the church through dialogue and enquiry. A forward-looking developmental, or evolutionary view of doctrine is presupposed here, such as that postulated by John Henry Newman in the 19th century and popularised thereafter, but far from current in the patristic understanding of the nature of tradition.

In the Byzantine church the perceived duty of those attending councils was to 'recognise', by comparison with past precedent, the faith of the church, and having recognised it acclaim it in the Spirit. This was the force and role of the numerous episcopal 'acclamations' that one finds within the acts of an ancient council, designed to evoke the way in which the apostles of old had been inspired by the Spirit of God to teach the faith in the orginal Pentecostal enthusiasm. It is an implicit, but nonetheless clear, claim to stand as bishops in the apostolic succession. It was not expected, therefore, that senior hierarchs should have to agonise about what that faith was, or search out its meaning, given that they had lived by it for years and were holding the ecclesiastical office as teachers of the faith. This important context holds true even in those cases, such as the present one, when the matters under discussion were highly complex. It was expected that theologians should articulate positions, but the 'acclamation' of them, by a supposedly unanimous episcopal voice, was the decisive factor. In short an open and neutral enquiry over doctrine that was designed to achieve an internationally acceptable compromise was never in the minds or expectations of any of those attending the council of Ephesus, except perhaps Nestorius. This concept of the definition of christianity by progressive compromise was, and still is, alien to the Orthodox and Catholic communions who have retained synodical process, but more importantly in the present instance it is an unsuitable standard of assesssment, both historically and ideologically, for the events that constituted ancient conciliar meetings.

If one wishes to assess the rightness or wrongness of Cyril's actions, in their historical context, it is necessary to do so in terms of the canons to which he and the other bishops of all parties felt themselves to be bound. In this case we need to assess Cyril's actions in the light of Imperial law and canonical precedent.

The position, then, was this: to fulfil the requirements of law the council needed the reading of the Sacra to legitimate its session. Count Candidianus who held it was determined to wait for John of Antioch. To fulfil the requirements of the ecclesiastical canons the senior bishop had to be selected as the president. Rome and Alexandria had ranked as the two most important sees from antiquity until the fourth century when the Council of Constantinople had given to New Rome great ecclesiastical status to reflect its position as capital of the Byzantine world, on the occasion of the golden jubilee of its dedication.

In all practical reality Byzantium had long displaced all other cities of the Roman world, but Old Rome clung to her ancient pedigree tenaciously, and no less to her ecclesiastical dignity as the first international focus of canonical discipline the christian world had known after the age of the apostles. Old Rome was determined not to have her ecclesiastical precedence undermined in the same way that her political prestige had been within the last century and a half since Constantine had transferred his capital definitively to the East. The results of the political demotion were symbolically obvious to all, and the population of Rome still bore the physical and mental traumas of merely two decades previously when the barbarians had brought the once proud city to its knees in a humiliating defeat.

Rome had never accepted the validity of the conciliar canons of 381 which displaced Alexandria from the hierarchy of prestige and placed Constantinople in her stead with equal privileges to Old Rome. The canon had the force of imperial law, and in the East, where conciliar theological decrees were never understood as separate from the canons which were allied with them, this ecclesiastical mode of governance eventually became an accepted fact of life. The decree did not constitute any strictly hierarchical order among the great patriarchates (Antioch, for example, did not automatically rank 'below' Alexandria) rather it clearly signalled that Constantinople's ecclesiastical standing had finally caught up with her political, military, and economic power.

Rome was running against the tide, in a certain sense, by refusing to acknowledge the canons of Constantinople, and the same policy was repeated later as an immediate response when the Council of Chalcedon in 451 reaffirmed the decrees of 381. This position suited the Western Emperor's court (as long as it survived) which shared the Papal aversion to regarding Constantinople as the real centre of world power. Rome made this defence of its traditional right to stand as supreme court of appeal in the face of several difficulties. Firstly it had to run against the increasing prestige that the council of 381 was beginning to attract as the great symbol of Trinitarian orthodoxy. As with its attitude to Chalcedon later, the eastern bishops thought it very odd indeed that Rome could accept the inspired nature of a council's teaching and then refuse to be committed to its disciplinary canons which were also considered divinely authoritative. Secondly, it had to run against the tide of the increasingly powerful political principle that a church's territorial jurisdiction, within the single imperium of God's christian people, should be co-terminous with civil boundaries and divisions. For some of these reasons Pope Celestine had regarded Cyril of Alexandria almost as his church's 'deputy', and while it was a role that Cyril never explicitly accepted or even acted upon, it was not one that he disclaimed either, as long as he felt it could strengthen his hand against Nestorius.

Cyril and Celestine were presuming, on the basis of ancient tradition, that Rome would have the right to presidency of an international synod, and in Rome's absence, Alexandria. Nestorius was clearly presuming that in line with the canons of 381 it would be Constantinople which would preside whoever attended. The conciliar canons, however, also forbade any condemned bishop from assuming any sacerdotal role until another synod had heard his case and cleared him. Nestorius had presumed that since Theodosius had overruled, in 430, the synods of Rome and Alexandria which had excommunicated him, then their canonical status was rendered void by the act. Legally this was so in the eyes of the imperial court. It was not universally understood to be the case in the eyes of many bishops, not least among them

Memnon of Ephesus, Cyril, Celestine, and the Macedonians. The canonical censure from two major sees that hung around Nestorius from the moment of his arrival at Ephesus counted against him and fatally compromised his claims for the presidential chair. This, and the absence of the Roman delegation, left Cyril next in line for consideration for the presidency besides John of Antioch.

Several of the Easterners, especially Nestorius, Andrew of Samosata, Theodoret, and Alexander of Hierapolis, regarded it as a task of the council to try Cyril for suspected Apollinarism. Cyril, while dismissing the charges contemptuously, had thought it wise to begin to answer them in writing even before the council opened. More importantly, as a skilled church politician Cyril knew that no such charge had been formally proposed, sustained, or delivered against him in any proper canonical forum. The preliminary meeting that John of Antioch had called before his delegation set off for Asia Minor had discussed the issue as a charge of Theodoret's but the imperial summons to Ephesus had pre-empted them from making that meeting into a separate synodical trial. No synod had moved against Cyril from the part of Constantinople either, and given the internal condition of that see within a year of Nestorius' arrival there, with his senior clergy in open revolt against him, it would have been a very unwise thing to have tried anything like it.

Moreover, all the official communications Cyril had received from Antioch had been cordial in tone, and he may even have known that John had been urging Nestorius to change his position while not suggesting the same to him. The most recent of all the letters from John to Cyril which had arrived in Ephesus on that morning of June 21st had even suggested the latter should proceed if John was delayed—surely a tacit acceptance of Cyril's ecclesiastical right of precedence? Not only was there no canonical charge to debar him from claiming the presidency of the synod, Cyril could now cite the acceptance of his right to proceed as given to him by Juvenal of Jerusalem, Celestine of Rome, John of Antioch (implicitly), and Memnon the local hierarch. Add to this Cyril's international reputation as scholar and theologian and it must be apparent that he was regarded as the natural leader of the council by the great majority of those assembled. Apart from his own seniority and the canonical debarment of Nestorius Cyril also had another card up his sleeve—and that was Celestine's letter asking him to represent the interests of the Roman church in the prosecution of Nestorius' heresy, which it felt should not be re-examined except to condemn it afresh. Even if Cyril had allowed Nestorius' right to attend the council as an equal delegate (as the Emperor had intended), instead of as a canonically deprived defendant, he could still claim the canonical right to the presidency of the assembly. As it was, he found he did not need to abandon his first position (which had refused Nestorius the right to attend the synod other than as a defendant) because this was widely accepted by the other bishops at Ephesus.

When he heard the reports from the Syrians, therefore, Cyril could only have felt that the pieces of the jigsaw had finally come together. All that legally stood in his way from summoning the council to decisive action (when for all the world it looked as if it would disintegrate before ever getting started) was the imperial representative Count Candidian. Cyril was one of the few hierarchs present at Ephesus who had long experience of dealing with even more powerful Byzantine noblemen than this—as all three imperial aristocrats at Ephesus, Counts Candidian, Irenaeus, and later Count John, each found to their annoyance.

On June 21st Cyril was no longer prepared to allow the military to determine the form of the council, and now that he felt absoutely sure of his ecclesiastical grounds, he decided to test his civil right, on the premise (which turned out to be correct) that the Emperor would follow the traditional religious policy of his Dynasty, allowing the bishops the full determination of the religious arguments without the interference of the court aristocracy. Accordingly he cast the die and, with the agreement of the senior hierarchs that comprised his majority, announced the beginning of the council that same afternoon of Sunday June 21st 431, and sent round formal summons to attendance.

Cyril could count, at that time, on at least 155 signatories, including the Deacon Bessula as representative of Capreolus of Carthage, plus two other proxies, Celestine of Rome, and Rufus of Thessalonike, taking his command of the initial vote to 157. He could also cite the presence of Constantinople (the attendant bishops who had come with Nestorius) Alexandria, Jerusalem, the presence by proxy of Rome, and the most recent agreement to begin sent by an advance group of delegates from the last remaining great see of Antioch. By the time of the final hours of the first session of the council, which confirmed Nestorius' deposition, Cyril would be able to demonstrate 198 episcopal signatures agreeing to Nestorius' anathematisation, and other proxy votes which would take the figures to over 200.[119]

When the news broke on that Sunday evening that Cyril was going to open the synod under his own presidency, vigorous protests were immediately lodged against the action by the Syrian delegation and Nestorius' party, and also a group of the still unaligned bishops who were unsure of Cyril's canonical position and preferred to wait for John's arrival, however late that might be. At first this protest group numbered 68 bishops but it deflated in the course of the synodical meeting in the same ratio that Cyril's voting register swelled. Theodoret of Cyr wrote to Cyril from his lodgings that very evening to demand a delay until John arrived, and threatened Cyril with canonical censure if he refused. But Cyr was an obscure and unimportant see in itself, and Cyril did not consider there was any need to reply.

Throughout the later part of that evening and into the night of June 21st final preparations were quickly instigated by bishop Memnon to make the great church ready for the delegates, and throughout the city factional meetings were held. Count Candidian moved quickly from group to group, sounding opinion, and trying to reverse Cyril's decision by appealing to the Emperor's intention that all should be represented. He was looking for a delay of four days, and to support his claim he threatened to nullify anything that was arranged by the synod without the presence of the orientals.

Late that evening Cyril sent a special delegation of four bishops[120] to Nestorius' lodgings to require his presence at the synod on the following morning. They found him in the presence of half a dozen other bishops who supported him, and on hearing the summons they discussed with one another before he replied: 'I will examine the matter and if I ought to come, then I shall come'.[121] Nestorius must have recognised the summons as the first of three solemn commands that constituted the arraignment of a bishop before a synod. His words were not a refusal, neither were they an acceptance. Their import suggests he must have consulted immediately with Counts Candidian and Irenaeus along with his remaining supporters. The busy sequence of events that unfolded that evening and in the early part of the following day are somewhat confused. The version in the Conciliar Acts puts everything into a clear sequential version but leaves

---

119 ACO 1.2.3–7 (155 signatories); ACO 1.2.54–64. (over 200 claimed).

120 Hermogenes of Rhinocourouros, Athanasius of Paralos, Peter of Parembolos, and Paul of Lampa.

121 ACO 1.3.3–5 para.3; ACO 1.2.9. (Doc. 38.) para.1.

out important aspects. This is partly because of the very nature of the Acts themselves.

Cyril had appointed the Alexandrian priest Peter to act as chief legal notary of the conciliar sessions. It is because of his skill as a legal secretary that we possess such a large body of texts dealing with the proceedings of Ephesus, the first great council whose records have survived in such detail. But the Acts of the Synod are quite obviously, in the main, an Alexandrian composition, and thus not a neutral account (which is not to say they are inaccurate). They present a varied and highly important assembly of crucial evidence. Where they give a report it can generally be relied on as an accurate record, for Cyril was determined from the very outset to have his path secured from every conceivable angle for what he knew without question would be a forthcoming legal hearing at the royal court after the council was ended. They need care in the reading for what they do not say, more than for any doubt over what they do say.

In the end the creation of this strong legal record secured Cyril's personal safety and ultimate success in making the Ephesian synod stand with oecumenical authority. His foresight in this respect was remarkable. When one collates the theological writings that Cyril prepared in advance of the council, the extensive patristic testimonies he had assembled for the first session, the acts of the proceedings themselves, the post-conciliar lobbying he directed from his imprisonment, and the major theological writings he undertook in the aftermath of the council, one can only stand in wonder before his indefatigable energy. In addition, for theological power and political acumen Cyril had no rival to come anywhere near him.

Nonetheless the Acts give a stylised view that glosses over some aspects, particularly how Cyril had duped Count Candidian. Having an eye on a future imperial reader, they are very careful to give the impression of a scrupulous and loyal regard for the Emperor's will, while clearly Cyril's major motivation came from elsewhere, from the ecclesiastical tradition he made it his life's passion to defend.

Taking its cue from the obvious change of tone in Nestorius' responses, between his second summons on the morning of June 22nd, and his antagonistic refusal to receive the third summons in the afternoon of the same day, the following account of the events presumes that the official protest (in person) of Theodoret and Count Candidian took place in the late morning of the 22nd, after the second summons had been delivered from a gathering of bishops already ensconced in the Great Church of St. Mary.

In one sense Cyril had opened the first session of the Council on the morning of June 22nd when the Gospels were solemnly enthroned in the centre of the church,[122] surrounded by the bishops, as the sign of Christ's presence among them as Risen Lord directing their administration. Canon law required three formal summons should be recorded for any bishop who was to be tried before a synod. Accordingly one of the first acts of the day was to decide that Nestorius' invitation of the previous evening could stand as the first summons, evidently refused since he and his party were conspicuously absent.

Flavian of Philippi moved that Nestorius should be summoned a second time by a new delegation of three bishops, this time in the company of a lawyer to witness the act.[123] On their arrival they found that Nestorius' lodgings were thronged with troops. Count Candidian himself was present. The bishops were refused an audience with Nestorius who seems to have been engaged in a meeting of his own. Eventually Candidian appeared to tell them that no audience with the archbishop was possible, although they should wait for further instructions. He later reappeared with some of Nestorius' clergy who gave them the message: 'When all the bishops have been gathered, we will engage in mutual communication'.[124]

The response was ambivalent. It was clearly not a straightforward rebuff, but did it mean he would not appear until John of Antioch arrived, or until he had gathered all the bishops present in Ephesus? for there were 42 of these, apart from his own party of 16, who were still not seated in the church of St. Mary. It seems quite possible he meant the latter, and if this is so, it could be concluded that he actually did attend (by proxy) after the second summons, even though it was only to refuse the legitimacy of the council. In any case his answers demonstrate that Nestorius was being careful to proceed with the due processes of canonical requirement at this stage.

It was probably after the second summons that the purpose of Nestorius' and Count Candidian's deliberations became evident. The group of 68 dissident bishops had been consulted, and with a military guard at their head their delegation progressed to the church to present the formal protest that had been drawn up by Theodoret of Cyr.

[122] The considerable ruins of the building are still visible in Ephesus.

[123] Theodoulos of Elousa in Palestine, Anderios of Chersonese in Crete, Theopemptos of Cabasa in Egypt, and the Notary Epaphroditus, a lector of the church of Rhodes who was present in attendance on his bishop Hellanicos.

[124] ACO 1.2.10. (Doc. 40).

As he had already warned on the previous evening, this insisted that Cyril should delay proceedings and threatened him with canonical sanctions should he refuse.

Cyril knew that his canonical grounds for opening the First Session on June 22nd were defensible, and the renewed objection of the minority bishops was not entertained. Nonetheless he must have been acutely aware that he could claim no legal status for his synod under imperial law until the official reading of the Emperor's Sacra had taken place. Candidian held the copy of this. How Cyril could organise the reading was beyond him until his opponents offered him the resolution of all his technical difficulties at a stroke, and his superior political experience enabled him to seize the advantage once offered.

Candidian and the party of bishops entered the church with a great flourish, and after Theodoret had read his demand, Candidian intervened to demand that all the presently assembled bishops should immediately disperse as they constituted an illegal and partisan assembly which the Emperor had forbidden. Uproar ensued. Even the moderate bishops took badly to being ordered about by the military in the church itself, and the action of Theodoret was generally seen as a rather impertinent communication from the Antiochenes, whose long delay was already widely resented. In the clamours of protests from the majority of bishops the formal response was given to Candidian asking by what right he judged their assembly to be illegal. His reply, that his personal instructions from the Emperor, as written in his copy of the official Sacra, did not permit him to validate such an assembly, was rejected as hearsay and merely a personal interpretation that carried little weight in the face of such a large number of bishops assembled for the purposes of being a supreme legislature. In short, his claim was rejected as not having the force of law. At this the bishops probably followed Cyril's lead in demanding they hear the terms of the Sacra for themselves, and in the sublime confidence of his annoyance Candidian proceeded to read it.

He intended to chastise the assembly but failed to see the implications of his act. The bishops who were now assembled represented everyone who had been summoned to Ephesus. Even the Syrians were there, represented by Theodoret and John's advance party. Not only were the Cyrilline majority seated in the church, but even the representatives of the dissident 68 who had not assembled for the enthronement of the Gospels that morning were now gathered in the church. The text he read[125] outlined his responsibility for providing good order in the city, his duty to clear the council of monastic or lay agitators, and to ensure no partisan factions disrupted the balanced adjudication of the theological issues at stake. In its second paragraph the Sacra contained a key instruction: 'In consequence the Most Magnificent Candidianus, Count of the Imperial Chamber, has received his instruction to be present at your very holy Synod though without taking part in any enquiry or motion relating to the all-holy dogmas, since it is not permissible for any who is not on the list of holy bishops to engage in such affairs . . .'

When Candidian finished reading the Sacra he surely realised the full extent of his mistake. The Bishops acclaimed long life to the Emperor in demonstrative professions of loyalty, but now with the text officially declaimed in the symbolic presence of the whole episcopal gathering, the Synod of Ephesus was in formal session, legally as well as canonically sanctioned. Pointedly referring to the second paragraph where the Emperor had forbidden lay involvement in the proceedings, one of the bishops demanded that Candidian and his troops should withdraw as the assembled bishops were eager to fulfil their own imperial instructions and discuss matters of theology which fell outside military competence—as the Emperor himself had explicitly stated. Theodoret withdrew, as did Candidian, doubtless in some considerable annoyance, but they had lost the confidence of many of the dissidents whom they had persuaded that morning. Accepting the inevitable, several of that number started to come over to the Synod and these accessions to the majority continued throughout the day. As they left the building they heard the sound of episcopal staffs beating the floor—the First Session of the Council of Ephesus was at last begun.

The notary Peter drew up the list of the 155 attendant bishops who were present that morning[126] and arrangements were made for the third and final summons to be sent to Nestorius at his lodgings. This third delegation of four bishops[127] had the least enviable task. They set off in the late morning but did not return until hours later. The military had regrouped around Nestorius' lodgings and when Candidian had reported his mishaps to Count Irenaeus the evident fury of both aristocrats was more than obvious to their men. They

---

[125] ACO 1.1.120 f.

[126] ACO 1.2.3–7.

[127] Anysios of Thebes, Dominus of Opontos, John of Hephaistopolis, and Daniel of Darnis.

not only felt the bishops' behaviour to be an affront to their own rank but a frustration of the Emperor's will as they interpreted it. From this time onwards Candidian joined Count Irenaeus and set all the troops in alignment with the Cyrilline opposition, regardless of the changing voting lists and the evident collapse of support for Nestorius that happened in the ensuing week. As a consequence, certainly from that time onwards (though Cyril had had his suspicions beforehand),[128] the conciliar party refused to accept Candidian's role as a neutral broker, and later the bishops would complain loudly of his biased reporting of events back to the royal court of Constantinople, especially when this led to the subsequent arrest of Cyril and Memnon. Such factors should perhaps cause us to be sceptical of Nestorius' later complaints in the Book of Heraclides to the effect that Cyril tyrannically forced the council round to his way of thinking, and threatened his own life and safety like a common villain. Neither the synodical process itself nor the final voting figures can allow such an interpretation in regard to the first premise, and in relation to the second it is important to note that the only armed factions that are known to have been highly significant at Ephesus, blocking off food supplies, disrupting communications, involved in other clearly illegal activities—were those associated with Nestorius.

The bishops who arrived with their summons at Nestorius' lodgings were treated with unmasked hostility by the troops there. They were refused admittance to the courtyard, and forced to stand outside the yard walls in the midday heat, a mark of humiliating scorn. When they complained of their long wait in the open sun they were given the message by the guards that they could stand there until the cool of the evening for all they could care—they would not be recognised or admitted to the building. They returned to the church in the late afternoon and the conciliar business began in earnest, without Nestorius being in attendance. The refusal to attend did not abort the trial, but by established law the process had to allow a full hearing for the accused. Cyril had already prepared, for the Roman Synod which had tried Nestorius *in absentia*, a full dossier of texts. These had been revised already in advance, with Cyril foreseeing his refusal to appear, and the fact that Nestorius had preached quite openly and provocatively in the city over the last two weeks meant that there were bishops

[128] His negative opinion of Candidian's honesty in fulfilling his supposed mission as arbitrator is given in his Letter 27.

present who could testify to what they had heard *viva voce.* Here the negative witness of Theodotus of Ancyra and Acacius of Melitene, his former colleagues, would prove more than enough.

The priest Peter read out a synopsis of the events that constituted the Nestorian affair to date (explicitly mentioning Cyril's two corrective letters to his errant brother)[129] up to the point of the Roman and Egyptian synodical condemnations of the archbishop and the Emperor's intervention demanding an oecumenical reassessment. Juvenal of Jerusalem then asked for the imperial Sacra addressed to the bishops to be read out. This not only served legally to validate the subsequent Acta but conveniently justified their refusal to wait any longer for John of Antioch by re-emphasising the Emperor's own words: 'For the great care we have for such matters let it be known that no-one shall absent themselves, and that no excuse will be accepted before God or before us for anyone who fails to present himself with all speed in that appointed place and on the determined date (June 7th).'[130]

Firmus of Caesarea brought the point home by formally asking Memnon of Ephesus to state for the record how long they had already been delayed, and Cyril added to his reply the background of the pressing needs of the Ephesian bishops[131] and their impatience to fulfil the Emperor's will—a pious desire that was now capable of being realized because Count Candidian had just read the official Sacra before them and constituted their assembly.[132] The opening passages are clearly designed as a preemptive apologetic tailor-made for reading in Constantinople.

The Acts then record that the emissary delegations were asked to give an account of how Nestorius had responded to his three formal summons, and the narratives of how the major part of the day had been spent in fruitless attempts to reach Nestorius served to harden attitudes against him. The version of the third summons in the conciliar acts attributes all the hostility of the troops to the hubris of Nestorius himself.[133] It is more than probable that Nestorius never had sight of this third delegation, but the account represents the genuine outrage

129 viz. The Second and Third Letters to Nestorius.

130 ACO 1.1.116.

131 Being careful to cite sickness and death as the exact balances of the reasons John of Antioch had submitted to him in his letter of the previous day as the reasons why he had been delayed.

132 ACO 1.2.8–9. Doc. 36.

133 ACO 1.3.3–5. para.4.

the bishops felt, and it was widely (and accurately) understood that the guards were refusing admittance on the direct orders of the lord of the house.

Monday June 22nd was wearing on into late afternoon by this stage when the Creed of Nicaea was read out at the request of Juvenal of Jerusalem, as the standard of orthodoxy to be followed in the subsequent adjudications, and immediately after this the notary Peter reminded the bishops once more of Cyril's Second Letter to Nestorius. Paragraph 3 of this text turns explicitly on the right interpretation of the Creed. Acacius of Melitene requested that the whole text should be read also, and Cyril immediately petitioned the council to adjudicate whether this letter was in accordance with the faith of Nicaea or not—the implication being that since it opposed Nestorius the latter's theology could hardly be in accordance with Nicaea if Cyril's exposition was accepted.

Firmus of Caesarea, Memnon, Theodotus of Ancyra, Flavian of Philippi, and Acacius of Melitene were the first to begin the formal acclamations of Cyril's letter as an orthodox exposition. So far, this was clearly a pre-arranged plan of procedure that the chief protagonists of the Cyrilline party should shape the synodical proceedings but, as the list of the subsequent acclamations of Cyril's letter demonstrates, no less than 124 personal interventions subscribing to the letter as a summation of orthodoxy (with the notary adding a note that the remaining (31) delegates also assented) makes it impossible to sustain any view that Cyril's theology was not wholeheartedly endorsed by the assembly. It was an extraordinary testimony, and a massive vote of confidence in Cyril's ability as a theologian. Some of the acclamations, like that of bishop Hermogenes recorded in the Preface to this volume, are far from being merely passive votes of agreement.[134]

After the acclamation of Cyril's letter the reply from Nestorius was called for, read out, and recorded in the Acts.[135] At this point Cyril again intervened and asked for a formal judgement on whether this text was in agreement with Nicene doctrine or not, and once again the bishops gave individual responses. That of Acacius of Melitene is the longest and most articulated in which he also defends Cyril's reputation against the charge that Nestorius raised to the effect that he taught the nonsense of a passible deity. Acacius concluded that

[134] ACO 1.2.29.
[135] ACO 1.1.29–32. cf. Translation in Ch. 5. following.

Nestorius' sense of the union of God and man in Christ was purely a nominal one.[136] Peter the notary recorded the details of 34 different interventions condemning the substance of Nestorius' letter, and then synopsised the general acclamations as a unanimous verdict: 'All the bishops acclaimed together: Whoever will not anathematise Nestorius let him be anathema, for the orthodox faith anathematises him. We all anathematise this letter and the doctrines of Nestorius . . .' and so on, giving an indication of the strength of the verdict against him.

The reading of the details of the synodical condemnation of Nestorius by Rome was then called for by Juvenal of Jerusalem, which culminated in its solemn *judicium* as given in the previous winter of 430: 'Know, then, that this is our public sentence, that if you do not preach the doctrine concerning Christ our God which the church of Rome holds, together with the church of Alexandria, and the whole catholic church, the same doctrine as the church of Great Constantinople has maintained perfectly well until your time, and if you do not anathematise with a sincere and written confession this unbelievable innovation which has attempted to divide what the holy scripture has united, then know that within ten days from the delivery of this injunction you will be expelled from all communion with the catholic church.'[137]

Already the legal case against Nestorius was piling up in weight, and immediately after the reading of the Roman synodical judgement, that of the Egyptian synod was read out.[138] At this instance in the Acts, the notary signified the reading aloud of the Third Letter of Cyril to Nestorius (which conveyed the judgement of the Egyptian synod), as he had that of Celestine earlier, by the same stenographical device of citing the opening line and then adding kai ta loipa . . . the Greek form of "etc." There is, therefore, no way of telling whether the Twelve Chapters were read out at this stage of the proceedings at Ephesus or not. The Chapters were conceived as an appendix to the Letter, and their omission would not frustrate the sense of the text. Equally, it has been suggested, Cyril might well wish to cast a discreet silence over the existence of the Chapters since he knew that they were to be the subject of special attack from the Syrians. On the other hand, it seems far more likely that the Chapters would have been read out at this stage, not only as part of the original text of the letter, synodically validated, but also because Cyril could

[136] ACO 1.1.32.
[137] ACO 1.1.77–83. para.18.
[138] ACO 1.1.36.

ensure no better defence of the Chapters than to have them endorsed by the council Fathers ahead of any negative critique which might still materialise on the arrival of the Syrians. There is no evidence to suggest that Cyril did suppress the Chapters at this juncture, and indeed the Manuscript heading of his subsequent 'Explanation of the Twelve Chapters' suggests that Cyril composed the latter work after the bishops gathered in Ephesus had asked him for a clearer elaboration of his meaning. This cannot mean during the First Session, but probably reflects the reality that after the arrival of the Syrians there was some misgiving about the Chapters they had earlier endorsed, when the orientals insisted they were heretical, and many bishops asked Cyril for an explanation—which he seems able to have given them later in the time of his house arrest. This would suggest that the Twelve Chapters actually did form part of the reading of the Third Letter during the first session of the council.

The council then moved on to enquire what was Nestorius' response to these canonically delivered sentences against him. The Emperor Theodosius, and Nestorius relying on him, might well have regarded the decisions of the two synods as having been 'set aside' by the subsequent convocation of a general council to adjudicate the matter. As all the other bishops knew, however, although it was within the purview of a council to set aside the condemnations if it saw fit, it was not within the right of the Emperor to nullify them in advance, in the way he had presumed. When the Egyptian delegation to Constantinople had been called to give evidence of how they had delivered the sentences, and how Nestorius had rejected them in the winter of 430, the council moved to confirm the sentence in full accord with the canons governing the prosecution of one who refuses to repent after receiving a synodical decree.

The Palestinian bishop Fidus of Joppa intervened to state that Nestorius had not changed his views even to the present moment in Ephesus, and Cyril called then upon Acacius of Melitene and Theodotus of Ancyra to give formal testimony to the discussions they had held with Nestorius in his lodging house over the previous fortnight. Their confirmation was given that his theology had been faithfully represented so far, and that he still persisted in it. Theodotus repeated what Nestorius said to him: 'I cannot describe as God, an infant of two or three months',[139] the *cause scandaleuse* that had precipitated the

[139] ACO 1.1.38.

opening of the council in the first place, and perhaps one of the most careless and damaging remarks Nestorius could have made.

After hearing this evidence, Flavian of Philippi moved that the council should hear a patristic synopsis of doctrine on the nature of the incarnation. The assemblage of texts that was then read out was the fruit of Cyril's earlier work gathering citations such as those demonstrated in the De Recta Fide. In Schwartz's edition the conciliar florilegium runs to approximately six pages of texts that were read out at this point, and lists as its authorities such luminaries as: Peter of Alexandria, Athanasius, Julius of Rome, Felix of Rome, Theophilus of Alexandria, Cyprian of Carthage, Ambrose of Milan, Gregory Nazianzen, Basil the Great, and Gregory Nyssa. Much has been made of Cyril's dependence on a few Apollinarist texts which resurfaced after Apollinaris' condemnation by disguising themselves as the works of orthodox Fathers.[140] The assonance between the pseudepigraphical texts and the writings of Cyril is beyond question, and Cyril actually felt secure relying on them precisely because he thought they were genuine patristic treatises. The argument that he 'utterly' relied on them is, however, so grossly overstated as to be capricious.[141] His use of these 'dubious texts' in the overall range of his citation patterns of undisputed Fathers is not significant, beyond the one instance of the treatise of Ps. Athanasius from which he drew his famous phrase: One Enfleshed nature of the Logos (which we shall discuss subsequently). In this latter context it has to be remembered that the pseudepigraphical texts were not those of the arch-heretic himself but of his later disciples who moderated his christological teaching considerably—precisely that assimilation of Apollinaris' insights on the unity of Christ to an orthodox conception that Cyril was himself aiming at.

The patristic authorities that he now presented to the assembled council for their consideration confirm the argument that he had no

---

[140] The texts are listed and discussed by P. Galtier. 'S. Cyrille et Apollinaire.' Gregorianum 37, 1956, 584–609.

[141] F. Young lists the Apollinarist treatises that Cyril used and concludes; 'These were the authoritative authors to which Cyril appealed, and the authoritative documents on the basis of which he composed his anti-Nestorian writings.' Young, (1983) p. 259. The partial truth is so twisted here as to suggest Cyril's use of such texts provided a significantly heavy input to his thought. The very opposite can be deduced when the pseudo-patristic texts are placed in the context of all his other unquestionably accurate patristic citations, and they emerge as a very small minority indeed, none of which have in them anything obviously objectionable in the sense, for example, that Apollinaris' early writings were objectionable.

need to fear that one or two base coins had devalued his impressive treasury. Far from it; the patristic testimonies which Cyril was able to cite, both here and in his large works such as the De Recta Fide and the Ad Reginas, demonstrate that he was no mere plagiariser of old formulae. His proof texts are far ranging and sensitively contextualised across the spectrum of the great teachers of the past. His own preparatory studies (as later instanced by his ability to write a digest of the whole debate in his Scholia on the Incarnation) indicate how systematically Cyril had thought through the issues and put his finger on the one central question—the single subjectivity of the Incarnate Lord—at a time when Andrew of Samosata, Theodoret, and Nestorius were still obviously boxing in the dark.

The florilegium that the council Fathers now received was deliberately chosen to represent the Eastern and Western traditions:

Peter of Alexandria.	On the Godhead. (3 citations).
Athanasius.	Contra Arianos III; To Epictetus. (2 citations).
Julius of Rome.	Letter to Prosdocius. (short citation).
Felix of Rome.	Letter to Maximus. (short citation).
Theophilus.	V & VI Paschal Letter.
Cyprian of Carthage	De Opere et Eleemosyne.
Ambrose of Milan.	De Fide. (2 citations).
Gregory Nazianzen.	Letter 101. (chief and longest citation).
Basil of Caesarea.	De Spiritu Sancto.
Gregory Nyssa.	Oration 1: De Beatitudine.

The most important of his proof texts was Gregory Nazianzen's letter To Cledonius, one of the major anti-Apollinarist writings of the patristic canon, and something that he had clearly studied in detail. Allied with this was Athanasius' Letter to Epictetus. Both texts Cyril regarded as his prime authorities, and accordingly have been represented in translation as an appendix to this present volume. The Western theologians largely appear, one suspects, to give colour and to please his Western allies.

After the patristic texts had been read, the notaries began to read out a number of passages selected from the works and sermons of Nestorius.[142] These were digested by Cyril, and by Nestorius' opponents in the church at Constantinople, and they evidently focus on those points held to be most objectionable—but this was entirely to the

[142] These texts are given in the section of translations following. cf. 'The Synodical Deposition of Nestorius,' p. 369f.

point in hand, to test his mind on the controverted question of the subjectivity of the Incarnate Lord. As such, while the prosecution's evidence might never have been erienical in intent, this is not the same as necessarily imputing substantial unfairness to it. Against six pages of the Schwartz edition given to the patristic citations, Nestorius was allowed a considerable say by proxy, his texts running to just over seven pages in length.[143] The selections, moreover, are governed by a definite sense of fairness: they are entirely representative of Nestorius' way of thinking. It was not the intention of Cyril to misrepresent this, only to demonstrate its incompatibility with the mind of the Fathers. The exposition of Nestorius' christology that follows in the present volume has (largely) been constructed independently of these texts by having direct recourse to Loofs neutral collection of the fragments of Nestorius' teachings. It is a relatively easy matter, then, to judge whether the synod heard an accurate sample of Nestorian teachings or not by comparing the collection presented in the subsequent chapter, with the collection assembled at Ephesus, which is offered *in toto* in the translated texts in chapter five.

After the lengthy readings were over the Acts record that a letter was read from bishop Capreolus of Carthage, excusing his absence and appealing for the council to allow no novelty in the faith. It looks, however, as if this text has been mislocated, for it seems to belong more fittingly to the opening business of that morning's procedure. If this suspicion is correct, the conciliar Fathers would have moved straight from the readings to a formal renunciation of Nestorian doctrine.

The notary drew up a document for all present to sign. It read as follows:

> Apart from other matters, since the Most Reverend Nestorius refused to obey our summons, and would not receive the most holy and reverend bishops whom we sent, then of necessity we have had to proceed to the examination of the impieties he has uttered and written in his epistles and in those writings which have been read out to us; [impieties] even in those things he has recently been speaking even in this very city in front of witnesses. All of this convicts him of thinking and preaching wickedly. We are compelled, therefore, by the canons and by the letter of our most holy father and fellow-minister Celestine, the bishop of the church of Rome, albeit with many tears, to come to this terrible sentence against him: Our Lord Jesus Christ, who has been blasphemed by this man, has decreed through this present most holy synod that

[143] ACO 1.1.45–52.

> the same Nestorius is excluded from the dignity of the episcopate and the whole assembly of hierarchs.[144]

Cyril, Juvenal, Flavian of Philippi, Firmus of Caesarea, Memnon of Ephesus, Acacius of Melitene, and Theodotus of Ancyra were the first seven to sign the document, either at the notary's table or on the altar of the church. They were followed in a subdued queue, that must have taken the best part of an hour to file past, by another 190 bishops in the church of St. Mary that evening. As the first session had progressed about forty of the 68 dissidents of the morning had come over to join the majority and signified their assent to the conciliar decree by signing the document. This is an extraordinary fact. It is not the case that Cyril added on names in the weeks ahead as he managed to find other supporters for from the notary's explicit scholion in the text 197 signatories were present on the evening of June 22nd 431, representing by proxy, as he says, a total of over 200 bishops; and in the days ahead he makes special note of the fact that 'other bishops came over to the council' and also signed their agreement—but these he did not record on the first list. The latter certainly included the Roman delegates. Cyril too, in his Letter 24,[145] states explicitly that 'there were more than 200 bishops' in the meeting, and he was talking about the first session of June 22nd. This means that the remnant of Nestorius' entourage must have largely abandoned him, and even some of John of Antioch's contingent must have broken ranks and joined the Cyrilline majority when they later arrived. At the end of that momentous first day of the council Nestorius was left with no more than 30 bishops still ready to support his cause. By any standards this was an extraordinary, as well as calamitous, collapse of support.

Crowds had been milling outside the church of St. Mary throughout the day, now as the doors opened the bishops looked out to a starlit summer's night and flickering illumination throughout the square and city streets from the torches of the enthusiasts who had been waiting expectantly all day for the outcome of the council. The result was greeted with great popular enthusiasm. Even apart from Cyril and Memnon's party of attendants it is clear that the celebration of the result was a genuinely popular affair. The women chanting in torchlit processions to honour the Virgin Mother of God resonated deep echoes

[144] ACO 1.2.54.
[145] ACO 1.1.1. (pp. 117–118).

for the Ephesians of the 'virgin mother of the god' Isis, whose cult used just such illuminated liturgies. It was also a cry of triumph that sharp-witted and intellectualist theology had not suppressed the people's own expressions of piety. Nestorius had never understood this depth of ordinary feeling; for years Cyril had known the ins and outs of it in his own church in Egypt, and was a past master in bending it to the service of the new gospel. In the common sentiment of the people Nestorius was thought of as one who had dishonoured the Virgin,[146] the patroness of the city of Ephesus, which prided itself on being a centre of pilgrimage to the site of her church and the tomb of her protector the apostle John.

Cyril wrote back to Alexandria shortly after the event and provides a graphic description of the scene:[147]

> The entire population of the city stood from dawn to dusk waiting for the decision of the holy council. When they heard that the wretched man was deposed, they all began, with one voice, to cry out in praise of the holy council, glorifying God because the enemy of the faith had fallen. When we came out of the church they made a procession ahead of us to the lodging house (for it was getting dark by this time) and even the women came out carrying incense to perfume the path before us. Our Saviour has demonstrated his power in the face of all who blaspheme his glory. Accordingly we will finish the legal papers necessary for his excommunication, and then by God's grace we will soon be with you again.

Cyril's hope for a speedy departure, in the event proved unfounded. He had yet to experience the full force of the troubles that were to fall upon him in the light of the protests which the Syrians and the military commanders delivered to the imperial court. Far from tidying up the papers and returning to Alexandria, the entire episcopal body was destined to be shut up in Ephesus for a total of four months to come.

On the morning of Tuesday June 23rd, the notice of deposition was delivered to Nestorius at his lodging house. It did not mince words:

> The holy synod gathered by God's grace in Ephesus, in accordance with the instructions of our most religious and Christ-loving Emperors,

---

[146] To this day one Greek tradition of icon painting of the Koimesis (death or assumption) of the Virgin has a wicked monk attempting to overturn the bier, as Christ takes her soul to heavenly glory; it is Nestorius, and he is chased away by an angel entering from the right.

[147] Ep. 24. ACO 1.1.1. pp. 117–118.

> to Nestorius, the new Judas. Know that because of your wicked preaching and disobedience of the canons, on this 22nd day of the present month of June in accordance with the ecclesiastical prescripts, you have been deposed by the holy synod and excluded from all ecclesiastical dignity.[148]

The notaries of the council proceeded to the Ephesian Agora to fix up the public proclamation of their result—a move that took events one stage further along the road to constitute the legal irreversibility of their acts, but were forcibly stopped by Candidian's soldiers who forbade the herald to announced the decree around the city, thus signalling the enforcement of his earlier threat to annul any proceedings of the assembled bishops that transpired before the arrival of the Syrians.

It is clear that Cyril must have acted with great alacrity at this point. He must have suspected that Candidian intended to blockade the bishops in the city, and thus immediately sent off letters to Alexandria and messengers to Constantinople informing the clergy there of Nestorius' deposition, and instructing them in the name of the synod to arrange, with the Emperor's consent, the election of a new archbishop. He evidently intended to broadcast the news as widely as possible so that it would not remain a straightforward legal matter that would rest entirely in the lap of the Emperor alone waiting for a resolution. Until the Emperor sanctioned the result of a council, as all sides knew, there was little weight in its decrees. By ensuring that the anti-Nestorian agitators at the imperial city had as much intelligence on matters as Theodosius himself, Cyril had struck a decisive blow by limiting Theodosius' room for manouevre. At the same time as he informed the clergy he forwarded a digested version of the proceedings against Nestorius to the court.[149] He wrote to the highly venerated abbot Dalmatius, a leader of the monastic clergy at Constantinople who had much influence with the Emperor and the Augusta Pulcheria alike, and subsequent reports he heard from the monastic party in the capital told him that public feeling was generally glad that Nestorius was gone. Cyril's hope was that Theodosius would accept his conciliar report immediately and then matters would be at an end. It did not prove so simple.

In the intervening days, waiting for news from outside the city of Ephesus, the relations between the two opposed camps deteriorated further. Candidian made it clear that he would continue to fulfil his

---

148 ACO 1.2.64.
149 ACO 1.3.3–5.

duties and refuse to allow any bishop to leave the city limits. For his part Cyril directed the notaries to collate the full acts of the council for future reference. The soldiers of Count Irenaeus made common cause with those of Candidian, regarding the Cyrilline majority as guilty of treasonable disrespect of the Emperor in their evident disobedience of their respective commanders. Henceforward, as the Cyrillines were to complain, Candidian was publicly allied with Nestorius' cause. Nestorius and his ten remaining companions spent the time composing a formal appeal to the Emperor dwelling, somewhat melodramatically,[150] on the violence that had been offered to them at Ephesus, and making it out to be as seditious and as partisan an assembly as possible.[151] The complaint was repeated by John's synod later, presumably taking Nestorius' words at face value, and it has become commonly accepted because Nestorius much later repeated the same assessment of events in his Book of Heraclides, where he points to the riotous events of the Synod of Ephesus in 449 and says that the same thing happened to him in 431. This version has no firmer historical weight simply because it is repeated three times, all from the same source, and ought to be taken with some caution. As John's later complaint makes clear, a sober charge could not lay the riotous factions at the door of Cyril (however much his enemies might wish to do so) they were attributed to Memnon. Visions of Cyril commanding large troops of Egyptian sailors, parabalani, and heavyweight monks to terrorise the neighbourhood are simply not supported by the evidence. He was not in Egypt but thousands of miles away from home. To speak of 'riotous factions' who were 'stirred up by Memnon' is another way of telling the story of widespread popular disapproval of Nestorius. The same is true at Constantinople where extraordinary demonstrations later demonstrated to Theodosius only too clearly that the archbishop was a widely hated figure even in his own church. To ascribe all these expressions of public dissent to individual figures such as Memnon or Cyril does not do justice to the important and volatile nature of the Vox Populi in fifth century politics and religion. Memnon certainly took advantage of the vociferous crowds and used the popular swell as a counterbalance to the forces of opposition but, again, the only significant body of armed men who unquestionably threw their weight around at Ephesus were the troops

---

[150] ACO 1.5. 13–15.

[151] 'The Egyptian and Asian bishops spread the soldiers of their escort through the market place and filled the city with tumult.' Ibid. para.4.

of Candidian and Irenaeus. Nestorius certainly found himself in an overwhelmingly hostile environment when he arrived at Ephesus, but with the garrison surrounding him there was never a time when he was in any serious personal danger.

At the end of his appeal to the Emperor Nestorius says that Cyril had so organised affairs that he could not gain a hearing at the council, but goes on to make a curious proposition. It is something of an indicator of his political naivety. He asked the Emperor to dissolve the Synod and convoke another council nearer Constantinople which would only admit, as he had originally intended, one or two learned bishops from each province who could debate the issues of faith calmly and without prejudice. The suggestion of another full-scale gathering of bishops would hardly be entertained with any seriousness by Theodosius in any circumstances. The theological presuppositions behind Nestorius' request are equally revealing of his understanding of theological method, which here makes a scholastic innovation. Instead of the traditional view of a general council that 'recognised' the abiding reality of the ancient faith and 'acclaimed' it, such as Cyril and the (none too learned) majority of the council were working from, Nestorius seems to have envisaged instead the nature of a council as an organ of royal policy—taking the council as the ecclesiastical version of the senate at the capital where royal policy was discussed and finely tuned. This kind of council would, by nature, be an aristocratic and elite body, in a sense a learned society questing for an uncertain end, a new credal definition or such like by means of rational discourse.[152] Here the unlettered would have no legitimate voice at all. Even Theodosius would find such a presupposition unacceptable, if not blasphemous. His own appeal to the 'holy men' around him, and even as far away as Syria where he had sent messengers to consult St. Symeon Stylites and the ancient Acacius of Beroea, demonstrates his allegiance to another method altogether. Like his sister Pulcheria, Theodosius was enough of a Byzantine to sense that orthodoxy and spiritual charism were indivisible, and thus the holy men stood even as arbiters of doctrine, not debarred from theological acumen because of their lack of formal education, but on the contrary

[152] The preferred theological method is one aspect of the affair that has made Nestorius such a positive icon for several commentators of the Anglican and Reformed churches, whose own traditions give a high predominance to speculative reason in their theological methodologies (even when citing the Scriptural text as 'authority') following a longstanding Western scholastic paradigm. Such a paradigm should not,

elevated to decisive spiritual understanding by God's inspiration of their lives of prayer and asceticism. At the end of the day the opinions of the recluses, ascetics, and pillar dwellers carried more weight with Theodosius than the arguments of Nestorius.

Nestorius' letter of appeal to the Emperor was presumably sent to Constantinople at the same time as Cyril's, before the arrival of John of Antioch's party which put such a different light on events. Both rescripts seem to have been motivated by a shared desire to circumvent the incompetent Candidian. That of Nestorius implies to the Emperor that he did not attend the council primarily on Candidian's instructions. By appealing directly to Theodosius he obviously intended to come straight back to the court. Candidian, by strictly applying the original prescript that forbade any bishop to leave Ephesus until the business was concluded, was seemingly now in his way as much as that of Cyril's.

When Theodosius received both contradictory rescripts from the principal protagonists he began to realise how his hopes for the council had gone badly wrong. As yet Theodosius had received no formal report from Candidian. The latter had been pre-empted by both parties, and was now finding that matters were passing more and more out of his hands. He prepared a report which justified his dismissal of the Cyrilline council on the grounds that it was only a partisan meeting. Theodosius was to find the receipt of these three very disparate views of the events greatly confusing. What seems to have been his earlier acceptance of Cyril's account of the conciliar action was changed to an attitude of considerable annoyance when he read in Candidian's report that only a partial meeting had taken place. Cyril's Letter 27 was later to show his alarm at the way Candidian's version had gained acceptance at the court. But this was only the beginning of a long and complicated series of events at Constantinople that was to determine the final imperial policy regarding the status of the conciliar findings. Meanwhile events were not standing still in Ephesus, and even as the imperial post stations were busy transmitting the reports, the situation in Asia Minor changed in such a dramatic way that the intelligence to which Theodosius was going to react was already obsolete, almost before it arrived.

---

however, be presupposed in the 5th century context. St. Gregory Nazianzen's Fifth Theological Oration (380 AD) presented the common 'patristic' archetype of theological method, and it departs considerably from the Nestorian paradigm. (E.T. of the Orations in E.R. Hardy, Christology of the Later Fathers, London 1954, pp. 128–214.).

In the midst of the stand-off at Ephesus John of Antioch's party finally arrived, as he had said that it would, within the week of his advance party, probably on Friday June 26th. He was escorted in to the city by the soldiers of Count Irenaeus, and doubtless by the time he had arrived at his lodgings he had heard the outraged complaints of Nestorius' group. In these circumstances he did an extraordinary thing, probably on the spur of the moment, for he held a synod on his own authority to excommunicate the leaders of the majority council. It was a testimony to his inexperience as a hierarch, to Nestorius' desperation (for the latter completely abandoned the policy he himself had initiated only a few days before by appealing directly to the Emperor) and to Candidian's incompetency in allowing an even more partisan group meeting than the assembly of the week before.

Delegates sent by the majority council had tried to see him on his arrival in the city, and attempted to communicate the synodical decrees, seeking his assent to them. These were refused admittance for several hours while John listened to reports from Nestorius, and then they were ignominiously turned out by the soldiers. The account of their expulsion with menaces soon turned the feelings of the Cyrilline majority decidedly against John.

John proceeded to convoke a formal gathering of his bishops, and those of Nestorius, there and then in his lodging house within hours of his arrival. Beginning with Candidian's account of his grievances, exactly as Cyril had done he demanded a reading of the imperial Sacra entrusted to the Count, and thus constituted his synod as the intended council of Ephesus. It has subsequently been known as the Conciliabulum (little council) to distinguish it from Cyril's synod.[153]

The 43 bishops who comprised the meeting accused Cyril and Memnon of fomenting disorder in the city against the ecclesiastical canons and against civil law, and of 'audaciously, and in a disorderly manner of having begun a council of your own in a spirit of heresy even though we were at the very gates of the city'.[154] The decree of the conciliabulum focused particularly on Cyril's Third Letter to Nestorius, which had been the object of Theodoret's close and critical scrutiny over the previous winter. The bishops declared Cyril's Chapters to be 'in agreement, in the main, with the wickedness of

[153] The Acts of the meeting are found in ACO 1.5.119–124.
[154] Ibid. para.5.

Arius, Apollinaris, and Eunomius',[155] and they went on to proclaim the penalty of excommunication and deposition against Cyril and Memnon, while attributing to the other bishops the milder sanction of excommunication 'until such time as having recognised your error, you repent, accept the faith of the holy Fathers gathered together at Nicaea (without adding or subtracting anything from it), anathematise the heretical chapters published by Cyril of Alexandria in opposition to the evangelical and apostolic doctrine, and concur with the Sacra of the most pious and Christ-loving Emperors who commanded that the problems of the faith should be examined in an exact manner in a peaceful spirit'.[156]

The legality of the conciliabulum, in civil terms, was even more questionable than that of the preceding council, but in ecclesiastical terms it was wholly invalid and certainly reckless since no formal summons had been delivered and no examination of Cyril's statements had been conducted within the synod before the condemnations were pronounced. These legal aspects fade, however, in the face of the extraordinary prospect of a meeting of merely 43 complaining of the partisan nature of their 200 opponents, representing as they did Africa, Rome, Egypt, Macedonia, and Asia Minor.

Nonetheless, John's sentence had one important effect on the Cyrilline party, and that was to alert them to the considerable feeling that ran against Cyril's 12 Chapters, and particularly to the charge of crypto-Apollinarism that had been levied against him. In the weeks ahead Cyril had to engage in many efforts to assure bishops in Ephesus that the Chapters were orthodox. For some of his supporters, not least the Roman delegates who were soon to arrive, the very existence of them was news. He was compelled to compose a lengthy explanation of his meaning and, as the manuscript tradition testifies, this essentially justificatory work was designed for the benefit of his own party as much as for the Antiochenes. Until this point Cyril had been entirely on the offensive, and largely successful. The next four months were to be his most severe trial and called for all the diplomatic skill and theological wit he could summon to keep his synod in a cohesive momentum.

In the immediate aftermath of the conciliabulum its notice of deposition and excommunication was announced. On the following

155 Ibid. para.11.
156 Ibid. para. 15.

day letters were prepared for the royal court, the clergy, senate, and people of Constantinople.[157] In these, the 'theologically ignorant Egyptian and Asian bishops' were portrayed as the chief causes of the disorder which had overtaken everything, and the Cyrilline council was described, highly tendentiously, as made up for the rest of an assembly of Messalian heretics and various excommunicates 'a mass of men completely ignorant of the divine doctrines, and full of restlessness and violence'.[158]

As that Saturday of June 27th grew late, the practicality of the conciliabulum's decision was to be put to the test. Memnon had control over his own great Church of St. Mary and the martyrium of St. John. From the outset he had refused Nestorius permission to celebrate the liturgy in any of his churches. As the time drew near for Vespers of the Sunday feast, John of Antioch asked Candidian to ensure that none of the Egyptian or Ephesian clergy should be allowed to celebrate the liturgy in the churches, since their hierarchs had been deposed. Candidian was evidently not convinced of John's ability to represent himself successfully as the true conciliar party because the demand he made to Memnon was that only the local Ephesian clergy should celebrate the liturgy that Sunday. Memnon refused his competence to give any liturgical instructions at all, and pointedly asked Cyril, as conciliar president, to celebrate. The local people from then onwards resisted all efforts by the Syrians to enter the Ephesian churches. The Syrian attempt, probably on the Sunday morning, to seize the church of St. John by force and use it to consecrate a new bishop to replace Memnon, stirred up the outrage of the whole town and the Syrians were ignominiously driven back to their lodgings[159]—an event which John independently described, assuming the role of the outraged innocent, as a violent and unreasonable refusal of the local bishop to allow them to perform their devotions at the Apostle's shrine.[160]

Cyril's letter to Constantinople announcing the deposition of Nestorius had arrived first in the capital and, according to the archimandrite Dalmatius' report to Ephesus, had apparently initially been favourably entertained by the Emperor. John's letters and news of the Conciliabulum were still on their way, but Nestorius' earlier appeal for a reconvening of the council, together with Candidian's subsequent

[157] ACO 1.5.124 f.
[158] ACO 1.5.126.
[159] As reported in Memnon's letter to Constantinople ACO 1.3.46.
[160] ACO 1.5.27.

complaint that only a 'partial meeting' had taken place had arrived on June 25th and caused Theodosius to hold the earlier reports from Cyril in suspicion.

Theodosius was determined that his original instructions should be obeyed, in spite of widespread delight in the streets of the imperial city when news of the deposition of Nestorius had leaked out (as Cyril had planned when he forwarded separate letters to the clergy of the royal city). Accordingly, on June 29th the Emperor sent an examining magistrate, Palladius, to Ephesus with the commission to find out exactly what was going on, and 'assist' Candidian in keeping order. The Emperor ordered all the bishops to stay in Ephesus until the investigation was complete. The tone of his letter was one of clear annoyance, and he berated them for not obeying his instructions. Until a free discussion had been held the results of the Cyrilline council were to be set aside.

Meanwhile the clergy of Constantinople, especially the monks, celebrated the Cyrilline council and greeted the news of Nestorius' deposition with undisguised delight. On June 26th, when it seemed that the Emperor was turning from his first policy of accepting the Cyrilline synod, the monks of the city organised a procession to the imperial palace to plead with him to confirm the result. The procession was led by the aged archimandrite Dalmatius (whom Theodosius held in high veneration as a holy man and had unsuccessfully requested to assume the throne of the church of Constantinople himself). This caused a sensation in the city for in fulfilment of a vow the aged monk had lived as a hermit in his own monastery, never leaving the confines of his cell for the last forty six years. His sudden appearance in public, to plead the cause of Cyril and the condemnation of Nestorius was still not enough to sway the Emperor. He received the delegation politely, asked for the prayers of the old man and dismissed them.

Palladius reported with great haste. On his return, in early July, he brought with him a protest delegation from the majority council telling him that in no way could the decisions of the synod be set aside since they had been canonically constituted. The delegation was instructed by Cyril to expose the falsity of Candidian's version of events. The latter was accused of presenting a completely false account of the happenings and of 'having preferred his friendship with Nestorius to righteousness',[161] a polite way of accusing him of blatant partisanship.

---

161 ACO 1.3. (84) p. 11.

The blame for the stirring up of civil discord was laid at the door of Count Irenaeus and his soldiers, and the Acts of the synod were presented to the Emperor so that it could be proven that Nestorius did in fact receive a fair judgement of his case. The bishops appealed to the international representativeness of their meeting, and ended by denouncing the actions of John of Antioch as wholly illegal.

A few days later Count Irenaeus made a personal visit to the court to plead for the cause of his friend Nestorius. By this time Theodosius had also received the acts of the Conciliabulum, and he complicated matters in an extraordinary way. He decided to ratify both synods in the form of accepting their respective depositions of Nestorius, Cyril and Memnon, and in so doing dismiss the whole assembly, probably intending to defer a resolution until new patriarchs had been chosen.

As the week drew to a close at the beginning of July the people of Constantinople were agitating in the streets.[162] The popular dissent was focused in a protest meeting in the Great Church to demand the dismissal of their archbishop. On Saturday evening on the 4th of July[163] the people occupied the church building and demanded assurances from the Emperor that the Cyrilline synod would be honoured. They stayed in the church for three days chanting acclamations in praise of Pulcheria whose policy favouring the deposition of Nestorius they identified as their own.[164] In response, the court official Domitianus was sent from the Palace to announce to the crowd the Emperor's decision. When he read out the confirmation of Nestorius' deposition the news was greeted with acclamations but the mood turned to one of fury when he proceeded to inform them that the decrees of the conciliabulum were also being confirmed and Cyril and Memnon were thus equally to be held as deposed. Continuing agitation at popular level gave Theodosius grounds for thought. The palace was also the scene of constant discussions as various factions urged conflicting advice on the Emperor.[165] One thing Theodosius knew, after receiving Palladius' report, and that was that Candidian's position was hopelessly compromised, so he arranged to send another and more substantial politician to replace him. He instructed Count

---

162 Kopt. Akt.(Kraatz) p. 49; ACO 1.1.3.(14.); Holum (1982) p. 170.

163 Thus Holum (1982) p. 170 dates the events between the Saturday and Monday of July 4–6th.

164 ACO 1.1.3. 14; cf. Battifol (1924).

165 ACO 1.1.5. 136.

John, the Imperial High Treasurer, to go to Ephesus in person and effect his policy.

Meanwhile, in Ephesus, the spirits of the Cyrilline majority were about to be lifted. At long last on Friday July 10th the Roman delegation, Arcadius, Projectus, and the priest Philip, arrived in the beleaguered city. Cyril, still unaware of the Emperor's decree against him, at once reconvened the Synod in a second session. All the original members reassembled in Memnon's episcopal residence to hear the letter of Pope Celestine read out in which he requested confirmation of the Roman Synod's earlier condemnation of Nestorius. It was a great boost to morale.

On the following day, July 11th, a third session reconvened in Memnon's residence at which the Roman legates formally accepted and signed the Acts of both the previous sessions of the council. Further letters were sent to the Emperor and clergy of Constantinople again requesting that the decrees of the synod should be ratified. The conciliar momentum was under way once more, and attention began to turn to John of Antioch's continuing refusal to negotiate with the majority. Even after the arrival of the Roman delegation John refused to acknowledge the bishops in Ephesus unless they abandoned Cyril and Memnon according to the terms set out by the conciliabulum. On Thursday July 16th Cyril summoned the council to its fourth session to settle the impasse with John. The bishops met in the church of St. Mary and delegates were sent out to summon John and the Orientals. The first delegation was chased away. The second received a reply from John that he could not in conscience communicate with excommunicates. In the light of these replies Cyril suspended his meeting for further discussions among his leading bishops.

On the following Friday July 17th the fifth session of the council was opened, and a third and final delegation was sent to demand John's presence. When they arrived at John's lodgings his archdeacon would not give them a verbal reply but tried to present them with a scroll that contained the archbishop's answer. Suspecting that it contained a formal sentence of condemnation against Cyril and Memnon, the conciliar delegates refused to accept it and the two sides parted acrimoniously. The council proceeded to judge John's actions against Cyril and Memnon to be wholly unjust and uncanonically performed, and then passed sentence against John and 34 of his companion bishops, excommunicating them and suspending their rights of ecclesiastical jurisdiction—a deliberate stage short of the irreversible decision to depose them. News of the actions were again forwarded to Constantinople.

On Saturday July 22nd a sixth session was held to discuss the petition of the priest Charisius who had been suspended by his bishop Theophanes of Philadelphia (one of the members of the conciliabulum). In this legal process Charisius gave a meandering testimony as to how Nestorius' chaplains Anastasius and Photius had been instrumental in imposing on the church at Philadelphia a baptismal creed composed by Theodore Mopsuestia—by now a bogeyman for the whole Cyrilline party. It was a symbolic tying in of Theodore to Nestorius and doubtless Cyril propelled the priest to such prominence in the Acts so as to have the connection formally stated. The session ended with a canon to the effect that the Nicene Creed alone was the legitimate symbol of the universal church. It was probably at this session that a petition was heard from the Pamphylian bishops seeking confirmation of their policy to readmit certain Messalian (or Euchite) schismatics to full communion.

On Monday July 31st[166] the seventh and final session of the council was convened in the church of St. Mary. This too was concerned with more generalised business and the composition of regulatory canons, but since some of these affected the rights of the church of Antioch they were celebrated as deliberate expressions of the decrees of the fifth session. Rheginus the archbishop of Cyprus took advantage of the occasion to petition the synod to accede to his church's longstanding claims to be independent of the patriarchal jurisdiction of Antioch. There was some debate over the validity of appealing to the canons of Nicaea in support of the claim,[167] but the Cypriot bishops testified that neither Rheginus' predecessor nor the earlier archbishops of Cyprus had actually been consecrated by the patriarch of Antioch. The outcome was the synod's recognition of the independence of the church of Cyprus. To this day it remains an autocephalous church.

Six other disciplinary canons were composed on the same occasion reinstating clergy deposed by Nestorius, and threatening deposition

[166] The copyist in the Acts mistakenly dates this to August 31st, but after the arrival of Count John at the beginning of August no further meetings of the council took place.

[167] Canon 4 of Nicaea had attributed the right to consecrate bishops to the bishops of the local province. But canon 6 of the same had also reserved to the great and ancient sees their longstanding metropolitan rights.

or excommunication on those who would not abide by the council's decrees. The Pelagian appellants to the court at Constantinople were also condemned, doubtless on the specific request of the Roman delegates. It was possibly at this same session that Juvenal of Jerusalem pressed his case (for which he had long been agitating) that his ancient see should be given independent patriarchal rights, and an extension of jurisdictional territory. The attempt was supported by dubious documentary evidence, and was robustly resisted by Cyril as an unwarranted innovation in canonical precedent. Cyril doubtless had no desire to undo all his careful canonical proceedings with a suspect move that could play into his opponents' hands. While Juvenal's attempt failed at Ephesus, he would be successful at Chalcedon, pressing the same petition twenty years later.

The heat of the summer in Ephesus proved very trying for many of the bishops, lodged as they were in cramped conditions. Count Irenaeus and Candidian, after the conciliabulum's decree, were more open in their efforts to harass and hamper the Cyrilline party in any way they could. Supplies were restricted to them, and many messengers trying to convey letters and appeals to Constantinople were intercepted both at the docks, and on the land routes. The Syrian party hoped that they could regain the political initiative by subverting Cyril's links with the outside world while concentrating all their own efforts now on petitioning the royal court. On one occasion Cyril had to resort to smuggling out a letter to Constantinople in the hollow cane of a disguised beggar. It told Dalmatius that the orthodox bishops were being persecuted by the military and could hardly bear to be imprisoned in such conditions any longer. 'We are being decimated by the heat here', he said, 'and almost every day we bury another of our number.' This pressure hold on the Cyrilline party was to be short-lived. At the beginning of August the High Treasurer Count John arrived and took control of the city with a firm hand in the name of the Emperor.

The imperial chancery had prepared letters for him to bring to the bishops whom they thought were the prominent leaders of the council: Pope Celestine, Rufinus of Thessalonike, and Augustine of Hippo. This was an inauspicious start. The first two had never been present at the council at any stage, and the third had been dead for a year. It serves to illustrate how difficult it was under the prevailing conditions of transport and communication to gain a clear picture of events.

Count John soon showed that he was made of sterner stuff than

Candidian, and knew the Emperor's mind quite clearly. The list of the letter's addressees, however anachronistic it might have been in parts, was quite clear in another respect, for no mention was made, quite deliberately, of Cyril, Memnon, or Nestorius. On his arrival he summoned all the bishops to his lodgings for a plenary session on the following day. Nestorius and the Syrians were ordered to attend first, in the early hours of the morning. When the Cyrillines turned up they entered the loggia of the building to discover, for the first time, their opponents already sitting. Memnon did not appear, later excusing himself on the grounds of illness when a detachment was sent after him. Cyril immediately demanded the exclusion of Nestorius from the meeting as being canonically and irreversibly deposed. John of Antioch rose in turn and demanded the exclusion of Cyril and Memnon on the same grounds, and a tumult ensued. Count John was not moved. He told the assembly that since the Emperor's commands were addressed to the bishops specifically excluding the aforenamed, it was of little moment to him whether they were present or not; and he proceeded to drop the bombshell of announcing the Emperor's decision to validate the acts of both councils in so far as he was going to confirm the sentences passed against all three. The bishops were ordered to leave for their homes, and the meeting was broken up by Count Candidian who had been ordered to escort Nestorius away to house arrest, and by Count James leading off Cyril under guard to his lodgings and then pursuing Memnon whom he similarly arrested, freezing the assets of the church at Ephesus.

Significantly, John of Antioch abandoned Nestorius at this juncture, and signified his agreement with the Emperor's policy. The Cyrilline majority at first were hardly able to take in what had happened, but steadfastly refused to abandon Cyril and Memnon, and being unable to criticise Theodosius directly, concluded that his policy could only have been formulated on the basis of false reports. Only a few days before, they had been agitating to leave Ephesus for their homes, now that they had been commanded to do so they were determined to sit it out in defence of their synod's legality.

It seems probable that the Emperor had believed the reports of Nestorius and Candidian and John of Antioch, all of which depicted Cyril as a tyrannical ringleader who had railroaded sheepish and ignorant bishops into submission by the force of his personality. He seems to have estimated that once the two hierarchs were under arrest and Memnon's access to finances had been cut off, the rest of the bishops would soon fall into line with a suitably severe demonstration of imperial disfavour. It was an estimate which proved totally misguided. In the weeks ahead he began to realise that the majority opinion was both substantial and deeply held, and that the opposing camp commanded very little support indeed.

From this time onwards the locus of events moved entirely to the capital where negotiations were conducted at an even more furious pace, in the usual Byzantine manner, mostly in secret and relying on varying channels of access to important persons. Count Irenaeus was lobbying for Nestorius, and at the end of August the Cyrilline council sent a formal delegation with a petition to the Emperor requesting him to disregard all 'false reports' and confirm only their decrees.[168] Pulcheria's influence was once again at work on her brother, and gave Cyril hope that the imperial decision could be changed. Although Memnon was effectively silenced by his house arrest, the same could not be said of Cyril. His network of agents in the capital was put to full use and their aim was to undermine all the influence Count Irenaeus might command at court to their detriment.

Still having access to the great fiscal resources which the see of Alexandria could command Cyril used his agents to petition influential aristocrats around the throne, and leading ladies of the entourage of Pulcheria, to support their cause, and the petitions were accompanied by lavish 'eulogiae' (blessings) in cash and kind. The use of donations to assist the progress of any petition through the corridors of the imperial court was fairly standard practice in fifth century Byzantium, but the scale of Cyril's largesse was extraordinary. It almost bankrupted the Alexandrian church.[169] Count Irenaeus soon found that his face was not so welcome among his colleagues in the palace.[170] The vacillating Theodosius was induced to review his position yet again, but he was insistent on one point, that the theological issues should be debated and not simply reduced to the matter of personal excommunications. He decided to summon a small group of delegates from each party to debate the case in his presence at the capital. For this purpose he set aside the Villa Rufiniana at Chalcedon which had been Theophilus of Alexandria's setting, years before, for the Synod of the Oak which deposed John Chrysostom. On Friday September 11th he opened the colloquy in person.

---

[168] ACO 1.3.32 f.

[169] Cyril Ep.96, E.T. McEnerney (1987) p. 151; see also Battifol (1919); Jones (1986) vol.1, p. 346.

[170] Count Irenaeus' letter: ACO 1.5.135 f. paras.2,5, passim.

The Cyrilline delegation, deprived of his presence since he was still held under arrest in Ephesus, was comprised of the Romans Arcadius and Philip, Firmus of Caesarea, Theodotus of Ancyra, Acacius of Melitene and Euoptius of Ptolemais in Africa. For their part the Syrian delegation consisted of John of Antioch, John of Damascus, Hierius of Nicomedia, Paul of Emesa, Macarius of Laodicea, Apringius of Chalcis, Helladius of Ptolemais in Phoenicia, and Theodoret of Cyr. Acacius and Theodoret were the main opposing theologians of the groups.[171]

The Orientals put the best face on things that they could but as soon as they arrived at the capital they found themselves unwelcomed by the people at large. Almost immediately they heard to their dismay that a week before, on September 3rd, Theodosius had re-confirmed the deposition of Nestorius. In response to the latter's much earlier petition to leave Ephesus for the sake of his own safety (sent to the court even before the conciliabulum took place) the Emperor finally sent the laconic reply that he was graciously pleased to accede. The Praetorian Prefect Antiochus had communicated the news to Nestorius that he was to be released from Ephesus, and to enjoy free passage back to his former monastery at Antioch. Antiochus added a touching personal footnote to the formal edict: 'I have prayed to God's kindness that your holiness may flourish and live in accordance with his will. Knowing the prudence of your spirit and your innumerable outstanding qualities we have every confidence that you stand in no need of consolation from us'.[172]

The letters of the Orientals back to their party at Ephesus were at first buoyant and hopeful. They tell how Theodoret bested Acacius in his arguments, how their opponents could only keep on 'praising Cyril to the skies' and how Acacius had scandalised the senate and the Emperor so much that 'his majesty's cloak fell off'[173] supposedly in horror at what he was hearing. Acacius' fault, apparently, was to teach that the divinity suffered, which probably means no more than that he defended the orthodoxy of the Twelve Chapters. The Orientals were clutching at straws. Theodosius ended that first session by requiring written positions to be drawn up by each side.

---

171 The texts representing the course of the debates are found in ACO 1.7.72–81.

172 ACO 1.7.71.

173 ACO 1.7.77. Fragments of Theodoret's speeches on this occasion are preserved in the Acts of the Fifth Oecumenical council of 553.

Four other sessions of the Chalcedonian Colloquy were to follow throughout September and October. Both parties had been refused permission to enter the city itself, partly because local feelings were still running very high against Nestorius and now against the Antiochenes in general whose condemnation by the synod had already been communicated to the clergy in Constantinople. While the Cyrilline delegates were popular and welcome, the Orientals found even the churches closed against them in the suburbs of Chalcedon. They made no less than three formal protests to the Emperor about unfavourable treatment but, ominously, none of them was answered. In the end they had to hire a private house for their stay using the courtyard as their church and the galleries as their pulpit, from which they delivered daily sermons to their curious visitors.

Neither side in the negotiations could convict their opponents of heresy, however hard they tried to do so. It was a lesson on whose significance both John and Cyril later had cause to dwell. The Orientals accepted the Theotokos title, taught the singleness of the Lord's person, and the inseparable union of the two natures. In response to their main attack on the Apollinarist character of Cyril's Chapters, the synodical party followed Cyril's directions as outlined in his extensive Explanation of the Chapters. They adopted what was to be, increasingly, his future position—that the anathematisms had been a strong statement designed specifically against Nestorius' personal heresies. Without abandoning the principle of their doctrine Cyril was ready to accept they could not be the base for rapprochement with the Syrians. To the external observers from the imperial diplomatic service the embryonic form of a compromise was clearly emerging, although the two parties were as yet unable to see it. Could not the continuing insistence of the Syrians on the condemnation of the Chapters be set aside? In return could not the demand of the Cyrillians that the Orientals should ask in writing for forgiveness from the synod for their behaviour at Ephesus, equally be forgotten? This much at least was clarified at a diplomatic level by the Chalcedonian Colloquies, and the imperial diplomats noted it for future reference. But in terms of the theological debate between the bishops the exchanges did little to induce any side to cease hostilities.

The Orientals knew that their cause had been lost at court. Understandably, they argued bitterly that Theodosius and his officials had been corrupted by Cyril's gold. In a later letter of Acacius of Beroea to Alexander of Hierapolis the old man presents this (as hearsay) to explain why the Emperor, apparently so favourable to their cause at first, turned against them so decidedly at Chalcedon.[174] He speaks there of Cyril's conviction of bribery, of his deposition being confirmed, and of his illegal flight from custody but all this represents more of the aspirations or fantasies of the orientals than the political realities. It did not need gold to change Theodosius' mind, he was a past master in the art of vacillating. In fact, before the Syrians had even arrived at Chalcedon he had confirmed Nestorius' deposition and sent him into exile. If he had intended to do the same with Cyril he would surely have done so at this time in September. Cyril's payments to the court officials undoubtedly smoothed the way for his cause, and given his own belief in the rightness of that cause he seems to have had no qualms about applying the money for that end. Nonetheless the key factor which swayed Theodosius was without question the solid determination of the Cyrilline party not to abandon their president whom they identified as synonymous with their cause. In contrast, apart from being a tiny minority, the Syrians vacillated over Nestorius, and John at least was known to be willing to abandon him to his fate, much to the disgust of some of his own party.

The church at Constantinople had by now lost interest in the Orientals, and was busy with the business of electing a new archbishop—no Syrian this time but one of their own, a native Roman, Maximian, who had been a cleric of the church since the days of John Chrysostom.[175] His consecration was arranged for Sunday October 25th,[176] and the Emperor asked the Cyrilline bishops to take part in the ceremonies. The Orientals received no invitation.

By this stage Theodosius' policy was finally to be published. He had largely come down in favour of the Ephesian majority. Nestorius' deposition was to be final, and the accusation of Apollinarism against Cyril was dismissed. On the other side he was determined that the Antiochenes should also be accepted as orthodox in their doctrine. The colloquies had proved to him that no further resolution of the matter could be expected in the short term and as he had no further hopes from the less-learned parties still in Ephesus, he sent back the

---

[174] cf. Hefele (1908) pp. 375–376.

[175] Maximian was a childhood friend of Pope Celestine's. He was a pious and affable man, but no great intellect. The aristocrats had lobbied for the election of Proclus but Theodosius passed him over, evidently favouring a more nondescript candidate in the circumstances, and perhaps one not so overtly allied with his sister.

[176] Socrates. Hist. Eccl. 7.37. 19.

command that all should finally disperse to their homes.[177] In the Sacra of the dissolution of the council he gave permission for Memnon to resume his duties at Ephesus, and for Cyril to return to Alexandria. The ancient editor of the Casinensis collection which preserves this text added a footnote: 'This was the last of the Sacras after the blessed Cyril, Patriarch of Alexandria, had already returned to his city.'

Cyril had left Ephesus on October 31st. From this it has sometimes been deduced[178] that he fled from his prison in defiance of the Emperor, but this is an unwarranted supposition.[179] Even before Maximian's ordination on October 25th, it was obvious which way the Emperor's decision had gone, and Cyril's postal service was far more efficient than that of the chancery. On October 31st he surely knew that the Sacra freeing him had already been composed and so he returned home to a welcome as victor of the day.[180] His reputation everywhere, except of course in the oriental patriarchate, both as an ecclesiastical leader and an eminent theologian had never run higher. But there was still one international crisis to resolve, for large parts of the church were now out of communion, and the Emperor was determined to see the rifts between the major Christian sees closed with the utmost urgency.

4. The Long Search for Peace, 432–444

From the time of his house arrest in Ephesus Cyril had realised the need to go further in answering the Syrian charge of Apollinarism than simply by dismissing the accusation as a patent nonsense (something that he always thought was the case). His Explanation of the Chapters of 431 reflects the political reality that on no account could he simply renounce the Anathemas. Much as he might regret the

---

[177] ACO 1.7.142; 1.3.67.

[178] See, for example, Davis (1987) p. 159.

[179] After his safe arrival back in Alexandria Cyril set to work composing an apologetic of his behaviour at Ephesus, seeking Theodosius' pardon for any faults he had committed. It is clear from the document that he was more worried about the annoyance he had caused the Emperor by his appeals to the Empresses and Princesses in 430, than by any supposed 'flight' from custody in 431 cf. Apologeticus ad Theodosium. ACO 1.3. 75–90, paras. 4–5.

[180] Davis (1987) p. 160, uses the evidence of Isidore of Pelusium's letter to Cyril ('a number of those who have been at Ephesus represent you as a man burning to avenge a personal injury rather than seeking in orthodoxy the glory of the Lord Jesus Christ. .') in order to argue that the Alexandrian church was 'unimpressed by his intrigues' when he arrived home. This is far from the truth. Isidore was quoting to Cyril reports he had heard from the Orientals, not from Egyptians.

way the argument had turned on these highly condensed propositions rather than on the discursive works in which he had set out his theological argument at considerable length, the fact was this was where the conflict had settled.

The orientals had determined, in the Chalcedon colloquies, to insist on nothing less than the condemnation of the 'heretical' Chapters, and force Cyril to a public recantation of them. On Cyril's part he stood by his synopsis as legitimately expressing fundamental truths of christology which someone who was not bent on dividing the personality of Christ would not find objectionable. In the two years following Ephesus there is, nonetheless, a new concern visible in his writings, to seek for a rapprochement with the Syrians as long as they recognised the central doctrine of the singleness of Christ's person. He had been convinced by the reports of his party at Chalcedon that such was indeed their intent, or at least that of John, Acacius of Beroea, and Theodoret who spoke for the Antiochenes in this exchange.

There was some confusion at the time, and has been since in scholarly opinion, as to whether the compromises reached by both parties in this period amounted to a substantial revision of theologies, or simply an acknowledgement of the essential orthodoxy of both the Alexandrian and Antiochene conceptual traditions, once each had been sufficiently explained to the other. Cyril was unrepentant and unyielding over his anathemisation of Nestorius. As far as he was concerned rapprochement with the Antiochenes was one thing, any compromise with what Nestorius had taught was something quite different: the key issue being the explicit acknowledgement of a single subject referent in Christ.

The historical developments of the years after Ephesus throw light on important issues involved in interpreting Cyril's later theology. In so far as the central issue at stake concerned the legitimacy of confessing two natures abiding in Christ after the incarnation, the events of the next four years were not so much laying the council of Ephesus to rest, as preparing the ground for three major councils to come; Ephesus 449, Chalcedon 451, and Constantinople II 553. The agenda of all of them was largely determined by Cyril's works, and their respective results similarly drawn from his suggestions, frequently using his very terms. Cyril's arguments on the fundamental issues in christology, therefore, echoed loudly for centuries to come in the Eastern Church.

Shortly after his arrival back in Alexandria in the early part of November 431, Maximian, the new archbishop of Constantinople, wrote to him a cordial letter[181] informing him of his election and praising him for having been an outstanding confessor of the faith in the recent difficult circumstances (a diplomatic reference to his imprisonment by the Emperor). Cyril replied in a letter of congratulation comparing him to the faithful Heliakim who replaced Shebna whom God had rejected.[182] The letter is a most careful restatement of his christological position explaining how he 'rejects the teachings of the mad Apollinaris'.[183]

The Syrians, who had been snubbed at Maximian's consecration, continued to regard Nestorius as having been uncanonically overthrown, and would not recognise the legitimacy of his successor. They had left the capital after several fruitless weeks of trying to change Theodosius' policy and induce him to outlaw Cyril. On their return home they passed through the town of Ancyra in Galatia where, to their scandal and great chagrin, they were treated by the clergy and townspeople as excommunicates. Theodotus, the bishop of the place, had been one of the leading Cyrillines at Ephesus, and from Constantinople had written a joint letter with Firmus of (Cappadocian) Caesarea to instruct all the churches of their jurisdiction to shut their doors against them.

In protest, they held a council there and, as soon as they arrived back in their own territory, another at Tarsus in Cilicia, and a third at Antioch in which they reiterated their condemnation of Cyril as a heretic and anathematised the bishops who had argued against them at Chalcedon. They circulated their synodical decisions widely throughout the Patriarchate and this was established, in the popular mind throughout the Syrian territory, as the published decision of the 'Council of Ephesus'. John of Antioch visited the centenarian bishop Acacius of Beroea whose moral authority ran very high throughout the international church, and gained his support.

In the meantime Maximian of Constantinople proceeded to apply the conciliar decisions of the Cyrilline council as the true canonical results of the synodical meeting at Ephesus. This policy he applied

---

181 Ep.30, ACO 1.1.3. p. 71. E.T. McEnerney (1987) p. 119.

182 Ep. 31. ACO 1.1.3. p. 72; E.T. McEnerney (1987) pp. 121–125.

183 Ibid. 'The Word of God became a perfect man for our sake, not by having endured a change or alteration, or any confusion as is often attributed [to me], or mixture, or a change into that which he was not, but rather by having remained what he was [ie. God] even in his humanity which is like us.' The final phrase radically distinguishes Cyril from later Eutychian Monophysitism.

throughout his own jurisdiction, and in consequence deposed four of the notable episcopal supporters of Nestorius within the region.[184] The rehabilitation of these dissidents soon became another of the causes of the Orientals.

By the middle of the year 432 Theodosius[185] decided to press for a healing of the rift with the Syrian bishops, and consulted Maximian and his local synod at Constantinople for the best way to proceed.[186] Shortly afterwards he wrote to John of Antioch deploring the continuing enmities and setting out the terms of his plan for reconciliation which the synod at Constantinople had drafted under the influence of bishop Proclus who had a large part in it. The Syrians were required to recognise the deposition of Nestorius (*de facto* by recognising Maximian) and condemn his teachings as heretical, whereupon Pope Celestine, Cyril, and all the other bishops would receive them into communion. The Emperor also wrote to the two outstanding spiritual authorities then recognised in the East—St. Symeon Stylites, and Acacius of Beroea, asking them to mediate in the dispute. He successfully won over both, and their influence was not negligible in bringing about the climate of a reconciliation. Acacius of Beroea in particular was asked to be a broker between John and Cyril in the cause of reconciliation and he performed this task faithfully and with no little skill.[187]

At first Theodosius seems to have decided to summon John and Cyril before him in person for a face to face colloquy at the palace in Nicomedia. He presumed that a reconciliation could be effected on the spot. There is no evidence, however, that such a meeting ever took place, and it was probably a first thought abandoned when it was made clear to him that more was at stake than a simple reconciliation between two individuals.

The imperial Notary and Tribune Aristolaus was given the commission of bringing about the unity. He brought the Emperor's instructions to Antioch, where John consulted with Theodoret and

---

[184] Dorotheos of Marcianopolis (who had preached against the Theotokos title in the cathedral at Constantinople in Nestorius' presence), Helladius of Tarsus, Eutherius of Tyana, and Himerius of Nicomedia.

[185] In response to a letter of March 432 from Pope Celestine who appealed to him to resolve the problem of the rupture of communion but to apply the decisions of Ephesus without compromise. The Pope wrote shortly before his death in July of the same year. He was to be succeeded by Sixtus III (432–440) the Pope who rebuilt St. Mary Major's in Rome.

[186] As in Cyril's letter to Acacius of Melitene, ACO 1.1.4. pp. 20–31.

[187] ACO 1.7.146.

others before holding yet another synod composed of his leading theologians.[188] The result, although it was not stated in so many words, was a rejection of the Emperor's overtures. In return the Syrian synod set out its basic terms for reconciliation which involved the rejection of Cyril's Letters and Chapters, and the use of the Nicene Creed and Athanasius' Letter to Epictetus as the sole standards of orthodox christology. The latter was the text in which Athanasius had attacked the Apollinarists. In this insistence that only these two ancient and hallowed texts should be elevated to confessional status, the Orientals were attempting tacitly to set aside the whole work of the Council of Ephesus, and the entirety of Cyril's christological work and doctrine on which it was based. Acacius of Beroea undertook to set out these terms in a letter to Cyril and his text, together with the Emperor's own letter demanding that a reconciliation be pursued, was brought to Alexandria by Aristolaus on the second stage of his mission.

Cyril replied to Acacius[189] with another carefully composed synthesis of his theology, set out to demonstrate why the accusations of Apollinarism against him were unfounded. In the letter he renounced the principles of Apollinarism, explained his understanding of the single subject of the incarnate Lord, and gave ground on the Chapters in so far as he admitted that 'the force of the propositions was written only against the teachings of Nestorius'. But he refused to abandon all his theological work, and told Acacius:

> Your Perfection sees that they seek an impossibile thing. So far are they from a desire to appease the discord between us that they have taken matters back to the very beginning of this incessant strife.[190]

Cyril was not so naive as not to have seen the implied basis of the rejection of the synod of Ephesus whose only christological statement was that of Cyril's own letters. If he renounced his own writings, he renounced the whole synod, and the condemnation of Nestorius it had pronounced.

This statesmanlike letter won Acacius over. At about the same time one of the most notable oriental theologians, Rabulla of Edessa, announced that he had decided that Cyril was right all along. It caused a great stir. These significant shifts of opinion among the orientals,

---

[188] Alexander of Hierapolis, Acacius of Beroea, Macarius of Laodicea, Andrew of Samosata, and Theodoret of Cyr.

[189] Ep. 33. ACO 1.1.7. 147–150.

[190] Ibid. Ep. 33. para. 3.

fostered by Acacius of Melitene who had long been Cyril's enthusiastic ally, began to signal the favourable time for a reconciliation might finally have arrived. Alexander of Hierapolis and Andrew of Samosata were still violently opposed to any rapprochement,[191] and were appalled at the shift they witnessed in the attitudes of John and Acacius. But soon Theodoret began to signify his acceptance of Cyril's explanations. As far as Theodoret was concerned Cyril's letter to Acacius of Beroea had signalled a complete volte face in his theology,[192] particularly in what he felt to be Cyril's abandonment of his Fourth Anathema. A close study of the actual text of the Anathema demonstrates that it was Theodoret who had misunderstood the argument, not Cyril who had changed his mind. Theodoret's general opinion that Cyril after the council had entirely abandoned the principles he set out in his Chapters is not a defensible view, and was partly caused by Theodoret's excessive reliance, for understanding Cyril's overall christological teaching, on the very limited range of texts he appears to have studied. When one considers the whole range of Cyril's extensive work it is clear that the Cyrilline positions of the years after 432 when he is seeking a resolution of the conflict with the Antiochenes are not based on abandonment of his principles and doctrine of the years before Ephesus. Theodoret's opinion, however, has continued to be sustained by several more recent commentators. Durand's[193] observation, relevant to this point, is very apposite when he notes that Cyril can hardly be said to have 'capitulated' in his theology at this period. In 433 he was in far less danger than he had been when under house arrest in Ephesus. Then he would not give an inch. Once he thought he could give ground without sacrificing the principle of the single subjectivity of the incarnate Lord he was ready to negotiate and settle.

In this climate of negotiation John of Antioch sent off a personal delegation to Alexandria in the form of the old and very diplomatic[194] bishop Paul of Emesa. In the letter that Paul brought to Cyril, John lamented the theology of the Chapters, requiring further elucidation

---

[191] Alexander said: 'I would rather lose my see and my right hand than enter into communion with Cyril.' He refused all appeals, and even the direct command of the Emperor, and was eventually condemned by the court to penal servitude, serving his sentence in the dreadful conditions of the salt mines in Egypt.

[192] Letter of Theodoret to John of Antioch. ACO 1.7.163.

[193] de Durand (1964) p. 26.

[194] Cyril was completely won over by him: 'I marvelled at the complete courtesy of the man, and was deeply sorry to see him leave.' Cyril's letter to John of Antioch, Ep. 89, ACO 1.1.7. p. 153; E.T. McEnerney (1987) p. 132.

of their meaning (that is a defence of their orthodoxy), but held out an olive branch in the form of a statement that he had rejoiced when he read a copy of the letter Cyril had recently sent to Acacius of Beroea. John's letter was vague on important doctrinal points. It kept silent on the issue of Nestorius, and concerned itself only with the question of the conditions necessary for the 'rehabilitation' of Cyril. To accompany the text John gave Paul the profession of faith which he and Theodoret had drawn up at the Chalcedon colloquy in response to Theodosius' demands for a written version of the respective positions of the parties. He requested Cyril to sign it now as a condition of restoring communion.

The negotiations with Paul were long and fragmented, partly because Cyril was bedridden with an illness he had contracted. When he studied the Antiochene profession he found it to be substantially orthodox and told Paul as much, but he wholly rejected John's accompanying letter since it evaded the issue of Nestorius' condemnation and had justified the conciliabulum at Ephesus as being 'motivated by a zeal for orthodoxy'. It was a point which had raised Cyril's temperature even more than his illness, and Paul had a task in hand to smooth matters over in Alexandria once the contents became generally known. Cyril made it clear that the doctrinal point was evident enough, and if the orientals would not distance themselves from Nestorius then there could be no hope of any reconciliation.

In reply Paul of Emesa told Cyril that it was not John's intention to be evasive and added, somewhat naively, that the 'whole of the Orient' shared his opinions and was ready to anathematise Nestorius. One suspects that the Tribune Aristolaus who had accompanied Paul was applying no little pressure for a solution. Taking Paul's statements at face value Cyril urged him to anathematise Nestorius publicly himself, there and then, as a token of the earnestness of his intentions, and then he would be restored to full communion with the church of Alexandria. And this Paul did, with Cyril subsequently sharing the eucharist with him, and inviting him to preach in his cathedral church. On Christmas day 432 Paul gave a sermon in the great church of Alexandria and described Mary as the 'Mother of God' to tumultous applause from the congregation.

Cyril was now anxious to keep up the momentum of what appeared to be such a favourable reconciliation and he tried to induce Aristolaus to go back to the Antiochenes after winter had ended, for he had heard that they were becoming dissatisfied with Paul's efforts as an emissary, given that several months had passed with seemingly no return. Accordingly, in the spring of 433, the imperial delegation prepared to return to Antioch.

Cyril would not accept Paul's verbal assurance that all the Orientals agreed to condemn Nestorius and required a formal signature from John of Antioch to this effect, on documents he prepared and entrusted to his two deacons Cassius and Ammonius. In reply to John's demands in his earlier documentation Cyril incorporated the Antiochene profession of faith and added futher explanations of his teaching, as required, designed to satisfy the Orientals that he had never taught an Apollinarist conception of the mixture or confusion of natures in the incarnate Lord. Confident of the success of the mission Cyril also prepared formal letters of communion which he entrusted to the Tribune Aristolaus. Even if the negotiations failed Cyril knew that by this action of taking the initiative first, he would secure himself at the royal court. He first made Aristolaus take an oath, however, that on no account would he betray the Alexandrian church by giving these letters to John without first having witnessed John's signature on the deed condemning Nestorius and his teachings.[195] Aristolaus assured him that this would be done and gave him to understand that if John did not accept the terms of the reconciliation thus set out, he would travel on directly to Constantinople and exonerate Cyril from all blame in the affair. There were thus grounds for Cyril, in the early part of 433, to be very pleased with the way negotiations had progressed.

When Aristolaus' delegation arrived at Antioch in the late Spring of 433, the terms were accepted. The Syrian determination to make Cyril recant the Chapters was quietly dropped. John signed Cyril's document with a few minor modifications, recognised Maximian, and condemned the 'blasphemous teachings of Nestorius.' When relations were thus formally restored Cyril sent his famous letter 'Let the Heavens Rejoice',[196] which has since been known as 'The Formula of Reunion'. It largely repeats the substance of his earlier submissions (including the Antiochene profession which emanated from the Chalcedon Colloquy). On April 23rd Cyril announced from his pulpit in Alexandria that communion had been re-established in the christian world, and then he composed letters informing Pope Sixtus III and Maximian

[195] As in Cyril's Ep. 37. To Theognostus. ACO 1.1.7. p. 154.

[196] Ep. 39, To John of Antioch. This text was canonised at Chalcedon as an authoritative expression of orthodox christology.

of Constantinople of the developments.[197] In his reply to Cyril the Pope told him: 'You can rejoice as the victor of the day'.[198] For his part John of Antioch announced the news to the Emperor, and sent an encyclical letter around his patriarchate informing his bishops that Cyril's orthodoxy had now been accepted. He published the letters that had been exchanged of late, to demonstrate that Cyril had sufficiently answered their demands for further explanation, and concluded by asking his bishops not to do anything that would upset the peace that had been so laboriously negotiated. He evidently sensed trouble ahead among his own party, and he was not mistaken.

The coherence of the Antiochene party was, by this stage, somewhat dissipated. John of Antioch took the majority with him, and it was generally interpreted, in the Orient at least, that Cyril had been forced to climb down, and then had been accepted back into the fold by John once he had complied. For several of the leading lights of the conciliabulum, however, John's acceptance of communion with Cyril without an explicit rejection of the Chapters was no less than an out and out betrayal of fundamental principle, and this party continued to press for Nestorius' rehabilitation and Cyril's condemnation. This was a small and hardline group which included Alexander of Hierapolis and, needless to say, Nestorius himself, who far from lying low in his monastery had begun a pamphlet war, much to John's embarrassment. A third element regarded John as dilatory, and of being swayed more by political expediency than a desire for justice, and these turned more and more to Theodoret of Cyr for intellectual guidance and for a representative who could be a proper spokesman for the Syrian tradition.

Theodoret accepted the reconciliation with Cyril, though he interpreted it as a complete turn-about on Cyril's part, symbolised in the latter's submission to the Syrian profession of faith which had originally been drawn up at Chalcedon.[199] For Theodoret, however, Nestorius' teaching contained nothing so objectionable that it merited his deposition, since it was substantially inspired by their mutual teacher

---

[197] ACO 1.7. 157–160.

[198] Ep. 51. ACO 1.2. 107–108.

[199] As far as Cyril was concerned he accepted the orthodoxy of the Orientals' statements but, as his letter to Eulogius shows, did not think that they had expressed matters particularly well: 'the easterners are somewhat obscure in their terminology', and at no stage did he have any intention of adopting their methods of speaking and theologising henceforth.

Mar Theodore of Mopsuestia, the great Syrian scholar who had died in the high reputation of sanctity. Theodoret refused to concur in any policy of abandoning Nestorius, and indeed was only compelled to do so in one of the final sessions of the Council of Chalcedon 18 years later. These varying degrees of the Syrian understanding of the reconciliation process (basically that Cyril had been brought to his senses by Antiochene theology) differed substantially from the way in which the other sees (Cyril, Maximian, Sixtus, and Juvenal) interpreted the events. For them, and the majority of the bishops, the reconciliation demonstrated that Antioch had finally recognised the issues and turned away from its former tradition of teaching, towards a commonly agreed doctrine emphasising the single subjectivity of Christ. Such massive and unspoken differences of judgement were bound to come to the surface in fresh conflict sooner rather than later.

News of the reconciliation, what it signified and on what basis it had been concluded, began to seep out through the churches in quite different forms. Rumours circulated (wrongly) that the new Pope Sixtus sympathised with Nestorius.[200] Acacius of Melitene and Isidore of Pelusium independently wrote to Cyril in some anxiety, seeking reassurance that mention of the 'two natures' of Christ in his letter of reconciliation did not signify a betrayal of his insistence that Christ must only be confessed as one—the dominant theme of all they had stood together to defend. Cyril's long reply to Acacius is an important text in the elucidation of how the Syrian agreement was to be harmonised with the resolutions of Ephesus. His two very significant letters to Succensus, also from this period, similarly concern the same question, as does his reassurance to Bishop Valerian of Iconium[201] where he complains of a proliferation of 'old gossips who have messed up the whole story'. The confusion was such that even Cyril's agents in Constantinople entertained the rumour that their archbishop had recanted. He wrote to them in some exasperation:[202]

> How is it I write to you about all our affairs, and then you write back to me as if you understood nothing at all?' [and he concludes], 'So do not give way to anxiety. We have not been so stupid as to anathematise our own writings. We stand fast by what we have written, by what

[200] Cyril accused the Orientals of forging a memorandum from the Roman legate Philip to signify Sixtus' disapproval of Nestorius' deposition.

[201] Ep. 50, ACO 1.1.3. pp. 90–101. E.T. McEnerney (1987) pp. 212–227; see also Scholia On The Incarnation 8.

[202] Ep. 37, ACO 1.1.7. p. 154. E.T. McEnerney (1987) p. 142.

> we have thought. Our beliefs are orthodox and blameless, in accord with the Holy Scriptures and the faith as set out by our holy Fathers.

To counter the growing force of hearsay Cyril wrote a round of letters, especially to Constantinople, trying to get Maximian more involved in the controversy. He had little success, and soon came to regard the latter as being too languid, and blind to what was happening around him. But some of his letters bore fruit, particularly the appeals he addressed to the royal court in the person of the Empress Pulcheria. Cyril's reputation was now gaining higher and higher currency, and his letters served to alert the imperial chancery to the fact that the Antioch-Alexandria reconciliation was far from secure. It also highlighted the problem that the aged and intellectually slow Maximian might not be up to the job in hand.

In the Orient, the Nestorian party were now focusing their efforts on demonstrating that Nestorius was essentially orthodox because he simply had restated the doctrine of their church's great teachers, Mar Diodore and Mar Theodore. Their writings, but especally those of the latter, were copied extensively at this period and circulated throughout the Syrian region. Nestorius' harmony with the tradition was emphasised, and Cyril's differences were highlighted as evidence of his innovation in matters of the faith.

At this juncture, in April 434, Maximian of Constantinople died, and Proclus (three times a candidate for the office) was elected in his place. Proclus was the same who had outraged Nestorius by preaching on the Theotokos in his presence at the very beginning of the controversy, and had proved himself a loyal ally of Cyril's ever since. In contrast to the simple Maximian, he was a highly polished orator and a consummate diplomat who had great influence at court, especially with Pulcheria. On top of all this he was a very good theologian. With his accession the royal court decided to speed up the process of pacification in the church. A policy was adopted of imposing the Formula of Reunion of 433 as a test of faith on all the oriental bishops, carrying the force of imperial law to sanction it.

Nestorius himself, who had kept up a stream of polemical writings since his deposition, was the first victim of the new crackdown. He was sent from his monastery near Antioch into a real penal exile this time, first to Petra, the Arabian caravan city, and subsequently (when he continued his agitation against the Emperor's policy) to the prison colony of the Great Oasis in Egypt, a dismal place reserved for high prisoners of state and fallen courtesans. It was a natural prison, a waterhole surrounded by a vast sea of desert. In the Roman estimation it was truly the end of the world, and here he had more than enough time to reflect on the events which had caused his downfall, composing his memoirs in the form of the Book of Heraclides.[203] The record of his exiles and the hardships he endured makes sad reading, and several commentators have noted the nobility of spirit with which he bore his sufferings.

For the previous two years since 431 Acacius of Melitene and Rabulla of Edessa had been publicising the terms of the council of Ephesus, as distinct from the conciliabulum, throughout the Syrian patriarchate. Like Cyril they had increasingly come to focus their opposition against the continuing influence of Theodore Mopsuestia's theology, refusing to allow that this could stand as the authentic representative of the whole Syrian tradition as such. It was at this time that the Armenian church had commissioned a series of translations to be made into its own language of a 'library of the Fathers of the church' to serve as the basic teaching materials in their schools of doctrine. The works of Theodore had been proposed to them as an essential part of this canon. Acacius and Rabulla warned the Armenians that Theodore was not regarded as orthodox at all[204] and a considerable argument blew up around the issue in the Syrian church. It was to prove the spark that re-ignited the wider controversy. A confused delegation from the Armenian church came to settle the matter with the new and learned archbishop of Constantinople and in response to their query, Proclus produced his celebrated Tome to the Armenians[205] in 435. This digested objectionable christological passages from the writings of Theodore (as anonymous propositions) and condemned them as blasphemies, thus throwing a diplomatic veil over the author's true identity and honouring his reputation for sanctity while leaving no one in any doubt as to his theological unreliability. Acacius continued to castigate the memory of Theodore openly,[206] but it was as vehemently defended by others such as Ibas of Edessa who had succeeded in

---

[203] French translation from the Syriac by Nau (1910). E.T. by Driver & Hodgson (1925). For a note on his subsequent adventures (being captured by a raiding party and held to ransom) cf. de Durand (1964) p. 25. n.2.

[204] cf. M. Richard (1948) pp. 393–412.

[205] PG 65.856–873; ACO 4.2.187–195. It was a text that opened up the way for a new settlement in terms of agreed terminology in the christology debate, and thus an important bridge between Cyril's work and that of the council of Chalcedon.

[206] M. Richard (1948); de Durand (1964) 27–31.

place of Rabbula, and held diametrically opposed theological opinions to those of his predecessor.

Continuing his royal commission to resolve the crisis in the eastern church Proclus proposed that John of Antioch should sign the Tome to The Armenians, and condemn another florilegium of texts he had prepared (from the writings of Theodore and Ibas of Edessa) which taught the double subjectivity of Christ. On the understanding that they would do so without condemning anyone by name, most of the orientals accepted this compromise, though Acacius of Melitene and several other Cyrillines regarded the coyness about Theodore's memory as an evasion of a central issue. So the argument rumbled on, with Theodore of Mopsuestia, Ibas of Edessa, and Theodoret[207] himself becoming increasingly identified as the Syrian 'alternative' to the more and more universally accepted doctrine of Cyril and the council of Ephesus.

In several letters Cyril expressed his unhappiness at the way the Orientals seemed to be ready to anathematise Nestorius yet carry on the substance of his doctrine by propagating Theodore's views as authoritative. He also complained about Theodoret's very public dissidence[208] wondering why John of Antioch did nothing to bring him into line. But Theodoret was unrepentant, and the initiative had now passed from Cyril to the royal court, in the hands of Proclus.

Cyril's personal standing had risen to an international level by this time. It was acknowledged publicly when Theodosius asked him to accompany his increasingly estranged wife Eudoxia on her pilgrimage to Jerusalem[209] in 438. When he was there, engaged in a grand tour on a lavish scale, where Eudoxia dispensed donations on ecclesiastical foundations and gathered relics like a new Helena, Cyril was met by a group of Antiochene dissidents. These informed him of the considerable disagreements in the Orient over the status that ought to be afforded to the teachings of Theodore, and gave him clear evidence of Proclus' policy to avoid further confrontation by avoiding any direct and explicit condemnation of Theodore's memory.

Cyril viewed the policy as misguided, and on his return to Alexandria later that same year he set to work in a new burst of literary efforts. The writings of this last period of his life turn more and more to

---

207 The works of these three became digested into the so-called 'Three Chapters', and they were anathematised at the council of Constantinople II in 553.

208 Ep. 63. E.T. McEnerney (1987) p. 51.

209 Ep. 70. PG 77. 341. E.T. McEnerney (1987) pp. 68–69.

attacking Theodore of Mopsuestia directly and openly in the harshest of terms, as a heretic. They include key works such as That The Christ is One, the Exposition of the Creed[210] and the Three Books to the Monks.[211] When the news got out that Cyril was now vehemently attacking the reputation of Theodore it fanned the flames of deep resentment among many of the Orientals who had only been lukewarm supporters of the union in the first place. Theodoret, for one, was barely able to contain his rage that Cyril should so presume to move against his own teacher and mentor. Proclus appealed to Cyril not to jeopardise the fragile peace and begged him to allow matters to rest. John of Antioch too made it clear to him that he would not be accountable for all his Syrian bishops' reactions if Cyril continued to pursue his policy of attacking their 'Fathers'. And so, while he made it abundantly clear to everyone, including the Syrians,[212] that he did not regard Diodore or Theodore in any sense as 'Fathers' of the church,[213] Cyril decided to accept the advice of Proclus[214] and John,[215] even though it was much against his better judgement, and dropped his assault on the reputations of the Syrian teachers by name.

He decided that perhaps it would be better after all to proceed quietly and condemn the propositions while allowing the memories of Diodore and Theodore to remain venerable in their own churches, since his earlier policy would serve to 'rekindle the flame that has started to die down.' As Cyril knew, it was a policy that deferred the problem rather than solved it, as events over the next two centuries would more than bear out. Edward Schwartz has suggested there

---

[210] ACO 1.4. 49–61.

[211] Now only surviving in fragments.

[212] Ep. 67 to John of Antioch and His Synod, ACO 1.1. 4. pp. 37–39; E.T. McEnerney (1987) pp. 61–64 (see para. 7.); Ep. 69 To Acacius of Melitene PG 77. 338–340, E. T. McEnerney (1987) pp. 66–67; Ep. 71 To Theodosius, ACO 1.4. 210–211, E.T. McEnerney (1987) pp. 70–71.

[213] And thus, implicitly, that their christological teaching was not an authentic 'tradition' of the church, such as could be compared, for example, with that of the Alexandrian Fathers such as Alexander, Peter and Athanasius. The issue is an interesting one in the consideration of the nature of christian tradition. Many recent studies simply presuppose that the christological crisis of this period is the result of a clash of two disparate christian traditions in the public arena. Cyril would have dissented from such an analysis in the case of Diodore, Theodore, Nestorius and Ibas, whose works he regarded as pseudo-traditions.

[214] Ep. 72. To Proclus. PG 77.343–346. E.T. McEnerney (1987) pp. 72–74.

[215] ACO 1.5.314–315. He agreed not to proceed any further against those who had died in the peace of Christ. The council of Constantinople II reversed this policy and anathematised the authors of the 'Three Chapters'.

was an undisclosed pressure on Cyril from the imperial court to adopt this change of attitude, and he named Pulcheria as the active agent behind it.[216] Given Cyril's obvious reluctance to leave off from the fray this is highly likely, and he continued to speak with evident scorn about the intellectual integrity of those (among the Syrians) who agreed to anathematise the teachings of Nestorius but would not anathematise the sources of those teachings which themselves even more blatantly suggested the double subjectivity of Christ. In a letter to Proclus he wryly quoted Homer on the subject:

> I have my doubts about many of them who would object to the action (against Theodore). But the whole business might serve as a pretence for them to reopen their grieving for the teaching of Nestorius, like that spoken of by the poet of the Greeks: They mourned in semblance for Patroclus, but really each one mourned her own sorrows.[217]

The final years of Cyril's life began to settle down to a semblance of relative calm after decades of energetic involvement at the highest level of international politics. He continued his literary works with unabated energy. The monumental work Against Julian the Apostate belongs to this final part of his life, when he once more redirected his attentions to the church's pressing need to offer a systematic cultural and missionary programme as an alternative to the pagan revival of the fifth century. He sent a copy as a peace offering to Theodoret, who congratulated him on his achievement.[218] A few letters remain from this period showing us how he intervened to settle disputes within his own patriarchal territory. His letter to Calosyrius of Arsinoe (Fayyum)[219] shows that crude forms of folk religion, such as those attacked by Theophilus a generation before, were still in evidence among the monks, most of whom were unlettered peasants. His letter also discusses the problems of Messalians in the monasteries (an issue that had featured at the council of Ephesus), and the treatment of Melitians—the remnants of the schismatic clergy who had so troubled the Egyptian church in the days of Alexander and Athanasius. Calosyrius set before him the theory that certain monks were propa-

---

[216] Konzilstudien, Strasbourg 1914. vol. 20, p. 36.

[217] Ep. 72. PG 77. 343–346. para. 5. Citing Homer's Iliad. 19.302;

[218] Cyril may have had an ironical motive in this, for he may well have composed this monumental work of anti-pagan apologetic to render the similar but slimmer work of Theodore Mopsuestia's on the theme, definitively superseded.

[219] Ep. 83. (Against those saying God is Anthropomorphic); Critical text and E.T. Wickham (1983) pp. 214–221; E.T. McEnerney (1987) pp. 109–112.

gating to the effect that the eucharistic elements lost their efficacy if they were reserved in the churches after the liturgy had finished, and in response Cyril restated his lifelong concern for the importance of orthodox eucharistic theology:

> They are insane who say these things. Christ is not altered, nor is the holy body changed, but the power of this consecration, his life-giving grace, is perpetual in his body.

He also wrote to the bishops of Libya and Pentapolis urging them to take greater care in the candidates they were advancing for ordination to the priesthood, since several of the monks had been scandalised by the appointment of newly married men and the ordination of ex-monks who even came back to monasteries from which they had been expelled, now in the role of celebrants of the liturgy.[220]

In 441 John of Antioch died and was replaced by his nephew Domnus. On two occasions[221] Cyril wrote to the new patriarch. The first occasion was to intercede for a certain bishop Athanasius of Perrha who had been deposed from his church, at the request of his clergy at a metropolitan synod in Syria, and who had appealed against its decision to Cyril. Cyril has sometimes been accused in these instances of interfering in Domnus' jurisdiction, but the appeal of bishops to eminent sees was long established custom, and Cyril's response was simply to urge Domnus to attend to the matter himself so that a proper synodical hearing could be held on the affair presided over by the patriarch of Antioch in due canonical order.In writing as he did, however, he deliberately passes over the canonical rights of the church at Constantinople, whose jurisdictional territory was being expanded at this period by the policy of Theodosius, to the detriment of the former Antiochene patriarchate. In writing this way to Domnus, Cyril is again demonstrating something that had motivated him at Ephesus—that the long established ecclesiastical canons were more important to him than current ecclesiastical policies emanating from Constantinople.

The second letter to Domnus resulted from an appeal he had received from an old bishop who had been dismissed from his see, apparently for incompetence in his financial administration. Cyril's letter to Antioch suggests that for justice's sake a proper canonical trial ought to have been held, for the old man now felt aggrieved at his dismissal. Cyril

---

[220] Ep. 79. PG 77.364–365. E.T. McEnerney (1987) pp. 97–98.

[221] Epp. 77 & 78. PG.77. 359–364; E.T. McEnerney (1987) pp. 92–96.

obviously felt a certain amount of pity for the petitioner, especially in the way that he had been turned out without any financial security himself. Once again he urged Domnus to reconsider the case in accordance with canonical law rather than by making executive decisions single-handedly. He did not necessarily want the judgement reversed, but he points up yet again the need to follow established canonical procedure, and simply urges that the old man be given something like a pension:

> May your Holiness, therefore, considering what is decreed in the holy canons, and what is proper for the church, and for those assigned to the sacred ministry, and in addition being moved by this letter from us, cause the old man's weeping to cease.

Like many others who have felt the advance of their years Cyril passes out from history[222] evidencing a keen sense of compassion for the old and dispossessed. It might have reflected a growing anxiety of his own, within his own church at Alexandria, that the reins of power were beginning to slip from his fingers, and more and more trouble was brewing not least on the financial front where day to day church administration was tested. The events immediately following his death suggest that his final year would have given him ample opportunity to realise that his archdeacon Dioscorus was growing restless with the old man, and perhaps too obviously eager to have a radical house cleaning of the internal affairs of the church, especially the finances which Cyril had lodged in the care of members of his own family. But whatever his age or his anxieties, in the final letters of his episcopate the old vigour is still there, the assurance of his international stature remains, and there is no wavering of his claim to a canonical right to supervise the ecclesiastical affairs of the East.

Cyril died on the 27th of June 444, a little short of his 70th year, and only five years before the christological controversy which had taken up so much of his life's energies was to flare up once more in a full scale international synodical crisis (The Council of Ephesus 449), and seven years before the great events of the council of Chalcedon. Perhaps its was providential that the voice which had determined so much of the agenda for the latter council was quieted in time for a later generation to take stock of the situation anew.

[222] Easter letters to Pope Leo, dated to 444, are not authentic, but 7th century Celtic compositions. See B. Krusch, Studien zur Christlich mittelalterlichen Chronologie: Der 84 Jahrig Ostercyclus und seine Quellen. Leipzig, 1880, 345–349.

At this time most of the central protagonists had died, with the exception of Theodoret and the Augusta Pulcheria. Her hand was still very much active in guiding the results of the subsequent synods. But even though Cyril's voice was hushed, it was his spirit which perhaps was still most in evidence even at the council in 451 and certainly at Constantinople II in 553.[223]

As soon as the funeral of Cyril was over, a purge was begun in Alexandria. Cyril's nephew, the priest Paul who was Econome of the church, was deposed from his rank and all the family connections were severed and uprooted as the archdeacon Dioscorus clawed back fiscal control of the treasury. A turbulent dynasty on the throne of Alexandria, begun by Theophilus sixty years before, was finally over. But power had passed to a man who had studied his master closely over the years and now tried to emulate him, without being possessed of all his qualities. Dioscorus was devoted to Cyril's theology which he identified as the sole standard of orthodoxy, though with much less personal ability and acumen than Cyril could command and, accordingly, with a narrower vision and less theological judgement. He regarded all Cyril's efforts of rapprochement with the Syrians as the misguided weakness of an old man who was sick at the time Paul of Emesa came to deal with him. He thus dismissed a significant part of Cyril's theology supposedly in the name of Cyril. Even worse, he was much less politically skilled than his mentor. He would soon bring the Alexandrian church into a ruinous decline from which it would never re-emerge as the great international christian power it had once been.

When the news of Cyril's death became known, some of his enemies wrote bitterly about him. One such letter which caustically asks the recipient to see that the largest stone possible was laid on his tomb so that he would never rise up again to trouble the church, was later attributed to Theodoret.[224] It caused such offence at the time in the general sentiment of the bishops that it was used against Theodoret

---

[223] See, for example, the balanced summation of P.T. Gray (1979) who, like Meyendorff, serves to lay the ghost of a very unneven reading favoured by previous English scholarship of the early decades of this century that sees Pope Leo's Tome as the most significant material presented at Chalcedon. Gray rightly brings out just how much Chalcedon was indebted to Cyril. The following council at Constantinople II (553) was even more so. The 1st Letter to Succensus in the present collection of translations shows Cyril at his most forward looking; it is almost a first draft of the Christological solution adopted in 451.

[224] Now Ep. 180 of Theodoret's corpus.

in his arraignment process at Chalcedon. There is a likelihood, however, that it was not originally written by him, and indeed his own general character as a man of discretion and charity would concur with this estimate. As Bright put it: 'If it were indeed the production of the pen of Theodoret, the reputation which would suffer from [such a coarse and ferocious invective] would assuredly be his own.'[225]

The proper estimate of Cyril's reputation was found in the massive international support that was given to his theology and his memory in the thick of theological conflicts over the following decades and centuries. Even at the time of his death, his reputation had achieved monumental status. The extent of his literary productions was staggering, and his enduring influence gave him a rank in importance for the subsequent history of christian theology among the giants of the patristic era, in the company of Origen, Athanasius, the Cappadocians, and Augustine. He stands among all the patristic writers as the definitive exponent of oecumenical patristic christology, and soon gained the title (particularly in the eastern church where his reputation has always reigned supreme) of the 'Seal of all the Fathers' (sphragis ton pateron). Given his devotion to the principle of tradition in establishing the authentic mind of the church, it is a title which would have pleased him immensely.

[225] 'Cyril of Alexandria' in DCB, 1877. p. 772.

CHAPTER TWO

THE CHRISTOLOGY OF NESTORIUS

1. Sources for the Reconstruction of Nestorius' Teaching[1]

From the surviving Acts of the council of Ephesus, the remains and fragments of Nestorius' own writings and sermons, and his correspondence with Cyril, John and Celestine, a basic picture of his original doctrine can be built up. He is largely in agreement with Theodore of Mopsuestia on all central points[2] and, following Theodore, he had advanced Antiochene theology to the point of regarding the more primitive formulations of Eustathius of Antioch and Diodore of Tarsus' Two-Son theory as crudely untenable. For the Alexandrian commentators such an advance had not been generally registered.[3] In the early part of this century the greater portion of Nestorius' last work, The Book of Heraclides,[4] thought to have been entirely lost in antiquity, was dramatically rediscovered surviving in a Syriac translation from a time just posterior to Nestorius himself. With this discovery a fuller resource became available for the reconstruction of his mind.[5] The work needs to be used with some caution because of its interpolations,[6] and because it generally represents the hindsight of Nestorius looking back on what he meant to say to Cyril perhaps more than simply

[1] In part the chapter is a revised edition of an earlier treatment McGuckin (1988).

[2] H.E.W. Turner (1976) p. 48, described the relationship as Nestorius following Theodore in all essentials but expressing it all with a sharper edge and narrower perspective.

[3] Certainly Cyril regards both Nestorius and Theodore as teaching a double-subject Christology which is tantamount to 'Two Sons', and this forms the main point of his intellectual attack on Nestorius.

[4] Because of an early mistranslation from the Syriac it was first propagated by Bethune-Baker (1908) and thereafter by Driver and Hodgson in their translation of it (1925), as the 'Bazaar of Heraclides'. The word that was taken for 'market place' (hence Bazaar) in fact represented the Greek 'Tomos', book or treatise.

[5] The Book of Heraclides: Syriac text Ed. P. Bedjan Paris, 1910; French Tr. F. Nau, Paris, 1910 (The French version has been used mainly as the basis for this present exposition); E.T. Driver and Hodgson (1925).

[6] See Abramowski (1963) and (1972, vol.2); also Grillmeier (1975) pp. 559–568; and Chesnut (1978) for a discussion of the textual tradition and authenticity questions.

what he actually did say on the occasion. The work thus represents a state of Nestorius' mind at its most 'clarified'. It was written in that island prison in a sea of sand, the Great Oasis in Egypt, after his final exile by the Emperor, perhaps fifteen years or more after the events it describes.

In the fourteenth century a Nestorian bishop, Ebed Jesus of Nisibis, listed the complete works of Nestorius[7] as: a Liturgy,[8] a Tragedy, The Book of Heraclides, The Letter to Cosmas,[9] a Book of Letters, and a Book of Sermons and Discourses. To this list we might add the so-called First Apology (the Book of Heraclides being considered as the Second) fragments of which, under the title of Hypomnemata are preserved by the monophysite theologian Severus of Antioch. In the same source there are also fragments of a work apparently entitled The Theopaschites, evidently designed by Nestorius as a refutation of the Chapters of Cyril.

The sources necessary for a Nestorian reconstruction had been painstakingly assembled by F. Loofs in the years just preceding the rediscovery of the Book of Heraclides[10] and several works both by Nestorius and his supporters have been re-edited since in a collection of texts and translations by Abramowski and Goodman.[11] Of Nestorius' many sermons, which Cyril complained had been circulated far and wide even by 429, only nine have survived intact, the rest are represented only by a few scattered fragments, from which Loofs claimed to be able to reconstruct at least three distinct homilies. There is also the complete Greek text of a Sermon on the High Priesthood of Christ which had been discovered in the nineteenth century and published as a work of John Chrysostom.[12]

Three of Nestorius' important official letters have survived thanks to the conciliar record-keeping, being his correspondences with Cyril, John of Antioch, and Celestine of Rome. A Latin theologian who

---

[7] cf. J Assemani, Bibliotheca Orientalis (4. vols. Rome, 1917–1928) vol.3.1. pp. 35f.

[8] Still in use in the Nestorian church but certainly not composed by Nestorius himself.

[9] This text is not by Nestorius but rather about him, giving us important information concerning his life, his character, and his subsequent exile. It is an apologia for his memory. The text is printed at the end of the Book of Heraclides in Nau's version.

[10] Loofs (1905).

[11] L. Abramowski & A.E. Goodman (1972).

[12] cf. Migne, PG. 64.453–492; Loofs (1914) p. 7; also S. Haidacher, Rede des Nestorius uber Hebr. 3.1., in Zeitschrift fur Katholische Theologie, 29, 1905, 192–195. For a review of the position see Bethune-Baker (1908) pp. 105–120.

lived in Constantinople during the period and who seems to have acted as the eyes and ears of Rome, Marius Mercator,[13] preserved some of Nestorius' work in so far as he translated a series of Nestorian propositions from the Greek for the benefit of Western readers. He seems to have taken many of his formulations from Cyril's collection of objectionable elements in Nestorius' writings—a collection which Nestorius complained was misleading in the way it took sentences out of context and interpreted them in the most damaging way possible. The Mercator source is, then, far from being a neutral text. The church historian Evagrius,[14] writing in around 590, preserved some correspondence of Nestorius in exile, and thus gives us an interesting record of his final days when, to add to his general problems as a state prisoner, he had to contend with being taken hostage by a group of marauding bandits and held to ransom. Loofs also draws attention to the Synodicon[15] discovered in 1873, which is a late adaptation by the Nestorian church of the late fifth century work The Tragedy, thought by some to be based on the original, now lost, Tragedy written by Nestorius himself.

From the remaining texts we may be able to piece together the doctrine of Nestorius on his own terms rather than solely as he was heard by others. It is a difficult exercise to reconstruct his thought coherently and sympathetically. The confusion of the church at the time, and the rapidity of events which overtook Nestorius may all play a part in this. It is difficult to decide whether the obscurity and confusion was the fault of simplistic christians in Constantinople who could not understand him and were shocked by the apparent implications of phrases they heard at random; the fault of opponents who did not really attempt to understand him (a not uncommon failing in most ancient, and indeed modern, debates); or the fault of Nestorius himself who could not fully express his mind and was working out the implications of his belief system as he went along, an understandable position, but fatal for one who arrived in the imperial city with the arrogance of a new broom, an expert determined to teach everyone the basics of christology.

All three are probably true in relative degrees. It was the last of the three that greatly concerned Cyril. Throughout his attack on

---

[13] Migne PL. 48.757f.

[14] Hist. Eccl. 1.7; cf. Loofs (1905) 198–201.

[15] cf. Quasten (1975) 515–519; Synodicon Orientale, ed. & tr. J.B. Chabot, Paris, 1902; cf. Abramowski & Goodman (1972).

Nestorius' christology, Cyril is far more concerned with the wider implications of the doctrine than with an academic desire to give his opponent an exact and scholarly exegesis. Cyril regarded the whole Antiochene tradition as irredeemably woolly in its expositions anyway, even when it was orthodox; he certainly regarded Nestorius as a poor theologian and was only roused to oppose him, not because of the thrill of academic exchange, but because his teaching had been given a wide audience an account of his elevation to the throne of Constantinople. He was extremely worried, from the beginnings of the conflict, about how this teaching would be picked up as a common tradition. To this extent criticisms which are based on the fact that no careful exegesis of each side's position was engaged in, slightly miss the point. The issue of how a doctrine was heard was, in effect, far more important that what a doctrine was. Cyril was quite right and very clear about this: that in christology the implications are crucial to the argument.

The literary style of Nestorius' writings explains the reason, perhaps, for the historian Socrates' testy remark that having had a first hand encounter with the texts (and he had them before they were fragmented, dissipated, and burned by Imperial censors)[16] he could only conclude that: 'the man was disgracefully illiterate'.[17] The Book of Heraclides is immensely repetitive, far beyond the norm for the expansively discursive patristic literature of the period. It is a diffuse and meandering book, whose lines of logical development are often tedious to trace. Given that this was a text written fifteen or twenty years after the events, in the enforced leisure of a life-long exile, and designed to present a definitive apologia for his own thought, the excuses for lack of focus begin to run thin. Perhaps the difficulties in arriving at a clear reconstruction of Nestorius' mind must be attributed to the original architect, and are not entirely due to the fragmentation of the literary sources.[18]

In the exposition that follows, the evidence of the Book of Heraclides is taken into account with the caveat that the doctrine of the mutual reciprocity of the prosopa which he there advances, seems to be an

---

[16] Edict of Theodosius II, 30 July 435, ordering the burning of all Nestorius' writings: Cod. Theod. 16.5.66.

[17] Socrates, Hist. Eccl. 7.32; E.T. Nicene & Post Nicene Fathers, p. 171.

[18] Roberta Chesnut (1978) has given a more positive and holistic account of his work, explaining his prosopon language in terms of a Platonic mirror-image theory of reality, which she believes was consciously operating in Nestorius' mind. Her work also represents an important discussion on the textual tradition and authenticity of the Book of Heraclides. See also Hodgson (1918) and Wolfson (1976) pp. 372–462.

afterthought in hindsight, which he has added to strengthen weak parts of his earlier teaching in the light of Cyrilline and later Antiochene criticisms after Ephesus 431. In spite of the fact that the book was composed so long after the events it describes, it still represents a substantial agreement with the other surviving fragments from 428–431, and fits exactly with the main intellectual objections of Cyril at that period. What then was the christological teaching that produced such a furore in Nestorius' own see that an oecumenical crisis resulted, involving his own political and ecclesiastical ruination?

2. Nestorius' Theological Presuppositions And Method

Of all the various axiomatic presuppositions in Nestorius' approach to the doctrine of Christ, the first and most important is that the one Christ of faith must be confessed as fully divine (since Nicene orthodoxy had already established that the Logos is consubstantial with the Father), and also fully human (in so far as the council of Constantinople in 381 had reiterated the synodical condemnation of Apollinaris and all attempts to present a scheme of incarnate deity devoid of a human soul). Nestorius insisted that both confessions were equally necessary for the redemption effected by the incarnation to have any real significance.[19] To be fully divine means that the Logos can in no sense suffer, be changed, limited, or historically relativised in the incarnation. This follows from the fact that he is consubstantial with the Father and thus impassible, unchangeable, unlimited in all ways, and eternally transcendent. To be fully human, on the other hand, demands that one must be ready to attribute to Christ the full panoply of human characteristics, excepting sin which is not a 'humanising' characteristic or even a defining human attribute in any case.[20] He must have a human mind, a human soul with human feelings, choices and limitations, both mental and physical, involving him in

[19] His initial axioms already demonstrate his reliance on the christology of the Cappadocian fathers, particularly the two Gregories, a point which will be further elaborated. But his refusal to permit the orthodoxy of any form of 'mixture' language in christology when he first came to Constantinople, was an unwitting refutation of his great predecessor, St. Gregory Nazianzen, who had applied such terminology extensively.

[20] Following the canons of Nicaea, Nestorius taught that Christ was always sinless. He regards Christ's human, moral, life as so unswervingly set on fulfilling the Father's will that no dissonance ever could, or ever did, exist in him. It is a preacher's approach and a moralist's perspective on the 'atreptos' of Nicaea (the unchangeability of the Logos).

a range of testing situations (the temptations of the Lord) which proved and refined his virtue as a man, and which involved him inexorably in all the sufferings consequent on being human. Nestorius was unswerving on the point that this demanded that the approach of Apollinaris represented a dead-end. The latter's theology is considered briefly in the following section outlining Cyril's christology, here it will suffice to remark that Apollinaris had found no place for a human limited consciousness in Christ, or for a human soul which could be considered as the seat of genuine human choices. Apollinaris' logic demanded that these things must be sacrificed in the interests of the unity of the person of Christ, if one were to accept that the infinite mind of the Logos inhabited his human frame. Nestorius took the earlier christological heresy of Docetism as an extreme form of the same tendency in Apollinaris to acknowledge merely the appearance of fleshly limitation in the divine Christ who was really unlimited.

For Nestorius it was this tendency to absorb or evaporate away the human reality in the face of the divine that was the chief deficiency of Apollinaris' heresy, and like Gregory Nazianzen before him he attacked such presuppositions on soteriological grounds, for a theory of incarnation that wiped away the human reality in the advent of the deity constituted not only a failure of revelation theology but an inability to value the extraordinary role which the christian Gospel gave to human experience in its conception of God's redeeming work. Nestorius taught that such 'absorption theory' in christology was sub-christian or mythological, inevitably involving its proponents in concepts of incarnation based upon Krasis[21] or mixture. He was ever on the look out for the 'mixture' or 'confusion' of divine and human spheres of reality in christological discourse, and regarded this as the most serious deficiency of Cyril's work. He regarded all sense of 'mixture' as inevitably connoting the change, and even the annihilation, of the individual elements that were so mixed. For this reason his great concern in all his doctrine was to insist on the abiding distinctive relationship of the two fully enduring spheres of reality (or 'natures') in the incarnate Lord. For Nestorius all christological language applying the term 'mixis' was irredeemably Apollinarist. In this rigid attitude he apparently had failed to notice that even Gregory Nazianzen's anti-Apollinarist writings had applied the term.

Cyril's stress on the union of the two realities in the incarnation,

---

[21] A mixture that inter-diluted both constituent realities rendering them both finally changed: like water and wine, or oil and honey, stirred together.

and his equal insistence on using this very term of 'unification' (henosis, that is 'making-one-reality' seemed to Nestorius to be logically synonymous with the doctrine of the mixture and confusion of those two natures—hence Apollinarism resuscitated, pure and simple. But this habit Nestorius had of positing only two alternatives; either an understanding of two distinct but related natures abiding in Christ, or an Apollinarist confusion of the two things into a third hybrid, was his fatal logical mistake, a narrowness of conception that did not open him to hear the subtleties of what Cyril was actually positing and, more problematically, that did not enable him to realise why Cyril or anyone else should have any anxiety about the apparent 'divisiveness' that his own christology of 'abiding distinctness' and 'separate natures' introduced into the church's understanding of the incarnate Lord. Cyril was concerned to preserve the singleness of the acting subject in the church's christology. Nestorius opposed him because of his method without fully realising his overall intent, but in return did not seem able (as far as Cyril was concerned at least) to give the necessary assurances that the single subjectivity of the incarnate Lord could be protected on his alternative grounds. For this reason Cyril concluded he must have abandoned the principle of single subjectivity in favour of the Two Sons theory of his Syrian predecessor Diodore. Although Nestorius protested on several occasions that this was not his teaching, he never convinced Cyril of the grounds why it was not. This is a key element which needs to be examined in his thought.

For Nestorius, the notion of the absorption of the humanness of Christ within the overwhelming presence of the divine Logos, was tantamount to the destruction of any meaningful sense of truly human reality in Christ. As in the Apollinarist scheme, he argued, such a conception would make a full range of authentic human experiences impossible for Christ, and he therefore set his face determinedly against anything redolent of a defective understanding of Christ's humanity. Following on from this, the more moderate view that proposed Christ could be conceived as fully human since he was the divine Logos who truly shared 'our flesh' was also challenged by Nestorius. This was a view that had long been classical in the school of Alexandria, taught by Athanasius and maintained by Cyril.

On this view, neither Docetic nor Apollinarist, it was enough for the divine Logos to know bodily experience. He himself did not suffer (qua God) but in so far as his body suffered he can be said to have suffered-in-the-body.[22] Such an approach can maintain that Christ is fully human, but it would never choose to say (without qualification) that Christ is a man, in case the statement was heard to imply either that he was 'only' a man, or that he was a man alongside the divine Word in a bi-polarity of subject. To avoid any risk of such misunderstanding the Alexandrian tradition consistently preferred to talk of the Word's humanity, and in all statements dealing with the subject of the incarnation, the personal pronoun referred strictly and unfailingly to the divine Lord who had assumed the flesh.

In this school of thought the divine Christ was said to be authentically human in so far as deity undergoes a more or less full range of bodily experiences. On these terms humanness is not so much defined as deficient in some sense (missing a mind or soul, for example, as with Apollinaris) but rather as entirely there but radically transformed by the incomparably greater power of the divinity which has assumed the flesh into its own orbit. A key element of such 'transformation theory' was the notion of the 'deification' of the Lord's flesh (and by implication that of the believer) which was achieved in the act of incarnation. This is one of the most dynamic insights of the Alexandrian school, and their chief goal in incarnational language. For Nestorius it was a lamentable deduction from a reliance on 'absorption theory'. And as he opposed the latter firmly and strictly, so he tended to disparage the former.

For Nestorius if the relationship beween the divine and human aspects of Christ was so unequal as absorption theory suggested (such as the analogy of the mingling of a winedrop in an ocean: the winedrop of humanity in the ocean of deity) then a full range of authentically human experiences would have been impossible for Christ. When Jesus appears in the Gospels to have been praying, for example, or searching for the will of God in his life, he could hardly have done this sensibly or honestly if all the time he knew exactly what the will of God was, being the eternal Logos and as such the very mind and will of God himself. Cyril would explain Jesus' prayer life as an economic exercise done largely for our instruction and edification.[23] Biblical statements of limitation such as: 'But as for that day or hour no one knows,

[22] cf.e.g. Athanasius. De Incarnatione 17–18. (E.T.) E.R. Hardy, The Christology of The Later Fathers, London, 1954, 70–73.

[23] As for example in Jn.11.42. where Jesus prays before the raising of Lazarus, and then adds that this was done for the benefit of his hearers.

not the angels in heaven, nor the Son, but only the Father',[24] were similarly interpreted as being real but not absolute limitations. Cyril argues, for example, that it was not fitting for humans to be told the date of the end of time, so Jesus replied to the question in an 'economic' or man-centred way, rather than in a divine manner. As Logos he had all the Father's knowledge, including the date of the last day, but as incarnate Lord he had assumed by free choice a full range of limitations and restrictions which he was self-bound to observe. For example, he chose to live a fully human life in the incarnation, and this meant that he walked and could not fly, he ate and drank and did not exist on air, and accepted ignorance within his human mental life as a 'kenotic' expression of his divine condescension which brought him to the incarnate state in the first place. This was, for the Alexandrians, why Jesus spoke in the latter instance about the end of time from within his chosen human limitations (which as freely chosen did not thereby imply that they were weaknesses on the part of the Godhead) and said that it was not for him to know the date of the last day—even though if he were to speak purely in terms of his position as divine Logos (apart from the flesh) he would admit that he knew when this date would be. Economically his knowledge was mediated through his human mental states, and thus limited, although in divine, or absolute terms, his knowledge transcended all mental functions in its immaterial omniscience. Modern readers find the distinction difficult to imagine, for personality is largely defined today in terms of subjective intellectual consciousness, but for Cyril intellectual awareness was not the defining factor of personhood, but one of its functions; and he certainly regards the immaterial person of the Logos as the creative originator of the human consciousness of Christ (the 'soul' in the terms of the ancient psychology) not the fruit of it. The Alexandrians, after their long struggle with the Arian exegesis of precisely just such biblical passages as Cyril is here dealing with, were determined to avoid any possibility of the attribution of change and limitation to the Logos, which would carry with it the immediate implication that the Word was not God. This traditional response dominated their biblical method.

Nestorius, on the other hand, seemed to regard such an exegetical approach as suspect and misleading. This resolute acceptance of the implications of all that 'fully human' might mean is an aspect of much

---

[24] Mk.13.32.

modern christological thought too, and in this respect Nestorius' doctrine has taken on a new relevance for many contemporary thinkers. Nonetheless, the argument serves to demonstrate why so much of the debate between Cyril and himself turned on the proper hermeneutic to be applied to biblical texts.

Given the understanding that Nestorius was no Arian, and had no intention of using the biblical statements of limitation to deny the divinity of the Logos, it becomes evident that the question of subjectivity of the incarnate Lord is now the key problem seeking resolution in such an exegetical method. Because of his insistence on the implications, as he saw them, of being 'truly human' Nestorius was led on to his second great axiom, that the deity and humanness are represented in the one Christ by two distinct, unaltered, and unconfused natures which abide in their respective spheres of operation throughout his life—the divine nature manifesting itself by correspondingly 'divine' works and claims,[25] and the human nature being seen in his evident earthly limitations.[26] The two natures, then, exist side by side in Christ, each retaining its proper characteristics, and neither being confused or limited in the exercise of its proper functions by the other. The divine nature remained omniscient, the human nature remained limited in knowledge.

Nestorius regarded such conceptions of the christological union favoured by Cyril, such as 'natural union' (henosis kata physin) or 'hypostatic union' (henosis kath' hypostasin) as fundamentally compromising the abiding separateness of the natures in Christ. In consequence he rejected any formula of christology which envisaged a union taking place on the level of the 'natures' (a union of the natures) in so far as it implied that the separateness was not continued in the life of Christ, and that some kind of third new nature must have been produced as a result of this form of symbiosis (a new kind of mutant nature which he doubted could be regarded either divine or human).

Since Cyril's party favoured a conception of the christological union based on the level of 'natural union', and had propagated the catch-phrase: union from out of two natures (henosis ek dyo physeon) to sum it up for the populace Nestorius in turn coined the radically different formula: 'Christ in two natures' (en dyo physesin). In this

---

[25] Such as Jn.8.58; Jn.11.25.

[26] Such as Jn.4.6

latter aspect of his christology Chalcedon would partially follow him,[27] at the cost of alienating the extreme Cyrilline party of the mid fifth century and causing the monophysite rift.

These two cardinal points of Nestorius' christology highlight a third and most critical element—that if it is important to preserve the sense of abiding distinctness of natures and operations in Christ, some account must now be made to explain how this bi-polarity can exist in Christ without his inner life being reduced to an intolerable dualism, that is 'Two Sons'. Nestorius is clear that orthodoxy demands that there can only be one Son, one Christ, who is fully divine and also fully human, in two distinct natures. His difficulty is to explain how, once he has renounced the validity of the Alexandrian approach with its vision of the divine Logos acting eternally as a single subject/person assuming a body to act in history, he is able to conceive of the subjectivity of this one Christ, one Son.

Here Nestorius came up against the main problem of fifth century christology, the necessity of articulating with more clarity than had hitherto been applicable in the church the 'how' of the incarnation. He himself stands in need of justifying his own faith in the oneness of Christ, more than others, in the light of the way he had repeatedly stressed the need to insist on the abiding separateness within the incarnate Lord's earthly existence.

The statement that Christ was truly God and truly man would have been generally accepted across a wide range of the fifth century church as a basic standard of orthodoxy, but with differing notions of what being 'truly human' involved. Only the Antiochene school would have concluded from the phrase that Christ was 'a man'; Alexandrian theologians, on the other hand, were satisfied that it primarily meant the divine Logos lived a completely human life and used an ensouled body as his instrument (organon) for experiencing realities in the extra dimension of 'a bodily manner'. They did so, not so much to baulk at the reality of the Lord's humanity as to

[27] Though having secured a firmer sense of single personal unity in Christ than Nestorius was able to do. Cf. Loofs (1905) p. 197f. where Nestorius argued: 'Look what Cyril says here: "Even if the distinction of natures is not misunderstood from which (ex on) as we say an inexpressible union is achieved..." But this phrase of his "from which", makes it sound as if he were speaking of the natures of the Lord as being parts which together made up a single whole. He should not have said "from which" but rather "of which an inexpressible union is achieved", because the inexpressible union is not made up from the natures, but rather is an inexpressible union of the natures.'

avoid the two unwanted implications they saw inherent in the confession of Christ as 'a man'; namely that he was 'only a man', or that he was a man alongside and distinct from the deity, and this they identified as the already rejected third century heresy of Adoptionism.

The statement that the two aspects of Christ abided on equal terms throughout the Saviour's life was, however, bitterly contested. The Alexandrian position was that the 'assumption' of the humanity by the Logos deified the flesh from the very instant of the conception in the Virgin's womb. From the moment of his birth, Christ was seen by the eyes of faith to be one reality. To speak of two abiding aspects or natures, for the Alexandrians, would utterly destroy any sense of the integral unity in Christ, the embodied Logos. As far as they were concerned two complete and distinct natures remaining within Christ was synonymous with two separate lives, especially if the doctrine of single subjectivity was not otherwise secured, and thus two persons. The Alexandrians understood Diodore's stress on the two natures to mean exactly the 'Two Sons' as he said it did. What they could not understand was how Nestorius could continue to insist on the two separate realities abiding and yet still insist that he did not mean two sons himself. The Antiochene position argued to the contrary that any theory which did not allow the two natures to abide fully and distinctly made nonsense of any claim that Christ was really human.

The third statement as to 'how' Christ united Godhead and humanness in his life was the new matter that was to play the role of the locked clasp of the chest. As yet a technical theological vocabulary had not been forged to serve as the key for this lock. Nestorius and Cyril's great public argument was to be largely instrumental in creating this vocabulary. It was to be Nestorius' destiny, as well as his great misfortune, to be the spark that ignited the volatile mixture.

For Nestorius the terminology of a theologian was all-important. It was one thing for simple christians to make faith-utterances in prayer, but once a theological dialogue began all protagonists must know what they were saying and ensure that their statements were 'fitting', that is reverent and sensible. For him piety could never be sufficient excuse for careless exposition, or sloppiness of thought that was unable to see its own implications. In his eyes the Theotokos title was an outstanding example of just such terminological carelessness. Before we can investigate the details of his argument, however, it will be important to scrutinise the technical terminology on which he himself was basing the logical case, and this will involve us in a short study of some key philosophical terms which, however abstruse they may appear to the modern reader, are absolutely indispensable for an understanding of the patristic debate in general, and Nestorius in particular.

In simplest terms the christological problem, as it was then discerned, was that certain statements were utterly inappropriate to God. God, for example, could not be said to be capable of any passions since he was changeless and self-moving by definition of being God. He could not be conceived as capable of any ignorance, being omniscient; or capable of any form of limitation, being omnipotent and omnipresent. If these attributes were seen to be essential to the very definition of the words 'God' and 'divine' (and they were all accepted as base axioms by all parties concerned) then what sense did it make to attribute human passions, limitations and sufferings to Christ (all of which were necessary corollaries of accepting him as being human) and then in the next breath still claim that this Christ was 'divine'? In other words descriptions of divineness and humanness conflicted in a most obvious way. How could they be posited of one being? This problem was not merely one of obscure semantics, it involved the whole sense of the rationality of a faith that held Christ to be at once divine and human, and it challenged that faith to articulate itself meaningfully as to how the two statements could be posited—or in other words to define the manner of the union of the two conditions in Christ.

In order to articulate this central issue of the christological union there were four terminological possibilities, or key terms, available to fifth century theologians. The possible range of meanings for these could be extended by a graded series of qualifying adjectives or adverbs. The exact combinations of these semantic variables came, in the end, to be a matter of critical importance. The four major terms were as follows:

Ousia:	Essence, substance, being, genus, or nature.
Physis:	Nature, make-up of a thing. (In earlier christian thought the concrete reality or existent).
Hypostasis	The actual concrete reality of a thing, the underlying essence, (in earlier christian thought the synonym of physis).
Prosopon	The observable character, defining properties, manifestation of a reality.

Even at first sight it is clear that the words bear a range of meanings that overlap in some areas so as to be synonymous. This is particularly so with the terms Physis and Hypostasis which in the fifth century simultaneously bore ancient christian meanings and more modern applications. In relation to Physis, Cyril tended to use the antique meaning, Nestorius the modern. In relation to Hypostasis, the opposite was the case. Since these terms were at the very heart of the debate no small confusion resulted. What is more, in the full force of the argument over christological terminology both Nestorius and Cyril used the same term in different ways—this mutual inconsistency and variety of use adding greatly to their difficulties in understanding one another, and to our problems in understanding them both.

Last, but not least, many modern studies on the controversy insist on translating the two cardinal terms prosopon and hypostasis (the preferred terms of Nestorius and Cyril respectively) by the same English word 'person' in spite of the fact that in many instances the two terms were not synonyms for either protagonist, and that neither of the words meant what the modern notion of 'person' evokes for the reader today. Because of these bedevilling problems in ancient as well as modern hermeneutic it is particularly necessary to distinguish the meanings of the words with precision. Let us attempt, briefly, to describe the applications of these respective terms in the context of the philosophical argument.

Ousia is the genus of a thing. One can think, for example, of the genus 'unicorn'. Such a genus exists, but only theoretically, not practically, or concretely. It does not exist, that is, 'in reality' as we would say today. Nonetheless, it makes sense to talk of the necessary characteristics of a unicorn such as its magical horn, its horse-like appearance, its whiteness, its beard and lion's tail, and so on. Thus, the genus of unicorn is the ousia, that which makes up the essential being of a thing. The notion of the physis of our unicorn is intimately related to this. It connotes what we might call the palpable and 'physical' characteristics of a unicorn such as outlined above—but always understanding that this possession of a physis-nature still does not necessarily imply that such a creature is real. The word physis, however, has taken our discussion of unicorns one step further into a more real or specific dimension than the base generic term ousia did.

In some circles, especially those represented by the christian thinkers of Alexandria following Athanasius, the word physis signified something slightly different from this sense of 'physical attributes' and had been used to connote the physical existent—in the sense of a concrete individual reality. In the hands of Cyril the word is used in two senses, one in what might be called the standard 'physical' usage where it connotes the constituent elements of a thing, and the other in which it serves to delineate the notion of individual existent—or in other words individual subject. This variability in the use of a key term on Cyril's part goes some way to explaining Nestorius' difficulties in following his argument over the single Physis of the Incarnate Word (Mia Physis tou Theou Logou Sesarkomene). By this Cyril meant the one concrete individual subject of the Incarnated Word. Whereas Nestorius heard him to mean the one physical composite of the Word (in the sense of an Apollinarist mixture or fusion of the respective attributes of the natures of man and God). What Cyril meant by this key phrase was to insist that the single individual reality of the Word of God, and no other, was the one who had now been incarnated: in other words that the sole personal subject of the incarnation was the eternal Word, and that there was no human personal subject alongside God in the incarnate Lord. He was entitled to use the term physis to signify individual existent in so far as that was the ancient tradition of his Alexandrian predecessors, but subsequent theological usage, culminating in the Chalcedonian settlement, restricted the significance of the term to the connotation of physical constituents, and Cyril himself, in the negotiations with the Antiochenes after the council of Ephesus, began to realise that for clarity's sake the use of physis as a subject-referent could no longer be sustained.

So much for the term 'physis' as used in the sense of subject referent by Cyril, but in terms of its more commonly understood sense, as a physical descriptor, it had some limitations in the way it could only connote a generic identity and to that extent describe an abstract level of reality. If we wanted to take our discussion of the 'nature' of a thing into a more specific domain, in this period, a further term needed to be employed. If, for example, we wished to discuss whether unicorns existed or not, the word that was needed was hypostasis which signified 'the making concrete, or real' of a generic thing, in the sense of individualising it in an existential way. If our ousia and physis of unicorn was hypostatised, if that is it had a unicorn hypostasis as well as unicorn genus (ousia) and unicorn's natural properties (physis), then we would be talking about a living, moving, unicorn, no longer a fantasy image or creature of the imagination.

The word physis has obviously carried some of this latter sense of making a generic thing specific, but hypostasis was soon to become the generally preferred term for 'individual specification' with an emphasis on realising an abstract reality into a personal existent. On the corresponding semantic rules it followed that any real existent had to be hypostatised, and here opened up the real chasm between Cyril's way of thinking and that of Nestorius. The former saw that there could only be one hypostatic reality in Christ, if indeed Christ was to be one (though he meant hypostasis to bear the weight of subject-centre) whereas the latter followed the logical thread more rigidly and argued that every ousia had to be hypostatised separately (and was thus meaning hypostasis to bear the sense of the physical grounding of a genus).[28]

Unfortunately the use of terms never did, and still does not, follow the confines of dictionary-like definitions, and in the period of the early fifth century hypostasis had other, older, meanings also attached to it. It had been used in the past as a straight synonym for physis. Even Athanasius, when explaining his doctrinal terms after the Synod of Alexandria in 362, had set out for his listeners that, 'hypostasis means ousia, nothing more.' The term had actually begun life in this way. Etymologically it consisted of the prefix hypo- meaning 'underneath', and stasis—meaning 'standing', and it was thus a direct parallel of the Latin word Sub-stantia (substance/ousia). However, in the Trinitarian debates of the late fourth century a great deal of theological effort, on the part of the Cappadocian Fathers among others, had succeeded in forging new technical senses for the word hypostasis. The trinity doctrine had thus defined that God was one ousia expressed in three hypostases. In this more modern sense, hypostasis was already well along the road to signifying individual concretisation, or subjectivisation, rather than connoting (as it had done once) the simple nature of a thing.

The double senses of the word again became a source of considerable

---

[28] This is for him a basic principle, and he says, in rebuke of Cyril: 'One must not conceive of an ousia without a hypostasis as if the union in Christ had taken place in an ousia.' Liber Heraclidis 305, Nau. p. 193; Ibid. 291, Nau, pp. 184,192. Cyril's point was not, of course, to posit union on the basis of ousia but on the basis of hypostasis understood differently: as the personalised centre of natures. Although Cyril would agree that all natures must be hypostatised he did not agree that this meant Christ must therefore have two hypostases. For him the whole point of the argument was that the two natures were not separate independent realities, and thus were both realised, in the one Christ, by one hypostasis. The use of monohypostatic language eventually won the day, but it took the next generation, at Chalcedon, to spell the argument out in the technical terms: Two natures (divine and human), one hypostasis (divine) in the one Christ.

confusions between Cyril and Nestorius. Cyril uses hypostasis largely in the newer sense to describe the manner of the union in Christ. He says frequently, for example, that the union took place 'Kath Hypostasin': hypostatically, or on the basis of a hypostatic level. What he means by this is to stress that the union of God and man in Christ is properly understood to have been effected precisely because it was a single individual subject (the hypostasis: God the Word) who realised the union of two different realities (divinity and humanity) by standing as the sole personal subject of both. This for him is the 'hypostatic union' which is the only proper way of securing an incarnational theology. Nestorius, on the other hand, consistently read hypostasis in the antique sense of meaning something closely allied to physis or ousia; either a synonym of the preceding terms, or the term that signified their concrete grounding in a precise 'nature'. He confesses at several points in his writings that he cannot understand what the term 'hypostatic union' can mean in Cyril, except to posit the union on the basis of the most mechanical way possible. In short he heard 'hypostatic union' to be a synonym of 'material union' a concept which Cyril abhorred, for the same reasons as Nestorius, because it would be a mythological notion involving the creation of a new kind of nature: neither divine nor human but divino-human, and thus neither one nor the other in any authentic sense. This latter position would indeed be Apollinarist. Nestorius believed Cyril was teaching this largely because he had misread the term's significance in Cyril's writings. Its use, however, alongside Cyril's other preferred phrase[29] of the Mia Physis (One Physis of God the Word made flesh) served to convince him as well as the other Antiochene theorists that this was indeed what Cyril meant: that his terms hypostasis and physis could only have such a material meaning, not the connotations of individualisation Cyril wanted them to have, and indeed felt he had a right to expect the terms to bear given their prior use within the tradition of his own church.

Nestorius had other problems with the terms of the argument, and he tended to see himself as someone who was long overdue in the church for the task of clearing up the inconsistencies of christian discourse on the incarnation. For him hypostasis was not a particularly good term to speak of the 'distinct reality' of a thing—its individualness—and this because of the term's close semantic associations with the

[29] Though the latter is less frequently applied.

words for overall generic nature (ousia, physis). He found it made much more sense to apply a different word altogether to signify the distinct individualness of a thing, and this was to be prosopon.[30] For Nestorius the meaning of hypostasis should be restricted to connoting the concretisation of a thing, and physis to signify the stuff of which it was made. He studiously avoided using the form hypostasis to describe the christological union, in direct criticism of Cyril's preferred language. When Nestorius did speak of the term it was only to make two points: firstly that the word was highly 'physical' in its associated meanings and utterly inappropriate for use in the christology debate since it could suggest an organic or chemical model of union; and secondly that any ousia without a hypostasis of its own would, therefore, not be a real existent. The latter point was a significant attack on Cyril who had argued that Christ's humanity did not have a corresponding human hypostasis of its own (and thus Christ was not an individual man, rather God the Word enfleshed). Cyril saw this argument as crucial in defending the single subjectivity of the incarnate Lord; Nestorius attacked it on the logico-semantic grounds that if Christ's humanity did not have its own hypostasis then that humanity was only notional, not real. Whereas Nestorius demanded logical exactitude in the theological exchange, Cyril preferred to defend an intuited principle of single subjectivity regardless of the strains his varied use of technical terms placed on his hearers or upon logic itself. Cyril always felt that the mysterious nature of the faith truly reflected the reality that discourse about the incarnation of God was not something that could be neatly packaged and wrapped up in a scholastic fashion; for his opponents this 'mystical' attitude in his theologising was frequently dismissed as obscurantism. There are undoubtedly several inconsistencies in Cyril's terminological use, although conversely they hardly make his meaning any less clear since he constantly repeated his point using a variety of metaphors and in an abundance of ways, refusing to rely on any rigidly consistent set of terms, almost as a protest against creating a technical christological scholasticism. By contrast Nestorius was a logician to his roots and for him prosopon was the new way forward in rationalising the church's doctrine of Christ.

[30] If the matter had only been a case of differences in terminology, Cyril would have let the argument rest. In his own writings he eventually uses prosopon as a synonym for hypostasis: both signifying individual reality. The argument could not rest, however, because at this critical juncture Nestorius began to speak of Prosopon in a way that gave Cyril grounds to think he did not mean a single unique prosopon.

The word prosopon was a traditional term for the Antiochene theologians. It literally meant a 'face' or an 'actor's mask', and its Latin equivalent was persona which had long been established in the West as a christological technical term since the days of Tertullian.[31] The prosopon is the external aspect or form of a physis as it can be manifested to external observation or scrutiny. It is a very concrete, empirical word, connoting what appears to outside observation. Each essence (ousia) is characterised by its proper nature (physis), everything, that is, which makes it up, and in turn every nature that is hypostatically real presents itself to the scrutiny of the senses in its own prosopon—that list of detailed characteristics or 'propria' that constitute this thing individually and signal to the observer what nature (physis) it has, and thus to what genus (ousia) it belongs.[32] In the system Nestorius is following, every nature has its own prosopon, that sum of proper characteristics (idiomata) by which it is characterised in its unique individuality and made known to others as such. The word carried with it an intrinsic sense of 'making known' and appeared to Nestorius particularly apt in the revelatory context of discussing the incarnation. Cyril too used the word, intending it as a synonym for his sense of hypostasis (or physis on occasion), meaning, that is, the individual subject centre. He only used it because he knew it was in the vocabulary of the Antiochenes, he certainly did not like it much and always had a sense that in the way it appeared in Nestorius' arguments it was a defective word in comparison to hypostasis precisely because it had such 'surface' connotations evoking 'appearance' perhaps more than 'reality'. Cyril wanted a word to define the personal-centre of Christ which was as ontologically grounded as possible, or in other words as 'substantial' a word as possible. This for him was admirably done by hypostasis. Moreover he was appalled by the way Nestorius kept referring to different prosopa as well as to the prosopon of union. Far from proving a consistent doctrine of single subjectivity Cyril felt

---

[31] Persona also meant an actor's mask in origin, but had come to be used as the grounding factor of a nature. The Latin formula had emerged since Tertullian as, Una Persona duae Naturae: Two natures one subject. Neither persona nor prosopon bore the weight of the modern term 'person'.

[32] Prosopon, like hypostasis, is related to physis in so far as it is a referent for concreteness and individuation, but it differs from the range of meanings attached to physis in being a more specific term, having a distinct sense of 'the individual character of something as manifested to observation'. For a fuller discussion of the precise etymological meanings see H.A. Wolfson (1976); Loofs (1914) p. 76f; Abramowski (1963) p. 217f.

this level of variability in key words at the very central point of the whole debate demonstrated that it was not Nestorius' intention to teach a single personal centre in any real sense at all, only in the apparent sense that Christ 'seemed' to unite two realities. In later theology the church generally followed Cyril's lead in preferring hypostasis, but Chalcedon also agreed with him that prosopon could also be used once it had been redefined as a synonym for hypostasis, and certainly vindicated his point that the term for union, be it hypostasis or prosopon, was so important that on no account could one apply it in any way that suggested a compromised attitude on the basic point of single-subjectivity.

Such then is a brief description of the terms available to Greek theologians in the fifth century with which to debate the christological issue. It might serve as a preliminary explanation of why there was so much ground for misunderstanding between two thinkers, such as Cyril and Nestorius, who were using different language codes to present their respective positions. It will also serve as the basic introduction to the following exposition of Nestorius' detailed argument about the person of Christ which rested upon these foundations. Nonetheless, the English equivalents of these four central terms: Ousia, Physis, Hypostasis, and Prosopon, and the philosophical sketch just offered can only have the status of tentative preliminary jottings to assist us to recognise the terrain and follow the turns in the ancient argument. This is because the real meaning of terms can not be found in the abstract definition but only in the actual semantic application of those terms in the precise context of a textual argument. Cyril, for example, despite all Nestorius' desires to standardise the vocabulary in a rigidly consistent way, does not have the same drive to do so. The primary way in which one ought to understand Cyril's theology is by reading a good deal of it. For centuries this option was not allowed to students who could not command Greek. In the modern era of translations of the major Fathers it is still the case that Cyril's writings are hard to access—a significant reason why section five of this book was thought appropriate. The texts of Cyril are not offered here as an adjunct to the critical discussion preceding them, but as the primary source to demonstrate the doctrine in hand. In the light of reading Cyril directly, at first hand, one may gain a sense of surprise at the way he has been summarised in doctrinal manuals. For Nestorius too, it is in the way he applies the technical terms in context that his real intentions will be further clarified for us, and the exposition of his thought which follows will attempt to present a fairly generous amount of primary citations.

Of the four cardinal terms so far discussed only three are capable of being used to describe the christological 'how', that is the manner of union between Godhead and Manhood in Christ. This is because the term ousia had been exhaustively worked out for christians in the earlier debates around the council of Nicaea in the fourth century, and by this stage all parties were agreed that it was the proper word to connote the very being of God, or the very being of Man. It was a word for irreducibility, not for unification. In other words, if christological union was posited on the basis of ousia, then an ontological union of God and Man would have been envisaged in Christ. If there was to be only one ousia in such a scheme it had to be either a divine ousia or a human ousia or a divino-human ousia. If it was divine then in no sense could Christ legitimately be called man. At best he could only have the appearance of a man while all the while he was really something else, that is God the Word posing as a man. Any sense of 'incarnation' would necessarily evaporate on such a basis and Christ would be better described as an 'epiphany'.[33] Such a view would be nothing more than a revival of the ancient heresy of Docetism, and no one was ready to conceive the union on these terms.

If the supposed ousia was human, however, then Christ could be called authentically human, but any attribution of divine honours would be blasphemous since in no sense would he be God, and thus the entire christian system of cultic liturgy would be contradicted. Again, if one tried to suggest that the single ousia was divino-human in the sense of a new unity composited of Godhead and Manhood at an ontological level, then such an ousia would be an altogether new and unique genus of existence. It would, however, not be divine in any proper sense since it would have changed from the pure conception of what a divine ousia was (that is before the incarnation) which involves unchangeability, and in the very act of changing demonstrated its non-divinity by being historically relativised. Moreover, whatever else such a divino-human ousia might have been it would certainly not have been human. On such grounds of a christological union in terms of ousia (kat'ousian), therefore, Christ would have been neither God

[33] A longstanding Hellenistic (pagan) term to describe the encounter between the gods and men, and even the demi-gods. It was a notion that the Church had resisted from the outset.

nor Man. This approach was regarded by all as a wholly impossible and inapplicable notion. To posit a christological union on this term was consequently regarded as the biggest and most naive blunder a theologian could ever make, and was ridiculed as inevitably transforming the Trinity into a Quaternity.[34] All sides in the christological argument of the fifth century took delight in trying to point out how their opponents had fallen into this massive and ridiculous mistake. Such an accusation lay behind Nestorius' and Theodoret's charge that Cyril was Apollinarist, and behind Cyril's charge that Nestorius' was an Arian. Neither accusation was strictly accurate, but they formed a large part of the methodology of ancient debating technique. One such accusation was to backfire very badly on Nestorius. In his writings before the council of Ephesus, and at Ephesus itself, Nestorius argued that Cyril had dragged down the whole Trinity into the incarnation event in a wholly illegitimate way. He expressed this charge in his usual sarcastic way of posing the problem to startle his hearers with the implications, intending to expose his opponents by this method. Unfortunately the collection of texts which Cyril presented to the council contained several such examples of Trinity-Quaternity sarcasm which the assembled Fathers, not recognising the sarcastic intent, took to be Nestorius' own sentiment, and regarded him as theologically illiterate. At Ephesus he did the same thing orally in the presence of Theodotus of Ancyra whose report of the event was a major factor in his synodical condemnation for blasphemy.

The term ousia, then, had a firm place in the established christian technical vocabulary. It signified what was essential and ontologically given—in the case of the doctrine of Christ, the essence of the unchanging, eternal divine nature on the one hand, and the passible human nature on the other. In no way, however, could the term be used to illuminate the manner of relating these two conceptions in the person of Christ confessed in the church as both human and divine.

This left physis, prosopon, and hypostasis, as three possible alternatives. None of these terms had as yet been developed in the christological arena in any agreed sense. The word physis had appeared previously in the work of Apollinaris who was led thereby to posit

[34] As, for example, in the Book of Heraclides 55–58, Nau pp. 35–36. Nestorius' point here is that if the christological union is 'substantially' conceived then it would involve the Father and Spirit too since there is only one substance (ousia) in God. This would relativise the absolute and destroy christian theology.

a Christ who was less than fully human. Apart from this ill-starred usage in the past, culminating in a christology which had already been condemned by numerous synods, the term also had unavoidable connotations (because of its very 'physicality') of an inevitable organic union, which several theologians found disturbing. Even though Cyril had applied it (in his Mia Physis formula) he noticeably backtracked from this usage in the aftermath of his dialogues with the non-Nestorian orientals. That seemed to leave prosopon and hypostasis as the two leading contenders in the struggle to find a meaningful christological vocabulary. Nestorius worked on the basis of the first. Cyril alternated between physis and hypostasis, refusing to surrender the former word simply because of its earlier heretical uses, but eventually realised its deficiency in being able to secure common agreement and came round to proposing hypostasis as the definitive key word.

Some of the meaning range of both terms hypostasis and physis overlapped onto the territory of the word ousia, as we saw in our earlier discussion of terms. Because of this Nestorius frequently (not entirely innocently perhaps, but part of an overall apologetic intent) claims to find Cyril's use of hypostasis to describe the christological union as 'wholly incomprehensible'. He wished his own readers to avoid such terminology for the dangers it had in suggesting the kind of ontological union in Christ that would make the Trinity into four, and leave Christ neither man nor God.

In the Book of Heraclides[35] Nestorius confesses that he did not understand what possible sense 'hypostatic union' could have when he first heard the notion from Cyril twenty years previously, and that he did not understand it now. This is, of course, not a straightforward confession of ignorance on Nestorius' part but a heavily ironic suggestion that Cyril was guilty of the biggest christological naivety possible, propounding an ontological term of union. He based this reading of Cyril on the antique use of the term hypostasis seen, for example, in the way the Nicene creed used it as a synonym for ousia, signifying 'real being'.[36] In fact Nestorius is refusing to allow the validity of a new technical use of the word hypostasis in Cyril's works, insisting on reading him in the antique sense of the vocabulary, on the grounds

---

[35] Book of Heraclides 228, Nau. p. 138: 'I Confess I never understood it then, nor do I understand it now.' For the relatively recent introduction of the word hypostasis into christological debate see Abramowski (1963) pp. 213–217; also M Richard (1945) pp. 5–32, 243–270.

[36] cf. Loofs (1914) pp. 70–72; Bethune-Baker (1903) pp. 235–238.

that he had not made sufficient qualifications in his writings to show a clear differentiation between any new sense he wished to emerge, and the old Nicene meaning of hypostasis. In this complaint Nestorius had some justification in Cyril's habit of using hypostasis and physis as interchangeable words (suggesting he too was following the Nicene sense) while simultaneously applying the newer significance of hypostasis as a reference to subject differentiation (in the way that the Cappadocian tradition had formulated the Trinity doctrine in the late fourth century—God as one identical ousia differentiated in three individual hypostases).

Cyril, on the other hand, had some justification in claiming that this 'new sense' of hypostasis to connote differentiated subject was already well established by the council of Constantinople 381 as the fundamental structure of the church's trinitarian orthodoxy. For Nestorius to regard it as a novelty of Cyril's own invention was thus hardly acceptable. Ironically Nestorius' dislike of the term hypostasis in theological discourse was an aversion that earlier had been shared by Rome. A generation previously when the Cappadocian Fathers had first tried to systematise the use of the word to signify the 'threeness' of God while using ousia to connote the essential oneness of God, Rome was at first dismayed by the doctrine. It had misheard the teaching of three hypostases and one ousia as the equivalent of three substances in God—hence three Gods,[37] and (at first) it regarded the whole Neo-Nicene movement as at best an incomprehensible use of theological terms. Nestorius still seems to be pursuing that line fifty years later. It had taken a long while for the meaning of the new trinitarian terms to be commonly agreed. What was in dispute now, between Cyril and Nestorius, was much the same issue—whether or not hypostasis should be imported into yet another theological arena to stand service as a key christological cipher. Nestorius was arguing that such an importation was indefensible and confusing. Cyril, on the other hand, was implying that the Trinitarian use of hypostasis had already defined it as indicative of the subjectivity of God, and in the case of the incarnation to speak about the hypostasis of God

[37] Etymologically hypo-stasis was equivalent to sub-stantia but in theological application the West used substantia where the Greeks applied ousia, and the Greeks employed hypostasis where the Latins used persona. The Greek etymological equivalent of persona would, strictly speaking, have been prosopon, not hypostasis. For a fuller discussion of the vexed terminological developments of this earlier era see Kelly (1978) chs. 5 & 10.

in the flesh meant precisely the Word of God. Thus, the doctrine of hypostatic union was, for Cyril, one of the strongest ways he could think of to argue that the personal subject of the incarnation was none other than the divine Word. His application of the Trinitarian hypostatic language is, therefore, entirely apposite. What Nestorius objected to was not really the terminology, but the doctrine he sensed behind that terminology, and thought to be alien to orthodoxy. For him, to make the divine Word the direct subject of the incarnate acts was not admissible.

Throughout the Book of Heraclides Nestorius returns time and again to criticise Cyril's notion of a christological union based on physis or hypostasis (henosis physike, henosis kath' hypostasin) as involving a necessary composition of elements devoid of any freedom of choice like a biological product or a chemical reaction or a mechanical union of incomplete parts to make up the new whole of a *tertium quid.* For Nestorius, any such intellectual model of the christological union provided neither for the abiding completeness of the respective natures in Christ, nor for the perfectly voluntarist character of the incarnation which hinged not on any form of physical necessity, but solely on the graceful free choice of God to reveal himself in human form.[38] In a fragment from his work Theopaschites Nestorius expressed his objection as follows:

> For you confess that Christ was constituted one nature (Mia Physis) from the incorporeal and the body,[39] and was a single-natural-hypostasis[40] of the divine enfleshment (Theosarkoseos). But to say this is a confusion of the two natures, a confusion which deprives the natures of their own respective hypostases[41] by confounding them with one another.[42]

---

[38] cf. R.A. Greer. (1983) pp. 82–98.

[39] In other words Cyril's position was attacked as maintaining that from the union of divine nature and human nature there results divine nature in the flesh. One plus one equals one, and the last one can only be a synthetic composite on these grounds. Cyril in fact would not allow that the humanity was a distinct and individual reality in the same way as the deity: it was not personalised independently, there was no human individual subject apart from the Word.

[40] That is, for Cyril physis and hypostasis were synonyms. One hypostasis, as Nestorius read him, would appear to mean only one nature in Christ, either an obliteration of the humanity (Docetism) or the result of a synthetic fusion of the two natures in a composite (Apollinarism). Nestorius is here ironically suggesting that Cyril's use of philosophic terminology is chaotic and tautologous.

[41] As Cyril understood Hypostasis largely to signify individuation it is easy to see how he heard Nestorius' doctrine to be teaching Two Sons rather than one Christ.

[42] Theopaschites. Preserved in Severus of Antioch, Contr. Gramm. 2.32. Tr. J Lebon, CSCO 112, p. 192.

In the Book of Heraclides he returns often to the same theme,[43] that if the christological union is posited as an ontological or 'natural' one by such terms as ousia, physis, or hypostasis, then it would be tantamount to saying the divine Logos was compelled by the tyranny of nature to suffer all that his body suffered. This would not only destroy any notion of the impassibility and transcendence of the Godhead, but equally would rob the incarnation of any religious significance it could have of God's freely chosen solidarity with us. One would no longer be able to speak at all of free choice in the incarnation on such a model of union. This was why he posited prosopon as the correct term to use in the christological debate. Let us see how he chose to use it.

3. Prosopic Theory: Associative Difference in Christ

For Nestorius, there are two distinct genuses in Christ, the two ousiai of divinity and humanity. It follows from this, on his terms, that there must be two natures (physeis) corresponding to the distinct genuses. Accordingly, these two physeis will be apparent to the external observer in their respective prosopa. One can look at the historical figure of Christ in the Gospels and see the clear signs of the two prosopa, divine and human. The fact that Jesus is a man with the human parentage of Mary, grows and advances as a human child should (Lk.2.49), shows true human emotions such as grief (Jn.11.35) and anxiety (Mk.14.34), all contribute to present us with a body of evidence that here before our eyes and senses are all the prosopic marks of a human physis. The prosopic reality of this human physis is known as Jesus, the man from Nazareth. On the other hand, this same historical figure of the Christ gives the observer another body of evidence that signals there is not simply a human prosopon here but another prosopon of a fundamentally different kind, the prosopon of a divine ousia. The latter body of evidence transcends the scope of a human prosopon and amounts to claims of pre-existence that human beings cannot rightly make (Jn.8.58), claims for absolute status (Jn. 6.54; 8.12.), and signs of awesome power such as raising the dead (Mk.5.35.) and walking on the sea (Mk.6.45.f). These are all things beyond the range of a human prosopon and they signal to the observer the existence of another kind of prosopon, one that manifests a divine physis behind

[43] Book of Heraclides 55–57. Nau. pp. 35–36.

it. This holy and powerful prosopon is recognised by faith as the divine Logos. An accurate scrutiny of the external visible signs and evidence concerning Christ, therefore, clearly tells the observer that there are two separate levels of reality in this figure; two prosopa (or prosopic sets of evidence) signalling to the intelligent exegete the fact that two different natures co-exist in this being. Yet it is equally true to say that one encounters unity as well as diversity in the single concrete figure of 'the Christ', for all the evidence also concurs that there are not two Christs, only one figure who stands before our scrutiny and somehow combines these two different sets of evidences. This experience our exegetical senses have of the one Christ must signify that Christ himself (that is 'he-who-combines-two-prosopic-realities') is in some sense a single prosopic reality, and this is the prosopon which is known to experience as, and commonly designated, 'Christ'.

Clearly the semantic rules become very important at this stage of the argument if one is to avoid a multitude of confusions.[44] For Nestorius, we are speaking about three central faith experiences: (a) Here is a man, limited by his humanness; (b) Here is also God the Logos, untrammelled in all his power; (c) Here is one and the same figure presenting this bi-polar reality to the eyes of faith and experience. In speaking of this complex phenomenon Nestorius insisted that the proprieties of language were of critical importance. Statements of type (a), for example, refer properly and strictly to the man Jesus of Nazareth. 'Jesus' should be the grammatical subject of all such sentences. Statements of type (b) refer strictly and properly to the divine Logos. Statements of type (c) which attempt to remind the hearer of the single and yet bi-polar compositeness of the Lord, are to be referred neither to Jesus, nor to the divine Logos, but to an appropriately bi-polar set of confessional titles, which Nestorius specified to be: Christ, Only Begotten, Son, or Lord. In consequence, he taught that if one observed these simple rules of language all theological improprieties could be avoided.

This meant, for example, that one should not say: 'Jesus raised Lazarus from the dead', because if Jesus was really a man then he would not be able to raise anyone from the dead since that is not a power within true human experience. When Lazarus was raised

[44] For all that Nestorius criticised Cyril for using the same etymological terms in different ways simultaneously, it is clear that he himself wished the term prosopon to do too much work: to signify individuation as well as unity in one and the same context of argument.

from the dead, it followed that it was the Logos who did it. Similarly, for Nestorius, it is wholly inappropriate to say: 'The Logos died on the cross', because if he is truly the Word of God then he is immortal and so cannot possibly die in any way whatsoever. In short it is as foolish to suggest that Jesus can raise someone from the dead as it is to suggest that the Logos can ever die. The man Jesus of Nazareth died on the cross, therefore, as a man subject to mortality like all other men. God the Word raised him from the dead as himself one who was beyond the power of death. The distinctive spheres and capacities of both (the distinct physeis) were always preserved, and their relationship constituted the history of salvation.

Attempts by christians to cross-exchange language categories (the so-called 'exchange of properties', or communicatio idiomatum)[45] were fundamentally misguided in Nestorius' eyes: no more than basic category mistakes to be avoided by intelligent christians. It was his habit of regarding Cyril as being so fundamentally unintelligent about this that greatly exacerbated their mutual correspondence, for Cyril felt that the language about bi-polarity was a thin veneer over a doctrine that quite openly spoke about 'the man Jesus' and the God 'Logos' in several contexts, which to him was nothing other than dual subjectivity, whatever the qualifications one might like to add. Moreover, the refusal to allow for cross-language references such as 'God the Word died on the Cross' (provided always that one either understood, or added the proper context 'as enfleshed in the incarnation')[46] was for Cyril not an attack on misguided piety but on the essential heart of the Gospel. The two theological schemes were quite

---

[45] The exchange of properties meant linguistically associating both sets of attributes (eg. divine attributes such as raising the dead and human attributes such as being weary, or weeping) indiscriminately as a result of the incarnation whereby they were concretely associated in the life of Christ. For Cyril, and for later theology after Chalcedon, this was permissible on the basis that both sets of differing characteristics could be radically associated on the basis of the single personality who stood as the active subject of them both. The viability of the entire method, however, stood or fell on this matter of single subjectivity. At the time of the present controversy that was the very issue that was being fought over. Cyril propounds the method of the exchange of properties as one of his main ways of promoting his doctrine of the single subject, but as far as Nestorius was concerned the linguistic method only served to confuse the issue of the distinctness of the different natures (physeis) visible in the incarnation.

[46] So, for example, in relation to the phrase 'One enfleshed nature of God the Word', Cyril freely admitted the sense could be heretical—but only if one deliberately omitted the key word 'enfleshed'. Since that word was one of the key elements of the phrase Cyril felt it could hardly be overlooked by anyone with a genuine intent.

decidely opposed on basic matters of the argument.

For Nestorius the language scheme of christological utterance was all revealing. Many of the traditional expressions of christian piety such as 'God wrapped in swaddling bands' would be far better laid aside, or rephrased with regard for theological exactitude as 'Jesus was wrapped in swaddling bands' (if one wished to consider the pathetic humanness of the Lord), or 'The Son of God was wrapped in swaddling bands' (if one wished to articulate a sense of the divine condescension involved in the incarnation). For Nestorius the phrase 'God wrapped in swaddling bands' was at worst blasphemous nonsense, or at best evidence of simple-mindedness and theological ineptitude. If such a phrase implied that the Logos was the direct 'personal' subject of the God-Man's human sufferings then it involved the impassible Logos directly in passibility[47] and this was heretical. All this kind of language, in any case, he considered contrary to scripture,[48] and being 'unbiblical' this was why it naturally came to grief. On Cyril's part such language was a natural progression from belief in the incarnation. He presumed that the context for all such statements (including the Theotokos) was self-evidently the incarnate state of God the Word, and to have to labour the point every time, as Nestorius seemed to be insisting, by such a rigid scheme of language rules, was simply not necessary, in fact it was detrimental to belief precisely because it weakened the sense of the paradox such language-crossing evoked, the paradox which enshrined the church's sense of the single subjectivity of Christ. For both Cyril and Nestorius, then, confessional titles and precise rules of exegesis became of cardinal importance. This can be seen in the very nature of the surviving polemical correspondence which is so largely taken up with the proper method of interpreting biblical texts, and on the correct use of titles. The argument of Cyril's Scholia on the Incarnation, and That The Christ Is One demonstrate this aspect quite clearly, but it is observable in almost all their mutual exchanges. The Theotokos title in particular became a flag around which both sides quickly drew up positions to make a stand.

The phrase 'Mother of God' for Cyril was a quintessential synopsis of his doctrine that the divine Word was the direct and sole personal subject of all the incarnate acts (including that of his own birth in the flesh). For Nestorius, on the other hand, it was a prime example

---

[47] Book of Heraclides. 59, Nau p. 37; Ibid. 133–135, Nau pp. 86–88.
[48] Loofs (1905) pp. 278, 295–297.

of a deeply wrong-headed approach to theology, a perfect example of non-biblical language that led christological orthodoxy astray. Nestorius had already pronounced on this word in the early days after his election to the throne of Constantinople. He felt it was always dubious to evoke the term unless the user was willing to add the necessary balance by also confessing Mary as 'Mother of the Man' (Anthropotokos).[49] This was substantially the position of Theodore Mopsuestia,[50] but Nestorius was particularly uneasy about the possible Arian or Apollinarist tendencies that could lie within the word.[51] Regarding the whole question of the communicatio idiomatum he determined that sets of attributes should be referred to the prosopon of each nature as appropriate, since neither of the natures was identical with the 'prosopon of union'—Christ. He nonetheless accepted that the singleness of the prosopon Christ allowed for a certain legitimacy in using the methodology of the 'communicatio' but stated quite clearly that it was 'only as words go' (homonymos), not something substantial. Cyril took this to mean he did not regard the christological union as something real, only a language game; not a union at all only a verbal manner of referring to an association of two subjects God the Word and the man Jesus.

This argument that the correct attribution of words was semantically and theologically critical is typical of all Nestorius' work. He says, for example:

> If you make your way through the whole of the (New) Testament you will nowhere find death attributed to God, but either to Christ, or The Son, or The Lord. For Christ, and Son, and Lord, when applied by scripture to the Only Begotten, are terms designed to express the two natures,[52] and reveal now the Godhead, now the manhood, now both.[53]

Again he makes the same point arguing against the Alexandrian position that the Nicene Creed (and thus, by implication, the ancient voice of orthodox tradition) had sanctioned a free use of the communicatio idiomatum in so far as its language implied that the Logos was one subject who pre-existed, came into history, suffered, and effected

[49] Loofs (1905) p. 167, 181f, 191, 252, & 273.

[50] De Incarnatione, fragm.15, (Ed.) Swete p. 310.

[51] Loofs (1905) p. 273. Nestorius certainly regarded Cyril's defence of the term as highly Apollinarist.

[52] Loofs (1905) Tōn physeōn esti ton dyo semantikon.

[53] Loofs (1905) p. 269; Ibid. pp. 181, 185, 203–204, 247, 252, 312–313.

salvation for mankind. Protesting against the semantic implications of such an interpretation Nestorius says:

> The Fathers did not say: We believe in One God the Word, but rather 'in Christ', which indicates the two natures, and thus they chose this term to connote both.[54]

And again:

> If you take a closer look at the statements (of the Creed) you will find that the choir of the Fathers did not say that the consubstantial Godhead is capable of suffering, nor that the one who is co-eternal with the Father was newborn, nor did they say that which raised up the destroyed temple (of the body) was itself raised up . . . . See how they use first the term Lord, then Jesus (Saviour), and Christ, and Only Begotten, and Son as their foundation—since these are the names common to the Godhead and to the Manhood. In this way and on this basis they build up the tradition of the incarnation, the passion, and the resurrection.[55]

For Nestorius, the terms Christ, Son or Lord, were thus the correct titles to connote the faith experience of the oneness of the incarnate Saviour. These terms alone were the proper designation of the 'prosopon of union'—that observable phenomenon of the one reality of Christ in whom was also experienced the reality of a single human life (the prosopon of Jesus) and the very presence of the Godhead (the prosopon of the Logos); thus two realities.

Central to the coherence of Nestorius' thought was his belief that all christological thinking should always begin from this concrete experience the church has of Christ in his double reality.[56] He felt that christology ought never to begin with the man Jesus (which would lead to Adoptionism) or with the divine Logos (which would lead to Docetism or Apollinarism). He complained, for example, that Cyril began the whole doctrinal process from the wrong premise and consequently deduced fallacious results:

> You start your account with the creator of the natures and not with the prosopon of union. It is not the Logos who has become two-fold, it is the one Lord Jesus Christ who is two-fold in his natures. In him are seen all the characteristics of the divine Logos who has an eternal, impassible, and immortal nature, and all the characteristics of the

---

[54] Loofs (1905) p. 295.

[55] Loofs (1905) p. 174; Ibid. p. 175: 'Christ is the common name of the two natures.'

[56] For Cyril the exact opposite was the case.

> manhood which is mortal, passible, and created, and lastly those of the union and the incarnation.[57]

To begin the christological process from any other starting point than the Christ who stands before the eyes of faith as God's unique statement of what the concrete realisation of 'divine' means is, for Nestorius, tantamount to disregarding the whole economy of salvation. But if one starts one's doctrine from Christ, he insists, then the principal lesson learned should be the sense of abiding distinctness in the one Christ's revelation of the divine, and his revelation of the human.

In so far as a prosopon signifies 'observable aspect' or 'communicable external appearance' then perhaps we can sum up Nestorius' position so far as follows: The eyes of faith recognise in Christ two clearly observed aspects of his reality, which signify to the beholder divinity as well as humanity. Christ, therefore, has two prosopa. At the same time the eyes of faith recognise that this Christ who has two prosopa is not the same as those prosopa themselves. In other words Christ is not the Logos as such. It would be bad theology, for Nestorius, to speak of the pre-existent Christ, since he is not eternal as the Logos is. Nor would it be right to make unqualified statements about the impassibility of Christ since the radical qualification of human limitations and sufferings is an integral part of what the mind understands by the word 'Christ'.

But in just the same way as the Logos is not synonymous with Christ, neither is the man Jesus of Nazareth. Christ, for Nestorius, was no mere man. The word connotes far more than the term 'the man Jesus'; in fact it connotes the whole mystery of the intimate relationship of this man with the divine Logos, and the union of the Logos with him. Christ is not only a word for the union of these two prosopic realities, it is also the concrete experience, in some way, of how that union has taken place, how it is to be conceived, and how it ought to be articulated by the church. The term Christ signifies the experience of the encounter with this unique composite figure of the Son of God. In the light of this it is not enough merely to insist that there are two prosopa in Christ, because the experience of the unique revelation of Christ calls for the confession that here there is also the 'prosopon of union' the one Christ who manifests in a single prosopon (observable reality) the differentiated prosopa

---

[57] Book of Heraclides 225; Nau p. 136.

of the divine Logos, and the human Jesus. There are two prosopa, and there is one prosopon. This is why the starting point of one's consideration is all-important. If one begins always with the concrete experience of the incarnate Christ, the paradox is solved: the one is revealed as two-fold. The awareness of the double nature, however, is secondary to the experience of the actual oneness of the incarnate Christ, and is only arrived at by deduction from that oneness.

It should be clear by this point, if not earlier, that Nestorius' christological argument is only supported by a highly complex hermeneutic that demands a sharp degree of precision in its usage. The question of how many ordinary bishops of the fifth century, let alone the common people, would ever be able to follow him was not something that seemed to have worried him greatly, but his awareness of the problem certainly explains why he did not wish the christological question to be discussed in a general forum of bishops, as in any ordinary synod, but only by the select few who could demonstrate their dialectical qualifications for the task. This intellectual abstraction from the realities of the world (if not to say downright arrogance) was to prove his political downfall. For all his intellectual subtlety, Cyril, by contrast, knew his audiences better. In addition it is clear that at many instances the highly complex language of Nestorius raises as many questions as it solves. Cyril's main point of criticism voiced the doubts of many others at Ephesus—does not talk of 'the man Jesus' not inevitably commit his scheme to a double polarity of subject despite all his qualifications? We might also wish to query whether, despite all the complexity of his semantic rules, Nestorius actually did achieve what he set out to do, that is clarify the christological discussion. If so, the complexity might have been a tolerable price; but in reality his scheme to clarify the semantics had a flaw in the heart of it.

The problem was that Nestorius was using one and the same technical term to connote the disparate concepts of differentiation and convergence: there are two prosopa (Jesus and Logos) and only one prosopon (Christ). There is, of course, no sensible context whatsoever that would allow one to speak of three prosopa. It may well be that this economy of language in Nestorius led to a fatal weakness in the coherence of his theory, as Cyril argued, but it is clear enough that the caricature of his teaching that described it as no more than a repetition of the old Two Sons theory is an uneven reading of his intent. To this extent Cyril's synopsis of his opponent was inaccurate. But Cyril had nonetheless put his finger on the key matter and his criticism still had force in the way he argued from Nestorius' explicit statements to his necessary implications. In this regard Cyril had posed the essential question and voiced the fears of many others when he asked whether such a theory had done enough to secure a concept of unitive subject in Christ.

For all the force Nestorius brings to insisting that there are two prosopa in Christ, the divine Logos and the human Jesus (which certainly appeared to suggest, on first reading, that he may be talking about two subjects), he time and again stressed that the church's experience of Christ is as a single prosopon—a single subject of reference. What seems to be at issue, however, is that he approaches the concept of subjectivity largely in semantic terms, as the grammatical subject of reference in discourse, whereas Cyril tended to understand the subject primarily as the initiator of actions, especially the spiritually dynamic action of redemptive restoration of communion. It was this latter sense of spiritual subjectivity that was destined to win the day in christian philosophy. From this period in Late Antiquity, even down to our own age which understands subjectivity predominantly in psychological terms, the emergence of the concept of 'the person' was to have incalculable importance for the European consciousness, and it was to emerge in Cyril's sense: as signifying dynamic spiritual subjectivity and consciousness that stands as the direct and unmediated initiator of actions, words, and intentions which describe its personhood but do not constitute it.

Nestorius not only relied on his own theory of prosopic unity to define his christology, he also took account of other analogies and technical terms drawn from the previous patristic tradition. He partly depended on St. Gregory Nazianzen's language for the distinction of the physeis.[58] Gregory had used Greek grammatical pronouns (capable of connoting 'things' by the neutral, and personal subjects

---

[58] Yet he alarmed his contemporaries in the way that he forcibly rejected Gregory's corresponding language for connoting the union through the term 'mixture' (mixis). Gregory had applied both concepts together in a consciously sought balance between Diodore's tradition of disparity and Apollinaris' excessive unitivism. Nestorius' uncompromising rejection of 'mixis' as a christological term on the grounds that it was hopelessly Apollinarist was an unwitting refutation of the important Gregorian resolution, and only served to signal to many of his opponents both in Constantinople (Gregory Nazianzen's former see), and in Alexandria, that he was consciously tipping the balance back again in favour of Diodore and the Two Sons theory. Theodotus of Ancyra and other 'Cappadocian' bishops present at Ephesus found his interpretation of Gregory to be alien to their tradition, and allied themselves decidedly with Cyril.

by the masculine forms) to argue that Christ is two-fold in so far as one thing (allo), divinity, is seen alongside another thing (allo), humanity, but this does not thereby demand that each of those distinct realties amount to two personal identities (allos kai allos). He had encapsulated this, with his usual rhetorical flair, in the brilliantly succinct formula: 'Christ is one thing with another thing, not one person beside another person' (allo kai allo ouk allos kai allos). Nestorius makes a resumé of this in the Book of Heraclides. Two things are noticeable, however, firstly that the perceived need to highlight the sense of personal unity only came to him late in the day, and secondly that even when he addresses the issue, the clarity of Gregory's dictinction is somewhat missed because of Nestorius' preference for his own prosopic theory. So, for example, he says:

> Christ is indivisible in that he is Christ, but he is two-fold in that he is both God and Man. He is one in his sonship, but he is two-fold in that which assumes and that which is assumed. In the prosopon of the Son he is individual, but as in the case of two eyes, he is separate in the natures of manhood and Godhead. The result is we do not acknowledge two Christs, or two Sons, or Only Begottens, or Lords. We do not say One Son and another Son, not a first and a second Christ, but one and the same[59] who has been seen in created and uncreated nature.[60]

The fact that Nestorius so regularly rejected the charge that he taught a double subject christology like that of Diodore argues that the prosopon of union should not be considered as a 'third' prosopon understood in the same sense as the prosopon of divinity and the prosopon of humanity,[61] though this is something that he does not spell out clearly in his own text. The selfsame word is being used analogously by Nestorius but in a different sense to connote a different referent, Christ—the fact of God's correlation of two hitherto disparate natures.

Critics who ask,'How many prosopa did Nestorius actually believe in: one, two, or three?' do not grasp his real point. He was arguing that the eyes of faith meet one clear prosopon, the one Christ. This is the first external, empirical fact (prosopic reality) that strikes one.

---

[59] Greek: 'heis kai ho autos', viz. 'one and the same (subject)'. This was very close to Gregory's 'ouk allos kai allos', and was integral to Nestorius' sense of the one prosopon of the union. cf. Book of Heraclides 323. Nau p. 206.

[60] Loofs (1905) p. 280.

[61] cf. Loofs (1914) pp. 77f.

The prosopon of union, however, as Nestorius constantly reiterates, should thereafter be the constant source of reference for all christological language, worship, and speculative theology. At the same time this experience of the one Christ opens up into the experience of two levels of reality within Christ (the prosopa of deity and humanity). These latter prosopa are not equal in significance to the prosopon of union simply because they cannot be experienced independently of the prosopon of union, but rather inhere within Christ: this alone is the medium of our experience of these two levels of reality. But since they do not exist *in vacuo*, rather co-inhere in the prosopon of union, they cannot be conceived as two independent subjects of reference in themselves when one is considering the incarnation of the Son of God as Christ.

What Nestorius clearly does not mean by prosopon of union is a third prosopon that results from the self-sacrificing fusion of the other two prosopa that belong to the natures. This would be no different from the Apollinarist Krasis doctrine that he felt Cyril was propounding by means of his formula of hypostatic union.[62] What he does mean, I suggest, is that the oneness of Christ is not compromised by being composited, which was essentially the matter on which the whole controversy was turning. Ironically, and sadly, it was the selfsame point Cyril was so passionately arguing, though by another route that was by no means synonymous in other respects.

As Nestorius had ruled out any approach that envisaged a unification (henosis) of natures producing a God-Man, he proposed instead the notion of 'conjunction by interrelation' (schetike synapheia) of the respective prosopa of the two natures. His preferred terms to describe this association and bonding were: conjunction (synapheia); indwelling (kat' enoikesin); appropriation (oikeosis); or by the habituated possession (schesis) of the human prosopon by the prosopon of the Logos. In each of the analogical models one discerns the central element of his thought to be an emphasis on the divine prevenience and initiative whereby the Logos binds himself to the man Jesus in an unassailably intimate union, without destroying any of the free capacities of the human life he graces with his unlimited power and presence. Christ is revealed to the church as the sign of the intimacy of that union. Whenever we speak of Christ, or Son, or Lord, Nestorius tells us,

---

[62] 'We do not speak of a union of prosopa,' he says, 'but of natures.' Book of Heraclides 252. Nau p. 152.

we presume and invoke it. This never means that Christ is simply the Logos, or that Christ is simply Jesus. It does mean that the Logos is Christ, and that Jesus is Christ, because Christ is all that we understand of the union of the two realities of divine and human existence which christians deduce to have been harmonised in the one Christ who presents himself to human history as Lord and Teacher.

This synapheia of two realities Nestorius depicted as founded on the freedom of mutual love,[63] not on the necessities of nature—at the level of prosopon not of ousia. He takes great care to qualify this central term of synapheia by a series of predicates such as perfect (akra),[64] exact (akribes),[65] or continuous (dienekes).[66] It is an 'association' rooted in the 'good pleasure' of God, that is, God's grace, favour, and loving delight wherewith he commits himself to the incarnate life of a man. This notion of 'association by grace/ good pleasure' (synapheia kat' eudokian) was to be Nestorius' central technical term to connote the 'how' of the christological union. He was to be attacked on the basis that it was not a term that could be 'ontologically' grounded, but in his eyes at least the fact that it was a union based on the love and grace of God made it incomparably superior to any conception of a union based on the dictates of natural demands. He posited a relation based on God's will as a more elevated notion, and arguably a more stable notion, than a relation posited in terms of nature.

As a result of this synapheia the prosopa of two distinct and unaltered ousiai are united so intimately by graceful love, given by the Logos, received and reflected back by the man, that the eyes of faith can recognise one single Christ presented to the church's contemplation with but a single will and intelligence, inseparable and indivisible.[67] This intimate union and singleness of subjectivity comes about not because all distinctions between essences have been abolished in a 'physical' synthesis, but because of the depth and rigour of the relationship of love. This one Christ is the prosopon of the union. As Nestorius says:

> He is the subject of the two natures which are separated in essence, but united by love, and in one and the same prosopon.[68]

---

[63] Loofs (1905) 220; cf. Book of Heraclides 81, Nau p. 52; ibid.210–211, Nau pp. 127–128.

[64] Loofs (1905) pp. 178,275.

[65] Loofs (1905) p. 357.

[66] Loofs (1905) p. 275.

[67] Book of Heraclides 316–317, Nau pp. 201–202.

[68] Book of Heraclides 81, Nau p. 52.

The synapheia involved such perfect unanimity in the life of Christ that the spiritual subjectivity of the prosopon of union was 'as it were' one single being.[69] Nestorius expressed it as follows:

> He was emptied out (Phil 2.6) in a wholly incomprehensible manner, in an emptying out that had no parallel, and thus was manifested as one single spirit, one single will, one single intelligence, inseparable and indivisible as in one single being. God's will was his will.[70]

Such a notion of the synapheia went far beyond an idea of two prosopa in any kind of loose alliance, as many understood him to be saying. Here was a single prosopic reality, that composite reality of Christ, who combined and related in himself the utterly distinct essences of God and Man, which both continued to abide intact throughout the incarnation. What is also clear, however, is that his language securing unity of subject was not firm. To continue to speak in terms such as 'God's will was his will', appears to attribute to the man and to the Logos a distinct will, and a distinct personal identity. His opponents thus had grounds for thinking he was maintaining Two Sons and arguing a moral association founded on grace and thus comparable to the manner in which the Logos inspired and indwelt the prophets.

Nestorius objected to this reading of his theology, and probably never meant it from the outset, but it was undoubtedly only after the events that he took time to elaborate how his theory could avoid falling into this category. He argued that on his schema Christ was no mere prophet since no 'inspired man' had ever achieved the synonymity with God which Christ manifested to the eyes of faith. He meets the charge when he says:

> Our reply to the simple[71] is this—never in truth has anyone ever made use of the prosopon of God in his own prosopon; none of the prophets, none of the angels, only Our Lord Jesus Christ has said: 'I and the Father are One,' and 'Anyone who has seen me has seen the Father'.[72]

---

[69] Cyril objects to the constant qualifications 'as it were'; and suspects Nestorius' semantic application of the notion 'as a matter of words'. This was one serious difference between them. Nestorius' thought on this point is comparable to Origen's notion of the soul of Jesus adhering in love so closely to the Logos that they became, 'as it were', one. Origen applied the exegesis of the marriage text in Mt. 19.5–6 to this context (De Principiis 2.6). The Cappadocians mediate Origen's influence on christology to Nestorius.

[70] Book of Heraclides 102, Nau p. 67.

[71] Ironically implying that anyone (ie. Cyril) who deduces this from his writings must have to be simple-minded.

[72] Book of Heraclides 76, Nau p. 49; Ibid 83, Nau p. 53.

It was to be one of Nestorius' most bitter complaints against Cyril and Eusebius (of Dorylaeum) that this version of his doctrine had been propagated. In the Book of Heraclides he was to insist that even a mind as closed against him such as Eutyches could at least recognise that he had never taught this.[73] It was Cyril's point, however, that a doctrine's implicit premises are just as important as its explicit intentions, and time and again Cyril lays bare the extent to which Nestorius speaks in terms which constantly suggest association of subjects, and thus asks how does he free himself from the charge of being comparable to the ancient adoptionist heretics?

Nestorius laid stress on prosopic association, despite his opponent's objections, precisely in order to refute the notion of union at any natural level. God did not take to himself another nature, Nestorius tells us (directly contradicting Cyril's central thesis) but rather took up into an intimate union of love another prosopon. This he regarded as synonymous with the biblical phrase (Phil. 2.7) 'assuming the form of a slave':

> The Logos took the form of a slave for his prosopon, but not for his nature, and not by any changing of essence. God the Logos is said to have become flesh, and Son of Man, as regards the form and prosopon of the flesh, and of the man, of which he made use in order to make himself known to the world.[74]

The singleness of this prosopon of unity is witnessed in the oneness of the worship that the church offers to Christ because it spiritually recognises the unity involved in the incarnation:

> God the Logos, and the man in whom he came to be, are not numerically two, for the prosopon of both was one in dignity and honour, worshipped by all creation, and in no way and at no time ever divided by difference of purpose or will.[75]

Hence he coined another catchphrase that was to have a wide circulation and form a particular target for Cyril's apologetic:

> I hold the natures apart but unite the worship[76]

---

[73] The same Eutyches who would form the occasion for the Councils of Ephesus 449, and Chalcedon 451. At the time he was one of Nestorius' most vociferous critics among the monks at Constantinople. cf. Book of Heraclides 462, Nau p. 296f.

[74] Book of Heraclides 230, Nau p. 139; Loofs (1905) p. 358.

[75] Loofs (1905) 224.

[76] Loofs (1905) 262.

This one worship and honour given to Christ by all those who held true faith in the incarnation testified, for Nestorius, that the acknowledgement of the abiding distinctness of the natures in no way compromised the sense of unity in the prosopon of Christ:

> Christ is indivisible in that he is Christ, but he is two-fold in that he is both God and Man . . . . We do not acknowledge two Christs. . . . . . but one and the same who has been seen in created and uncreated nature.[77]

There are, accordingly, not Two Sons as far as Nestorius was concerned: that is not two independently conceived personal centres in Christ. He knows that this was a regular charge against him by his opponents[78] and he was most concerned to answer it.[79] He says, for example:

> I did not say that the soul was one and God the Logos another. What I said was that God the Logos was by essence one thing, and the Temple (Jn.2.19–21) by essence another, but that there was one Son by conjunction (synapheia).[80]

The unitive function of worship should not be underestimated in Nestorius' christology, for he believed that it was in the church's confession of praise that the true understanding of Christ's oneness was maintained. It was the matrix of all correct thinking about Christ:

> We acknowledge the difference of natures within the indivisible power of worship.[81]

The worship addressed to the one Christ thus draws into its ambit even the manhood, because the disparate essences have been joined, but even in the oneness of worship the difference of the natures is not abolished. But he expressed this in a syllogism that was to give his hearers the grave suspicion that he had Adoptionist intentions, or at least was indisputably wedded to the idea of Two Sons, no matter how many protestations he gave to the contrary:

> I worship him that is borne (ton phoroumenon) for the sake of Him who bears (dia ton phorounta), him that is visible for the sake of Him who is hidden.[82]

---

[77] Loofs (1905) 280.
[78] cf. Cyril. Epistles 3 & 10. and passim throughout the translated texts.
[79] Loofs (1905) 259, 275, 299.
[80] Loofs (1905) 308.
[81] Loofs (1905) 327; cf. Grillmeier (1975) p. 457.
[82] Loofs (1905) 262. This and several comparable texts are found in the translation,

The citation of this text, and many others like it, at his trial in Ephesus counted against him very badly indeed. Taking it in the most empathetic way we might agree that it was, nonetheless, not meant to convey an Adoptionist theory. It refers, yet again, to the enduring distinctness of ousiai and their respective prosopa which was a basic theological axiom for Nestorius. The prosopon of the man could not be called God (this for him would be an illegitimate use of the communicatio idiomatum but rather was God-bearer (theophoros) or possessor of the Godhead (ktetor tes theotetos). Nestorius, then, appears to be using the notion of the commonality of worship in a very similar way that Cyril was to apply the full range of communicatio idiomatum language. It is an important avenue for him to stress the subjective unity of the Christ. As he said:

> The prosopon of both was one in dignity and honour (cultus), worshipped by all creation.[83]

And again:

> Two natures have but one Lordship, and one power or might, and one prosopon in one and the same dignity and honour.[84]

This shows Nestorius' sense of the unity of Christ to have been a dynamic concept (based on power, might, will, prosopic manifestation) rather than an essentialist one. The force of the prosopic union was supplied by the moral power of the adhering love of God to the human life he had chosen to adopt as his manifestation to the world. The theory, to that extent, had a long pedigree behind it. Its problematic was that it was unclear, at least as far as the majority of its hearers were concerned (including Antiochenes as well as Alexandrians), on how far the humanness with which the Logos united was so discrete a reality as to be more than a merely grammatical subject of reference. Nestorius' way of referring to 'the man Jesus' only served to sharpen the question, and many found that his replies to the criticism were more in the form of dismissals than answers.

Nestorius' preferred manner of posing the christological issue has

---

following, of the Synodical Deposition of Nestorius. The considerable number of such texts which sounded for all the world like acknowledgements of double subjectivity in Nestorius' incarnation thought were simply assembled by Cyril and presented to the conciliar Fathers at Ephesus. They are, unquestionably, a hostile collation of Nestorius' thought. They are equally a clear indication of how vague he was over such a central issue.

[83] Loofs (1905) 224.

[84] Loofs (1905) 196.

evidently laid great stress on the axiomatic fact of the abiding distinctness of the two natures in Christ. In so doing he followed Theodore Mopsuestia's refusal to reduce any of the force involved in confessing Jesus as a man. He is not just 'Man' in general, he must be seen as 'a man' in particular. He was determined on arguing this, perhaps not fully recognising the problematic involved in it. The meaning of 'truly human' for Nestorius was more than symbolic, in the sense that it would have sufficed for many of his day to admit that the Logos assumed a generic human nature as a vehicle of revelation. Nestorius invariably speaks about the Logos uniting himself with the life of 'a man', and thus attributes to Jesus, as that man, the full range of authentic human experiences.

In holding firm to the sense of the abiding duality of natures in Christ we saw how Nestorius absolutely ruled out any legitimacy in considering the locus of christological union within the domain of a 'naturalistic' analogy such as that of Krasis (the fusion together of elements—such as mixed wine and water). He regarded any form of absorption theory as unable to preserve the distinctness of the ousiai, and if the manhood did not fully endure in Christ the moral freedom of the union would have been destroyed since he did not see how anyone could posit a free human will in Jesus if such an unequal Krasis had taken place, with the immense power of the deity absorbing and drowning the fragile humanity in some envisaged process of deification. This latter approach Nestorius constantly disparaged while for Cyril it stood as one of the central values and achievements of the Gospel of incarnation.

Replacing the notion of deification of manhood, as too dangerously suggesting some alteration in one or both of the ousiai, Nestorius instead pointed to the perfectly free will of the human Jesus, wholly obedient to the will of God (the Logos) and intimately united with him as the excelling sign and means of salvation. Nestorius offered such a vision of Jesus as the Leader and Guide of the ethical life, at once our greatest example and our teacher, mainly because he was at heart a reformist preacher and as such concerned primarily with Christianity as a moral paideia.

In short, rejecting the possibility of a christological union based on natural/ousia[85] terms, Nestorius had turned instead to the notion of will and love, the moral domain, as the locus of his christological

[85] In natura et secundum naturam: as was the case with both the Arian and Apollinarist christologies. See Book of Heraclides 250–251, Nau, pp. 151–152.

theory. Theodore had already pondered on what basis the christological union could be posited, and had considered three alternatives:

(a) a union by nature (kat'ousian);

(b) a union by mutual engagement (kat'energeian);

(c) a union by God's good favour/grace (kat' eudokian).

He had determined that the third was the only feasible option, a view with which Nestorius concurred, as we have seen. The natural union implied such mechanical necessity, for the Antiochenes, and seemed to threaten the very survival of at least one of the natures as an objective reality, that the incarnation might be left without real moral significance. A union by mutual engagement made no allowance for the fact that any human moral striving (energeia) was wholly unequal to the power and capacity of the deity, and no real meeting of the Godhead and manhood could take place on this level with any suggestion of balance or encounter, let alone equality. Only in the third category, God's infinitely compassionate condescension in love and grace to his creatures, did a viable model emerge. The unequal equation between God and man is even partly levelled here by a meeting of loving wills that unite at the highest committment of each capacity, a meeting that is made possible and initiated by the condescension in love from the part of God. The grace of God the Logos, therefore, ennobles the man Jesus in the totality of its love so that each reality abides wholly in the other.

Nestorius seems to have made a move here which Augustine independently had reached for in his De Trinitate that, contrary to the traditional canons of Aristotelian logic, Grace (charis) could be posited in relation to God as a more fundamental category than nature (physis). In the case of christology, Nestorius, in following Theodore's lead, posed the terms of the union precisely on this basis.[86] It has been a theological insight which has attracted much recent christological attention and no little interest[87] in how it could be reapplied in the cause of restating a contemporary christology. By this theory of graceful

---

[86] cf. R Greer (1983) 82–98.

[87] D.M. Baillie's elegant book, God was In Christ, London, 1956, is much concerned with the implications. It is often erroneously thought that Cyril's preferred stress on a natural basis for the christological union divorces him from this insight. In fact Cyril regards human nature as the primary gift of God's grace, and its restoration in Christ as the primary end of the incarnation. He regards the divine nature, however, as the source of all grace, and thus does not believe that the concepts nature and grace can be separated in any meaningful sense. Nestorius' attitude in the distinction he made was one that Augustine shared independently because of his particular theology

conjunction Nestorius envisaged the two realities of Christ, the divine and human life, seamlessly joined but never confused, or diminished, or hindered in their respective abilities. Both are perfectly harmonised like two notes sounding together clearly as one pure sound, and mutually bound together by the unshakeable force of divine grace and love. In ruling out a natural union it seemed to many of his opponents that Nestorius had adopted a merely voluntarist conception of the incarnation, a moral union which however fruitful it might be in offering exemplarist possibilities of meaning for the incarnation, could never hope to match the force, stability, and grandeur of a theory of union based on an ontological foundation. He, on the other hand, did not wish to differentiate too rigidly an ontological union from the use of grace-union. If the christological union was founded on God's grace and choice then this was as ontologically stable and unshakeable as could be, and on a higher level than anything within the creation. The difference between the opposing schemes of christology is probably beter seen, not as a conflict between ontological models of union on the one side, and voluntarist models on the other, but a choice between analogies of the christological union based on notions of what things are, and how things are. Nestorius tended towards the latter, his opponents believed the former included it and did not feel the distinction to be worth the complications it introduced in other areas of the debate.

The main question in the face of all this, is whether or not Nestorius has done enough to convey a clear sense to his hearers of how such a theory accounts for a united 'personality' of the Redeemer. We have seen how, in the aftermath of his deposition, he insisted that he had meant to teach that Christ was one, meaning that there was only one centre of personal action, will, and understanding in him formed of an intimate union of two distinct realities that had been perfectly harmonised in love. It was his language about 'the man Jesus', however, that seemed to many of his contemporaries at Ephesus, an unavoidable lapse into a double subject christology. This might not have been his intent but three factors weakened his logical position in this regard.

The first was his rigid sense of what christological statements were permissible and on what terms. This was his severe view of the

---

of grace as utterly distinct from nature. Following in this Western Augustinian tradition Baillie rightly sees a strong connection between Nestorius and many of the Western presuppositions.

limitations of the communicatio idiomatum which we have noted. The second was the inflexibility of the only available technical term he had to connote the union—prosopon. He had made it central to his doctrine that a union based on ousia or hypostasis or physis was illegitimate, but this effectively left him with only the one term to connote differentiation (the prosopon of each ousia) and convergence (the prosopon of the union) in the one Christ. To put one word to work so hard gave rise to no small difficulties. Even long years after the events he seems, in the Book of Heraclides, still to have difficulties clarifying his different uses of prosopon. The third was his excessive schematisation of religious language, which denigrated statements of popular piety and called for intellectual or rational exactness. While in one sense this was (and still is) a laudable aim in theology, in another sense it neglected the fact that christian spirituality and worship was the primary articulator of orthodoxy. Whereas for Nestorius attempts to cross over language categories referring to the incarnate Lord were fundamentally misguided, for Cyril they were the very heart of prayer, and the foundations of an orthodox christology: one, that is, that safeguarded and conveyed the power of the christian doctrine of salvation. In the end, at Ephesus, despite his protests, Nestorius was not judged by academics but in the main by simple bishops on the grounds of the familiar pieties and prayers that had formed their own spiritualities, and on which grounds they felt far closer to Cyril than to the rather scornful and elitist patriarch of Constantinople.

On the one hand Nestorius had presented an interesting doctrine of the single Christ (the prosopon of union) which rejected any form of synthesis by essence or nature. The unity of these two disparate essences was achieved at the level of prosopic manifestations:

> The natures are not known in their respective diversities as if without prosopon or without hypostasis. One does not conceive of two prosopa of sons, nor again two prosopa of men, but of a single man who is moved in the same way by the other. The union of prosopa took place in prosopon (at prosopic level), not in essence or nature. One must not think of an essence without a hypostasis[88] as if the union had taken place in an essence,[89] and that there was a prosopon of a single essence.

---

[88] This was the natural result of Cyril's theology of hypostatic union—the human nature did not have its own human hypostasis, and was thus not a separate human entity (the man Jesus), simply the human nature of the divine Word; and the Word hypostatised it.

[89] The opposite of what Cyril said, though an indication of how Nestorius misheard

> The natures subsist in their prosopa, and in their own natures, and in the prosopon of union. As for the natural prosopon of each one, then one makes use of the other by virtue of the union. In this sense there is only one prosopon for the two natures.[90]

On the other hand, the clarity of his insistence on the oneness of Christ seemed hopelessly compromised to many, not only by his insistence on the abiding duality of discrete natures but also by his language on the duality of the natural prosopa abiding in Christ, which seemed to argue a plurality of subject. His frequent references to 'the man Jesus' did nothing to disperse such suspicions.

In the Book of Heraclides, the fruit of his long exile, and the result of considerable afterthought on the events that had transpired, Nestorius had more time to devote to elaborating how the prosopon of union could be conceived. Abramowski[91] thought that much of the work was inauthentic, or at least the result of very considerable hindsight, but later studies have since argued for a more positive view of the evidence.[92] It would seem reasonable to suppose, however, that the doctrine of the 'mutual reciprocity', or 'mutual prosopic interchange', which Nestorius proposes in this text, is the result of further theological thought on his part as he tried to strengthen the weak point of his doctrine. This elaborated notion argues that:

> The prosopon of one essence even makes use of the prosopon of the other essence.

and that the mutual use is so intimate an appropriation that:

> The prosopon of one is also that of the other.[93]

The key notion in this concept is mutual interchange and dynamic involvement:

> The divinity makes use of the humanity's prosopon, and the humanity that of the divinity. In this way we say that there is only one single prosopon for both. In such a manner is God shown to be complete, since his nature suffers no diminishment from the union. In the same way the man is complete and lacking nothing (as a result of the union)

---

his intent. Nestorius thinks Cyril's hypostasis is a synonym of ousia, whereas it was meant to signify concrete individuation (the 'person' of the divine Logos).

90 Book of Heraclides, 305, Nau pp. 193–194.

91 Abramowski (1963).

92 Scipioni (1975); Chesnut (1978).

93 Book of Heraclides 305, Nau p. 144.

> of all the functions and limitations of his nature . . . . . The natures are united without confusion and make mutual use of their respective prosopa.[94]

He had evidently designed this strengthening of his model of the union without having to abandon any of his rigour in insisting that the two natures in Christ endured unaltered and unconfused. One notes, yet again, the influence the Kenosis hymn in Philippians 2 had on his mind:

> We do not speak of a union of prosopa but a union of natures, for in the union there is only one prosopon but in the natures there are two, such that the prosopon (of union) should be recognised in them both. The prosopon, in short, is common, one and the same. The form of the servant (Phil.2.7) belongs to the divinity, and that of the divinity belongs to the humanity. So, the prosopon is one and the same but not the essence, because the essence of the form of God, and the essence of the form of a servant abide separately in their hypostases.[95]

To what extent did Nestorius succeed in presenting a credible and comprehensible picture of the christological union? Modern scholarship has been divided on both issues.[96] L. Scipioni has defended his intention to present a logical single-subject doctrine:

'It is clear that it is always a matter of the same person, except that the term Logos sees this person in his divine nature as such, whereas the terms Son, Lord, and Christ, see him directly as a person. For this reason Nestorius is able to predicate of the person existence in both natures, human and divine.'[97]

Scipioni, however, has the modern advantage of using the word 'person' as a strong psychic subject referent, a terminological possibility not open to Nestorius in his time. Nestorius' insistence that he did not mean to teach Two Sons, his use of the notion of worship to demonstrate and celebrate the unity of will and operations in Christ, and his argument that there was but one seat of understanding in Christ, amount to a considerable body of evidence demonstrating he had moved away from the crude and antique sense of Two Sons christology. On the other hand his bluster of technical terms, where he seems to be ready to move mountains rather than face the issue

---

94 Book of Heraclides 333–334. Nau p. 212 f.

95 Book of Heraclides 252, Nau p. 152.

96 L. Wickham (1983) describes Nestorius' system as 'incredible' and innately obscurantist, pp. xix–xx.

97 Scipioni (1975) qv. pp. 386–392.

of subjectivity directly (for he senses that the Logos as personal subject cannot be directly attributed with the works of the flesh), argues that he never grasped the solution of the problem really clearly. H.E.W. Turner's comment was entirely apposite in this regard when he noted that Nestorius' failure did not lie in positing a double personality in Christ, but rather in being unable to offer a convincing explanation, on his logical terms, of why there should not have been one.[98] This was certainly Cyril's consistent and sustained reaction to everything he read in Nestorius.

The christological scheme which Nestorius proposed is complicated, at times highly obscure, and always obsessively demanding of semantic exactness in the formularies the faithful may or may not hold about Christ. To this extent it was an intellectual's christology, unable to tap the deep springs of popular imagination and mysticism on which Cyril was able to draw. Nestorius occupied a position which was difficult to state but only too easy to misunderstand, and equally easy to misrepresent in the most damaging ways. The way he preferred to debate, with heavy use of sarcastic *reductio ad absurdum* did nothing to endear him to his intellectual opponents. His unquestioning belief in the all sufficing brilliance of his own mind and his arrogance to those he regarded as his inferiors, could be said to be the direct causes of his downfall, politically as well as doctrinally. He had clearly raised some extremely important issues in his teaching. He exposed the problems and aspects of christology that the fifth century church urgently needed to address. His own exposition had so many difficulties in it that it was inevitably misheard, and rejected because it was misheard. But this is not the whole matter, and one ought to be wary of those studies which hail him as a misunderstood genius who has much to offer contemporary theology.[99] Even with the most sympathetic and patient of exegeses, which he did not receive in antiquity needless to say, the fact still remains that time and again one senses that he is deliberately arguing around central issues instead of facing them plainly.

Cyril maintained that he was so 'slippery' in his use of language that he would not be satisfied with his orthodoxy of intent unless Nestorius signed a prepared statement (The Chapters). But he also

---

[98] Turner (1976) p. 51; Wickham too (1983. p.xx.) regards Nestorius' doctrine, behind all its bluster of technicalities, as entirely unable to explain subject unity in Christ.

[99] As for example, A.R. Vine (1948); or Anastos (1962).

argued from start to finish that he was attacking this whole tradition (Nestorius as well as Diodore and Theodore) because of fundamentally unacceptable implications in its doctrine. To this extent, however much one may clarify Nestorius, or read him in the best light possible, it was Cyril's thesis that his whole christological scheme did not, and was not able to, represent the mind of the church on one of the central dogmas of the faith. It was this conviction that spurred on Cyril to compose, after 429, the most coherently sustained and brilliantly argued christology the church had yet witnessed. It is to this that we shall now turn.

CHAPTER THREE

THE CHRISTOLOGY OF CYRIL

1. Redemptive Deification: Cyril's Presuppositions and Major Concerns

The christology of St. Cyril is the driving force of his entire theological vision. Like Athanasius before him, Cyril understands the church's christological doctrine to be the central point to which and from which all other comprehensions run. It is the central resolution of all thought about revelation, atonement, and the ascent to the life-giving vision of God. The christological argument is, thus, fundamentally about soteriology and worship, and this is why these aspects feature so strongly in Cyril's argument with Nestorius. In this profoundly dynamic coherence that characterises Alexandrian thought, something in which Cyril shares in abundance, this great patristic tradition approaches the grandeur of the theology of the Fourth Gospel.

Cyril's thought shows a remarkable consistency both in its tenor and direction.[1] He is a subtle thinker who reacts and adapts to circumstances, especially in the crisis years of the Nestorian argument, when his thought responded to the twin stimuli of criticism from determined theological opponents, as well as a major programme of patristic reading which he imposed on himself as preparation for the battle he knew was to come. In these years, especially 430 to 438, the pace of the political and theological exchange was fast and furious. Clarifications were made on terminology, central issues were established, and compromises reached in appropriate areas. Cyril's was not a rigid mind. For him the words were less important than the essential theological truth they were attempting to enshrine. Like Athanasius, Cyril was ready enough to be flexible on terms if and when he felt his basic point had been secured. He has attracted criticism for this, as someone who was confused or inconsistent, but the criticism frequently betrays an ignorance of the 'economic' nature of most

[1] cf. Liebaert (1951) p. 237; De Durand (1964) pp. 149–150; *pace* those who think that the writings of post 431 demonstrate a radical shift of direction.

patristic writing, as well as sometimes a careless exegesis of Cyril's texts, and it is also important to keep in mind that one of the central aspects of this whole fifth century controversy was the way that it showed up the church's universally pressing need for a commonly agreed technical language. It is not entirely apposite, in such circumstances, to accuse Cyril of terminological inconsistency, when he and all his contemporary protagonists are labouring towards this end, none being able to presuppose it. In fact, despite sharing in the common semantic disorganisation of the day (and using some terms at times as inconsistently as any of his contemporaries)[2] Cyril does succeed in establishing a terminology which, in the main, was to emerge as having classical and oecumenical status for subsequent christianity.

Behind the words, however, and in spite of his slightly varying analogies, Cyril's central ideas and his narrative discourse remained remarkably consistent from beginning to end. It is sufficient proof of this to be able to offer any of Cyril's main christological writings to random scrutiny, for there one sees the same dominant concerns arising time after time. The extensive body of work in translation offered in this present volume covers a decade of his writings from 429 onwards, the total extent of the Nestorian controversy. Readers can see for themselves, without any difficulty, this essential consistency of argument, and how it transcends a dependence on narrow formulas in the spaciousness of its christological design.

The early works, before 428, are largely exegetical, and his christological ideas are more abstractly presented there than in the specific and apologetical context of the Nestorian debate. Nevertheless, it is still clear that even before 428 Cyril's mind had already been shaped, formed in the living christological tradition of his church, summarised in the great Athanasius. This Alexandrian tradition, from Clement and Origen, through Alexander, Athanasius, and Didymus, was characterised by its realist and dynamic soteriology. It began its consideration of all theology in terms of the narrative of the eternal Lord's acts of salvation towards his people. Adopting the biblical and philosophical conception of the divine Logos who communicated the vision of the invisible God to earth,[3] the Alexandrians went on

---

[2] For a good analysis of the various Cyrilline employments of the key term 'hypostasis' see Du Manoir (1944) p. 126f.

[3] As, for example, in the Sophia figure of the Wisdom literature (Prov. 8.22, Sir.24, and passim) interpreted by Philo as the Logos; or in Jn.1.1–14; or 'pre-existence' texts such as Ephes.1.3f; Phil.2.6f; Coloss. 1.15f. The Apologists develop the terms

to expound the implications of this essential paradox in God's providential revelation.

In patristic Logos doctrine the incommunicable gulf between the absolute simplicity of the transcendent God, and the diffused world of immanent reality (the distance between the unchanging One and the variable Many),[4] had been bridged by the divine Logos. From the time of Origen onwards, it had been established in christian discourse that the Logos shared the nature of God's transcendence and yet (and here the paradoxical qualification was crucial) was the creative force of God who thus, in his very act of creation, established a rapport between himself and that relative or non-absolute order of being which he had instituted. The most frequent way this was conceived in Alexandrian patristic thought, again on the basis of the scriptures, was the doctrine of the Image.[5] On this understanding, the invisible and unapproachable Godhead was fully 'imaged' in the Logos. This image retained the character of the Absolute One, but was not specifically ontologically characterised, as was the One, by its unapproachable invisibility and, in consequence, when the divine image 'imaged itself' in creating the world, it thereby became the one source and medium of all divine revelation. The Supreme God was revealed to the world only through the Logos, and the world could only approach the unapproachable through the divine Logos who had given creation (particularly the soul of man) the capacity to relate to him through the mirror of his own life-force which he had left within the human soul, that is the spiritual intellect or Nous of man. Thus, the One and the Many were bridged in a way that did not compromise God's transcendence, nor weaken the biblical sense of his providential nearness to his people.

The rise to prominence of this fundamental structure of Alexandrian thought on the nature of God's self-revelation to the created order, was of momentous significance in the history of christian doctrine, because on its way to a clear articulation it passed through the fires of the great fourth century controversies it had engendered, notably

of Logos theology into the first christian system and the great work of Clement and Origen ensures that it will have a dominant influence as a way of interpreting the biblical texts referring to salvation and revelation in Christ.

[4] For an exposition of the later Platonic doctrine of the One and the Many cf. Wolfson (1956); also J. Bussanich, The One and Its Relation to Intellect in Plotinus, Leiden, 1988.

[5] As, for example, in Coloss. 1.15; cf. Roldanus (1968); P.E. Hughes, The True Image, Grand Rapids, 1989.

Arianism, Macedonianism, and Apollinarism. The theological scheme of the divine Logos had emerged from all this debate as a basic interpretation of the church's understanding of God as Trinity, and of his historical manifestation in time in an incarnation.

The very scheme of Logos theology had been attacked on different grounds by Arius, the Macedonians,[6] and Apollinaris, because of its central paradox—the Logos as Image of the Invisible who at once retained the full character of the divine (impassible, unchangeable, unapproachable, invisible) and yet was manifested to the creation as the revealer-God. Athanasius and the Cappadocian Fathers[7] had fought hard to preserve this paradox, not as an illogicality as their opponents had argued, but as the dynamic heart of the mystery of God's self-disclosure, but up to the time of Cyril it would be fair to say that the scheme had been able to clarify its doctrine of the 'Eternal Logos' (the Trinitarian relationships) far more satisfactorily than it had its conception of how the Logos entered into full communion with a particular historical and relativised life in the incarnation. The first great attempt to do this latter task, undertaken by a significant member of the Alexandrian school, Apollinaris of Laodicea, had come to grief publicly and disastrously.

Apollinaris had sensed the inherent paradox of the scheme and recognised its dangers. As the Arians had pointed out, if the Logos is the direct subject of a limited life and it is he who is said, as in the scriptures for example, to suffer and die, then how can there be any logical way to retain a belief in the Logos as impassible and immortal? For the Arians the scriptural references to Jesus' death, as attributed to the Logos as a synonymous subject with Jesus, were proof positive that the Logos was not impassible, and thus not divine. Accordingly, for the Arians and Pneumatomachians, this aborted any further speculation on the Trinity as unnecessary.

Apollinaris knew rightly enough that any equivocation on the central point of this argument (that there was a synonymity of subject between the Logos and Jesus) would ruin the entire religious force of the Alexandrian theology, that is its dynamic understanding of salvific revelation and its directness of the encounter between God and Man

---

6 Extreme later form of Arianism, otherwise known as Pneumatomachianism (Spirit-fighting), because it denied the deity of the Spirit and the very need for a doctrine of Trinity.

7 Sts. Basil the Great, Gregory the Theologian, Gregory Nyssa and Amphilokius of Ikonium.

in Christ. And he knew, equally well, that an urgent answer had to be given to the problem of subject reference thus posed. Apollinaris' solution was to cut the Gordian knot. If the essential constitution of man included the image of the Logos in the soul or Nous (the spiritual intellect) of man, and it was this that formed the link between man's limited life and his transcendent aspirations to the divine vision, then surely man's soul or Nous was an 'image of the image (Logos) of God'? On the basis of this[8] Apollinaris went on to suggest that the christological problem as it now stood at the end of the fourth century was how to avoid a doctrine of two subjects in the incarnation, on the one hand, and on the other hand a single subject doctrine which would hopelessly relativise the Logos in a changeable human life, in a way that could only demonstrate his essential non-deity.

Apollinaris had correctly isolated the the key problem of the day, that is the manner of the subject-unity or personal integrity of the incarnate Lord. His progress towards a solution, however, alienated both his Arian opponents and his orthodox Nicene friends, such as Athanasius. From the outset, the very notion of a single subject christology was anathema to his Antiochene contemporaries, such as Diodore of Tarsus, whose own theology of Two Sons Apollinaris, in turn, abhorred. Athanasius' letter to Epictetus and Gregory Nazianzen's letter to Cledonius represent the late fourth century realisation that Apollinaris' approach must not be allowed, any longer, to carry the flag on behalf of the Logos theology.[9]

Apollinaris' way out of his christological problems was to posit a single-subject christology where the subject was purely the Logos as existing eternally in his pre-existent state—for example, omniscient, impassible, immortal. He explained the incarnate union of the Word on the grounds that when the Logos relates to human beings generally, it is on the basis of the Image of God relating to the image of the image within the human constitution. In the case of the Logos' particular relation to man in the precise act of his own incarnation, the same general rules were held to apply. But, for Apollinaris, here in this particular case the Image of God has no need whatsoever to unite

[8] For a closer study of Apollinaris' thought cf. Raven (1923), Grillmeier (1975), Muhlenberg (1969).

[9] Both texts became classical in patristic literature; they were also of importance in Cyril's debate with the Antiochenes. They have, accordingly, been reproduced in the Appendix. Their foundational value for much of Cyril's christology can be readily discerned.

with any 'image of the image', for what need would there be for this? In the case of the Logos' personal incarnation the human 'image of the image' was thus dispensed with as an unnecessary factor once the Image itself had come to be present. Put in other terms, if the Logos is the archetype of all human spiritual intellects, or souls, then in the case of the divine incarnation the archetype simply replaced the soul of Jesus, it did not unite with it. The soul of Jesus was, therefore, unnecessary from the outset and never actually existed, since the Logos himself always supplied the spiritual intellect of the incarnate Lord. For Apollinaris, this secured the single subjectivity of the incarnation. It was, moreover, an improvement on the general run of things as he saw it, for who would not prefer the design archetype to the imaged model? Was not the Lord's humanity, on this conception, a 'divine improvement' on the general quality of human nature?

No less importantly, he argued that this conception of ontological unity, not association, (a 'physical' model of the incarnation), secured the necessary transcendence of the Logos. Since there was no human psyche in Christ, there was no meaningful way in which one could say that the Logos suffered, or was relativised by his incarnate acts. Suffering, fatigue, age and change, all of which were witnessed in the biblical accounts, were all entirely referable to the body alone, aspects of a corporeal existence. The Logos himself might 'be said' to suffer but he did not really suffer at all, only his flesh suffered, as is the wont of flesh. Yet at the same time that flesh was animated (en-souled) by the infinitely powerful deity of the Logos, and was accordingly a divine instrument that showed its transformed nature by its ability to heal, to raise the dead, and ultimately to crush all suffering and death in the glorious resurrection. Apollinaris insisted that this sense of the incarnational relation between God and man in Jesus was not simply a theory of flesh 'added on' to the Logos, but very much a composited unity. The flesh formed 'one natural reality' (Mia Physis) with the Logos. It was ontologically, naturally, united with him (synousiomene kai symphytos).[10]

Hand in hand with Apollinaris' stress on the single subjectivity goes a very tight conception of the incarnate union on the basis of a compositional model, naturally posited. He uses words such as 'mixture' and 'fusion' (mixis, synkrasis, synchysis) between the Logos and his

[10] Cf. Lietzmann (1904) pp. 257–260 (the standard collection of the fragments of Apollinaris).

flesh, quite deliberately and provocatively, to heighten what he saw as the soteriological power of his theological model. He played with the paradox of how the unchangeable Logos could be said to be 'fused' intimately with the flesh, by stressing, all the time, that the apparently shocking implication of the relativisation of the Logos (his being 'changed' into fleshly reality) could not apply, given that the flesh in question had no independent or personal reality, outside the Logos' own life. So, for example, he says:

> The flesh, being dependent for its motion on some other principle of movement and action (whatever the principle may be), is not of itself a complete living entity, but in order to become one enters into fusion with something else. So it united itself with the heavenly governing principle[11] and was fused with it. . . . . . Thus out of the moved and the mover was compounded a single living entity—not two, and certainly not a singleness that was composed of two complete self-moving principles.[12]

If Apollinaris felt he had secured the pass against his opponents, others were not so sure. Even his Nicene friends were antagonistic. They felt that his point about single subjectivity and his refusal of bi-polarity in Christ were both quite right, but they did not like the way he had arrived there.[13] What Apollinaris saw as the 'improvement' of human nature in the Logos' dismissal and personal replacement of the Nous in Jesus, was seen by others to be the destruction of the quintessential part of the humanity. Gregory Nazianzen was later to sum up this objection in perhaps the most famous phrase of all patristic soteriology: 'What he (the Logos) has not assumed, he has not healed.'[14]

Apollinaris had implicitly preferred a philosophical model of the constitution of man to the less sophisticated biblical anthropology that characterises, for example, Athanasius' and Gregory Nazianzen's doctrine, despite all their philosophical flirtations. For Apollinaris,

---

[11] The hegemonikon of the Logos as its animating force.

[12] Lietzmann (1904) fragm. 107, p. 232.

[13] Accordingly, when Cyril maintains both principles of single subjectivity, and refusal of bi-polarity, he is not per se, being Apollinarist. It is only the inability of some critics to separate out from Apollinaris' doctrine the heartland of the Alexandrian tradition from his own heavily platonising elements, that has led them to see in Cyril's maintenance of the old tradition a revival of Apollinarism. Cyril is able to rescue the Alexandrian tradition precisely because he can express these main points without having to subscribe to the damaging implications of Apollinaris. In this, Cyril follows the tradition of Athanasius and Gregory Nazianzen.

[14] Letter 101 to Cledonius, see Appendix.

following a Platonic lead, the Nous was not just an essential part of man, it was the essential man. The body was subordinate to it as an ontological accident. If the Logos was enfleshed, then he was genuinely living a human and corporeal life, and yet, equally, was not subject to its limitations. In the letters to Epictetus and Cledonius, respectively, Athanasius and Gregory basically dissent from the Platonic premiss that man is his Nous, and instead they remained faithful to a biblical, semitic, anthropology that demanded a more composite reckoning-in of the body as a fundamental part of the anthropological equation.

In a real sense, however, Apollinaris had tried, more elaborately than they, to elucidate this problem of integral subject-unity in the incarnation. The later Athanasian and Cappadocian christology signals the perceived failure of Apollinaris' attempt, on important grounds that carried with them a central body of orthodox assent that culminated in Apollinaris' international synodical condemnation between 377 and 381.[15] Nonetheless, even after the late fourth century orthodox restatement of the need for a human soul to secure a full sense of the Lord's incarnate humanity, there still remained a need to arrive at a clear articulation of how the doctrine of single-subjectivity could be reconciled with the presence, in Christ, of this human soul which was now required of any orthodox christology. The central problem Apollinaris was addressing had now re-surfaced. As he saw it, if Christ had a human soul he was a human person, and thus there was no way out from an incarnational scheme that would have to admit two persons in the incarnate Lord, or two sons. If his solution of denying the soul was refused, the problem rose again with even greater urgency.

This was the face of the impasse in the generation of Cyril. Not much had been done to advance the argument since the Cappadocians, but the fifty years intervening had undoubtedly created a new climate of Alexandrian thought, and a new context of argument as signalled by Athanasius' letter to Epictetus and the treatises Contra Apollinarem.[16] This new context is witnessed in Didymus the Blind, the leader of the catechetical school in Alexandria and possibly one of Cyril's early

[15] At the Synod of Rome in 377, Synod of Alexandria 378, Synod of Antioch 379, and the Oecumenical Council of Constantinople in 381.

[16] Even if not by Athanasius, certainly Alexandrian and 'Athanasian' in their theological scope. For a defence of the possible Athanasian authorship of the treatises cf. Dragas (1985). The introductory study of this latter work elucidates a far truer conception of Athanasian christology than is gained from the currently popular Grillmeier and Richard 'mythos' of Logos-Sarx Logos Anthropos schematisations, which have been so artificially imposed as a straightjacket on so much of the debate.

tutors, and not least in the thought of Cyril himself. Cyril moves across the whole range of the Alexandrian insight and finally completes the system as a result of the great controversies which embroiled him in the decade after 428. By this stage the Apollinarist heresy had been isolated and identified as essentially the denial of the soul in Christ and the notorious mixture or fusion theory of the christological union. For Didymus and Cyril these are now well-charted rocks that are to be avoided. Time and again Cyril explicitly affirms the necessity of a soul in Christ, and condemns the notion of 'confusion' of natures in the one Christ. Technically this exonerates him from the charge of Apollinarism *per se*. It remains to be seen whether he was able to meet the challenge Apollinaris had posed any more successfully than he; that is, how the existence of a soul in Christ could be reconciled with a single-subject christology.

As Cyril pointed out to those who accused him at every turn of being Apollinarist:[17] 'Not everything a heretic says is necessarily heretical'.[18] This is a basic fact that has been too often ignored in the argument about the so-called Apollinarism of Cyril. As far as Cyril was concerned, even if Apollinaris' overall scheme had been a failure, his fundamental insights that the church's faith demanded a confession of a single subject in the incarnate Lord, and also his fidelity to the Alexandrian tradition (at least in his desire to safeguard a dynamic soteriology) were both absolutely and uncontrovertibly right. Cyril was determined to preserve a theological insistence on both these premises, and did not feel indebted to Apollinaris for them, despite his opponents' accusations. He rightly regarded them as the common inheritance of the Alexandrian tradition as a whole, and thus as rooted, ultimately, in the scriptures themselves. He frequently sums up the claim to authentic intellectual and theological pedigree by his scriptural exegeses, as well as his appeals to the creed of Nicaea (whose champion Athanasius had been) and the tradition of the 'Fathers' before him.

In terms of the 'dynamic soteriology' that was so fundamental a part of Alexandrian thinking, we ought primarily to understand the deification[19] theory of the eastern Fathers.[20] Athanasius summed this up as the entire point and meaning of the incarnation understood

---

17 ie. the Antiochenes, whom he, in turn, accused of being guilty of proposing a double-subject christology: Two Sons.

18 Letter to Eulogius, para.1.

19 Theopoiesis.

20 cf. V. Lossky, The Mystical Theology of the Eastern Church, London, 1973.

as a salvific encounter and exchange between God and man. He did so most succinctly in his De Incarnatione by quoting Irenaeus' famous apophthegm: 'He (the Logos) became man that man might become god.'

In Cyril's thought this transforming mediation[21] is the motive that gives credibility and purpose to a scheme of incarnation that would otherwise be pointless, even offensive. The Logos had no need whatsoever to appear as man. Two deductions thus followed inevitably about the incarnation: firstly that it was an entirely free act of divine power, a Charis, or gracious act, of God. Secondly, that it was not for God's benefit but mankind's. Thus the incarnation was a restorative act entirely designed for the ontological reconstruction of a human nature that had fallen into existential decay as a result of its alienation from God.[22] This is what Cyril means by the incarnation as being fundamentally an 'Economy'. In our present context the word means a 'working-out' and carries the pregnant soteriological connotation of the deification of human nature, by virtue of the divine presence within it, as we have previously noticed. This is the way he answers two key questions about the incarnation: 'Why did it happen?', and, 'How did it happen?' To both queries he replies: 'As an economy of salvation.' To say that the Logos was born is, for Cyril, not the nonsense Nestorius thought it to be, any more than to say the Logos suffered or died, because the apparent paradox brings home to the believer the constantly presumed context—that these things, birth, suffering, death, and resurrection, took place 'economically', that is as a practical exercise of the Logos who assumed a human bodily life not pointlessly but in order to work out the salvation of the human race in and through that bodily condition; first in the divine transformation of his own authentically human life, and then (as he was the paradigm of salvation in his resurrection) in the transformation of christians.

In the case of the incarnation, the divine Logos appropriates[23] human nature. This human nature becomes none other than the human nature of the one who is God, and is thereby lifted to an extraordinary glory. More than this, it becomes the economic instrument[24] of the divine Logos; that is, the primary way the Logos has chosen to effect the

---

[21] For Cyril the whole incarnation demonstrates Christ as supreme mediator between God and Man. cf. Liebaert (1951), 218–228.

[22] The entire argumentation of Athanasius' Contra Gentes & De Incarnatione.

[23] Oikesis.

[24] Organon.

regeneration of the human race, concretely, intimately, and personally. The human nature of the Logos is, therefore, an instrument of the divine energy. The human nature in itself and on its own terms is not possessed of unlimited scope. Indeed it would be a contradiction of everything the words 'human nature' meant even to suggest that it could command unlimited powers such as impassibility, omniscience, or omnipotence. On its own terms human nature, in fact, connotes the exact opposite of these things, as all human beings know from experience.

Nonetheless, Cyril insists that while of itself human nature is not powerful but passible, in its union with the godhead, as in the dynamic act of incarnation, the human nature of the Logos thereby becomes an instrument of omnipotent power and thus, in a real though paradoxical sense, an 'omnipotent instrument'. It is at once powerful and fragile, majestic and humble. Cyril loved to press the force of this economy by the use of strong paradoxes. One of his favourites was: 'The Logos suffered impassibly'.[25]

He has often been accused, largely by those who have not read him in context sufficiently, of trivialising the sense of incarnate reality in Christ by meaningless conundrums—as if 'impassible suffering' meant nothing other than 'impassibility'. This is certainly not the case for Cyril. To say that 'he suffered impassibly' deliberately states both sides of the paradox with equal force and absolute seriousness of intent, refusing to minimise either reality. The point he wishes to make is that of the intimacy of the connection between two realities in Christ: one a reality of the glorious power of the godhead, and the other the tragic reality of the suffering human condition. In the incarnation of the Logos, Cyril posits the intimate union of the two realities as a salvific act or life-giving transaction. The power of the one heals and transforms the fallibility of the other. The fragile passivity of the other makes possible a revelation of the incomprehensible power of the one in a suitably 'fragile' and approachable medium for other fallible and fragile human beings. Both aspects were crucial for the very possibility of this revelation, and both contributed fully their respective characteristics; but by their mutual union they created the new possibilities and conditions of this revelation of the eternal within history.

This mutual sharing of the capacities, power and fragility, is seen

---

[25] Apathos epathen. cf. Scholia 33–35.

in the case of the incarnate Lord, whose human nature is depicted as powerful in its life-giving abilities. Cyril, for example, points regularly to the biblical texts depicting Christ's physical healings and resurrection miracles in the historical ministry (and not least his own death and resurrection). Here was a human nature that was at once fallibly fragile (for it suffered and died) and yet powerful beyond the capacity of a human nature, for it healed by its touch, raised the dead with its spoken words, and reanimated itself after its physical destruction.

For Cyril, this was paradoxical, or better 'mysterious', but not illogical, because Christ's human nature did not exceed the limits of its own capacities (or 'proprieties') on its own terms—something that would indeed have been nonsensical—but precisely because it was being used as an instrument within an infinite design. The human nature is, therefore, not conceived as an independently acting dynamic (a distinct human person who self-activates) but as the manner of action of an independent and omnipotent power—that of the Logos; and to the Logos alone can be attributed the authorship of, and responsibility for, all its actions. This last principle is the flagship of Cyril's whole argument. There can only be one creative subject, one personal reality, in the incarnate Lord; and that subject is the divine Logos who has made a human nature his own. Equally, however, the incarnated Logos cannot be sensibly understood purely in terms of his own 'proper' divine characteristics (as he would be before the incarnation) since he is now the Logos-acting-in-the-flesh, and in accordance with the conditions of the flesh which he willingly assumed, precisely to make use of those capabilities directly. In other words, for Cyril the Logos did not simply assume a body, as Apollinaris imagined, he assumed a human life and all the relativised conditions that are applicable to that. Cyril constantly reminds his readers that in christology one must not speak of the Logos as 'Gymnos' (ie. naked, in his divine characteristics) but as 'Sesarkomene' (enfleshed). The subject is unchanged, the divine Logos, but that subject now expresses the characteristics of his divinely powerful condition in and through the medium of a passible and fragile condition. Cyril, by preference calls this economy a Kenosis or self-emptying, following the terms of Philippians 2.6–11, a central text in the debate.

For Cyril, this economy, or transaction that constitutes the incarnation, is nothing less than a wonderful transformation of human nature. He points, in the person of Christ, to the paradox of a true human nature (the historically concrete Christ who is genuinely human with all the human emotions, human fatigue, and human passibility) that is at the same time transformed in divine glory (the radiant figure of Christ in glory on Mount Thabor, or the Christ who shows unlimited authority against the forces of evil even in his human limitations). This transformation which happens 'naturally' in Christ because the divinity has appropriated a human nature to itself, makes the flesh of Christ 'Life-giving', replete with all the glory and majesty of the Godhead. Indeed, for Cyril, the flesh of Christ is the worthy object of the christian's most profound worship and adoration.

Always being careful to secure himself against the Apollinarist sense of the confusion of natures, Cyril frequently presses the point of this paradox home with great vigour: the flesh of Christ is divine flesh, inherently life-giving, though evidently and necessarily human, that is 'flesh', for if it were not given in material fashion, as for example as the christian's food in the eucharist, the transforming blessing could not begin to be communicated to material creatures. Cyril appeals, among other ideas, to the analogy of the stick that has just caught alight from the fire. In that moment, the wood of the material reality is perfectly preserved, and yet the fire has become at one with it.[26] Likewise the divinity plays through the flesh of Christ like a lancing flame to deify his own body in a most natural and intimate way, and yet also fires out from this source to restore and heal his contemporaries in Galilee, and thence to the redemption of the whole human race. What Christ has naturally deified in his own flesh he 'gratuitously' deifies in the human race at large. The appropriation of human nature in the particular, that is in his own birth in time and space, is also a real sacrament of the Logos' appropriation of human nature at large. And his appropriation of it gives to human fallibility a new-found infinite worth.[27]

For Cyril, the salvation offered universally, the 'deification by grace' that amounts to the restoration of mankind to union with God in and through Christ, is the cosmic gift of the metaphysical transformation effected in the act of incarnation. In other words christology is the paradigm of all salvation, and that salvation is understood as an ontological rescue of the race. What Christ was and did naturally, he transfers to humankind as an inheritance (kata thesin).[28] This, quite

---

[26] Scholia. 9.
[27] See, e.g. That The Christ is One. PG.75.1332; 1st Ep. To Succensus, para.9.
[28] Thesaurus. PG.75.561; That The Christ is One, passim.

simply, is the reason why the eucharistic elements, unarguably material and unarguably humble, are also, for Cyril, unquestionably divine and adorable. The physical interchange that occurs when the believer communicates with his Lord in the eucharistic mysteries is no less than a metamorphosis—healing and salvation are given. The believer is deified by the encounter, for the encounter brings him into life-giving proximity with the Logos, and this proximity (for all the Alexandrian theologians) was the metaphysical root and sustenance of all being. Eucharistic theory is a key element of Cyril's anti-Nestorian thinking, and can be observed explicitly at several points of his correspondence.[29]

We might sum up Cyril's predominant christological vision, then, as a 'mysterious' transformation of the human race according to the paradigm of the divine appropriation of a human nature in the incarnation. His precise theological arguments time and again, appeal to the mysteriousness, or ineffability, or inconceivability, of the whole operation. This is not so much a pious obfuscation, as an earnest of his desire to avoid a mechanistic conception of christology, such as that posited by Apollinaris, and Cyril holds to it in the interests of securing the authentic Alexandrian understanding of the incarnation as an act of divine freedom and power. The repeated reminders of the 'ineffable mystery' give his thought a doxological character, for 'mystery' in the patristic tradition did not primarily connote an unsolved riddle or intellectual problem, but the biblical sense of that mystery which is Christ's redeeming presence in the church, as transcendent Lord of time, and following from that, his presence as Risen Lord in the church's timeless liturgy. The very word was often used as a synonym of the liturgy—the church's mysteries. This theme of the ineffable mystery marks a significant difference in theological methodology between Cyril and Nestorius. The former appeals to tradition and the church's sense of the mystery of Christ that quells human voices in the sense of numinous presence (in fact the two things are really as one for him because the 'tradition of the Fathers' is predominantly a tradition of the inspired saints of Christ),[30] whereas the latter appeals to semantic clarity and logical necessity like a true scholastic.

One final aspect of the controversy which ought to be considered

---

[29] E.g. in the Third Letter to Nestorius, para.7; Explanation of the Twelve Chapters (no.11).

[30] cf. Scholia 35.

in this general review, is the extent to which it was also a dispute about biblical interpretation. This can be seen in all Cyril's christological work, and never more clearly so than in the Scholia, and The Christ is One. Patristic theology is, in a sense, wrongly (though commonly) presented when the works of the ancient writers are looted for systematic formulas for specific doctrines (frequently on the terms set by later systematicians more intent on confirming their own theories than listening to the voices of the past). Such an approach, a scholastic rapine of the Fathers, has been typical and widespread in European scholarship of the last few centuries, but when one reads the patristic texts expansively and in context, it is abundantly clear that the exegesis of the scriptures was their common point of origin, even in the most technical and apparently philosophical of their discussions.

In the Nestorian controversy both sides of the argument instinctively appeal to the scriptures to justify their respective christological positions, or rather maintain that they hold to these positions as part of their faithful interpretation of the biblical witness. As in the Arian controversy, a few key texts soon came to prominence, and their interpretation was behind many of the precise arguments. In the case of Cyril, Jn.1.14 and Phil.2.6–11 feature time and again. For Cyril the notion of the Eternal One's self-emptying (Kenosis) as outlined in Phil.2.6f. rises to the status of a master theme throughout his thought—to such an extent that the earthly economy of the Word made flesh is often simply referred to as the Kenosis. Nestorius makes great use of the texts in Hebrews which refer to the High Priesthood of Christ, and these too become familiar texts to Cyril as he brings them into the scheme of his apologetic response. The manner of using the biblical citations often appears oddly de-contextualised to the modern reader, as if they have been dragged in to the argument artificially, and yet it would be a mistake to regard the biblical references that abound in the discourses as mere garnishing. There is a genuine concern on all sides of this debate to bring to the fore the biblical text as the primary authority of the church's tradition, and to explicate how new problems are to be illuminated and resolved by it. The main difference with patristic, as opposed to modern, exegesis, lies in what one might call 'historical method'. The patristic writers, especially the Alexandrians[31] such as Cyril, regard the text as a continuous narrative of the Logos

[31] Yet the perspective, as related to an eternal revelation historically transmitted, is equally shared by the Antiochenes, despite their (sometimes) less allegorical approach.

himself. It was the Word who spoke through all the prophets, the Word who inspired the psalms, the Word who appeared to Abraham Moses, and Jacob, and so on. In every instance the text (be it Old or New Testament) relates to the Logos' revelation of God, whether in the life of the Trinity or the earthly economy of salvation. The modern reader begins from a concrete historical perspective, the patristic writer began from an 'eternal' perspective and related everything to the revelation of the Logos, culminating in the historical manifestation of the Word in the flesh. This thoroughgoing christocentricity, and different understanding of historical reality, marks off their exegeses from contemporary interpreters; it makes them unfamiliar and strange, but it does not necessarily make them any less valid.

Here, in the case of fifth century christology, the argument came to be particularly focused on two biblical aspects. The first was the nature of the scriptural witness to Christ's subjectivity. Exegesis of the last two centuries, and its concern with the 'historical Jesus' has re-opened this debate, and this explains why much of the Cyril-Nestorius controversy has the ability to create resonances in modern theological discourse. The widespread distinction in contemporary critical biblical interpretation between the Jesus of History and the Christ of Faith frequently betrays, in the hands of its exegetical users, an undisclosed christological anthropology that is much more like that of Nestorius than it is of Cyril. The usual divorce between biblical specialists and systematicians today, does nothing to resolve the large theological issues that are thereby exposed.

The second issue is what has since come to be called the 'Exchange of Properties' or 'Communion of Idioms',[32] that is the precise debate over the legitimacy of cross-referencing the different characteristics (properties, or idiomata) of divinity and humanity if a single subject was posited as the personal referent of both. In other words could what is characteristic of the divine be attributed to the human, and vice versa, if the one Christ was both God and man? Was the Communicatio simply a sloppy way of doing theology, or did it preserve an insight basic to christianity? Nestorius took the first line, Cyril the second. And yet, both Nestorius and Cyril agree that some form of cross-referencing is made permissible by the very fact of the incarnation considered as God's approach to the human race.

---

[32] Antidosis Idiomaton, or Communicatio Idiomatum. cf. Manoir (1944) p. 148.

Where Cyril maintained that the doctrine of the single subjectivity of the incarnate Lord meant that a free and untrammelled exchange of attributes is possible, and that this (often paradoxical) language protected the doctrine by proclaiming its implications, Nestorius was not so sure. He was very cautious about the interchange permissible in theological discourse (so cautious that Cyril suspected he doubted the doctrine of the single subject that lay behind it) and he felt that Cyril's use of paradox manifested an unskilled theological mind, one that had secured a single subject doctrine at the cost of mythologising christianity with its talk of a suffering God and other such things, most notably language about 'the Mother of God'—Theotokos.

For Cyril, if God is the single personal subject of the incarnation, then when Jesus is said to weep in the Gospels (Jn.11.35), the christian can rightly conclude that 'God wept'. The latter statement is an exegesis of the scripture, an interpretation that rises out of the christian's faith in, and recognition of, the deity of Jesus. The same exegesis of other texts, on the same basis, might lead the christian to speak of God's sufferings, God's death on the cross, and so on. Cyril is well aware that this language had a very shocking aspect; its paradoxical nature brings one up sharply against the problem that 'God' is a term that connotes a transcendence of all suffering. If 'God' means 'to be impassible' then to speak, for example, of a God who suffers, is simply to say 'the Impassible is passible', and that would be nothing more than nonsense-talk. There is only one possible way out of the dilemma thus caused by this language of cross-referencing, and that, as Cyril never tired of repeating, is the realisation that the statement 'God suffered' is only apparently self-contradictory, because the word 'God' is being used in a different way to normal. In fact in all incarnational language Cyril says that it is being used as a synonym for 'God-in-the-flesh', and this crucial qualification is given in the very paradox itself, since all christians will, or ought to, admit that suffering, death, sorrow, and suchlike, are inapplicable to 'God-in-himself', but no longer inapplicable to God-made-man, in so far as he has appropriated, along with a human body, all that goes to make up a human life, that is soul, intellect, emotion, fragility, even mortality.

This marks Cyril's profound divergence from Apollinaris, but also might explain why Nestorius thought him to be at his most Apollinarist when he used the language of the communicatio. In Cyril's hands the exchange of properties is like an intellectual firework, a condensed cipher of all that he holds to be important in christology and faith.

It is a statement full of power, that by its inherent paradox forces the hearer to reflect on the fact that a single subject christology means a dynamic and intimate union of different conditions in the one life of God. As such, the communicatio is shorthand for his whole doctrine of the incarnation itself as a transforming transaction whereby human nature is appropriated by God and deified in the process. Cyril's Twelfth Anathema was to become famous both before and after Ephesus as his most provocative use of this schema. It still serves as a litmus test of people's christological positions.

For Nestorius, the language of the exchange of properties was generally suspect, and often odious. He found, in the expressions 'Mother of God' and 'God suffering', little more than an ignorant piety that had cut so many corners in its implications that it stood very close to pagan mythical conceptions of the deity: such as Isis being the 'mother of the god' Horus, or Hercules as a 'suffering god' on Mount Aetna. Nestorius wished to see clean and coherent distinctions made between characteristics appropriate to the human condition, and those appropriate to the divine condition. In his exegesis, therefore, he attributes the biblical ascriptions (Phonas) quite decisively to their respective, and different, personas. So, for him, God the Logos raised the dead Lazarus, while the man Jesus wept at the tomb.

This is the argument that brings Cyril and Nestorius into their immediate conflict. Cyril summarises his objections to Nestorius' biblical method in his Third Letter and the Anathemas, but the argument runs throughout his writings. His chief worry was that such a divisive method of attribution signalled a double subject christology. Since he was using his method of biblical ascriptions primarily to enshrine his own single-subject doctrine, it seemed reasonable to deduce that of Nestorius from the latter's preferred methodology too. On this basis he characterised Nestorius as condemning the exchange of properties because he did not believe the underlying principle of the single subject. From this it was a short leap to surmise that Nestorius had resurrected Diodore's Two Sons doctrine—one of whom did divine things, as God, and the other who seemed to do human things as man.

The resolution of this argument was long in coming, but it is interesting to trace Cyril's growing sense, in the post-Ephesus correspondence, that a more strictly defined form of the exchange of properties language than he himself preferred was still within the bounds of orthodoxy—once given an agreement over the issue of single subjectivity in Christ. On this basis he was ready to acknowledge the orthodoxy of John of Antioch. Cyril's Explanation of the Twelve Chapters, as well as his letters To Eulogius and To Succensus, and the letter To John of Antioch, all demonstrate this formal mutual recognition of the terms and significances of the attribution language henceforth permissible in christology. Several comentators (following Theodoret's lead) have regarded this later rapprochement as Cyril's climb-down from his fourth anathema. A close reading of that text will show, however, that such an analysis was, and is, misguided. Cyril was maintaining the point of not referring different attributes to different subjects, rather than refusing to allow that the different attributes could be referred to the two conditions, if it were agreed that there was only one subject of reference in Christ.

Leo's Tome is much concerned with the same issue, but it greatly overstates the case to argue that it was Leo's contribution which resolved this argument at Chalcedon. Cyril's later writings had elaborated it clearly enough, and with the stress more successfully placed on the implications of Christ's personal unity, than Leo managed to do in the Tome, which largely reproduced Augustine's less focused christology. The Eulogius letter demonstrates how extensively Cyril's text became the real basis of the Chalcedonian settlement of the communicatio argument.[33] It is an issue to which we shall return in the subsequent discussion of the oecumenical reception of Cyril's theology.

Having set out, as briefly as possible, the general topography of Cyril's christology, it may be useful to turn now to the specific assessment of some key aspects of his thought.[34] The following discussion may illuminate somewhat our earlier question: To what extent did Cyril advance christological understanding from the impasse it had reached, poised uncertainly between the Apollinarist confusion of natures, and Diodore's separate subjects?

2. Henosis Theory: Cyril's Christological Argument

Cyril's thought has not been served well by those who have pillaged his work for the formulas it contains on the subject of the christological

[33] Pace C. Moeller's thesis of the Roman theology's predominant influence in the Chalcedonian settlement: cf. Le Chalcédonisme et le néo-Chalcédonisme en Orient de 451 à la fin du VIè sieclè. In Grillmeier-Bacht (1951) vol.1, pp. 638–720. For a revision of this thesis see P.T. Gray, The Defense of Chalcedon in the East, Leiden, 1979.

[34] A synopsis and review of the key terms, more balanced than that of Grillmeier, can be found in Du Manoir (1944) pp. 114–162.

union. His christology is is simply not so much formulaic as discursive, and his analogies are always subordinate to the general line of his narrative. If the formulaic sections alone are isolated this leads to a considerable distortion of what Cyril is quite plainly saying, at great length, and with many repetitions, throughout a considerable body of writing. The formulaic method, however, can often dispense a commentator from the burden of having to read the texts, and thus has always been popular. It is partly because of this quest for formulas, a preferred text-book method, that so much attention has been given to Cyril's phrase on the Mia Physis: One Enfleshed Nature of God the Word.

In situ, in the context of all his work, the phrase merges unremarkably with a number of other idioms, analogies, and suggested similes, that together make up a dynamic coherence. What is more, the qualifications Cyril attaches to this, and his other analogies, in the surrounding text of his argument, are always crucial. It is precisely these subtle qualifications that are often jettisoned by a formulaic analysis. The method thus tends to falsify the picture from the outset, for there are remarkably few formulas in Cyril as a whole, and the evidence does not justify a commentator propelling them to the forefront as the mainstay of his argument.

Nonetheless, with Nestorius christian theology had come to a new watershed. Three key issues were now challenging the theologians of the day: firstly the concept of personal identity in Christ, in terms of the active subject referent of the deeds of the incarnate one as described by scripture; secondly the problem of the manner of the relationship between the divine and the human in Christ (the 'how' of the christological union); and thirdly the need to settle on an agreed terminology with which to discuss and define the issues in question. If Nestorius had attempted to apply a strictly logical method to resolve the problems, it is a legitimate question to ask how better did Cyril fare in tabling the same issues, in his preferred non-scholastic style of theologising?

For Cyril, three principles form the pillars of his entire christological doctrine. They may be summarised as the 'what' of Cyril's christology, the 'why', and the 'how' of it. In the first place he holds fast to the primary proposition that there is only a single subject referent in all the incarnate acts, in all the psychic and intellectual life of the incarnate Lord, and that this personal subject is none other than the eternal Word of God. For him, this primary principle had to be defended against the very suspicion of any compromise, and he did so throughout his life however many paradoxes necessarily had to be invoked to keep it intact. This determined focus explains all his theological motivation.

Secondly, he holds that this doctrine commits one to a certain position on its purposefulness. In other words, to understand the manner of the incarnation it is first of all necessary to understand the reason for it: the 'why' thus explains the 'what'. As we have seen, Cyril, from start to finish, envisaged the incarnation as a dynamic soteriological event. This 'why' of incarnation theology represents the internal flow of his thought, and often explains why he sometimes seems to be unnecessarily obscure in certain local arguments, for he is not so concerned with meeting all his opponents' precise objections as with preserving the integrity of this general movement of his theology as religious confession. As in our earlier section we might sum up for him this 'why' of the incarnation as a dynamic transaction stimulated by God's redemptive mercy, such that the particular incarnation of the Logos becomes the principle cause of a universalised divinisation of the believer by grace.

This second major premiss commits him, in turn, to his third; for if the goal of the incarnation is transforming intimacy with God then the manner of conceiving the particular case of Christ must demonstrate its status as paradigm for the universal hope of the believer. In short, Cyril's 'how' of the union has to draw the connecting line between his christology and his soteriology. He does this by arguing strongly, and consistently, that only one term is at all suitable for depicting the 'how' of the incarnation and that this is 'Henosis', union or unification. At one and the same instant the term describes the general soteriological principle of the incarnation, and the particular method of how to conceive the relationship of divine and human realities in the person of Christ. Sometimes he adds qualifiers to the notion of union; some of these are sustained, some abandoned, but he would never compromise on the necessity of a christology of henosis. In this latter context the concept of economic appropriation is particularly important for him, an aspect that shall be elucidated shortly.

So far, Cyril has perhaps demonstrated that he was the true successor of Athanasius and Didymus, now in the Nestorian controversy he was particularly called upon to prove that the Alexandrian mystical tradition had not been fundamentally compromised by Apollinaris. Cyril's originality lay in his demonstration that the concept of Christ's union of two states did not necessarily connote the destructive absorption of its constituent parts, but at its best signified the enhancement of individual elements within the union and precisely because of their mutual involvement. To elucidate his sense of the christological union he applied several analogies, or christological models. It will be instructive to review them.

Minor Analogies

Cyril describes the nature of the union of God and man in Christ in several graphic images. In the case of each of them the point is to describe how two things, notionally discernible or intellectually distinct in themselves, can nonetheless be combined in one concrete reality, so as to make a singular subject referral evidently necessary. Christ, for example, is like the Ark of the Covenant.[35] The Ark is wooden but was covered inside and out with beaten gold, thus it was golden too. Was it gold or was it wood? The observer would say it was gold, and the scripture so describes it, but this does not mean that it ceased being wood. Nonetheless all would agree that there was only one single Ark. In the same way, Cyril argues, the one Christ was both God and Man. The wood symbolises his humanity, the gold his deity. Yet the wood is covered in gold and made indestructible and precious in the process, just as the humanity was transfigured in its adoption by the Godhead.

In the first of his anti-Nestorian writings, the 17th Paschal Homily[36] he describes the union as a like a precious stone, and the radiant coloured light it emits. The two things cannot be separated. They constitute the single reality and character of the precious stone—and so it is with Christ; composited of Godhead and manhood, he is but one with the radiance of divine light shining through his material form.

Cyril was really looking for analogies of inherent attributes. One of his most effective was the lily and its fragrance.[37] The perfume is an 'incorporeal thing', while the lily flower and stem are corporeal. The two are quite different in state, immaterial, and material, yet they are inseparable and the lily is evidently a single reality. Without its perfume or without its specific corporeal shape it could not be a lily. Two different things combine here inseparably as one, and

---

[35] De Adoratione In Spiritu et Veritate. PG 68.596, 661; Scholia 11. PG 75.1381.
[36] Hom. Pasch. 17, PG 77.776; Con. Nest.II.54, PG. 76.61. (Pusey, vol.7. p. 95).
[37] Scholia 9.

their dynamic interpenetration constitutes the one reality—and so it is with Christ. The perfume is his Godhead, the corporeal matter his bodily form, with the perfume of the deity emanating from all the earthly acts of the one Christ.

Cyril took the idea of interpenetration one stage further in his use of the analogy of fire and wood.[38] Here his point is to speak of the active interpenetration which transforms but does not thereby destroy. The image is itself a fragile one, as he knows, for fire actually does consume and change, even destroy, its original combustible material. But Cyril is careful to point specifically only to a stage in the process, that instant when the fire catches on the wood and first blazes around it. For that moment the object is all itself, a wooden stick say, and yet also radiant with flames of fire. Here are two things, but one is transforming the other while it has not changed it from being wood. It has preserved its essence as a wooden thing and worked from this basis (and because of it) to metamorphosise it into fire. So it is with Christ: the wood symbolises the humanity, the fire the transforming power of the Godhead which deifies the flesh without destroying its essential humanity.

He also uses the image of the live coal of Isaiah's vision[39] to sustain a similar point. This was coal, certainly, but suffused with fire, and in the same way Christ was man, yet suffused with the deity. Was the live coal fire or was it coal? It was both, but it was only one thing, not two. And so was Christ one from two realities. Cyril wishes to highlight the dynamic nature of fire suffusing something, but he knows that the instance of the fire and the wood (or even ultimately the fire and the coal) is a somewhat defective image since fire inevitably does destroy its host object, and for this reason he does not develop the image very extensively.

He had the example of the Burning Bush,[40] which Moses saw in the desert, to use if he so desired. It had been applied in the christological context before but, significantly, he himself does not wish to use it. Here the Bush was burning, suffused with fire, but the fire did not consume it. Far from being useful, Cyril seems to have thought this image even more defective when applied to Christ, because the fire

---

[38] Apol. Ad Theodosium. PG. 76.408; Con. Nest. PG.76.56; Scholia 9. PG.75. 1398; De Recta Fide ad Reginas, PG.76.1364.

[39] Is. 6.6.

[40] Ex. 3.1–6.

in this case did not touch the Bush, and can hardly be said to have provided the concept of dynamic interpenetration he was looking for. He did regard it as a christological type[41] but he applied it not to signify the union of the two natures, but rather the manner in which Mary gave birth physically, and yet remained a virgin.[42]

In all the images he applied to the union, the points he wished to get across were; firstly, that two inherent realities are often more properly seen as one; secondly, that the composited union is thereby often a 'natural union' which witnesses the composited realities mutually engaging and acting on one another to produce a visible function; and thirdly, that this mutual engagement (as in the case of fire) can be a radical transformation of the one element by the other, without necessarily implying its destruction in the process. These three key arguments Cyril applies to the union of God and man in Christ.

To an extent, however, they remained material analogies. He was really looking for an image of dynamic spiritual transfiguration, and he seized upon it in the concept of the soul's relation to the body it indwells, informs, and transforms by vivification.

Soul and Body

Cyril's most recurring image[43] of the union of godhead and humanity in Christ is thus the manner of the union of soul and body in man. This is so extensively applied that it can be said to sum up the others, and frequently even the others are synopsised at the end of his discussions by comparison to this as the essence of his point. He prefers it to the material analogies because he senses it to be a spiritually dynamic type of a profoundly spiritual mystery, and one that has its end result in the gift of life. In the case of the soul's relation to the body, the distinctness of the two realities is taken for granted as an obvious and self-evident thing.[44] Deity is not humanity, as soul is not flesh. They are both distinct and discrete realities. To go on to insist that they cannot be mixed, however, as if the whole notion

---

[41] As in Glaphyra in Exod. PG.69.

[42] Con. Anthropomorphitas. PG. 76. 1129; In That The Christ is One, the figure was applied once only to signify the way the divinity is not defiled by contact with affairs of the flesh; it was, for Cyril, not an image of union, but of discreteness.

[43] cf. Scholia 9; Letter to The Monks, para. 12; 1st Letter to Succensus; Explanation of the Twelve Chapters (Expln. 3) and passim.

[44] It was partly because it was such an obvious thing to him that Cyril took so long in appreciating the extent of the Antiochene fears that his theology had not done enough to articulate the distinctness of the natures.

of mixture had been utterly compromised by the way Apollinaris used it to connote 'mixed up', was in Cyril's eyes a serious mistake. The analogy of the soul and the body demonstrated for him how two distinct realities can be mixed together without destroying or compromising the integrity of either. In fact, far from assailling the natural integrity of the flesh, or soul, in the case of a human being, the 'mix' of the two here constitutes an enhancement by creating the very conditions of a human being's life. For Cyril, the notion of the mix or relation of the two is best described as a union (henosis), and in so choosing to elevate the concept of *henosis* over that of *mixis* he advances on the christology of Gregory Nazianzen.

When the soul is united with the flesh a new condition is created, the life of a human being. The union of the two elements produces a single reality by means of their dynamic interpenetration. The human soul is spiritual in essence, but not spiritual in the way an angel might be understood to be such, for in life a human soul is inescapably bonded to the flesh, and the affairs of the flesh affect it directly. A purely physical or fleshly event such as toothache could demonstrably produce an effect on the soul (as the ancient psychology held to be self-evident) such as grief or depression, even though this latter condition was regarded as a psychic and non physical state in itself. Similarly, psychic states had their direct physical expressions too; the soul's sorrow (a peculiarly psychic and non-physical reality) could produce the body's physical tears, and the soul's elation might result in laughter or dancing, both of which were entirely physical activities.

This discrete existence of a spiritual reality (soul) and a physical reality (body or flesh) was never compromised in the union of the two that constituted a human being (an embodied soul), for even in the union the two realities existed discretely. Nonetheless, the fact of the union made it equally obvious that the discrete existence of the two was by no means the same as their separate co-existence. An individual human being could not do any single act which was either purely spiritual or psychic (only a soul-act) or purely physical (merely a body-act). Everything a human did consciously involved the body and soul in a continuous and unbroken union, everything was, thus, a body-soul act, although the extent of the respective influences might vary widely. So, for example, a human's prayer was both a physical and a spiritual act but the latter predominated, and there were also many actions where the physical aspects predominated over the psychic.

Cyril's conclusion was that in the body-soul analogy he had a concrete demonstration of an important christological principle—that a union of two things, which were discrete in terms of their respective natures, could be envisaged where a union of those different things took place that effected a new condition and new possibilities by virtue of the union, yet did not destroy the integrity of the respective elements that came together to form the union. So it was, he says, in the case of the incarnation. Deity and humanity were different things in terms of their discrete natures. In coming together in union in the incarnation they constituted a new condition, that of 'God-enfleshed-in-history', without destroying the integrity of either element. The fact that God is enfleshed means neither that human nature is destroyed or obliterated, nor that the divine nature is compromised or altered as such. As Cyril puts it:

> He (the Word) underwent a birth and came forth as man from woman. This did not mean that he abandoned what he was, for even when he came in flesh and blood, even so he remained what he was, that is God in nature and truth.[45]

Equally, however, within this new condition and new possibility of being God-enfleshed, the deity now works in continuous and unbroken union with the humanity, and vice versa. There is no instance of a purely divine act in the incarnation (no sole Logos-act), nor is there any instance of a purely human deed (a man's act), just as as any ordinary human being cannot choose to do anything that is either purely psychic or merely physical. Each and every single act of the incarnate Lord was, for Cyril, an act of God enfleshed within history; and thus an act where deity and humanity were synchronised as one theandric reality. This synchronic interpenetration was the essential mystery that at once allowed the divine majesty to stoop down to the encounter with humanity at a direct and personal level, and the humanity to be caught up in this divine condescension[46] so as to be elevated into a new condition and a realm of utterly new possibilities. The point of the incarnation is thereby demonstrated. God in his own being (the eternal and impassible Logos) cannot be directly

[45] Third Letter to Nestorius, para.3.

[46] Synkatabasis: in patristic thought the word does not connote any sense of arrogance, as it often does today. It is the biblical word for the mother's 'condescension' to the cradle of her infant, as an analogy of God's loving care for his people, despite the inequality of their respective conditions.

impinged on by human events (historical and passible). Similarly human nature, within its own terms, cannot exceed its own limitations. In the unique union of the two in the incarnation, a wholly new condition is created. Deity is now able, through its union with humanity, to experience historical and conditioned reality directly and personally (without being historicised and relativised in itself qua divine nature) because the union (or incarnation) is in a real sense a historical and de-limiting reality.[47] Likewise human nature, which in itself cannot exceed its natural limitations, is able, by virtue of the new conditions created by the union, to be so enhanced that it transcends its original condition, again because the union is in a real sense a transcendent and infinitely liberating reality. The one reality of the incarnation can have both characteristics simply because it is a composite reality. What was impossible before the union can, therefore, become possible after it.

God enfleshed within history, is both God and Man. The same one now exists within two conditions. God suffers, and man conquers death. God, who could not suffer in his own nature is enabled to suffer because of the intimacy of the union with the humanity which does suffer in terms of its own nature. Humanity, which in terms of its own nature is radically limited by its physicality and passibility, transcends its limitations by virtue of the union it enjoys with the Godhead. The body of Christ, for example, heals the sick, and rises immortal from its own death.

Appropriation Theory

For Cyril, the union of the two realities opens out radically new conditions of existence that would otherwise be seen as impossible, and when these are demonstrated they strike the beholder as mysterious, or paradoxical. He argues strongly, however, that their paradoxical character does not make them nonsensical or inappropriate, if one always remembers that these things are the logical results of a particularly new condition of existence: the fruit of the henosis. The cross and resurrection demonstrate this.

In the torments of the cross God is said to suffer. But God cannot suffer in his own nature, and evidently does not, or he would not

---

[47] It is a real but not an absolute limitation on the Godhead because the Godhead chooses to adopt the limitations that apply to humanity as an exercise of its omnipotent freedom.

be God. Yet, the one hanging on the cross is not God-in-his-own-nature but rather God-enfleshed-within-history, and within this new condition of existence God suffers in so far as his own body suffers. He does not suffer in his deity, but he does suffer in his humanity which he has appropriated as his own. Like any ordinary person, the physical act is attributed to a single personal reality. Arthur's tooth may hurt him, but it is not Arthur's tooth which has toothache, it is Arthur who is said to suffer. The psychic personal subject Arthur, however, does not suffer the pain in his psychic reality, he suffers in his physical reality, nevertheless because this body is Arthur's own, it is Arthur who is doing the suffering, no one else. Similarly, Cyril argues, we must understand it to be in the case of Christ, and in so doing he marks another radical corrective of Apollinaris, who wished to attribute the suffering only to the mindless flesh. For Cyril, suffering is entirely a matter of humanity; it emanates from the body of Christ which is in torment on the cross and is felt by the soul that animates the body; but the one who suffers is the Word, because the Word is the direct personal subject of all the acts and experiences of his own life, whether that life is lived out in the conditions of deity or humanity.

In the latter case, where humanity is engaged in sufferings and joys that are peculiar to it, the Word's intimate appropriation of the bodily reality has made it his own, and thus he, and no other, is the one who suffers or rejoices. Cyril says he suffers impassibly. That does not mean it is a play act; it means he does suffer, but does so qua man, not qua God, but neither, because of the intimate union, does he suffer in a discontinuous (or unengaged way), rather in a direct fashion in so far as he has made the body his very own and because of it now exists in two conditions. Because of the incarnate henosis, and the appropriation, the Word indeed suffers, as Cyril says, but his divine impassibility is not affected (in his life and condition qua God) and this is brought out by the explanation of 'how' he suffers in the incarnation, that is 'economically', or 'by appropriation', or 'in the nature of his flesh'. By adding these important qualifications Cyril does not intend to diminish the reality of the Word's engagement with suffering, in fact the opposite is the case, for he considers the Word's engagement in human sorrows to be the supreme redemptive principle, nonetheless he is teaching the basic principle that the union of the two conditions (like the relation of soul and body in an ordinary man) which allows such perfect interchange between them, still does not obliterate the necessary and discrete characteristics of each of them. Cyril expresses it as follows:

> So it is we say that he both suffered, and rose again, not meaning that the Word of God suffered in his own nature.... but in so far as that which had become his own body suffered, then he himself is said to suffer these things, for our sake, because the Impassible One was in the suffering body.[48]

This does not mean to say that the sufferings of God are merely a matter of words, as Nestorius would have it. For Cyril it is a dynamic act of the Word of God, a central act of the economy of salvation. The flesh allows the Word of God a new condition of expression. In his divine nature he could not possibly suffer, in his human nature he can.

Cyril understands the suffering as a mode of God's very impassibility, or in other words, the passivity is an expression of the perfect power of the Godhead whereby it appropriates to itself the fragile and powerless flesh. By suffering in the flesh, the sufferings of the flesh are transfigured, and by dying in the flesh the Godhead definitively conquers death. Thus even the limitations the Word assumes along with the assumption of the flesh are not expressions of God's impotence but of his redemptive power. The paradox of the suffering God is part of that vital interchange which Cyril understands as the union of the two conditions of Godhead and manhood, or as the 'economic appropriation':

> (God) ever remains what he is and does not change or undergo alteration. Moreover all of us confess that the divine Word is impassible, even if in his all-wise economy of the mystery he is seen to attribute to himself the sufferings that befall his own flesh (1 Pet. 4.1.). He bears the suffering of his own flesh in an economic appropriation to himself, as I have said, so that we may believe him to to be the Saviour of all.[49]

So when Cyril applies suffering to the Word he does so with two key qualifications: it applies to the Word made flesh, and it happens economically (for a salvific purpose of transfiguring mankind) not absolutely. Both things are almost synonymous.

Alternatively, instead of the sufferings attributable to the enfleshed

---

[48] Second Letter to Nestorius, para. 5; see also Homily on St. John's Day (in translated texts); and Explanation of the Twelve Chapters (Expln. 12).

[49] Letter to John of Antioch, para.9.

Godhead we might consider the issue from the perspective of the human nature. A human being is mortal, and immortality cannot be attributed to human nature as such because to do so would contradict the very definition of that state. In the case of Christ, the natural limit of human nature was demonstrated by its real, physical, and definite death. The body was cold in the grave. By virtue of its union with immortal deity, however, that experience of death (permanent and irreversible in the natural condition of all human beings) was made temporary and reversible in Christ. In just the same physical way as the body died, so it came back to life. The union with the deity effected a new condition and new set of possibilities for the body. In short, it was affected by its intimate union with the Godhead and was enhanced by the conditions and possibilities of the latter. In Christ, Godhead was directly affected by the terms of manhood, and manhood was by Godhead. The infinite power of the Godhead empathetically stood in union with the trials of the body, and the fragile passibility of the body was enhanced and glorified by the divine power.

The union is, therefore, all about interchange and transformation, and was initiated by God for the purpose of transfiguration and regeneration. Like Athanasius, Cyril sees the entire incarnate economy, not merely the atoning death of Jesus, as the act of God's redemption. But Cyril stressed the reality of the union with great force. If it was self-evident that more than one thing is involved in the very notion of a union, then it was equally self-evident (as far as he was concerned) that once a union had been accomplished one was subsequently committed to talking in terms of a singular reality, not a double reality. Cyril argues, for example, that it is simply pedantic to keep on referring to the two constitutive elements of a human being. The union of body and soul is expressed more truly when, instead, we simply refer to one single being. Similarly in the case of the incarnation, the union of Godhead and manhood is expressed by the singleness of Christ. As he puts it:

> Each nature is understood to remain in all its natural characteristics, though they are ineffably and inexpressibly united, and this is how he demonstrated to us the one nature of the Son; though of course it is the incarnate nature I mean. The term 'one' can be properly applied not just to those things which are naturally simple, but also to things which are compounded in a synthesis. Such is the case with a human being who comprises body and soul. These are quite different things,

> and they are not consubstantial with each other, yet when they are united they constitute the single nature of man, even though the difference in nature of the things that are brought into unity is still present within the system of the composition.[50]

He consistently describes the union in this dynamic sense. It is not an abstract reality for him, but an economic action, or 'an unspeakable consilience into unity',[51] and he regularly defends it as the sole way that one can understand the basis for personal unity in the incarnate Lord; just as the union of body and soul accounts for personal unity in a human being.

In his Third Letter to Nestorius Cyril argues the point by refusing to weaken the sense of union by the divisive biblical attribution of some texts to two subject referents, God and man:

> We do not divide out the sayings of Our Saviour, in the Gospels, as if to two hypostases or prosopa. The one and only Christ is not two-fold, even though he is understood as compounded out of two different elements in an indivisible unity, just as man is understood as consisting of soul and body, and yet is not two-fold, but rather is one from out of both. No, we think correctly, and so we must maintain that both the manly as well as the godly sayings were uttered by one subject.[52]

What he is insisting is that the term 'union' is a very precise one. It means nothing less than it suggests. If two things are 'joined' to one another, or related in any other kind of fashion, it might be logically possible still to continue to call them, and regard them as, two. But if a 'union' takes place, something that by definition means 'a making one of different realities', then there is no sensible point in calling them two after the union has been effected. To insist that they are one does not deny the inherent characters of what has been united, on the other hand to keep on talking about those different characters separately, as if they had not been united, suggests to the hearer that the speaker does not really admit that a union has taken place at all. This is exactly what Cyril accused Nestorius of believing, and found all the latter's insistence on the discrete natures to be merely a smokescreen for his refusal to accept the notion of the personal unity of Christ.

After Richard and Grillmeier it has become something of a cliché

---

50 Second Letter to Succensus. para.3.
51 2nd Letter to Nestorius, para.3.
52 Third Letter to Nestorius, para.8.

to speak of Word-Flesh and Word-Man christologies: a pseudo-category of patristic analysis which has been strictly avoided in this present study, as something that is artificially imposed on the subject in hand, quite anachronistically, and which distorts the context of the ancient debate more than it informs it. Nonetheless, it has sometimes been raised as a criticism of Cyril (and Athanasius) that the soul of Christ did not play a greater role in this analysis of the christological union, such as it had, for example, in the christology of Gregory Nazianzen, where it became (through Origen's influence) the 'meeting ground' of the spiritual and the corporeal in Christ. It is not the case that Cyril failed to see the opportunity such an avenue presented, but rather that he saw the further implications of the approach and chose not to develop it because of them. Grillmeier's[53] analysis of the development of christology almost makes this soul-christology a mark of authentic progress, and so describes Cyril as an antiquated thinker who delayed the development of the church's theology, because he did not teach the doctrine as the central core of his theory. Such a view is decidedly odd, despite the fact that it has become so often repeated in subsequent European analyses depending on him.

Cyril certainly taught the existence of a soul in Christ as the focus for the affective life—emotion, sensation, and empathy. In the same way he taught the existence of a human Nous in Christ—as the focus of his human spiritual and intellectual functions. This was part of his overall strategy to refute Apollinaris' attempts to reduce the impact of Christ's humanity: an intent that could hardly have been further from Cyril's mind. Nonetheless, neither the soul of Christ, nor the human Nous were, for Cyril, the ultimate locus of personhood. For him this was to be strictly reserved for the hypostasis of the Logos. The modern philosophical contexts wherein personhood is predominantly defined in terms of psychic emotional capacities (the ancient psychology's realm of the Soul) or in terms of intellectual judgement and consciousness (Nous), makes it particularly difficult for modern readers to realise that Cyril does not wish to reduce what he means by 'person' to these previously mentioned 'functions' of person. It is a critical factor which will be touched on further in the following section. Ultimately, I suggest, Cyril is not positing personhood on the basis of either psychic or intellective states, but on the basis of the act of divine power which first creates man. Neither the soul nor

[53] Ibid (1975), p. 446.

the Nous nor the flesh is the real subtrate of the person, but the divine hypostasis which has imaged itself in the human hypostasis. This is a thorough reworking of the Athanasian anthropology, in the De Incarnatione for example, where the great Alexandrian theologian had taught that man's ontological stability utterly depended on the human person's spiritual relation to the creative Word. When Cyril reapplies it to the context of christological anthropology, far from being an antiquated dead end as Grillmeier suggests,[54] because he has not elected to make soul the primary christological category, this is rather a profoundly new and thoroughly christianised sense of the doctrine of personhood, and one that was to suffuse the consciousness of the whole Byzantine oecumene for centuries to come. This was the very heart of Cyril's genius.

Mia Physis

If the image of the Henosis of body and soul clarifies his application of the notion of union throughout Cyril's exegesis of the Christ-event, it also explains his use of the Mia Physis formula. Cyril, for a while, failed to take seriously enough his opponents' accusations that he taught an Apollinarist-like confusion or melding of the two realities of God and man, by his insistence on the union of the two so as to form one Christ. He did not grasp their point, and thus made little moves until after Ephesus 431 to allay their fears, largely because he could not bring himself to treat the accusation as anything other than a rhetorical nonsense. He himself took for granted that the natures were intact and distinct, and so regarded the statement as a mere truism,[55] which he did not wish to waste time on. For him, the point of christology was to go on to insist on the fact of union, not to spend one's efforts defending the distinctness of two obviously different things. This was why he posited what, for the Antiochenes, was the very provocative formula: The One Enfleshed Nature of God the Word.[56] This had Apollinarist pre-echoes, and the Antiochenes, in their usually careless way of reading Cyril's context, heard him as merely repeating it in the way Apollinaris had intended. For if, for example, God the Word became flesh in such a way as simply to be one physical reality (and

[54] Presumably because he sees personality as fundamentally a question of psychic consciousness.

[55] Scholia PG.75.1385; 2nd Letter to Nestorius. para.3.

[56] cf. van den Dries (1939); Wickham (1983) fn.3, p. 62.

how that could happen could either be by adopting a soulless flesh, or by being confusedly mixed to a new kind of God-man-like nature, or even by sending down a new nature hybrid of heavenly flesh from heaven to earth) then the whole Apollinarist scheme could be succinctly expressed by the phrase 'One Nature of God the Word' or even 'One Nature of God the Word Who is made flesh' (Mia physis tou Theou Logou Sesarkomenou). What Cyril's phrase meant, on the other hand, was something quite different to this[57] and to see that, it was necessary to listen to his words quite carefully for he taught: One Enfleshed Nature of the Word (Mia Physis Tou Theou Logou Sesarkomene). That is, he used the the adjective 'enfleshed' to qualify the word nature, not the personal pronoun Logos. It made a world of difference. What was the significance of it for Cyril?

For him the phrase was ideally suited to signify the reality of union. Union means one, whereas partnership or association means two; and if a union is what it claims, it can be referred to, after the union has been achieved, by a singular verbal reference. If two countries politically united (rather than merely entered association through treaty), then after the Henosis they could not be referred to again as two countries—perhaps two different parts of the same country, but no more than that. For Cyril, if the christological union means anything it means that there is only one reality to be affirmed henceforth. This concrete reality (physis) is what stands before the christian observer; it is a single concrete reality enfleshed before us: Mia Physis Sesarkomene. What is more, that concrete, fleshed-out reality, is that of the Word of God, none other. In short, by using the phrase Cyril is attributing the person of the Word as the single subject of the incarnation event. He does so in a phrase which is highly succinct (a good rallying phrase for his party), provocatively robust (using concrete physis terms as opposed to the semantic word-plays of Nestorius), and radically insistent on the single subjectivity of the divine Word (the direct personal subject of the incarnate acts).

For Cyril, the physis in this sense of concrete personal individuant is synonymous with hypostasis. Both are referring to individual and

---

[57] So too did the moderate Apollinarists invent the phrase Cyril uses for exactly the same strategy, to distance themselves from the earlier theandric confusion of their founder, Apollinaris, and to move closer towards meeting the neo-Nicene resolution of the later Athanasius, the Cappadocians, and Didymus. Cyril mistakenly thought the phrase he used had an Athanasian provenance, but the source did not compromise the clear and orthodox way it is is used in Cyril.

real personal subjectivity, and in the way he uses them they are synonyms of 'the Logos' as subject. He says so himself quite explicitly in his Defence Of The Anathemas Against The Orientals where he starts his process of ordering and explaining the somewhat free terminology he has been using so far:

> Thus, there is only one nature (physis) of the Word, or hypostasis if you like, and that is the Word himself.[58]

A similar readiness to substitute hypostasis for physis (or prosopon) in this context can be seen in his Third Letter to Nestorius where he says:

> This is why all the sayings in the Gospels are to be attributed to the one prosopon, and to the one enfleshed hypostasis of the Word.[59]

The Mia Physis phrase was, and still is, if correctly understood, a brilliant encapsulation of his point, but was a formula that to a certain extent distracted the christological debate during his life, and even more so after it. In his own time, particularly because the phrase had an unwanted tonnage of prior heretical use, it was never able to command a role as an internationally agreed technical formula, even in spite of Cyril's authoritative endorsement and rehabilitation of it.

One large part of the problem was that Cyril used physis here in its antique sense as concrete reality, suggesting 'individual subject', whereas the Antiochenes consistently read it in the technical Aristotelian sense of 'physically constituted nature' or 'defining natural qualities'. When Cyril proclaimed 'One enfleshed nature of the Word' he thus meant that there is only the one subject concretely presented to us here who is God the Word (though God the Word now made flesh). His opponents, however, heard him in a different way, to be saying: 'The incarnation merges God and man into a single reality of a new divino-human nature', which was evidently Apollinarism revisited.

Cyril was also (though less frequently) capable of using physis to connote 'natural quality', and in the literature specifically relating to the Orientals, such as the Letter to John of Antioch, and the Eulogius and Succensus letters, he even admits that there can be two physeis in Christ, of God and man, though inseparably united (and thus

---

[58] PG.76. 401.

[59] Third Letter to Nest. para. 8.

ultimately one). Nonetheless, on his own terms, he generally prefers other ways of describing 'humanity' or that natural condition understood in the Aristotelian sense as a collection of attributes making up a genus. His preferred terms for this are: 'flesh', 'body', 'the manly element', 'manhood', 'the form of man', 'our own condition', 'that which he assumed', 'that he became like us', and 'the form of a slave'.[60] The obvious advantage of them all, and it was critical for his anti-Nestorian case, was that they did not carry any implicit sense (as he was well aware that *physis* did) of any necessary individual subjectivity in the humanity (that is other than the Word's). And so, when Cyril asserted the full humanity of Christ he was not implicated, by the logic of his semantic, in asserting the fully individualised human subjectivity of Christ, that is as an individual man distinct from the Word of God. For Cyril, the fully human Christ was not a human person, but a divine person who had chosen to live in the human condition. Thus, he never speaks of God assuming a man[61] (anthropon analambanein), and indeed regards it as Nestorius' major error.

It was not until after Ephesus that Cyril realised how his words had been misinterpreted by the Orientals. He begins to clarify his meanings in his 1st and 2nd letter to Succensus, perhaps the second of those, together with the Eulogius letter, is the clearest exposition of what he means by Mia Physis. Although he still regards his original point as entirely right and proper, and still justified his phrase as being sufficiently distinguished from Apollinarism by the use of the qualifying adjective 'enfleshed', something he felt ought to be readily apparent to all who read him without malicious intent, it was nonetheless brought home to him between 432 and 433 that the formula did not have a future. He was willing to let it fade away as long as its main point, the single personal subjectivity of the incaranate Lord, was secured by all parties concerned. The refusal of many elements in his own party, Dioscorus chief among them, to be ready to abandon the formula in the light of possible misinterpretations, caused great problems in the christological argument after Cyril's death, and grew eventually into the Monophysite resistance of the council of Chalcedon.

In the First Letter to Succensus, after re-stating that he preferred to use the Mia Physis as a rallying point to defend the two key issues

---

[60] Sarx, soma, to anthropinon, anthropotes, anthropeia morphe, ta hemetera, to pheroumenon, gegone kath' hemas, he tou doulou morphe.

[61] Defence of the Twelve Chapters: Against Theodoret, PG. 76. 429; 1st Letter to Succensus, para.4; et passim.

of the debate (single subjectivity in Christ, and the fact that a union occurred not an association), Cyril turns, in a revealing passage,[62] to meet the Antiochenes' objection that the incarnation demonstrates two distinct natures (physeis) in Christ, and thus cannot be properly summed up in the 'One Nature' catch-phrase. Here Cyril falls back again on the paradigm of the body-soul union and maintains that there is both 'one nature' (Mia Physis) and 'two natures-united'. The one nature is the primary reality of the incarnation, the 'two natures united' are deducible from the former. It is, therefore, only possible to speak of two natures after the union in a theoretical or deductive sense, precisely because the union has made them 'united', thus one reality, even though a composited one. So, for Cyril, just as it would be foolish for a person to say: 'I will take my body for a walk', instead of, 'I will go for a walk', just so to speak of two realities in Christ is unnecessary except in theoretical or technical discussions which want to state the obvious fact that Godhead is different to manhood. So he says:

> And so, they are simply splitting hairs when they talk about him suffering in the nature of the manhood, which serves only to separate it from the Word, and set it apart on its own, so that one is led to think of him as two, and no longer the one Word of God the Father, now incarnated and made man.[63]

It is his point that in all normal christian conversation, Christ should be referred to only as singular, and the fruits of the union recognised. Thus, Jesus is no less than God enfleshed (Theos sesarkomenos) and so the virgin is the Mother of God. Likewise God died on a cross, and a human voice called Lazarus back to life. For Cyril, all these statements express faith in the act of union, and all of them always presume the context of the incarnation.[64] To quibble with them in the manner of Nestorius seemed to Cyril to be motivated only by a refusal to accept the doctrine of single subjectivity. Thus, if Jesus was a different person to the Logos there would be a point in being worried about Theotokos language, or other such statements; on the other hand if Jesus was exactly the same person as the Logos (except

[62] See 1st Letter to Succensus, end of para. 6 & para. 7.

[63] 2nd Letter to Succensus, para.5; Epistle to the Monks, para.11; Explanation of the 12 Chapters, (Expln. 4).

[64] This too he thought to be obviously self-evident: if, for example, one was talking about Mary as Theotokos, how could one pretend it to be otherwise? The context of the nativity at Bethlehem was absolutely obvious.

that Jesus was obviously referring to the Logos as made man within history) what could there be that was objectionable in such titles as Theotokos? or in such phrases as the Mia Physis? As with many other catch phrases (such as Homoousios at Nicaea) their very succinctness and pugnacity was ideal for first annoying and then exposing the vaguenesses of heretical dissidence. And indeed Cyril certainly used several key phrases and titles, like the Theotokos and the Mia Physis, to serve precisely as this kind of 'test of faith'.

Hypostasis—Hypostatic Union

Closely related to his concept of the Mia Physis signifying the single subjectivity of the incarnate Lord, was his use of the term hypostasis.[65] This in fact was more commonly proposed in Cyril's works than the Mia Physis, particularly in the Nestorian correspondence, and he clearly regarded it as a more useful basis for wider terminological agreement, as well as a much better term with which to replace Nestorius' preferred concept of prosopon.

Cyril primarily uses hypostasis to connote individual reality. To speak of the one hypostasis of the Word was thus a simple way of connoting the single divine subjectivity that constituted the incarnation. In other words, the Logos was the direct and single personal subject of the incarnation and every incarnate act. Cyril also applied the word to denote the manner of the christological union: it was a hypostatic union (henosis kath' hypostasin), that is one that was based and founded on the singleness of hypostasis. This means that, for Cyril, the union of two distinct levels of reality, Godhead and manhood, takes place dynamically because there is only one individual subject presiding over both, the one person of the incarnate deity. He was well aware, however, that hypostasis had another technical meaning (as we saw earlier) connoting 'concretely realised existence' or simply 'real'. He delights in running the two associations together in his use of 'hypostatic union'; that is (a) the union is effected because there is only one personal subject of the divine and human actions, the same one being at once God and Man, and (b) the union is a real and concrete event, or as we might say 'a substantive reality' not a cosmetic exercise.[66]

---

[65] For a fuller technical and historical analysis of the term see Richard (1945).

[66] In the Third Letter to Nestorius (para.4) he talks of the hypostatic union as a 'natural union', by which he means a radically concrete union 'such as the soul of man has with its own body'.

Nestorius, as we have seen, read Cyril's 'hypostatic union' only in this latter sense, and understood the word in its most severely 'physical' connotation. When Cyril demanded he give his assent to the notion of hypostatic union (as in his Third Letter) Nestorius felt he was being pressed to accept Apollinarist Krasis doctrine, and refused to do so, thus exacerbating the conflict in the immediate prelude to Ephesus. In his Second Letter to Nestorius, Cyril proposed the concept of hypostatic union to summarise his central objections to Nestorius' theories:

> Because the Word hypostatically united human reality to himself 'for us and for our salvation', and came forth from a woman, this is why he is said to have been begotten in a fleshly manner[67] . . . . . but if we reject this hypostatic union as either impossible or unfitting, then we fall into saying that there are two sons.[68]

The hypostatic union demands a clear affirmation that the Logos was the sole direct subject of all the incarnate acts, and this was something Nestorius was loathe to admit so simply. Again, in his 3rd letter, Cyril used the phrase to push him towards such a view:

> We reject the term conjunction (synapheia) as being insufficient to signify the union . . . . . As we have already said, the Word of God, hypostatically united to the flesh, is God of all and master of all.[69]

In short, hypostatic union epitomised Cyril's key point about the Christ being one. It has thus survived in the history of doctrine to be the quintessential mark of orthodox christology, and from Chalcedon onwards it displaced the Mia Physis formula to assume the role of an internationally agreed technical christological language.

Unfortunately the Antiochenes, in Cyril's time, applied the term to signify 'concrete realities', and it was, thus, for them almost a synonym for physis understood in the sense of natural properties constituting a genus. Just as they insisted on two natures (God and Man) so they insisted that there had to be two hypostases in Christ. They were applying hypostasis in its technical philosophical sense of that which made real a physis and presented it to observation as a concrete entity. In his correspondences relating to Theodoret, Cyril acknowledged

---

67 2nd Letter to Nestorius, para.4.
68 Ibid. para. 6.
69 Third Letter to Nestorius, para.5; cf. Anathemas 2 & 3.

this different use of hypostasis.[70] He himself wished to reserve the word to signify subjectivity not natural property, but he meets Theodoret's objections to his own insistence on the single divine hypostasis of the Christ.

Theodoret's problem was that if a physis was not hypostatised, it was simply a notion, not a reality. As in our earlier semantic discussions in regard to Nestorian doctrine, we could argue about a unicorn's physis without ever having to believe that unicorns 'really' existed. The notional unicorn was fantastic because it was not hypostatised. If there was only one divine hypostasis in Christ, Theodoret argued, then Cyril's Christ was certainly God, but he could not be a real man because his human physis had not been made real by having a corresponding human hypostasis. Cyril meets that objection in two ways. In the first instance a human physis humanly hypostatised must be a distinct human being. Like a generic unicorn that does not really exist, once it has been hypostatised it is a real unicorn. More precisely, it now has a name and an identity. So, Cyril argues, if Christ's humanity was defined as humanly hypostatised then Christ would be a human person, the man Jesus. But in that case the christological union would necessitate the destruction or abolition of the divine person (for a human person cannot be a divine person and vice versa) which is offensive to christianity, or alternatively necessitate the acquiescence in having two personal centres in Christ. If this is the case, Cyril demands that the Antiochenes should openly admit that they teach Two Sons, and admit accordingly that in no sense can Christ be called one. If this were to happen, however, then the incarnation does not represent a dynamic interaction between God and Man at all, it is reduced to yet another prophetic epiphany, where God associates himself with a human being in a discontinuous parallel relationship—the inspiring God to the inspired man.

Theodoret, of course, did not want to accept these christological implications, but Cyril pressed him to admit that his own logic of double hypostasis demanded it. In his later writings, notably the Eranistes, Theodoret took the point and used Cyril's terminology of the single hypostasis. If, however, one accepted the overriding principle that there was only one hypostasis in Christ, and that a divine one, did Theodoret's criticism, that this implied a merely notional

[70] For a fuller discussion see Manoir (1944), p. 129.

or abstract humanity, have a real force? Cyril argued, no.

To assume that a hypostasis had to correspond with its own generic type was a generally applicable principle. So, a cat physis with a cat hypostasis becomes a real cat, and so on. But Cyril argues that the same rules do not apply in the case of the incarnation which is a unique ontological event. A cat physis cannot be realised by a human hypostasis, or a man's physis by an elephant hypostasis, simply because these created realities are set within the bounds of their generic limitations, and these limitations are a fundamental part of creaturehood. All created things must obey the limits their nature sets upon them. In the case of the divine hypostasis, however, his nature sets no limit upon him whatsoever; as God he is untrammelled in power and actually expresses that power to create all kinds of natures and their corresponding hypostases. It is thus nothing extraordinary (except for its extraordinary particularity) that God the Word should create a human physis for himself. This he does, outside the normal generic processes, in the particular act of the direct fashioning of a human form in the womb of the virgin. He did not displace a human foetus that had a human hypostatic reality of its own, because there was never an instant when this human foetus existed independently of his personal creative act. It was a human foetus within Mary because it was created in the perfect attributes applicable to the human genus, and within a human womb, but it was unique in that it was the direct and personal presence of the Logos on which it depended for the inception of its existence, not on human insemination. This was why Cyril maintained that the baby born from Mary after nine months of gestation was a fully formed member of the human genus, a baby with all the characteristics of a member of our species, a human baby indeed, but not simply any human baby, or merely a human baby. For Cyril, this baby was God in the flesh, who also possessed, as his direct personal attributes, all the characteristics of the deity.

In short, this human baby was personally hypostatised, directly and immediately, by the Word of God. He was human in so far as this meant he lived and moved within the attributes and conditions of the human genus, but he was also divine in so far as he lived and moved in the power of the Godhead which was 'his own nature'. The divine hypostasis of Christ moved and lived within human form, in the incarnate life, realising an individual human and historical existence; but some important facts demanded notice, and chiefly that this living out of a human life was an exercise of divine power. The

Word initiated the incarnation and sustained an incarnate life as an act of his own omnipotence. To this extent we have the paradox of a human (thus limited and fragile) life lived out as a direct expression of God's power (so, the limited humanity walks on the sea and rises from its own death). What this amounts to is that Cyril's doctrine of the single divine hypostasis insists that although Christ is entirely human, he is not a man, rather he is God made man, God enfleshed, God assuming humanity, or however else one cares to express it so as to bring out the centrally important notion that it was none other than the eternal Word of God who was the sole active subject of the human life of Jesus of Nazareth.

Cyril's doctrine has been attacked on the basis of two critiques related to this mono-hypostatic theory. The first, developing from Theodoret, is that Cyril's idea of the humanity without a human hypostasis (often, though wrongly for reasons which we shall see, called the 'non-hypostatic doctrine') meant that he saw Christ's manhood as abstract and notional, and to this extent defective. The second is that if Christ is God made man, but not particularly and precisely 'an individual man', then Cyril is again guilty of diminishing the concept of Christ's real humanness to the point of Docetism: he is merely an apparent man.

Neither criticism strictly applies to Cyril's theology. Despite many avowals by later critics, Cyril did not believe that Christ's humanity was non-hypostatic or merely generic simply because it did not possess an independent human hypostasis of its own. For him the whole point of the incarnation was that Christ's humanity was individual, and concrete, and real in the fullest possible sense, precisely because it was hypostatised by the Logos himself. This was no defect of humanity but rather an assumption of the whole range of human experience (including the proper limitations of humanity such as ignorance and mortality) by a person who at once lived within them, and yet lived beyond them because of his nature as God.

Christ's Limitations

We might take the test case of Christ's knowledge.[71] Cyril often speaks of Christ 'seeming' (dokein) to pray,[72] appearing to grow in knowledge,[73]

---

[71] cf. Manoir (1944) pp. 150–162.
[72] In Lucam 22.19, PG.72.908; In Joannem 17.2, PG. 74. 481.
[73] Adv. Anthropomorphitas. 14, PG.76.1100; Adv. Orient. PG.76.340; Quod Unus

seeming to be humiliated,[74] appearing to be troubled and sorrowful,[75] seeming to succumb to death,[76] and appearing to be exalted in the resurrection.[77] In fact Cyril says that he seemed to undergo all the limiting experiences proper to humanity.[78]

What he means, quite evidently, from all this, is certainly not that Christ 'seemed' to do these things whereas in reality he was not doing them at all, merely pretending to do so as a stage-act for the benefit of others. This is not the only application of the word 'dokesis', or 'seems to', although it is certainly the major application of its current English usage, which has thus sometimes been read back anachronistically into the text of Cyril. Cyril's 'docetism' has been disproportionately overemphasised by selecting out such passages referring to Christ's prayer, or Christ's knowledge, and reading him in the English usage of the words, as suggesting that when Christ prayed he only did so as a pious fraud. Being God he had no need to pray, and only prayed so as to offer an example to mankind on how to pray. Being God, he knew all things and so when he said in the Gospels that he did not know some things (such as the time of the end) this was only a pious subterfuge. Such an interpretation reads Cyril wholly out of context and radically distorts his true meaning in the texts in question.

If not only the texts relating to Christ's prayer, and knowledge, are treated, but the others are read in to the equation too, then it soon becomes abundantly clear that Cyril is not simply speaking of random incarnational activities being 'docetic' (particularly the spiritual or intellectual activities) but actually describing the whole economy in this way. When he speaks of Christ seeming to die, and seeming to be raised in glory, he has another intention than to deny the historical reality of these things, which for him were fundamental to the faith. Cyril believed absolutely in the reality of Christ's death. For him the body was truly cold in the tomb, and truly rose alive in glory on the third day. This is, in his estimate, the entire point of the incarnation and he had no intention of weakening its effect like any second century

---

Sit Christus, PG.75.1332; Adv. Nest. PG.76.153; Ad Reginas 2.16, PG.76.1353; Thesaurus PG. 75. 421; Adv. Theodoretum PG. 76. 416. and passim.

[74] De Recta Fide ad Theod. 28, PG. 76.1173.

[75] In Joannem 11.33, PG. 74.53; In Joannem 13.21, PG.74.136; In Lucam 22.39, PG. 72. 920.

[76] In Joannem 6.38, PG.73.532.

[77] Ad Reginas 2.50, PG. 76.1405.

[78] In Lucam 22.39, PG.72.920.

gnostic shying away from its physical veracity by denying the material reality of the events.

We conclude then, that when Christ seemed to die, Cyril means he did in fact die. In exactly the same way, when Cyril teaches that Christ seemed to pray, and so forth, he means that Christ actually and genuinely did all these things. Like his death, his prayer was no mere formality or charade. As a human being he died, similarly as a man he expressed his duty of religious reverence to God his Father, as the true Israelite. And in the same vein, he did in actual fact suffer in the garden and on the cross, and experienced all the limitations of mankind's natural capacity for knowledge.

All the limits proper to humanity were really his. In terms of grief, then, his tears at Lazarus' tomb were real and heartfelt. They were the natural and fitting human responses of that situation. His human knowledge was also limited to that appropriate for his time and upbringing—he knows only Aramaic and perhaps a little Greek; he has no mental awareness of electronics or nuclear physics, things which were not applicable to men of his day. So, if these experiences of limitation are real, then why does Cyril habitually use the phrase 'seemed to'?

What he means by it is not to deny the genuiness of the experiences *per se*, but to insist that they do not tell the whole story. This is simply because they are focusing on the limitations of the human economy and Cyril wishes to remind his readers that although the Word assumed those limits in his earthly condition, he did so as an act of power that did not negate his unlimited condition as God. Just as a mountain, from a distance, seems to be small, but on approach its great size makes us reconsider our judgement, so in the case of Christ, his full reality would make us reconsider any definitive statement that he was ignorant because he only knew two languages at most in his lifetime. To say 'he seemed to be limited' means, then, that although he was limited in his human life, he remained unlimited as God, and the observer is required by the terms of his faith to discern the deeper reality behind the material forms: the deity veiled in the flesh.

Cyril was feeling towards an assertion that Christ is genuinely, but not absolutely, limited. Limited as man he is untrammelled as God. Although Christ expresses those limitations such as grief, or mental doubt, authentically as far as Cyril is concerned, nevertheless he argues we must be tentative in definitively stating that Christ was ignorant, grief stricken, or so forth, because in referring such characteristics to the person, there was the risk that the speaker might forget that this single person is none other than the unlimited Word of God himself who, in his own nature, can never be subject to limitation. In short, the device of his phrase 'seemed to' does not argue against the authenticity of Christ's human experiences at all, even though several commentators have misinterpreted him along these lines, but on the contrary is a device that he applies to underline his doctrine of the single subjectivity.

To avoid this christological approach lapsing into either an unconvincing play-act, or an intolerable dualism, Cyril explains how one can order one's experiences of Christ, and does so by applying the adverb 'economically' (oikonomikōs). It becomes a cardinal christological term in his system.[79] To the same end he also applies the adverbs anthropoeides, and theikōs: Christ does some things godly-wise, and some things manly-wise, but never in an oscillating sense of discontinuous states. Even in the godly acts the humanity is active (his human feet walk on the sea) and in the human acts his deity is present (Lazarus obeyed Jesus' voice by coming back to life). Cyril's dominant and powerful sense of the union (such as the lily and its fragrance) saves his scheme from lapsing into such artificial duality. The limitations of humanity are appropriated by the Logos in just the same way (and for the same reasons) as he appropriates the body. They are thus real, but not the full story, for he who chooses to be limited is always the one who as God knows everything. The chosen limitations of his humanity are, however, not embraced for the sake of a pious play-acting, but are entered into seriously for the sake of redemptive deification:

> He who alone was more worthy than all others laid down his life for the sake of all, and for a short time, in an economy, allowed death to pull down his flesh. But then, as life, he destroyed death, refusing to suffer anything contrary to his own nature,[80] and he did this so that corruption should be weakened in the bodies of all, and so that the dominion of death should be destroyed.[81]

---

[79] Particularly notable in his That The Christ Is One, where he treats the theme at some length. cf. McGuckin (1994).

[80] Always in Cyril 'his own nature' means the deity; the humanity 'is his appropriated nature.'

[81] Letter to The Monks, para.25.

Even within his human limitations, Cyril argued, the Word was recognisable as God, and the limitations were, paradoxically, themselves manifestations of his great power in so far as the Word freely chose to subject himself to those economic limitations when he committed himself to an earthly life. So, for example he says:

> When he speaks of himself in a god-befitting way, 'Whoever has seen me has seen the Father', then we are given to understand his divine and ineffable nature.... On the other hand when, not despising the limitations of the manhood, he speaks to the Jews, 'Now you seek to destroy me, a man who has told you the truth,' we nonetheless recognise him as God the Word, despite the limitations of his manhood. For if it is necessary to believe that he who is God by nature became flesh, or rather became man ensouled with a rational soul, then what reason could anyone have to be ashamed of these sayings of his if they were made as befits a man? If he had refused to use words that are proper to a man, who was it that was forcing him to become a man like us in the first place?[82]

This is Cyril's constant stress, that the human limitations are genuinely assumed, but do not absolutely condition the life of the Saviour in the way they do the life of a normal human being who has no choice but to acquiesce in the limitations his nature imposes. The Word's transcendence of the limits of the human nature is not arbitrary, or magical, in such as way as to diminish the significance of his earthly experience so radically that it was not a real human life, but on the other hand the divine Word only experiences these very limitations in order to be able to transfigure them for the sake of the human race he desires to lift beyond the corruption of nature into which it has declined. The whole of the earthly limited experience, as he has so often said, was for this economic motive:

> When he became like us, even though he always remained what he was, he did not deprecate our condition. No, for the sake of the economy he accepted, along with the limitations of the manhood, all those things which pertain to the human condition, and he regarded nothing therein as unworthy of his personal glory or nature; for yet, and even so, he is God and Lord of all.[83]

As Cyril maintained, in his explanation of the twelfth anathema,[84] and frequently throughout the Christ Is One, this economic motive

---

[82] Third Letter to Nestorius. para.8.
[83] Explanation of the Twelve Chapters, Expln. 2, para.9; see ibid. Expln. 10, para.27.
[84] op. cit. para.31.

of salvation explains the apparent paradox of the Unlimited One in limitations, and gives what seem at first sight to be odd or unfitting conclusions, their true depth and grandeur as acts of God. This, then, is his general conclusion, that the limitations of the divine Word in the flesh are not absolute, although they are genuine; rather they are economically real. Critics who have read Cyril as trying to dispense the Logos from the full thrust of earthly experience and human limitation have, accordingly, misinterpreted in a quite radical way, the entire drive of his thought. For Cyril, the sufferings and limits of the earthly economy are no less real than the divine power that effects that economy. What he wishes to insist on, however, is that neither condition destroys or dispenses with the other, even though the divine power is the unerring hegemonikon of the whole composite economy. He is able to express this dynamic paradox at times in fine style:

> How could anyone doubt that the nature of God the Word is filled with true and regal dominion? Certainly we must understand this nature as being in the very highest heights befitting God. Since he appeared as man, however, a being upon whom all things are said to be bestowed as gifts, he received as a man, even though he is full and gives to all from his own fullness (*Jn.1.16*). He made our poverty his own, and we see in Christ the strange and rare paradox of Lordship in servant's form, and divine glory in human abasement. That which was under the yoke in terms of the limitations of manhood, was crowned with royal dignities, and that which was humble was raised to the most supreme excellence. And yet, the Only Begotten did not become man only to remain in the limits of the emptying (Kenosis), the point was that he who was God by nature should, in the act of the self-emptying, assume everything that went along with it. This was how he would be revealed as ennobling the nature of man in himself, by making it participate in his own sacred and divine honours.[85]

After this passage, Cyril goes on to explain in his That The Christ Is One that the economic working out of salvation through the human limitations had also a pedagogic value. Christ demonstrated in all aspects of his human life, the proper responses of of the sanctified Israelite, as an example for his disciples:

> Thus, the Word of God became an example for us in the days of his flesh, but not nakedly[86] or outside the limits of the self-emptying. This was why he was quite properly able to employ the limitations of the

[85] That The Christ Is One. PG.75.1377.
[86] Gymnos: that is in the nature of his deity *per se*.

> manhood. This was why he extended his prayer, and shed a tear, at times even seemed to need a saviour himself, and learned obedience, while all the while he was the Son.[87]

In short, the Word of God assumed the limitations of the human condition in just the same way, and for the same end, as he committed himself to that condition in the first place in a personal incarnation. But he did so as God to transfigure that limited state. This is the 'economic appropriation' in a nutshell:

> We say that these human things are his by an economic appropriation,[88] and along with the flesh, all the things pertaining to it.[89]

This appropriation is evidently an aspect of Cyril's overriding vision of the purpose of the entire incarnation as the redemptive deification of mankind. The Antiochenes had asked him, 'How can the same one both suffer and not suffer, be ignorant and be omniscient, if there is only One Christ and him the incarnate Word?' His answer was that in his own nature he was impassible and omniscient, and yet he became fragile and passible 'economically', and by appropriation, as the central strategy of his Kenosis, to redeem the world by this appropriation. This, for Cyril, was why christians could speak of the 'victory of the cross'. The Kenosis of the Word was no less than the raising up of human nature to a transcendent condition (hyper physin)[90] where the supreme limitations of that nature, corruptibility and death, would be abolished root and branch. And as these were annihilated, far from being the end of the human genus (because two of its defining characteristics were thus transfigured), it would indeed be the arrival of the entire human race at the perfection of its being. As it would be for the race, so it was for Christ in the particular case of the incarnation, because Cyril saw him as the personal paradigm and architect of the ontological rescue he had set in motion. Though he was genuinely limited as man, he transcended those limitations as God, and so brought the flesh to heavenly glory at the right hand of the Father, as the symbol of the transformation of human nature he had effected universally.

---

[87] That The Christ Is One, PG.75.1321.

[88] Kat' oikeiosin oikonomiken; cf. Manoir (1944) p. 133.

[89] That The Christ Is One, PG. 75. 1329.

[90] De Ador. in Sp. et Ver. PG.68.653; In Joannem PG.73. 153; cf. PG 74. 89; Glaphyra, PG.69.48; Dial. 4, PG 75.881.

3. The Cyrilline Construct

We concluded our introductory review of Cyril's christology with a question, and now that we have regarded some of the key elements of his doctrine in more detail, it may be apposite to re-state it, so as to focus our assessment of what he has achieved: To what extent has Cyril advanced christological understanding from the impasse it had reached poised uncertainly between the Apollinarist confusion of natures, and Diodore's separate subjects?

Perhaps the brief answer to that question is that Cyril's greatest achievement was to reorientate the classical Alexandrian scheme after it had been in great danger of being grounded by the careless piloting of Apollinaris; and having been rescued it was able to come alive and vibrant into the oecumenical forum where its voice and cadences dominated the agenda of the international church, literally setting the tone for a universally recognised christological orthodoxy for centuries to come, through the councils of Ephesus, Chalcedon, and Constantinople II.

After Cyril's defeat of Nestorius, the Two Sons approach to christology was utterly wrecked, and exiled from the bounds of classical orthodoxy. To this extent christians came into the full inheritance of the Athanasian and Cappadocian establishment of Nicene christological orthodoxy. Then, the full deity of the Logos had been fought for, now Cyril had completed their work in presenting an unquestionable icon of a Christ who was fully divine in and through his humanity, not in spite of it. The assuredness of this vision gave the christian consciousness of Christ a new stability and force of endurance that cannot be underestimated. In the impact of the Islamic invasions of the seventh century, Cyril's own christian domains of Egypt were flooded with a monolithically simple doctrine of Allah. The Alexandrian patriarchate, and increasingly the entire Byzantine domains, found in the warmth and religious mysticism of their belief in the divine Christ, a rock which secured them, and preserved their identity and existence, against adversely changing political destinies. It is highly doubtful whether a prophetic or charismatically based christology, such as that favoured by several of the Antiochenes (once it had permeated from episcopal salon to street level), would ever have survived its reinterpretation by Islam. This is another way of saying that it was Cyril's vision and concept of the divine Lord that authentically articulated the faith of the entire eastern church, and gave voice to the warmth of his people's religious commitment to a God who had so willingly, and personally, committed himself to the vagaries of their life.

Cyril's christology is not only filled with a profoundly mystical grandeur (one that can be seen graphically and immediately in the Byzantine icons of Christ Pantocrator which sum it up) but it also has a moral impact of considerable weight. In his doctrine of God's personal adoption of human life Cyril presented a paradigm wherein all human life was raised to a transfigured level, and endowed with a potentially divine significance. The most insignificant human act was thereby given an ultimate status and worth. As with Christ's spittle, for example, it meant nothing of any real value, and yet it also meant the gift of vision, physical and then spiritual. So with Christ's voice; how many million spoken words of his lifetime, so many of which were trivial and perishable as is the case with all human words? asking how to spell as a child, asking how to tie on his clothes, and yet that same voice was also asking the ultimate questions and posing the ultimate challenges. The Lord became, for Cyril, the epitome of all that was truly human, but humanity defined on a new premise—a transfigured humanity that came alive (as it had in Christ's case in the virgin's womb) in its communion with God, and was 'made personal' precisely in and through that communion.

Cyril's focusing of the christological debate on the issue of single hypostatic reality, or single subjectivity, within the composite life of the incarnate Lord, had inestimable effects on christian philosophy for subsequent centuries, in so far as it centred profound attention on the concept of the Person as the locus of the true self, and the holy place of the encounter with the divine. Prior to Cyril's insistence that the Logos himself was the personal subject of Jesus' life, Christianity had still been largely under the sway of either a Semitic or a Platonic type of anthropology. In the former, great stress was laid on the composite nature of human identity. Man was not simply soul, or flesh, or spirit, but a relation of all three, whose fragile communion, once disrupted, reduced him to the dust of the earth. In the latter, man was not, in reality, anything to do with his body or the animal soul this required to function, he was merely a captive in this alien bodily form, quintessentially a pure mind, untainted and ill at ease in its imprisonment.

Christian anthropology, under the twin stimuli of philosophical thought and biblical exegesis had, until Cyril's time, moved uneasily between the two. It was Cyril's ultimate achievement to present the blue-print for a final resolution of a definitive christian anthropology—one that was wholly re-defined in terms of the incarnation, and which synthesised the biblical and Hellenistic insights. Now, in the emerging concept of Person as dynamic agent of conscious action, spiritually exemplified in the hypostasis of Christ, Cyril had found a focal point which was as central and coherent an anthropological understanding as the Hellenistic elevation of Nous, yet which did not have to sacrifice the evident bodily reality and culture of mankind in the process of its self-identification. Cyril's rescue of christology from the distorted Hellenistic centralism of Apollinaris, and the unresolved semitic compositedness of the Antiochenes, presented a new and hopeful definition of the human person—the one who has the potential to transcend. As such it was quite distinct from the Platonic, Aristotelian, or semitic archetypes the church had previously been working from, and it gave to the christian world an unquestionably powerful way in which to articulate its spiritual and cultural identity.

The divine Lord, deifying his flesh for the sake of the ontological rescue of the human race, became at once the universal and particular paradigm of this. He who transcended his own fragility and death thus calls out to the whole race to become greater than they know themselves to be, and in this becoming, to become alive. To locate such an optimistic and religiously powerful concept of person at the living heart of Christianity was a factor that shaped the psychological structure of subsequent christian society, and formed its moral values around the concept of a self-giving personal identity and authenticity.

Cyril's vision of Christ has attracted its critics, mainly on the basis that somehow or other he did not do justice to the 'full humanity' of Jesus.[91] Such an approach presumes, however, that 'humanity' is to be defined on the basis of our common experience of humankind—a static and reductionist model of analysis arrived at by levelling down. Cyril's point was that Christ was fully human because he offered the possibility of human transcendence. Far from being less than human, because he was God, Christ demonstrated, for Cyril, the most quintessential human life of all, a life that was fully alive, vibrantly

[91] eg. F. Young (1983) p.260: 'Cyril is incapable of doing real justice to the humanity of Christ, and his rejection of Apollinarism is merely superficial.' Needless to say, for reasons I hope have become evident in the previous expositions, I dissent radically and *toto caelo* from such an analysis.

merciful, and sublimely compassionate, precisely because it had transcended all its tendencies to the self disintegration and moral compromise that so often disfigure humanity.

It is, in a sense, analogous to the old rabbinic proverb that says: 'The opposite of the human is not the animal, it is the demonic.' In Cyril's case the definition was more optimistically simple: it is the destiny and definition of the human to become divine. What He was by nature, to this he summons us by grace.

Cyril's language and preferred formulas were, as we have seen, sometimes responsible for causing more confusion than illumination in the camps of his opponents. Unlike Nestorius, however, his essential meaning always tended to emerge clearly enough from the discursive flow of his text, and so, while he cannot justly be called a confused thinker, at times he can be rightly accused of being a diffuse and discursive theologian. In this he is not unlike many other contemporary patristic rhetoricians, despite the Antiochenes' delight in caricaturing him as rambling and woolly. Some have accused him of protracting the christological controversy more than resolving it.[92] It would, nonetheless, be truer to conclude that it was only Cyril who possessed the moral and intellectual authority to bring matters to a head, at precisely the necessary time, by stating the issues so forcefully and so brilliantly.

When all is said and done, for the mystical and moral power his icon of Christ bears, for the profundity of his christian sense, the power of his intellect, and the unfailing purity of his literary purpose, then surely all his faults are diminished in significance.

His greatness cannot be denied.

---

[92] Scholarly hindsight is, of course, a very cheap commodity, as in Grillmeier's claim that Cyril 'delayed' the christological resolution; Grillmeier (1975) p. 446.

CHAPTER FOUR

THE OECUMENICAL RECEPTION OF CYRIL'S THEOLOGY

1. From Dioscorus to Chalcedon

Cyril's theology was destined to have great implications for the future development of Christianity. Even before the end of his own lifetime he was regarded as the authentic representative of the christological tradition. This was not only true in his enthusiastic endorsement and acclamation at Ephesus, by the bishops assembled there, but to an extent even by the Antiochenes themselves where opposition to his thought was localised. Significant oriental thinkers came increasingly round to his point of view, such as Acacius of Melitene, and Rabulla of Edessa, then even Acacius of Beroea, John of Antioch, and not least Theodoret himself who ended up by defending the very Cyrilline terms and construct he had once attacked, for the Eranistes adopts the language of the single hypostatic reality of the Word incarnate. Cyril's instinct in regarding the school of Diodore and Theodore Mopsuestia as not being a substantive 'tradition' in itself was largely proven right by the way in which this school had well and truly collapsed by the late fifth century, hardly sustained even by the tiny Nestorian minority outside the imperial borders in Persia and Arabia. After Cyril, and largely because of him, the Alexandrian schema of the pre-existent Word's Kenosis to humanity and his deification of the flesh became the standard canon of christological language for the church universally.

Cyril's construct had not depended on its formulas, rather on the clear passion of its narrative of the descent of the divine person, to save. As a result of the conflict over terminology from 431 to 433, even Cyril had come to admit that if his opponents agreed the central principle of single subjectivity, he would admit a flexibility in the terms he used to describe that event. So, in his later correspondence with the Antiochenes, Cyril eased away from using the Mia Physis as a catch phrase (though he unapologetically applied it even in one of his last great writings, That The Christ Is One) and moved, with them, towards the commonly agreed language of single hypostasis.

Accordingly, he allowed the point that Christ was possessed of two natures (dyo physeis) as a concession to the Antiochenes which he felt was quite compatible with the general run of his theology, given the other concessions the Antiochenes themselves had made after the Nestorian debacle. He only admitted the diphysite position in terms of the validity of the Antiochenes to talk that way if they so wanted. He had no intention of using such language himself and, in the Letter to Eulogius and That The Christ Is One, he says explicitly that he regarded their whole way of thinking and arguing as obscure.

He admitted the diphysite terms could be orthodox on two grounds. The first was that the 'natures' in question meant natural properties (idiomata) not independent subject entities (in the way he habitually preferred to regard the connotation of physis), and therefore one was talking about states, or conditions, not persons. The second was that their continuing co-existence should be radically qualified by sufficient indications that these two realities had actually been united, made one, were inseparable in mutual communion, or only 'notionally' separable (like body and soul) not practically divisible. Such a profound stress on the union of the two, such that 'the two were really one' was, of course, typically Cyrilline, but there is no doubt that some of the Antiochenes, and perhaps some of the Latins later, did not share the same passionate commitment to emphasising the unity of Christ that animated Cyril, and were more ready to identify him as a single subject presiding over a bi-polar reality than Cyril cared to do, who felt that the two realities of Godhead and manhood, though distinct, were synchronised by mutual perichoresis far more substantively than such a bi-polarity suggested.

Even when he admitted the diphysite point, as for example in the Succensus letters, or his letters to Eulogius and Valerian of Ikonium, he admits its validity only through the perspective of his overall intent, as set out in the mainstream of his writings. He did not, therefore, really retreat from any part of his earlier doctrine in accepting the Antiochene argument. At the time of the Antiochene rapprochement in 433, his own supporters such as his archdeacon Dioscorus and his adviser Isidore of Pelusium, even his own agents in Constantinople, expressed alarm that he might have given away too much in his diphysite concessions. He seems to have reassured them on the basis that it was a concession to be understood in terms of his previous teaching, not as an amendment of it. Such was the policy directly continued by Dioscorus, his successor in the see of Alexandria.

Dioscorus sometimes has wrongly been accused of misinterpreting Cyril's mind on this point, but in fact he consistently applied Cyril's ideas and interpreted all christology on the basis of the pure Cyrilline canon, with one significant exception. What he did was to attempt to delete Cyril's Antiochene negotiations from the picture. He came to regard all the Syrian 'variations' on the Cyrilline theme as dispensable. This was a fatal emendation of his teacher's life's work. Dioscorus regarded the rapprochement of 433 as merely the result of an imperial pressure placed on a sick old man, whose judgement had accordingly lapsed. In consequence, he cut across the diphysite literature of Cyril and thus abandoned the policy of mutual search for an agreed terminology that had been slowly bringing the churches together in common agreement after the council of Ephesus. In this, he not only abandoned a part of Cyril's legacy, but made a large departure from Proclus too.

It was Proclus who had been largely instrumental in that international process of brokering Cyril's principles for the vast areas within the sway of the imperial city, not least the Syrians and Armenians, and his celebrated Tome[1] developed the central idea that Cyril's vision could be authentically expressed in the terminology of one person hypostatising two natures in a mutual communion of interchange (antidosis idiomaton). Such was to become the classical resolution at Chalcedon, but before this happened two significant events occurred. Firstly, in 446, Proclus died, and was succeeded by the more ambivalent Flavian. Secondly, in 447, the Syrians, under the stimulus of Theodoret and Ibas of Edessa,[2] reopened the argument for a diphysite christology that owed little respect to Cyril's memory. At the same time, a dyed-in-the-wool Cyrillian was pushing for a christology that pressed Cyril's implications alone, and brought the scheme back to a proximity with Apollinaris that Cyril himself would have resisted.[3] The latter was the archimandrite Eutyches, at Constantinople, one of the original dissidents who had started the process of complaints against Nestorius back in 428. Theodoret was probably attacking him as the 'beggar man' of the title of his Eranistes, but as far as Disocorus was concerned

[1] ACO 4.2.191; PG.65.864.

[2] Theodoret published his Eranistes that year, and Ibas of Edessa had succeeded, in 435, the strongly Cyrilline Rabbula, and completely reversed his theological policy, becoming a new Syrian leader of the Cyrilline opposition.

[3] In fact Cyril does resist, in advance, several of the tendencies of Eutyches, in his 2 letters to Succensus.

Eutyches was a martyr to be defended, and with Alexandrian backing, that of the Emperor Theodosius (now a convinced Cyrilline), and powerful court aristocrats including the Grand Chamberlain Chrysaphius the Eunuch, it seemed as if Eutyches' star was now in the ascendant. In February 448 a law was promulgated that forbade any christological scheme not in accord with Nicaea or Ephesus, or the 'faith of Cyril of blessed memory'.

Despite the strong signal from the court that Cyril was to be the sole canon, Eutyches' enemies were strong enough to force a revision of the issue,[4] and in November of 448 the archimandrite was tried by a very reluctant Flavian, for doctrinal aberrations, at the patriarchal synod at Constantinople. Flavian, knowing that the Syrian and Alexandrian schemes were once more coming closer and closer towards an explosive clash, as they had earlier under his unfortunate predecessor Nestorius, tried to propose an eirenic compromise that would appease both sides. Melding the terms and statements of Cyril's letter to John of Antioch in 433, and the ideas of Proclus' Tome, Flavian tried to settle the argument over christological polarity once and for all.

He censured Eutyches for having an unbalanced theology, and imposed on him as a test of faith, if he wished to be reinstated to his priestly functions, the symbol: 'We confess that the Christ is of two natures (ek dyo physeon) after the incarnation, and one hypostasis, one person'.[5] Flavian's 'of two natures' was, in context, clearly weighted towards being an affirmation of the christological formula 'one person subsisting in two natures', which was becoming increasingly the standard profession of the Syrians; but Eutyches adamantly refused to accept this, on the grounds that he felt it weakened the sense and reality of the union with which Cyril had qualified the post-incarnational state of the one Christ. Eutyches stood by Cyril's idea of the 'out of two natures' but pressed it rigorously to a sense that puzzled many of his hearers:[6] as meaning two natures before, but only one nature as a result of, the incarnation. From this time onwards, the issue of the 'out of two natures', as opposed to 'in two natures', became the new storm centre of the debate.

---

[4] The Augusta Aelia Pulcheria was an implacable enemy of Chrysaphius, who had ousted her influence at court, and thus an enemy of all the power bases Eutyches was relying on for his support. Chrysaphius was Eutyches' godson.

[5] ACO 2.1.1. p. 114, paras. 8–10.

[6] Giving rise to the opinion of Leo, among others, that Eutyches was a very muddled old man.

If Christ was 'in two natures', a preferred perspective of the Syrians, and to an extent of the Latins who were to feature now more directly than they had in 431, then the stress was placed on the abiding integrity of the natures after the incarnation. If Christ was 'of two natures', the preferred perspective of the Cyrillines, then the stress was placed on the incarnation as an act of union, thus a corrrelation of two natures into a consilience, a unity. The two positions were not mutually incompatible, though many of their respective protagonists thought they were, but they certainly represented different approaches to the issue with notably differing emphases, and this time, unlike 431–433, there was no strong pressure coming from the Emperor to reach a compromise. This time Theodosius was more inclined simply to impose Cyril's work as a universal standard, and unfortunately regarded Dioscorus as not only Cyril's episcopal successor but even his legitimate intellectual heir.

Despite his appeals to Rome, Eutyches was condemned, and Pope Leo entirely concurred in his deposition,[7] deciding himself to compose a definitive solution to the christological problem, from the Roman perspective.[8] The Roman tradition was an element that had so far played little role in what hitherto had mainly been an Alexandrian—Syrian debate. When the Roman digest was presented, however, it seemed, to the great surprise of many eastern bishops that it was much closer to the Syrian perspective than that of Alexandria, whose policy Rome had been so adamantly defending in the time of Cyril himself.

Dioscorus, with the Emperor Theodosius' approval, supported Eutyches wholeheartedly, and after he had received an official appeal from the archimandrite, the prospects for any continuation of the fragile peace of Ephesus seemed very slight indeed. On March 30th 449, Theodosius and Chrysaphius set aside the legal condemnation of Eutyches and called for a full synodical review of the issue (by implication, on the standard of Cyril's theology) back in the metropolis of Ephesus. So opened the second council of Ephesus in 449, under the presidency of Dioscorus. It was intended, from the beginning, to be a re-run of Ephesus 431, and Dioscorus' presidency made it a trial of Flavian, Theodoret and Ibas, more than an examination of Eutyches, who, thus, had merely a symbolic role in the whole affair.

---

[7] Leo, Ep. 27, June 447.

[8] The Tome of Leo, E.T. in Bindley (1950). It is largely a digest of selected passages from Augustine; see McGuckin (1990), also Liebaert (1966) p. 213, fn.4.

At the council Dioscorus restated Cyril's doctrine, without the Antiochene concessions, and similarly abandoned all the lines of development drawn by Proclus and Leo.[9] Eutyches was restored, and then the blood-letting began. Theodoret, Ibas of Edessa, and their patriarch Domnus of Antioch (for tolerating them) were all deposed. Flavian of Constantinople was also deposed along with Eusebius of Dorylaeum who had first accused Eutyches. Dioscorus privately read Leo's Tome which had been sent to him as the council president (in the expectation that he would simply endorse and promulgate it) with a scandalised disbelief, that soon turned to hostility. He did not condemn Leo out and out, for political reasons, but cast aside the Tome despite all the protests of the Roman delegation, and refused to acknowledge its existencee, let alone have it read at the council. He thus saved himself the embarrassment of having to censure the Pope in synodical process at the same time as deposing two other patriarchs.

The atmosphere at Ephesus was extremely tense. Dissenters were heavily repressed by the imperial troops sent to ensure uniformity under Dioscorus' directions. Soldiers armed with cudgels beat up several of the condemned bishops who carried on protesting, including Flavian of Constantinople. This time Theodosius was determined that his second Ephesian council should follow his policy without demur. The soldiers did their job so well that Flavian died a few days later of the shock to his system, to the great scandal of the bishops, both present and afar. In his fury on hearing the results of this synod Pope Leo called it a den of thieves rather than a synod (Non concilium sed latrocinium) and to subsequent history it has since been known as the Latrocinium, the Robber Synod, or Brigandage of Ephesus.

Even so, for all Leo's objections, the council was vindicated and endorsed by the Emperor. Theodosius, for once, had his face set on

---

[9] Leo's Tome, despite its robust application of the distinct properties of each nature remaining intact after the incarnation (more so than Proclus or Flavian) still showed Leo as in essential harmony with Cyril's point, for he spoke of the natures 'running together in one person' (in unam coeunte personam). Leo's notion of the Word performing the godly acts, and the flesh performing the human acts of Christ was, however, an undoubted diminution and regression from Cyril's sense of the personal unity of the hypostasis. It seemed odd that the Romans should wish to fall back to an attibution of conscious action to a 'nature' rather than the person, in some parts of their discourse, and many found the teaching to be in opposition to Cyril's Fourth Anathema, though strictly speaking (like the Formula of Reunion of 433) it was not, in so far as it referred both sets of actions back, ultimately, to the same person.

something. But the plans of men and their destinies do not always agree; and on the 28th of July in 450 the imperial lord of the world fell from his horse and broke his neck. The head of the odious Chrysaphius was impaled on a stake hardly before his master's body was cold, for thus the Augusta Pulcheria moved out from her enforced retirement, with the connivance of the imperial Chief of Staff, Aspar. She assumed the absolute power in alliance with the popular General Marcian, whom she symbolically married,[10] and raised to the purple. The empire was in a parlous state; the Huns closing in on its north-eastern borders, the western provinces in fatal decline in the face of waves of barbarian migrations and incursions. Royal policy had to be decisive, and a definitive resolution to bring harmony to the christian world was to be Pulcheria's main intent. She would accept no contradiction, and made it clear to all concerned that a settlement acceptable to Rome was a priority, for both she and Marcian were currently negotiating to have his imperial elevation acknowledged by the surviving western Augustus, Valentinian III. Soon the imperial couple reconvened an international synod to meet at the capital, in the suburb of Chalcedon. It opened on the 8th of October 451. Its story would need another book in the telling, but it already commands many excellent studies outlining the historical and theological aspects.[11] Our account here is mainly concerned with its relevance to the reception given to Cyril's theology.

2. Cyril and the Chalcedonian Settlement

Through several of the opening sessions at Chalcedon, the synodical bishops resisted the imperial demand for a definitive statement of faith. The fathers present simply refused, at first, to create any new statement, but the profession of Flavian was accepted as orthodox, and he was posthumously rehabilitated.[12] In the second session, on October 10th,

[10] She retained her vow of virginity and never actually co-habited with him, but the alliance was (probably) the occasion for the exiled Nestorius' bitter accusations against her as an adulteress.

[11] cf. R. V. Sellers, The Council of Chalcedon (1953); The key documents are translated in Bindley (1950); Full study by Grillmeier-Bacht (1951–1954); other analyses by Meyendorff (1969) and more recently, ibid. 'Imperial Unity and Christian Divisions', NY, 1989; Pelikan (1971) pp. 263f Kelly (1978); Liebaert (1966).

[12] Subsequently so too were Theodoret and Ibas. But when the former entered the synod to take his seat, the outraged uproar of the bishops demonstrated that it was a generally unpopular and forced decision.

the Second letter of Cyril to Nestorius, the Formula of Reunion (433), and finally Leo's Tome, were presented for acceptance as definitive statements of christological orthodoxy. One of the bishops present cried out for the Anathemas to be added to the list of authoritative texts, but he was not successful in his ploy. Several of the Illyrian and Palestinian bishops expressed their grave disquiet about the apparent dualism of Leo's Tome, and blocked its immediate acceptance by the council. They were particularly concerned about this phrase:

> Each form[13] effects what is proper to it in common with the other; that is the Word operated what belongs to the Word, and the flesh operated what belongs to the flesh. One of these shines forth in miracles, the other succumbs to injuries.[14]

The intent of Leo was to teach substantially the same doctrine as Cyril, that is the single subjectivity of the Word presiding over his incarnate condition, perhaps with a more stressed sense of the distinction of natures, which in common Latin parlance had no other meaning attached to the word than 'natural properties'. To the Cyrillines at Chalcedon, however, and these undoubtedly formed the great majority of the bishops present, the use of the pronouns in the final phrase was alarming. With a close exegesis of: 'One of these shines with miracles, the other succumbs to injuries', it is evident that the pronoun does not refer to personal subjects (God the Word, the man Jesus) but to the respective 'forms' (the form of God, the form of a slave) and thus the Tome was in substantive agreement with the Formula of Reunion. Nonetheless, the stress it gave to the abiding distinctness of forms seemed to be both a contradiction of the Fourth Anathema and a betrayal of Cyril's fundamental insistence on the union, despite Leo's language of concurrence and union in one person.[15]

After Dioscorus' trial and deposition in the third session of the council, the leadership of the Cyrillines passed to the Illyrian and Palestinian bishops and they kept up their attack on the Latin definition, forcing the Roman delegates to justify themselves. It was only after the Romans had given them assurances that their suspicions did not represent the true intent of the Tome, and after several committees had discussed the issues over the best part of a week, that they agreed to sign the

---

[13] ie. that of God and that of the slave (Phil.2.6f.)
[14] ACO. 2.1.p. 28., 12–14.
[15] In unam coeunte personam (concurring in one person); natura inviolabilis naturae est unita passibili (an inviolable nature is united with a passible nature).

Tome[16] at the Fourth session. Its orthodoxy was affirmed here, but (to the growing embarrassment of the Roman delegates) only after five days had been devoted to a close scrutiny of the Tome's text in comparison with Cyril's writings, so that the consonance of the one with the other could be confirmed. The bishops were particularly keen to see how Leo's 'in two natures' could be reconciled with Cyril's 'out of two natures'.

When the Tome was finally acclaimed, of the one hundred and sixty one bishops who registered their official 'acclamations' in the Acts of the council, almost every one of them included a specific judgement that Leo had been faithful to Cyril.[17] Gray's judgement is highly pertinent here:

> Much is usually made of the cry which greeted the reading of the Tome: 'Peter has spoken these things through Leo'. It is often forgotten that that was not all they said; they went on to say: 'Cyril so taught. Eternal be the memory of Cyril. Leo and Cyril taught the same thing. This is the true faith. . . . This is the faith of the fathers.'[18] It was indeed complimentary to suggest that the bishop of Rome was living up to the reputation for orthodoxy of his see's founder, but it involved something more important than a compliment to compare Leo with Cyril the obvious meaning of those exclamations is that the bishops accepted and praised Leo *because* he taught the same thing as Cyril. Cyril was the test for christological orthodoxy, and Cyril alone.[19]

Even so, the Leonine 'in two natures' was not adopted at that session.

The fifth session of the council represented the continuing insistence of the Emperor Marcian that a simple and short definition should be published by the council, one that could be promulgated throughout the empire. With considerable reluctance the bishops agreed to do so, in principle, though several false starts ensued before a commonly agreed text emerged. The first draft proposal has not survived in the records but it certainly contained Cyril's own formula that Christ was 'out of two natures'.[20] The Syrians vetoed this and in the ensuing deadlock a committee was established by imperial decree to compose the council's final statement. Marcian threatened the bishops that if they could not agree on a text he would dissolve the council and

---

16 ACO 2.1.2. p. 102. 22–41.
17 Chalcedon: Actio 4.9; ACO 2.1.2. pp. 94–109; cf. Gray (1979) pp. 9–16.
18 Chalcedon, Actio 3.23. ACO. 2.1.2. p. 81.
19 Gray (1979) p. 9.
20 ACO 2.1.2. p. 124, no. 13. cf. Cyril's Second Letter to Succensus.

reconvene it in Italy. Since everyone knew that this meant an Italian council would simply rubber-stamp Leo's Tome, and its dogmatic profession wholesale, the bishops sudden willingness to accept the committee's decision is yet another indication that they were generally unhappy with the thought of having the Tome as the final word on the subject. This is one of many indications that the common European interpretation of the Acts of Chalcedon as the triumphant vindication of Leo's theology,[21] is historically misplaced. This subsequent western reading of Chalcedon, although it accurately depicts the manner in which christology was received in the western provinces from the fifth century onwards, does not do justice to the way the Chalcedonian fathers approached the texts on the occasion. Nor does it represent, at all, the way in which Chalcedon was interpreted in the East. Moreover, the detailed terms of the Chalcedonian decree, as we shall see, demonstrate that it was meant as a deliberate corrective of several of the Tome's aspects.

More careful studies, such as those of Diepen,[22] Meyendorff,[23] and Gray[24] have demonstrated that Chalcedon, despite the influence of the Roman and Syrian voices in its deliberations is still, in the main, defending a Cyrilline perspective on the canon of christological orthodoxy[25] and, thus, in the direct line of development between Ephesus 431 and Constantinople 553, not in aberration from it.

The imperial commission of eighteen commanded by the emperor to draw up a conciliar draft statement, was instructed to affirm the enduring identity of the 'two natures.' The bishops would accept this, however, only on the basis of the strictest qualifications and safeguards (such as those agreed by Cyril himself in the Succensus letters). The adverbs of Cyril they had in mind were that the two natures endured in the one Christ: unchangeably (atreptōs), undividedly (ameristōs), and unconfusedly (asynchytōs). They were trying to move on a mean

---

[21] e.g. Kelly (1978) pp. 341–343, esp. 341—though Kelly himself admits that this is not a balanced view of the proceedings.

[22] H. Diepen, Les Trois Chapitres au Concile de Chalcédoine, Oosterhout, 1953.

[23] Meyendorff (1969) chs. 1–4.

[24] P.T. Gray, The Defense of Chalcedon in the East. Leiden, 1979.

[25] Gray, for example, argues from the way the bishops at Chalcedon regarded Theodoret's presence, the way they received the Tome with qualification, and the actual construction of the Chalcedonian decree, that the Cyrilline theology (understood in the sense Proclus and Flavian had mediated it rather than Dioscorus and Eutyches) was the conciliar majority view. Ibid.pp. 7f, and thus the original 'intention' of the council.

between Nestorian duality and Apollinarist fusion. The prelude to the final definition at Chalcedon had involved the solemn reaffirmation of Cyril's Second and Third Letters to Nestorius (without the Chapters) and Leo's Tome as definitive standards of orthodoxy. The symbol of faith then went on to declare:

> In agreement, therefore, with the holy fathers, we all unanimously teach that we should confess that Our Lord Jesus Christ is one and the same Son, the same perfect in Godhead, and the same perfect in manhood, truly God and truly man, the same of a rational soul and body, consubstantial with the Father in Godhead, and the same consubstantial with us in manhood, that is like us in all things but sin; begotten from the Father before the ages as regards his Godhead, and in these last days, the same one begotten from the virgin Mary, the Theotokos, as regards his manhood, for our sake and for the sake of our salvation; one and the same Christ, Son, Lord, Only Begotten, who is made known[26] in two natures, without confusion, without change, without division, without separation; the difference of natures being by no means removed because of the union, but the property of each nature being preserved and concurring in one prosopon and one hypostasis, not parted or divided into two prosopa, but one and the same Son, Only Begotten, Divine Word, the Lord Jesus Christ, as the prophets of old and Jesus Christ himself have taught us about him, and the creed of our fathers has handed down.[27]

It is remarkable in the light of this text how many European scholars have concluded that 'the converging influence of the western tradition and the diphysite tradition of Antioch was the determinant factor' here.[28] Even more peculiar is the judgement of Pelikan, who seems in this instance to be leaning heavily on Liebaert: 'Even though it may be statistically accurate to say that "the majority of the quotations come from the letters of Cyril",[29] the contributions of Leo's Tome were the decisive ones, in the polemic against what were understood to be the extreme forms of the alternative theologies of the incarnation. . .'[30] By the time that the afterthought of the final clause has been lost in the idea's subsequent cloning and dissemination, such a judgement can emerge in the even more unbalanced assessment of Davis[31] as: 'The contributions of Leo's Tome were the decisive ones.'

---

[26] Gnorizomenon: intellectually perceived.
[27] ACO 2.1.2. p. 129, 16–22.
[28] Liebaert (1966) p. 220.
[29] I. Ortiz de Urbina, in Grillmeier-Bacht (1951) 1.389–418.
[30] Pelikan (1971) p. 264.
[31] Davis (1987) p. 187, quoting Pelikan out of context.

In fact, Leo's attribution of separate actions to natures had been decidedly dropped, and his terms only inserted as one key sentence[32] in a sea of Cyrilline citations, for the skeletal elements of the symbol are all, in spirit and largely in terminology, clear resumés of Cyril's writings. Even the Leonine contributions that were accepted, were admitted only after the conciliar fathers had seen how their Cyrilline sense could be established. The second and Third letters to Nestorius were the main quarries, but other Cyrilline sources, evidently less familiar to some of the commentators, are significant too.

The recurring drive of the text's 'one and the same' is pure Cyril, as was the central doctrine of the one hypostasis of the Word as single subject, the virgin as Theotokos, and the utter rejection of the Antiochene Two Sons christology. Yet, as Liebaert has pointed out, it was, in a sense, the acceptance of 'in two natures' that was the sticking point of the council, and thus the critical element of its symbol. In the aftermath of the council of Chalcedon many Cyrillines in Egypt and Syria thought that this was an essential betrayal of Cyril's theology, and separated into the Monophysite schism. Were they right to interpret it in this way? Had the western addition so qualified Cyril's intention that it represented 'the triumph of diphysitism'? On the basis of an accurate exegesis of Chalcedon's text it would seem not. Liebaert puts it as follows: 'The following expression "made known in two natures" is the most original element of the definition: these are the terms which the [Roman] delegates, the Orientals [ie. Antiochene party] and the imperial magistrates had demanded to be inserted instead of the expression "out of two natures" proposed by Anatolius.'[33] Well, if the 'out of two natures' is rightly seen as Cyril's phrase, which Anatolius was still offering even at the last stage of the draft, was its replacement a decided shift from Cyril's point? To qualify the 'in two natures' in such an extraordinarily tight way by the famous sequence of four consecutive adverbs seems a highly emphatic point and if Liebaert is suggesting that this was a western or Antiochene contribution, in this, Chalcedon's key phrase, he could not have been more mistaken. In fact the adverbs are deliberate, though often unrecognised, quotations of Cyril himself—primarily from the First Letter to Succensus, which was very much in the mind of the Chalcedonian draft-writers at this point.

[32] The main Leonine contribution to the Chalcedonian settlement is the phrase: 'the property of each nature being preserved and concurring in one prosopon.'

[33] Anatolius was the head of the commission of eighteen. Liebaert (1966) p. 220.

In this text[34] Cyril himself explains exactly on what terms the 'in two natures' can be accepted as orthodox, and on what terms it would be a fallacious theory. Here he says:

> And so we unite the Word of God the Father to the holy flesh endowed with a rational soul, in an ineffable way that transcends understanding, without confusion (asynchytos), without change (atreptos), and without alteration (ametabletos), and we thereby confess One Son and Christ and Lord. The same one God and Man.[35]

To have supplied, in substance, three of the four so-called 'Chalcedonian adverbs' already, and with the fourth missing adverb emphasising Cyril's basic point of the inseparability of the natures, is hardly, on anyone's terms, a 'triumph' of western and Antiochene christology. It is surely the complete vindication of Cyril's overall ideas, and shows that the Chalcedonian commission constantly attempts to use his terms even in those critical instances where they were ordered not to. In this, Cyril stands out, unarguably, as the primary authority for the Chalcedonian decree, and this, I think, was the deliberate intention of those who framed it.

In his immediately following context, in the Succensus letter, Cyril goes on to say that this is what 'out of two natures' means, but then adds his famous qualification, in the same text, that the proper understanding of this does not deny that the two natures endure within the one Christ (in two natures) but only denies that they endure separately. Cyril admits that notionally, or 'in theory', one can speak of two natures, but that to do so in common and habitual parlance would lay one open to weakening the belief that a union has occurred, as if the natures were 'practically distinct', as it were, rather than being 'one in practice'.

He says:

> As to the manner of the incarnation of the Only Begotten, then theoretically speaking (but only in so far as it appears to the eyes of the soul) we would admit that there are two united natures, but only one Christ and Son and Lord, the Word of God made man and made flesh.[36]

And he concludes by comparing the notional distinctness and practical

---

[34] Ep. 45, ACO 1.1.6, 151–157; PG.77.228–237.
[35] 1st Letter to Succensus, para.6.
[36] 1st Letter to Succensus, para.7.

union as similar to the relationship of soul and body in a man. Now this, in a strict sense, is not the di-physite language. He is really teaching the Mia Physis, *in loco*, and preferring the 'out of two natures' while allowing that his opponents' language of 'in two natures' can be orthodox under certain conditions: that is if they are understood to be 'natural properties' that endure notionally rather than practically. What that means is that they abide without being mutually destroyed or altered in the union (something that he never tired of insisting in his doctrine of the economy) but are only 'discerned to have endured' by intellectual scrutiny, since to all intents and purposes they have been united, that is 'made one' in the one Christ.

But this, nothing else, is what the Chalcedonian text teaches, at least when it is read apart from the Leonine Tome, which has too often been taken as its exegetical commentary, but rather should be taken out of the interpretative picture since the Chalcedonian symbol was more in the manner of a corrective of Leo than a substantiation of him. This can be seen nowhere more clearly than in the verbal form which drives that whole central clause containing the four adverbs qualifying 'in two natures'. It is none other than 'Gnorizomenon': 'made known to the intellect.' Chalcedon, therefore, teaches that Christ is 'made known (to the intellect) in two natures'. It does not simply teach that 'Christ is in two natures' as the Antiochene system had suggested. Those who do not recognise or understand the importance of the difference are those who have not followed the whole fifth century christological debate, but this certainly did not include the bishops present at Chalcedon. And so, the Chalcedonian decree, at this critical juncture, is clearly, and deliberately, a profession of Cyril's understanding of the union and, again, largely on his terms. The 'made known' of Chalcedon is substantially the 'notional scrutiny' (oson men heken eis ennoian) of Cyril's First Letter to Succensus. Even when Cyril's terminology was felt to be in need of correction, or clarification, whether to placate the West, or to exclude a Eutyches or a Dioscorus, it was instinctively to Cyril that they turned to supply the correction.

3. Cyril in the Chalcedonian Aftermath

As far as the West was concerned, Chalcedon was Leo. It is, therefore, not surprising to find the West continuing to read the intent of the council of Chalcedon almost exclusively through the Tome, and this can also partly explain the long subsequent history of an uneven

European exegesis of the council. Alternative views have long been standard in eastern christian theologies, but until recent decades these have largely been in unaccessible languages. In the East, from the time of Ephesus 431 onwards, Cyril was, and remained, the chief christological canon. In the East, hardly anyone was happy, in the long term, with the so-called 'Chalcedonian settlement'. Marcian had been so anxious to establish a Roman voice at the deliberations because of the political needs pressing him and the Empire at that time. In the aftermath of Chalcedon (with the short-lived exception of Justinian's reign) the West became increasingly sidelined from the affairs of the Empire because of the barbarian conquests. It continued to exercise an influence on the subsequent debate, but largely in terms of a conservative weight that insisted on the Chalcedonian decree as the central canon, whereas the East wished, generally speaking, to turn back to Cyril pure and simple.

Large parts of Egypt and Syria preferred to remain with Cyril's language of the Mia Physis and the Ek dyo physeōn, instead of the terms that had been proposed for the reconciliation of the Antiochenes, and those offered by the Latins. Moreover in the eastern territories of Byzantium, in the aftermath of Chalcedon, neither the Latins or the Syrians were any longer of great political or theological moment. The western church, to its great surprise, found itself having to re-fight the Arian crisis, since the barbarians had brought the ancient heresy back into everyday life, and for these purposes they were glad of the di-physitism of Chalcedon in a way that the eastern church did not appreciate, since its own apologetic context, contained within an orthodox imperium, was so different. In the East, from the time of the break-up of the council, the Monophysite schism can be dated, and it grew in significance and effect generation by generation, still to be one of the key divisive factors of the eastern christian church to this day. The long, troubled, story has been admirably described in several recent studies,[37] and will not be engaged in here, for it is time to draw our narrative to a close.

It will suffice to single out the real 'settlement' of the 'christological settlement of Chalcedon', which was the Fifth Oecumenical Council of Constantinople in 553, under the Emperor Justinian.[38] It would

[37] J. Meyendorff, Imperial Unity and Christian Divisions (1989); P.T. Gray, The Defense of Chalcedon in the East (1979); W.H. C. Frend, The Rise of the Monophysite Movement (1972).

[38] cf. Davis (1987) pp. 207–257.; E.T. of the Acts in H. Percival (Ed.), The Seven

be fair to say that this has attracted little attention in western christological scholarship, again as part of that overall tendency to read all through the somewhat narrow lens of the Tome of Leo. And yet, the decrees of this primarily christological council demonstrate with abundant clarity how Cyril's memory and reputation had remained alive, and more to the point, how even more than a century after his death his theology had been adopted as the oecumenical standard for an orthodox christology for both East and West.

At Constantinople II the reputation of Theodoret and Ibas of Edessa, both of whom had been grudgingly rehabilitated at Chalcedon, was formally anathematised. To complete the triumvirate[39] twelve anathemas were pronounced against the person and theology of Theodore Mopsuestia. Thus, the three most significant theologians of the Antiochene school were publicly excluded from the orthodox canon. What Cyril had felt to be necessary in 438, in terms of the doctrine of Theodore, had been implemented over a hundred years later, demonstrating how much the whole East had come round to his mind in the intervening years.

At this council the theology of Cyril formed the obvious and explicitly acknowledged standard of all its work. Here the Twelve Chapters of the latter part of Cyril's Third Letter to Nestorius were formally accepted as a definitively orthodox expression of the faith, something that had not happened at Chalcedon. The decrees of 553, thus represent the final and complete triumph of Cyril's theology, even at its most robust apologetic level, and it was subsequently accepted, on those terms, by the eastern and western churches in the eventual admission of Constantinople II as having oecumenical authority.

Cyril's reception in the christian oecumene, then, was an advance of increasing momentum from 431 to 553. From the time of his death in 444, his personal charism and the massive weight of his theology had given him the status of a saint in areas far beyond his native Egypt. In short, Cyril's christology had risen like a star in the ascendant, quite extraordinarily, in a way that has no comparison with any other ancient christian thinker, except perhaps for the influence of Origen in the East, and Augustine in the West. Cyril stands, therefore, as one of the greatest of all christian theologians, and unquestionably as the chief protagonist of the classical doctrine of Christ. This is

Ecumenical Councils, Nicene & Post Nicene Fathers, vol.14, Oxford, 1900.

[39] The issue was known subsequently as 'The Three Chapters.'

true not only in terms of the power of his individual intellect and religious significance, but also in terms of the impact his life had on the history of his own age, and even on the arguments of centuries to come: a destiny that is not afforded to many.

In the West his liturgical feast is celebrated on February 9th. In the East he is remembered on two specific occasions in the liturgical year; on June 9th, as his own day, and on January 18th, in the company of Athanasius the Great, as the two great defenders of the deity of Christ. His festal Troparion acclaims him in the following words:

Hail translucent star,
defending warrior to the Holy Virgin,
who shouted out above all the hierarchs at Ephesus
that she was the Mother of God. . . .
Rejoice most blessed Cyril,
spring of theology and
river of the knowledge of God.
Never cease to intercede with Christ on our behalf.

CHAPTER FIVE

TRANSLATED TEXTS

Cyril's Letter to the Monks of Egypt.
The Second Letter of Cyril to Nestorius.
The Third Letter of Cyril to Nestorius.
Cyril's Letter to Pope Celestine.
Festal Homily at St. John's church, Ephesus.
Explanation of the Twelve Chapters.
Scholia on the Incarnation.
Cyril's Letter to Acacius of Beroea.
Cyril's Letter to John of Antioch (Formula of Reunion).
Cyril's Letter to Eulogius.
First Letter of Cyril to Succensus.
Second Letter of Cyril to Succensus.

Nestorius' Reply to Cyril's Second Letter.
The Synodical Deposition of Nestorius.

As Appendices:

Athanasius' Letter to Epictetus.
Gregory Nazianzen's Letter to Cledonius.

CYRIL'S LETTER TO THE MONKS OF EGYPT[1]

Cyril to the priests and deacons, to the fathers among the monks and to those following the solitary life with you, established in the faith of God, beloved and longed-for; Greetings in the Lord.

1. Some of your number, as is the custom, came to Alexandria and when I asked and earnestly enquired of them if, walking in the noble steps of your fathers, you too were eager to distinguish yourselves by an orthodox and blameless faith; whether you held in highest honour this beautiful way of life; whether you were proud of the toils of ascesis, truly regarding as your delight to choose to suffer bravely for the sake of the good, then these brethren told me that this was indeed the case with you. They said, moreover, that you competed with the exploits of your predecessors not without distinction. I could not but rejoice, therefore, and my heart leaped for joy at the thought that my children's [achievements] were my own. This is only right, for if gymnastic trainers can take delight in the contests of their young men, and themselves put the crown on their heads if they should win acclaim because of their valour; and if they can take a share in their vaunts of manliness, why should not we do the same who are spiritual fathers, who rub you down with words to give you good courage so that you can carry off the prize by quelling the urges of the flesh and refusing to fall into sin or yield to Satan's temptations? This is why I am filled with a God-beloved contentment, no less than these trainers.

2. As our Saviour's disciple said: 'With all zeal add virtue to your faith, to your virtue knowledge, to your knowledge self-control, to your self-control endurance, to your endurance godliness, to your godliness care for the brethren, to your care for the brethren add love. For if these things are present among you in abundance they will establish you as active and fruitful in the knowledge of our Lord

[1] Ep.1. PG.77.9–40; ACO 1.1.1. pp. 10–23. The letter dates from the Spring of 429 when Cyril had heard of Nestorius' teachings infiltrating Egypt, his own province, and thus first coming under his canonical remit. The Letter (together with Paschal Letter 17, PG 77,768 f.) marks the opening of the Nestorian controversy.

Jesus Christ' (*2 Pet.1.5–8*). And on my part I say that those who have chosen to tread that illustrious path of the spiritual life in Christ, that path we ought to love so much, must first of all be adorned with a simple and pristine faith, and then add on to it virtue, and when this is done, try to gather the riches of the knowledge of the mystery of Christ, and strive vigorously for perfect understanding. For this, I think, is what it means 'to arrive at the perfect man, and reach the measure of the state of the fullness of Christ' (*Eph.4.13*), with that sobriety which is fitting for monks, girding your loins well and fighting manfully against the passions of both body and soul. In this way you shall be shining lamps, well regarded, and established in the good things of that hope which has been prepared for the saints. But before anything else let there be among you an orthodox and unadulterated faith that is absolutely blameless. For in this way you too will follow in the footsteps of the godliness of the holy Fathers, and will dwell with them in the heavenly mansions and abide in those heavenly tabernacles of which the divine Isaiah reminds us when he says: 'Your eyes shall see Jerusalem, that rich city, whose tabernacles shall not be shaken' (*Is.33.20*).

3. I make it my concern, therefore, that your life may be radiant and worthy of all admiration, and that your faith should be established as orthodox and unadulterated. But I was greatly disturbed to hear that some dangerous murmurings had reached you and that certain people were circulating them, destroying your simple faith by vomiting out a pile of stupid little words and querying in their speech whether the holy virgin Mary ought to be called the Mother of God or not. It would have been better for you to have abstained altogether from such questions which are only contemplated with difficulty, 'as if in a mirror and an enigma', (*1 Cor.13.12*) by those whose intellects are prepared and whose minds are advanced, or else they cannot be plumbed at all. For these most subtle arguments exceed the mental ability of the simple. But since you have now heard these arguments, and given that some seem to have deliberately chosen to foment discord, wounding as it were those of weaker minds with the same hurt they themselves have already embraced, then I have judged it necessary to say a few things about these matters to you. This is not so that you yourselves might join in the verbal fight, rather that if any such people come to you, you will be able to oppose their foolish ideas with the truth, and escape the harmfulness of their deceit. In this way you may yet help others, as brethren, with suitable arguments

and persuade them to hold in their own souls that heavenly faith that was handed on to the churches from the holy apostles like some pearl of great price.

4. I was completely amazed that certain people should be in any doubt as to whether the holy virgin ought to be called the Mother of God or not. For if our Lord Jesus Christ is God, then how is the holy virgin who bore him not the Mother of God? The divine disciples handed on this faith to us even if they did not make mention of the term. We have been taught to think this way by the holy Fathers. Our Father Athanasius, of illustrious memory, was an ornament to the throne of the church of Alexandria throughout forty six years in all. He opposed an unconquered and apostolic wisdom to the sophistries of the evil heretics, and refreshed the whole world with his own writings as if they were some most fragrant balsam. His orthodoxy and godliness in teaching are confessed by all, and he composed a book for us concerning the holy and consubstantial trinity where, throughout the third discourse, he calls the holy virgin the Mother of God. I will make use of his own sayings and the exact words are these: 'This, then, is the purpose and essential meaning of the divine scripture, as we have said many times, that it contains a two-fold statement about the Saviour; firstly that he is eternally God, and that he is the Son being the Word, the Radiance, and the Wisdom of the Father, and secondly that later for our sake he took flesh from the virgin Mary the Mother of God and so became man' (*Con. Arianos 3.29*). And again, further on, he says: 'But there have been many holy men who were even pure of all sin. Jeremiah was sanctified even from the womb, and John still inside his mother leaped for joy at the sound of the voice of Mary the Mother of God.' (*Jer.1.5; Lk.1.44; Con. Arianos 3.33*). This man is trustworthy and we ought to rely upon him as someone who would never say anything that was not in accordance with the sacred text. For how could such a brilliant and famous man, held in such reverence by everbody at the holy and great Synod itself (I mean that which formerly gathered together in Nicaea) be mistaken as to the truth? At that time he did not occupy the episcopal throne, but was still only a cleric. Nonetheless because of his shrewdness, his purity of life, and his sharp and incomparably penetrating mind, he was taken along on that occasion by bishop Alexander of blessed memory, and he was to the old man like a son to a father, guiding him in everything useful and admirably showing him the way in all he did.

5. But since certain people seem to think that such discourse on these matters needs to be sanctioned for us from the holy and inspired scriptures themselves, and since they say that the holy and great Synod neither called the Lord's mother 'Mother of God', nor defined anything at all like this, well then, come, yes come even now, while we demonstrate as far as we can how the mystery of the spiritual economy in Christ is proclaimed to us by the divine scriptures. This is something which the Fathers themselves have spoken about, setting out the definition of the blameless faith while inspired by the truth of the Holy Spirit. For they were not speaking as from themselves, as the Saviour said, but it was the 'Spirit of God the Father speaking in them' (*Mt.10.20*). And when we have thus demonstrated that he who is born from the holy virgin is God by nature, I would think that absolutely no one could have any hesitation that we ought to consider and indeed profess that she may be called Mother of God, and rightly so. Our Symbol of faith puts it in this way:

6. I believe in God the Father almighty, the maker of all things seen and unseen; and in One Lord Jesus Christ the Only Begotten Son of God, begotten of the Father, that is from his essence; God from God, light from light, true God from true God, begotten not made, consubstantial with the Father, through whom all things were made, things in heaven and things on earth; who for us men and for our salvation came down, was made flesh and made man, suffered and rose again on the third day, ascended into heaven; who is coming to judge the living and the dead; and in the Holy Spirit.

7. But the inventors of heresies who dig ditches of destruction for themselves and for others, have fallen into such stupidity in their conceptions as to think and say that the Son is recent and that he was brought into being from God the Father on the same level as the other creatures. These wretched people are not ashamed to circumscribe within a time-bound beginning him who is before all ages and time, or is rather the maker of the ages. But having thought fit to drag him down from glory and equality with God the Father, even then they barely concede him precedence over others. They say that he is a mediator between God and man, but has not obtained the glory of divine transcendence fully, just as he does not fully rest within the limits of the created order. Who is this, then, who falls short of the divine transcendence, yet surpasses the limits of the creation?[2] The whole business is absolutely incomprehensible. No one

[2] Cyril is evidently characterising the christological implications of Nestorianism

can see any place or purpose for such a mediator between the Creator and creation. So, dragging him down from the divine throne (for this is what they have done) they name him Son and God, thinking it necessary to worship him even though the law cries out openly: 'You shall worship the Lord your God and adore him alone' (*Deut.6.13*). Also God says through the voice of David to the Israelites: 'Let there be no new god among you, and do not worship any alien god' (*Ps.80.10*).

8. But these people have abandoned, as it were, the straight highway of truth and have rushed into ditches and onto rocks, which is what Solomon says: 'They have strayed from the tillage of their own field, and shall gather sterility in their hands' (*Prov.9.12 LXX*). But we whose minds have been illumined by the divine light, who have preferred incomparably better conceptions than their stupidities; we who follow in the faith of the holy Fathers, we say that the Son was truly born in a God-befitting and ineffable manner from the essence of God the Father, and is to be conceived of in his own hypostasis, yet united in an identity of essence with his Begetter. We say that he is within him, but again that he has the Father in himself, and we confess that he is the light from light, God from God by nature, equal in glory and power, God's impress and radiance (*Heb.1.3*), having equality in all things, and inferior in no way at all. And if we go on to include the Holy Spirit, then we have the holy and consubstantial trinity, united in one nature of deity.

9. But the God-inspired scripture says that the Word of God became flesh, which means he was united to flesh endowed with a rational soul, and following the evangelical proclamations the holy and great Synod said that it was the Only Begotten himself who was born from the essence of God the Father. It is he 'through whom and in whom are all things' (*Col.1.17*), who came down from heaven for us men and for our salvation, was made flesh and made man, suffered and rose again, and in due season will return as judge. And the Synod called the Word of God 'One Lord Jesus Christ'. Notice, then, how by saying that there is One Son, and by calling him Lord and Christ Jesus, they have said that he has been begotten from God the Father,

---

as, logically, the same as Arianism whose doctrine he outlines here. Just as Athanasius called upon the assistance of the desert monks in the period of struggle after Nicaea (most notably on Antony the Hermit, the father of all monks), to help him oppose his arch-enemies, the Arian bishops, so now Cyril sees himself entitled as the legitimate successor of Athanasius' doctrine and throne, to call upon the monks of his province. The analogy gains in force since the see of Constantinople was, until 380, a stronghold of the Arian movement.

and is the Only Begotten, God from God, light from light, begotten not made, and consubstantial with the Father.

10. Nonetheless one might say that the name 'Christ' is not just applicable to the Emmanuel for we can find it attributed to others. For somewhere God says in regard to those elected and sanctified in the Spirit: 'Do not touch my Christs, and do no harm to my prophets' (*Ps.104.15*). Indeed, when Saul was anointed as King by God at the hands of Samuel the divine David called him the 'Christ of the Lord' (*1 Sam.24.7*). What does this mean? Well, is it not perfectly clear, for anyone who wishes to see, that those who have been justified by faith in Christ, and sanctified in the Spirit, are honoured with this designation? In any case the prophet Habbakuk announced the mystery of Christ and the salvation that comes through him long in advance when he said: 'You came forth for the salvation of your people, to save your Christs' (*Hab.3.13*). And so, the name Christ is not attributable solely and properly, as I have said, to the Emmanuel, but also to everyone, whoever it might be, who has been anointed with the grace of the Holy Spirit. The name originates from what it signifies, for the term 'Christ' comes from the verb to anoint. The wise John confirms that we too are thus enriched with this wonderful and truly desirable grace, when he says: 'And you too have an anointing from the Holy One' (*1 Jn.2.20*), and again: 'You do not need anyone to teach you, for his anointing teaches you' (*1 Jn.2.27*). But it is written of the Emmanuel: 'Jesus from Nazareth, how God anointed him with the Holy Spirit and with power' (*Acts.10.38*). And indeed the divine David says to him: 'You have loved justice and hated iniquity, and this is why God, your God, has anointed you with the oil of gladness beyond your fellows' (*Ps.44.8*). In that case what pre-eminence could one see in the holy virgin beyond other women, even if one says that she gave birth to Emmanuel? For it would not be silly, in fact, to call the mothers of each and every person who has been so anointed 'Mother of Christ'.

11. But there is a vast distinction that separates with irreconcilable differences the glory and transcendence of our Saviour from our human condition; for we are servants, but he is Lord and God by nature, even if he did come with us economically and in our condition. And this is why the blessed Paul called him Christ, when he said: 'Understand this closely, for no fornicator or impure man or any rapacious idolator shall have an inheritance in the Kingdom of God' (*Eph.5.5*). And so, while all others, as I have said, may quite rightly be Christs on

account of being anointed, the Emmanuel is the only Christ who is true God. And while one does not err from the truth if one should choose to say that these mothers of the other ones are 'Mothers of Christ', they are certainly not 'Mothers of God'. But in comparison with them, only the holy virgin can be said to be both Mother of Christ and Mother of God, for she did not give birth to a mere man like us, but rather to the Word of God the Father made flesh and made man. Even we are called 'gods by grace'; but the Son is not God in this way, but rather in nature and in truth, even if he did become flesh.

12. Perhaps you will say: 'Then tell me, did the virgin become the mother of the Godhead?' And to this we reply: There can be no doubt that the living and enhypostatic Word was begotten from the very essence of God his Father, and has his existence without beginning in time, eternally co-existing with his Begetter. He is conceived of as existing in him and with him, but in these last times of the age since he became flesh, that is was united to flesh endowed with a rational soul, he is also said to have been born of a woman in a fleshly manner. This mystery concerning him is in some ways like the mystery of our own birth, for earthly mothers, assisting nature as regards the birth, have the embryonic flesh in their wombs, which in a short time by certain ineffable workings of God, increases and is perfected into the human form. Then God introduces the spirit to this living creature in a manner known to him alone; for 'he fashions the spirit of a man within him' (*Zech.12.1*), as the prophet says. Nonetheless, the Word is different to the flesh, and equally different to the soul. But even if these mothers have produced only the earthly bodies, nonetheless they are said to have given birth to the whole living creature, I mean that of soul and body, and not to have given birth to just a part. To take an example, surely no one would say that Elizabeth was only the mother of the flesh, but not the mother of the soul, since she gave birth to the Baptist who was already endowed with a soul? Surely she is the mother of one thing constituted from both realities; that is a man, of soul and body. We take it, then, that something like this happened in the birth of Emmanuel. As I have said, the Only Begotten Word was born from the essence of God his Father, but since he took the flesh and made it his very own, he is also called Son of Man, and he became as we are. So, there is nothing foolish, I think, in saying (in fact it is necessary to confess it) that he was also born from a woman according to the flesh. Indeed,

in the same way the soul of a man is fashioned along with his own body, and is conceived of as one with it, even though it is reckoned to be, and is by nature, different according to its inner constitution. If anyone should want to insist that the mother of such and such a person is the 'flesh-mother' but not the 'soul-mother', what a tedious babbler he would be. As I have said, a mother gives birth to one living creature skilfully composited from diverse factors and truly forming one man out of two things, each of which remains what it is while concurring, as it were, into a natural unity, and each one mingling[3] its specific and proper characteristics with the other.

13. What an easy and completely effortless task it is to show that in the case of Christ the union was exactly determined. Let us consider, if you like, the sayings of the blessed Paul, giving them our most exact and careful attention. He says in regard to the Only Begotten: 'Who being in the form of God did not count equality with God a thing to be grasped, but emptied himself, assuming the form of a slave and coming in the likeness of men, and being found in fashion as a man, he humbled himself' (*Phil.2.6–8*). Who is it, then, who is 'in the form of God' and who 'did not count equality with God a thing to be grasped'? Or in what manner is he 'emptied out'? Or how did he descend to humiliation even in the 'form of a slave'? There are some who divide the One Lord Jesus Christ into two, that is into a man alongside the Word of God the Father. These people maintain that it was the one who came from the holy virgin who underwent the 'emptying out', and in this way they separate him and the Word of God. But if this is so, let them show how beforehand he could be conceived as being in the form and equality of the Father, in order that he could then undergo the manner of the self-emptying so as to establish himself in a state which he did not formerly enjoy? For there is nothing of all that is created, if understood in terms of its own nature, which is in the equality of the Father. How then could he be said to have been 'emptied out' if he was a man by nature, and was then born of a woman like us? Or how could he be understood as 'assuming the form of a slave' (implying that he

[3] Lit. 'anakirnamai': commingling or mixing. Cf. Lampe, Patristic Greek Lexicon, p. 106. which gives references for Cyril's use of the term elsewhere. The Antiochenes accused Cyril on this point—of mixing up the natures indiscriminately. When he does use the word, in this instance, note how he refers to the propria: he is not teaching a mixed nature but rather shared characteristics: the doctrine of the 'communicatio idiomatum' or exchange of properties.

did not have this in the beginning) if by nature he was already among the ranks of the servants and lay under the yoke of slavery?

14. They would reply: 'Ah, yes. He who in nature and in truth is the free Son, that is the Word of God the Father who is in the form of his Begetter and is equal to him, dwelt in the man who was born of the woman, and this is what it means to 'empty himself', and this is the essence of the humiliation, and the coming in the form of a slave.' Well my friends, would the fact that the Word of God only dwelt in a man be enough to connote his self-emptying? Would it be safe to say that this was how he assumed the form of a slave? or that this was how he underwent humiliation, even though I can hear him saying to the holy apostles: 'Whoever loves me shall keep my word, and my Father will love him, and we shall come to him and shall make our abode with him' (*Jn.14.23*). Do you hear how he tells us that in those that love him both he and God the Father himself will co-habit? Then shall we concede that the Father himself has been emptied out and has undergone a similar emptying out to the Son and thus has taken up the form of a slave, because he too makes his dwelling in the souls of those that love him? And what about the Holy Spirit who dwells within us? Did he too accomplish the economy of the incarnation which we say was effected by the Son alone for the sake of the life and salvation of us all? Away with such futile and completely stupid nonsense.

15. It was the Word, therefore, who is in the form of God the Father and equal to him, who humbled himself, and then became flesh, as John says, born through a woman, yet also having a birth from God the Father, who undertook to endure our condition for our sake. Let these people teach us how we can call, or conceive of the Word of God the Father as Christ? For if he is called Christ in terms of the anointing, whom has the Father anointed with the oil of gladness or rather with the Holy Spirit? If they say that it was only and specifically the divine Word born of God who was anointed, then in their ignorance they have wronged the nature of the Only Begotten and have perverted the mystery of the economy with flesh. For if it is the Word who is anointed with the Holy Spirit then they confess, like it or not, that the Word existed in former times (when he had not yet been anointed) as wholly lacking in holiness, and was non-participant in this gift which was later bestowed on him. But anything which is lacking in holiness is changeable by nature and cannot be considered as altogether sinless or beyond the capability

of transgression.[4] In such a perspective he would, therefore, have been susceptible of turning to the better, but in that case how could he be ever the same and changeless? And if the Word (being God and in the form and equality of the Father) was anointed and sanctified, then someone could equally say, led away as it were from reality into foolish conceptions, that perhaps even the Father himself stands in need of sanctification, or even that the Son is here shown to be greater than the Father since he himself was sanctified although even before this sanctification he was equal to the Father and in the form of God, while his Father simply remains in the state he was always in, that which he is and ever shall be, not yet having received this progress towards better things through sanctification, in the way that the Son has. And then the Spirit would be seen as greater than both of them since it is he who sanctifies them, if the following is true: 'It cannot be doubted and it is beyond any contradiction, that the inferior is blessed by the superior' (*Heb.7.7*). But all of these arguments are humbug, clap-trap, and the whinings of madmen; for the consubstantial trinity is holy by nature. The Father is holy, and in the same manner the Son is essentially holy, and the Spirit likewise. In what pertains to his own proper nature, therefore, the Word of God, considered on his own, is not sanctified at all.

16. If anyone should think that the one born of the holy virgin was separately anointed and sanctified and was called Christ for this reason, then let him tell us further whether this anointing was sufficient to reveal the anointed one as equally glorious as, and co-throned with, God who is over all? And if the anointing is enough and they tell us that this is the case, then note that we too have been anointed as the divine John will bear witness saying: 'And you have an anointing from the Holy One' (*1 Jn.2.20*). Does it follow that we ourselves should perhaps be on the same level as God? for in my opinion there would be absolutely no reason to stop us sitting down with him in the same way as Emmanuel himself. God said to him: 'Sit at my right hand while I set your enemies as a footstool under your feet' (*Ps.109.1*). And should the holy assembly of heavenly spirits worship us too in that case? for it also says: 'When he introduced the first-born into the world he said: Let all the angels of God worship him' (*Heb.1.6*). But in our case, even if we are anointed by the Holy Spirit, and

[4] Cyril is arguing, once again, that logically speaking the position of his opponents is Arian in substance.

enriched with the grace of sonship, and even if we are called 'gods', nonetheless we are not unaware of the limitations of our own nature. We are of the earth and we stand in the ranks of servants, but he is not within the limits that apply to us, but is Son in nature and in truth, and is the Lord of all, and from heaven.

17. Since we have elected to think correctly we certainly do not say that God became the Father of the flesh, nor again that the nature of the deity was born through a woman before it had assumed the human condition. No, instead we worship One Lord Jesus Christ, for the Word born of God and the man born completely of the holy virgin, come together in unity. We do not exclude him from the terms of the divinity because of the flesh, nor do we reduce him to the level of a simple man because of his likeness to us. This is how you should think that the Word born of God willingly underwent his voluntary self-emptying; and this is how he humbled himself, assuming the form of a slave, even though in his own nature he is free. This was how: 'He took descent from the line of Abraham' (*Heb.2.16*) and the Word of God participated in flesh and blood. For if we understand him as a mere man like us, how was it that he took descent from the line of Abraham as if it were a different nature to him? And how could he be said to have participated in his own flesh so that he: 'could be made like his brethren in all things' (*Heb.2.17)*? For something said to have been made like something else must necessarily pass from a state of non-resemblance to resemblance.

18. The Word of God, therefore, took descent of Abraham's line and participated in flesh and blood, making his own the body from a woman, so that through the union he might be understood as God who has also become a man like us. Most assuredly the Emmanuel is from two realities, that is of Godhead and manhood. Indeed the One Lord Jesus Christ who is the one true Son, is at once God and man. He is not made God in the way that others are 'by grace', rather he is true God revealed for our sake in human form. The divine Paul confirms this for us when he says: 'But when the fullness of time came God sent his Son, born of a woman, born subject to the law, so as to redeem those subject to the law, that we might receive adoption as sons' (*Gal.4.4–5*). Then who is it who is sent subject to the law and born from a woman, as I have said, if it is not again him who as God is beyond laws, but who is said, since he became man, to be subject to the law 'so that he might be made like his brethren in all things' (*Heb.2.17*)? In any case he pays the didrachma

along with Peter in accordance with the law of Moses. But he teaches us that he is free as Son, and greater than the law as God, even if he became subject to the law as man, for he says: 'From whom do the kings of the earth receive taxes and tribute? From their sons or from strangers?' And Peter replied, 'From strangers.' So he went on: 'The sons, therefore, are free' (cf. *Mt.17.25–26*). So it is perfectly clear that the Word of God would not have been called Christ in so far as he exists outside the flesh and, as it were, independently, but rather such a designation is fitting to him when he became man. Come then, come, let us demonstrate, taking our proofs from the sacred scriptures themselves, that he is God by nature and has come together into unity; I mean in a unity with his own flesh. And since this has been clearly demonstrated as true, then it follows that we can quite rightly call the holy virgin the Mother of God.

19. This was why the prophet Isaiah announced beforehand that the Son had not yet become man but was soon to appear, when he said: 'Be strong you quivering hands and trembling knees, and be comforted all you who are fainthearted in your minds. Be strong and do not fear. Behold our God vindicates his judgement and shall vindicate us. He shall come and save us. Then shall he open the eyes of the blind and the ears of the deaf shall hear. Then the lame shall leap like a deer and the tongue of the dumb shall be clear' (*Is.35.3–6*). Note how when he speaks in the Spirit he calls Emmanuel Lord and names him as God, because he knew that he was not simply a God-bearing man, nor someone assumed in the order of an instrument, but was truly God made man. For it was then that the eyes of the blind were opened, and the ears of the deaf heard, and the lame man leaped like a deer, and the tongue of the dumb became clear. This was how the Holy Spirit instructed the holy evangelists to proclaim him, saying: 'Climb to a high mountain, you who bring good news to Zion; lift up your voice in strength, you who bring good news to Jerusalem. Lift up your voice and do not be afraid. Say to all the cities of Judah: Behold your God, behold the Lord is coming with strength and his right arm has dominion. Behold his reward is with him and his work is before him. As a shepherd he pastures his flock and he shall gather his lambs in his strong right arm' (*Is.40.9–11*). Indeed Our Lord Jesus has appeared to us having a godly strength and in his right arm was dominion, that is authority and sovereignty. And this is why he said to the leper: 'It is my wish: be made clean' (*Mt.8.3*); and he touched the coffin and raised up

the dead son of the widow (*Lk.7.14*).

20. He also gathered together the lambs for he is the Good Shepherd who lays down his life for the sheep, and this is why he said: 'Just as the Father knows me and I know the Father, and I lay down my life for the sheep. Yet I have other sheep which are not of this fold and I must lead these too, and they will listen to the sound of my voice, and there shall be one flock and one shepherd' (*Jn.10. 15–16*). And when the divine John the Baptist began preaching about him he did not proclaim him as an organ of the deity, or merely a God-bearing man, as some would have it, but rather he proclaimed him as God with the flesh (that is made man) to all the inhabitants of Judaea when he said: 'Prepare the way of the Lord. Make straight his paths' (*Mt.3.3*). Whose path did he command to be prepared if not that of Christ, that is the Word revealed in the form of man? In my opinion the divine Paul is a sufficient witness of the faith when he says: 'What then shall we say? If God is for us who is against us? He who did not spare his own son but gave him up on behalf of all, how will he not grace us with all things along with him' (*Rom.8. 31–32*)? Moreover in what way can he that is born of the holy virgin be understood, tell me, as the proper Son of God? It will be in the same way as someone who is called a proper son of man, or generally a proper offspring of any of the animals, that is if it is born from that very thing by nature. This is how he is said and understood to be the proper Son of God, as from his own being. So in what sense is Christ called the proper Son of God, he who was given by God the Father for the salvation and life of all? For 'he was handed over for our transgressions' (*Rom.4.25*) and he 'carried the sins of many in his own body on the wood', as the prophet says (*Is.53.12; 1 Pet.2.24*). It is evident, then, that once the union occurs it necessarily reveals the Emmanuel (who is born of the holy virgin) as the proper Son of God, since it was not the body of anyone else that was born from her: no, it was the very own body of him who is the Word of the Father.

21. So if anyone attributes to him only and solely the function of an instrument, he thereby denies, like it or not, that he is the Son in truth. Let us suppose, for argument's sake, that we take a man. Let him have a son who is skilled on the lyre and is able to sing most beautifully. Would such a man consider that the lyre and this functional act of singing were on the same level as his son? Would not such a thing be the height of absurdity? For the lyre is taken

up to demonstrate a skill, but the son, even without the instrument, is still the son of his parent. But if one argues that the one born of a woman was assumed for a service, so that wonders could be accomplished through him, and the proclamation of the evangelical oracles could shine out, then it follows that we ought to call each of the holy prophets also an instrument of the deity. Does not the mystical priest Moses stand out before all the others here, for he lifted up his staff and changed the rivers into blood; he divided the very sea and told the people of Israel to pass through the midst of the waves. By striking his staff against the rocks he made them into fountains of water and showed forth the rocky places as a spring of water. He became a mediator between God and men, and was a servant of the law and a teacher of the people. But was there anything greater in the case of Christ? If he was just like all the others who came before him, and had only received the rank and role of an instrument then he has not surpassed them in any way at all. And it would seem that the divine David was talking nonsense when he said of him: 'Who among the clouds is the equal of the Lord? And who will be likened to the Lord among the Sons of God' (*Ps.88.7*)?

22. But the most-wise Paul shows that Moses is classed among the servants, and he calls him that is born of a woman economically, that is the Christ, both God and Lord. For he writes: 'And so, holy brothers, you who share in a heavenly calling, consider Jesus, the Apostle and High Priest of our confession, who was faithful to him who constituted him, as Moses was too in all of his household. For he was judged worthy of a greater glory than Moses, to the same extent as the builder of a house has a greater honour than the house itself. For every house is built by someone, but God is the builder of all things. And Moses, indeed, was faithful in all his household as a servant, and as a witness of all that had been said. But Christ was as a son over his household, and we are that household' (*Heb.3.1–6*). Notice then how he has maintained both the limitation of his manhood and also attributes to him the pre-eminence of heavenly glory and God-befitting dignities. For saying that he is 'High Priest and Apostle' and having clearly affirmed that he was 'faithful to him who constituted him' he is saying that he was much more highly honoured than Moses, to the same degree that 'the builder of the house has a greater honour than the house itself'. Then he goes on: 'For every house is built by someone but God is the builder of all things'. The godly Moses, therefore, is ranked in the number of those things that are made or

built, but [Christ] is shown to be the builder of all things. And since he says all things were built by God it is indisputable that [the Christ] is true God. 'Moses indeed was faithful in all his household as a servant', but 'Christ was as a son over his household, and we are that household'. For as God said through the sayings of the prophets: 'For I shall dwell with them and shall walk with them and I shall be their God and they shall be my people' (*Lev.26.12; 2 Cor.6.16*).

23. Perhaps someone might say: But how can we conceive of the difference between Christ and Moses if both of them are born of a woman? How is the one a servant and faithful in the household while the other is Lord by nature, as a son over his household, that is us? In my opinion the whole business is perfectly clear for everyone if they have good sense and share the mind of Christ, as the blessed Paul says. For the first one was a man, under the yoke of slavery, but the other was free by nature as God, and the maker of all things who undertook a voluntary self-emptying for our sake. But this did not deprive him of his God-befitting glory, nor did it alienate him from his preeminent transcendence over all things. For just as we are enriched by his Spirit (since he dwells in our hearts) and are numbered among the children, and yet are not thereby alienated from what we are, since we are men by nature though we say to God—'Abba Father'; in just the same way he, the Word of God who is born ineffably from the being of God the Father, has honoured our nature by taking up the human condition, but he did not thereby become alienated from his own transcendence but remained God even in his manhood. This is why we do not say that the temple born from the holy virgin was assumed in the order of an instrument, but rather we follow in the faith of the sacred scriptures and the sayings of the saints and we maintain that the Word became flesh in the senses already exposed by us so often before. He has laid down his life for us, for since his death was to be the salvation of the world he 'endured the cross, scorning the shame' (*Heb.12.2*) even though, as God, he was Life by nature. How can Life be said to die? It is because Life suffered death in its very own body that it might be revealed as life when it brought the body back to life again.

24. Come now, and let us carefully examine the manner of our own deaths. Is it not the case that men of good sense say that souls are not destroyed at the same time as are bodies that come from the earth? In my opinion this is something no-one questions. However, what befalls us is still called the 'death of a man'. This is how you

should understand in the case of Emmanuel. For he was the Word in his own body born from a woman, and he gave it to death in due season, but he suffered nothing at all in his own nature for as such he is life and life-giver. Nonetheless he made the things of the flesh his own so that the suffering could be said to be his. The same is true of his rising up on behalf of all, having died for the sake of all to redeem all that is under heaven with his own blood, and to acquire for God the Father all that is on the face of the earth. The blessed prophet Isaiah proclaimed the truth of this when he said in the Spirit: 'For this reason he shall inherit many and shall divide the spoils of the mighty, because his life was handed over to death and he was reckoned among the lawless and he himself bore the sins of many and was handed over because of their transgressions' (*Is.53.12*).

25. He who alone was more worthy than all others laid down his life for the sake of all and for a short time, in an economy, allowed death to pull down his flesh. But then, as Life, he destroyed death, refusing to suffer anything contrary to his own nature; and he did this so that corruption should be weakened in the bodies of all and so that the dominion of death should be destroyed. 'For just as all men die in Adam, so all of us shall be made alive in Christ' (*1 Cor.15.22*). For if he had not suffered for us as man he would not have achieved our salvation as God. So first of all he is said to have died as a man, but then to have come back to life again since he is God by nature. If he did not submit to die in the flesh, in accordance with the scriptures, then neither would he have been made alive in the Spirit, that is would not have come back to life. And if this were so 'then our faith is in vain and we are still in our sins' (*1 Cor.15.17*), for we were baptised into his death, as the blessed Paul says, and we have obtained the forgiveness of our sins through his blood (*Rom.6.3*).

26. But if the Christ is neither true Son, nor God by nature, but merely a man like us and an instrument of the Godhead, then we are certainly not saved in God but rather saved by someone like us who died on our behalf and was raised again by external powers. But in that case how could death have been destroyed by Christ (*1 Cor.15.54*)? Nonetheless I hear him clearly saying about his own life: 'No one takes it from me for I lay it down of my own accord. I have the power to lay it down and I have the power to take it up again' (*Jn.10.18*). For he who did not know death descended into death alongside us through his own flesh so that we too might rise up with him to life. And coming back to life he despoiled Hell, not

as a man like us, but as God alongside us and for us in the flesh. Our nature is enriched with incorruptibility in him as the first, and death has been crushed since it launched a hostile attack against the body of Life itself. Just as death conquered in Adam, so was it ruined in Christ. In any case the godly singer has dedicated songs of victory to him who rose up for us and on our behalf to God the Father in heaven so that he could render heaven accessible to those on earth, and he says: 'God goes up with shouts of triumph, the Lord goes up with the sounds of trumpets. Sing praise to our God, sing praise. Sing praise to our King, sing praise. Sing praise wisely, for God has reigned over the nations' (*Ps.46.6–8*). And the blessed Paul also said about him somewhere: 'He who came down is the one who ascended above the heavens in order to fulfill all things' (*Eph.4.10*).

27. So, because the crucified one is truly God and King by nature, and is also called the Lord of Glory (*1 Cor.2.8*), then how can anyone have scruples about calling the holy virgin the 'Mother of God'? Worship him as one and do not divide him into two after the union. Then the insane Jew shall mock in vain, for only then indeed shall he be convicted of having sinned not against a man like us, but against God himself, the Saviour of all. Then let him hear this: 'Woe sinful race, people full of sin, evil lineage and lawless children. You have abandoned the Lord and angered the Holy One of Israel' (*Is.1.4*). Likewise, the children of the Greeks will in no way be able to ridicule the faith of the Christians, for we have not worshipped a mere man, God forbid, but rather God by nature, because we recognised his glory even though he came as we are while remaining what he was, that is God.

And so, glory be to God the Father, through him and with him, with the holy and life-giving Spirit, to the ages of ages. Amen.

THE SECOND LETTER OF CYRIL TO NESTORIUS[1]

Cyril to the most Reverend and God-beloved fellow minister Nestorius. Greetings in the Lord.

1. It has come to my attention that certain persons are quite repeatedly bringing my character into disrepute before your Holiness, taking their opportunity particularly when synods are being held.[2] Thinking, perhaps, to bring you welcome news they are making groundless claims, for they suffered no injustice whatsoever, although they were rightly convicted, for one defrauded the blind and the poor, the other drew his sword against his mother, and the third (apart from having always had the kind of reputation one would not care to wish upon one's worst enemy) stole someone's gold with the connivance of a serving girl.

Nonetheless, what people like that say is of no great account to me. I must not rate my insignificant self above the Lord and Master, or even above the Fathers. However a man might order his life it is not possible to avoid the malice of the wicked. As for them, their

---

[1] Ep.4. PG 77.44–50; ACO 1.1.1. pp. 25–28; Pusey Vol.6. pp. 2–10; Wickham 2–11; Bindley 94–104 & 209–211; Kidd II 251–255. In the Acts of Chalcedon the text is dated Mechir 430 (26th January—24th February) cf. ACO 2.1.p. 104. When this letter was formally read out at Ephesus on June 22nd, 431, Bishop Valerian of Ikonium acclaimed it with the words: 'This letter refreshes the faith of the Fathers like a beautifully scented perfume.' ACO 1.2.16. para.16.

[2] The throne of Constantinople originally had no ecclesiastical territory assigned to it, and so developed the custom from early times of holding regular synods comprised of the numerous visiting bishops who came to the capital. This custom (The Resident Synod) was continued in Nestorius' time even when an extensive ecclesiastical territory had been acquired by the imperial see, and this regularity of meetings, allied to their proximity to the court, was one of the reasons why Constantinople had come to surpass even old Rome in its reputation as the major court of appeal for the Byzantine Christian world. This matter of the real, as well as the notional, and historical, precedence of sees was an important sub-text to the whole christological controversy. Cyril opens this letter to Nestorius determined to head off any plans the latter might have to subject him to a synodical judgement using the excuse of 'official complaints' received about Cyril's administration. On technical grounds Nestorius might claim such a right of precedence by virtue of the canons of the Council of Constantinople 381, giving his see precedence over Alexandria in the East. The canons, however, were not acknowledged in practice either by Alexandria or Rome at this period.

'mouths full of curses and bitterness' (*Rom.3.14*), they will have to answer to the Judge of all.

2. On the other hand, I will turn to what really concerns me, and even now I urge you as a brother in Christ to conduct your manner of teaching the people, and the way you envisage the faith, with all possible exactness. Remember that 'whoever scandalises even one of the least' of those who believe in Christ (*Mt.18.6*) will fall under the unbearable anger (of God). And when the number of those who have been distressed is very great, surely we stand in need of all the skill we can muster to remove the scandals prudently and to expound the sound doctrine of the faith to those who are seeking the truth? And we shall do this most correctly if we are very careful, when we encounter the teachings of the holy Fathers, to hold them in the highest regard. 'We should test ourselves to see whether we are in the faith' (*2 Cor.13.5*), as the scripture says, and thoroughly conform our own opinions to their correct and flawless ideas.

3. Well, the great and holy Synod[3] said that it was the Only begotten Son himself, naturally born from God the Father, true God from true God, light from light, through whom the Father made all things, who was the one who came down, was made flesh, was made man, suffered, rose again on the third day, and ascended into the heavens. We must follow these words and teachings, and realise what is meant by the Word of God being made flesh and made man. We do not say that the nature of the Word was changed and became flesh, nor that he was transformed into a perfect man of soul and body. We say, rather, that the Word, in an ineffable and incomprehensible manner, ineffably united to himself flesh animated with a rational soul, and thus became man and was called the Son of Man. This was not effected only as a matter of will, or favour, or by the assumption of a single prosopon. While the natures that were brought together into this true unity were different, nonetheless there is One Christ and Son from out of both. This did not involve the negation of the difference of natures, rather that the Godhead and manhood by their ineffable and indescribable consilience into unity achieved One Lord and Christ and Son for us.

4. For this reason, even though he existed and was begotten of the Father from before all ages, he is also said to have been begotten

[3] Nicaea, 325 AD.

from a woman according to the flesh. This does not mean that his divine nature received the beginning of its existence in the holy virgin or that it necessarily needed a second generation for its own sake after its generation from the Father. It is completely foolish and stupid to say that He who exists before all ages and is coeternal with the Father stood in need of a second beginning of existence. Nonetheless, because the Word hypostatically united human reality to himself, 'for us and for our salvation', and came forth of a woman, this is why he is said to have been begotten in a fleshly manner. The Word did not subsequently descend upon an ordinary man previously born of the holy virgin, but he is made one from his mother's womb, and thus is said to have undergone a fleshly birth in so far as he appropriated to himself the birth of his own flesh.

5. So it is we say that he both suffered and rose again; not meaning that the Word of God suffered in his own nature either the scourging, or the piercing of the nails, or the other wounds, for the divinity is impassible because it is incorporeal. But in so far as that which had become his own body suffered, then he himself is said to suffer these things for our sake, because the Impassible One was in the suffering body. We understand his death in the same manner. By nature the Word of God is immortal and incorruptible, and Life, and Life-giver, and yet since his own body 'tasted death by the grace of God on behalf of all', as Paul says (*Heb.2.9*) then he himself is said to have suffered death for our sake. This does not mean he underwent the experience of death in terms of his [own] nature for it would be madness to say or think such a thing; rather, as I have said, it means that his flesh tasted death. Similarly when his flesh was raised up, once again we say that the resurrection is his. This does not mean that he fell into corruption, certainly not, but again that his own body was raised.

6. And so we confess One Christ and Lord. This does not mean we worship a man alongside the Word, in case the shadow of a division might creep in through using the words 'along with'; rather that we worship one and the same because the body of the Word, with which he shares the Father's throne, was not alien to him. Again this does not mean two sons were sharing the throne, but one, because of the union with the flesh. But if we reject this hypostatic union as either impossible or unfitting, then we fall into saying there are two sons, and in that case we will be compelled to make a distinction and say that one of them was really a man, honoured with the title of Son,

while the other was the Word of God who enjoyed the name and reality of Sonship by nature.

7. And so, we must not divide the One Lord Jesus Christ into two sons. To hold this in no way benefits the correct exposition of the faith, even if certain people do declare a unity of personas; for the scripture did not say that he united the persona[4] of a man to himself, but that he became flesh (*Jn.1.14*). Yet the Word 'becoming flesh' means nothing else than that 'he shared in flesh and blood like us' (*Heb.2.14*), and made his very own a body which was ours, and that he came forth as man from a woman, although he did not cast aside the fact that he is God, born of God the Father, but remained what he was even in the assumption of the flesh. Everywhere the exposition of the orthodox faith promotes this doctrine. We shall also find that the holy Fathers thought like this, and this is why they called the holy virgin 'Mother of God'. This does not mean that the nature of the Word or his divinity took the beginning of its existence from the holy virgin, rather that he is said to have been born according to the flesh in so far as the Word was hypostatically united to that holy body which was born from her, endowed with a rational soul.

I write these things to you out of the love which I have in Christ, and even now I beseech you as a brother and 'charge you before Christ and the elect angels' (*1 Tim.5.21*) to think and teach these same things together with us so that the peace of the churches might be preserved and that the bond of harmony and love between the priests of God might remain unbroken.

---

[4] Prosopon.

THE THIRD LETTER OF CYRIL TO NESTORIUS[1]

1. Cyril and the synod of the diocese of Egypt assembled at Alexandria, to the most Reverend and God-beloved fellow-minister Nestorius. Greetings in the Lord.

Since our Saviour clearly tells us that: 'Whoever loves son or daughter more than me is not worthy of me' (*Mt.10.37*), then what censure would we incur in acquiescing to your Reverence's demand that we should prefer you in love to Christ the Saviour of us all? Who would be able to help us on the day of judgement, or what excuse could we find for having kept silent so long while you have raised up blasphemies against him? We would not be so concerned if you were only injuring yourself by thinking and teaching the things you do, but you have scandalised the entire church and have cast among the people the yeast of a strange and alien heresy, and not only among the people [at Constantinople] but everywhere the books of your sermons have been circulated. So how could we justify our silence any longer? How could we not recall the saying of Christ: 'Do not imagine that I came to bring peace on earth, but a sword. I came to set a man against his father, and a daughter against her mother' (*Mt.10.34f*). When the faith is being harmed then away with any stale and fussy reverence for parents, then let the law of affection for children and brethren be set aside, and let men of reverence prefer death to life that 'they may obtain a better resurrection', as it is written (*Heb.11.35*).

2. Take note, therefore, that in agreement with the holy synod gathered together in Great Rome,[2] under the presidency of our most holy and religious brother and fellow-minister bishop Celestine, we also charge and warn you, in this our third letter, to dissociate from these utterly wicked and perverse doctrines which you both think and teach, and instead to embrace the correct faith which has been delivered

[1] Ep. 17, PG.77.105–122; ACO 1.1. pp. 33–42; Pusey vol.6. 12–38; Bindley 105–139 + 212–219; Kidd II 255–265; Wickham 12–33. The letter was delivered to Nestorius after morning service in the cathedral at Constantinople on Nov. 30th 430.

[2] In August 430. cf. Cyril's letter to Celestine, Ep.11.

to the churches from the beginning by the holy apostles and evangelists, the 'eye-witnesses and ministers of the word' (*Lk.1.2*). If your Reverence does not do so by the time determined in the letters of our aforementioned fellow-minister Celestine, the most holy and religious bishop of Rome, then know that you will have no clerical standing whatsoever among us, and no place or status among the priests and bishops of God. For we cannot endure seeing the churches thus thrown into confusion and the people scandalised, and the correct faith set aside, or the flocks scattered by you who ought to be saving them; which you would do if you were a lover of correct doctrine, and followed in the path of the religion of the holy Fathers as we do. On our part, we all stand in communion with all those who have been excommunicated or deposed by your Reverence for the sake of the faith, whether lay people or clergy. It is not right that those who have had the wisdom to think what is correct should be wronged by your judgements because they justly opposed you. This is something that you yourself have signified in the letter which you wrote to our most holy fellow-bishop Celestine of Great Rome. It is not enough for your Reverence only to agree in confessing the Symbol of the faith previously set out in the Holy Spirit by that holy and great Synod formerly gathered in Nicaea, for you have not understood or interpreted it correctly, but have perverted it even though you may have confessed it verbally. Consequently you must confess in writing and on oath that you anathematise your foul and profane teachings and that you hold and teach what we all do, the bishops and teachers and leaders of the people throughout the West and the East. Moreover, the holy synod at Rome, and all of us here, agree that the letters written to your Reverence by the church of Alexandria were correct and unimpeachable, so we attach to this letter of ours the doctrines which you must hold and teach, as well as those you must dissociate from. For this is the faith of the catholic and apostolic church in which all the orthodox bishops throughout the West and East concur.

3. We believe[3] in One God, the Father Almighty, maker of everything visible and invisible, and in One Lord Jesus Christ, the Only Begotten Son of God, begotten of the Father, that is from the essence of the Father, God of God, light of light, true God of true

---

[3] The Nicene Creed is set out as the standard. Cyril has previously argued explicitly, as he here implies, that the single subject reference throughout the creed (the one son of God before the ages who is the one who comes down to suffer and so redeem the world) sustains his point about the hypostatic union exactly.

God, begotten not made, consubstantial with the Father, through whom all things were made, things in heaven and things on earth, who for us men and for our salvation came down, was incarnate and made man, suffered and rose again on the third day, ascended into the heavens and will come to judge the living and the dead; and in the Holy Spirit. But those who say, 'There was when he was not', and 'Before he was begotten he was not', and that 'he came to be from nothing', or those who maintain that the Son of God is from a different subsistence or essence, or that he is mutable or changeable, these the catholic and apostolic church anathematises.

We follow in every respect the confessions of the holy Fathers which they made with the Holy Spirit speaking in them. By following the path in which they understood these things we come, as it were, along the Royal Road, and we declare that the Only Begotten Word of God himself, who was begotten of the very essence of the Father, the true God of true God, the light of light, he through whom all things in heaven or on earth were made, himself came down for the sake of our salvation and lowered himself into a self-emptying, and was incarnated and made man. That is, taking flesh from the holy virgin and making it his very own from his mother, he underwent a human birth and came forth as man from a woman. This did not mean he abandoned what he was, for even when he came as man in the assumption of flesh and blood even so he remained what he was, that is God in nature and in truth. We do not say that the flesh was changed into the nature of Godhead, nor indeed that the ineffable nature of God the Word was converted into the nature of flesh, for he is entirely unchangeable and immutable, and in accordance with the scriptures he abides ever the same (*Heb.13.8; Mal.3.6*). Even when he is seen as a baby in swaddling bands still at the breast of the virgin who bore him, even so as God he filled the whole creation and was enthroned with his Father, because deity is without quantity or size and accepts no limitations.

4. So we confess the Word to have been united hypostatically with flesh, and we worship One Son and Lord Jesus Christ. We do not separate or hold apart man and God as if they were connected to one another by a unity of dignity or sovereignty (for this is babbling and nothing else); nor do we designate specifically a Christ who is the Word of God and then specify another Christ, the one who is born of a woman. No, we know only One Christ, the Word of God the Father with his own flesh. He was anointed alongside us in a

human manner, even though he himself gives the Spirit to those who are worthy to receive it, and gives it without measure as the blessed evangelist John says (*Jn.3.34*). We do not say that the Word of God has dwelt in him who was born of the holy virgin, as if in an ordinary man, for this might imply that Christ was a God-bearing man. Even though is is said that: 'The Word dwelt among us' (*Jn.1.14*) and 'all the fullness of the Godhead dwelt bodily' in Christ (*Col.2.9*), nonetheless we understand that in terms of his becoming flesh we must not define the indwelling in his case as if it were just the same as the way he is said to dwell in the saints; for he was naturally united to, but not changed into, flesh, in that kind of indwelling which the soul of man can be said to have with its own body.

5. There is, therefore, One Christ and Son and Lord, not as though a man simply had a conjunction with God as though in a unity of honour or sovereignty, for equality of honour does not unite natures. Indeed Peter and John have equality of honour with one another since they are both apostles and holy disciples, but these two are not one. We do not conceive the manner of the conjunction in terms of juxtaposition (for this is not enough for a natural union), nor indeed in terms of a relational participation in the way that 'being joined to the Lord we are one spirit with him' as it is written (*1 Cor.6.17*). In fact we reject the term 'conjunction' as being insufficient to signify the union. We do not call the Word of God the Father the 'God' or the 'Master' of Christ, and again this is so that we might not openly divide the One Christ and Son and Lord into two, and then fall under the charge of blasphemy for making him his own God and Master. As we have already said, the Word of God, hypostatically united to the flesh, is God of all and is Master of all, and he is neither his own slave nor his own master. To hold and say this would be foolishness, or rather blasphemy. He did say that the Father is his God (cf. *Jn.20.17*) even though he himself is God by nature and from his essence but we do not overlook the fact that as well as being God he also became man and as such was subject to God according to the law which befits human nature. Yet how could he possibly become the God or Master of himself? It is, therefore, as man and in so far as pertains to what is fitting to the limitations of the self-emptying, that he says that he is subject to God alongside us. This is how he also became subject to the law (*Gal.4.4*) even though, since he is God, he himself pronounced the law and is the law-giver.

6. We refuse to say of Christ: 'I venerate the one assumed for

the sake of the one who assumes; I worship the one that can be seen for the sake of the one that can not.' It is a frightful thing to go on to say: 'The one assumed shares the name of God with the one who assumes'. Whoever says such things again makes a division into two Christs, and posits a man distinctly separate, and a God likewise. Such a person is unquestionably denying the very union which determines why we do not give asssociate-worship to someone alongside someone different, and why we do not designate someone as God-alongside-with. In contrast, we understand that there is One Christ Jesus, the Only begotten Son, honoured together with his flesh in a single worship, and we confess that the same Son and Only Begotten God, born from God the Father, suffered in the flesh for our sake, in accordance with the scripture (cf. *1 Pet.4.1*) even though he is impassible in his own nature. In the crucified body he impassibly appropriated the suffering of his own flesh and 'by the grace of God he tasted death on behalf of all' (*Heb.2.9*). He surrendered his own body to death even though by nature he is life and is himself the Resurrection (*Jn.11.25*). He trampled upon death with unspeakable power so that he might, in his own flesh, become the 'first-born from the dead' (*Col.1.18*) and the 'first fruits of those who have fallen asleep' (*1 Cor.15.20*), and might lead the way for human nature to return to incorruptibility. This was why 'by the grace of God he tasted death on behalf of all', as I have just said, despoiling Hell and coming back to life on the third day. And so, even if it is said that the resurrection of the dead came about through a man (*1 Cor.15.21*), nonetheless we understand this as meaning the Word of God became man and the dominion of death was destroyed by him. And he will come at the appointed time as Son and Lord in the glory of the Father 'to judge the world in righteousness', as it is written (*Acts 17.31*).

7. We must, however, make this further point. We proclaim the death according to the flesh of the Only begotten Son of God, and confess the return to life from the dead of Jesus Christ, and his ascension into heaven, and thus we perform in the churches an unbloody worship, and in this way approach mystical blessings and are sanctified, becoming participants in the holy flesh and the precious blood of Christ the Saviour of us all. We do not receive this as ordinary flesh, God forbid, or as the flesh of a man sanctified and conjoined to the Word in a unity of dignity, or as the flesh of someone who enjoys a divine indwelling. No, we receive it as truly the lifegiving and very-flesh of the Word himself. As God he is by nature life and since he became

one with his own flesh he revealed it as life-giving. So even if he should say to us: 'Amen, Amen, I say to you, If you do not eat the flesh of the Son of Man, and drink his blood' (*Jn.6.53*), we must not consider this as if it were the flesh of any man like us (for how could the flesh of a man be life-giving from its own nature?) but rather that it has truly become the personal flesh of him who for our sakes became, and was called, the Son of Man.

8. We do not divide out the sayings of our Saviour in the Gospels as if to two hypostases or prosopa. The one and only Christ is not twofold even though he is understood as compounded out of two different elements in an indivisible unity, just as a man is understood as consisting of soul and body and yet is not twofold but rather is one from out of both. No, we think correctly and so we must maintain that both the manly as well as the godly sayings were uttered by one subject. When he speaks of himself in a God-befitting way: 'Whoever has seen me has seen the Father' (*Jn.14.9*), and 'I and the Father are one' (*Jn.10.30*), we are given to understand his divine and ineffable nature in which he is one with his own Father by identity of essence, the 'image and impress and effulgence of his glory' (cf. *Heb.1.3*). On the other hand when, not despising the limitations of the manhood, he speaks to the Jews: 'Now you seek to destroy me; a man who has told you the truth' (*Jn.8.40*), we nonetheless recognise him as God the Word in the equality and likeness of the Father, despite the limitations of his manhood. For if it is necessary to believe that he who is God by nature became flesh, or rather became man ensouled with a rational soul, then what reason could anyone have to be ashamed of these sayings of his, if they were made as befits a man? If he had refused to use words that are proper to a man, who was it that was compelling him to become a man like us in the first place? But since he abased himself for our sake into a willing self-emptying, what reason would he have for refusing these words that were proper to that very self-emptying? This is why all the sayings in the Gospels are to be attributed to one prosopon, and to the one enfleshed hypostasis of the Word, just as according to the scriptures there is One Lord Jesus Christ (*1 Cor.8.6*).

9. If he is also called 'apostle' and 'high priest of our confession' (cf. *Heb.3.1*), in so far as he ministers to God the Father, on our behalf, that confession of faith which is rendered for him and through him to God the Father, and indeed to the Holy Spirit as well, again we insist that he is by nature the Only Begotten Son of God; and we

do not attribute the title or reality of the priesthood to any man different to him, since it was he who became the mediator between God and men (*1 Tim.2.5*) and a reconciler for peace (cf. *Acts 7.26*) by offering himself up as a fragrant sacrifice to God the Father (cf. *Eph.5.2*). This is why he said: 'You did not want sacrifice or offering, but prepared a body for me. You took no pleasure in holocausts and sin offerings. Then I said: look I come. In the scroll of the book it stands written of me, O God, to do your will.' (*Heb.10.5–7; Ps.39.7–9*). For he offered his own body as a fragrant sacrifice on our behalf, not indeed for himself, for what offerings or sacrifices did he need for himself since as God he is greater than all sin? Even if 'all sinned and fell short of the glory of God' (*Rom.3.23*) in so far as we became prone to stray, and the nature of man was infected with sin, nonetheless he is not like this. This is why it is his glory that we fall short of; and so how could any doubt remain that the true lamb has been slain for us and on our behalf? To say that: 'He offered himself for his own sake as well as ours' cannot fail to incur the charge of blasphemy, for he was guilty of no transgression whatsoever and committed no sin (cf. *1 Pet.2.22*), so what offerings did he need when there was no sin for which they had to be made?

10. When he says of the Spirit: 'And he shall glorify me' (*Jn.16.14*), if we want to think correctly we will not say that the One Christ and Son received glory from the Holy Spirit as if he stood in need of glory from another; for his own Spirit is neither greater than him nor above him. But since he used his own Spirit in great miracles for the manifestation of his own Godhead, this is why he says that he is glorified by him, just as any one of us might say about our internal strength, perhaps, or a special skill we have, as being 'our glory'. Although the Spirit exists in his own hypostasis and is indeed recognised in himself, that is as Spirit and not Son, nonetheless he is not alien to the Son; for he is called the Spirit of Truth (*Jn.16.13*) and Christ is the truth (*Jn.14.6*), and he is poured forth from him just as he himself is from God the Father. This was how the Spirit worked wonders through the hands of the holy apostles after the ascension of our Lord Jesus Christ into heaven, and so glorified him. He himself was believed to be God by nature because he worked personally through his own Spirit. This is why he said: 'He shall take from what is mine and shall announce it to you' (*Jn.16.14*). Not for a second do we admit that the Spirit is wise and powerful by participation, for he is all-perfect and wanting in no good thing

whatsoever, and since he is the Spirit of the Father's wisdom and power (*1 Cor.1.24*), that is the Spirit of the Son, he himself is wisdom and power itself.

11. Since the holy virgin gave birth in the flesh to God hypostatically united to flesh, for this reason we say that she is the 'Mother of God'. This does not mean that the Word's nature took the beginning of its existence from the flesh, for he 'was in the beginning' and 'the Word was God, and the Word was with God' (*Jn.1.1*) and he is the maker of the ages, coeternal with the Father and maker of all things. As we have said before, it means rather that he hypostatically united the human condition to himself and underwent a fleshly birth from her womb. He had no natural need, or external necessity, of a temporal birth in these last times of this age, but he did this so that he might bless the very beginning of our own coming into being, and that since a woman had given birth to him as united to the flesh, from that point onwards the curse upon our whole race should cease that drives our earthly bodies to death. He did it to annul that sentence: 'In sorrow shall you bring forth children' (*Gen.3.16*), and also to demonstrate the truth of the prophet's words: 'Death swallowed us up in its power, but God wiped every tear from every face' (*Is.25.8 LXX*). This is why we say that in the economy he himself blessed marriage, and being invited went to Cana of Galilee with the holy apostles (*Jn.2.1f.*).

12. We have been taught to think these things by the holy apostles and evangelists, and by all the God-inspired scriptures, and from the true confessions of the holy Fathers. It is necessary that your Reverence gives assent to all of these things and accepts them without any evasion. All that your Reverence must anathematise is appended to this letter of ours:

1. If anyone does not confess the Emmanuel to be truly God, and hence the holy virgin to be Mother of God (for she gave birth in the flesh to the Word of God made flesh), let him be anathema.

2. If anyone does not confess that the Word of God the Father was hypostatically united to the flesh so as to be One Christ with his own flesh, that is the same one at once God and man, let him be anathema.

3. If anyone divides the hypostases of the One Christ after the union, connecting them only by a conjunction in terms of honour or dignity or sovereignty, and not rather by a combination in terms of natural union, let him be anathema.

4. If anyone interprets the sayings in the Gospels and apostolic writings, or the things said about Christ by the saints, or the things he says about himself, as referring to two prosopa or hypostases, attributing some of them to a man conceived of as separate from the Word of God, and attributing others (as divine) exclusively to the Word of God the Father, let him be anathema.

5. If anyone should dare to say that Christ was a God-bearing man and not rather that he is truly God as the one natural Son, since the Word became flesh and 'shared in flesh and blood just like us' (*Heb.2.14*), let him be anathema.

6. If anyone says that the Word of God the Father is the God or Lord of Christ, and does not rather confess the same one is at once God and man, since according to the scriptures the Word has become flesh, let him be anathema.

7. If anyone says that Jesus as a man was activated by the Word of God and invested with the glory of the Only Begotten, as being someone different to him, let him be anathema.

8. If anyone should dare to say that the assumed man ought to be worshipped along with God the Word and co-glorified and called 'God' as if he were one alongside another (for the continual addition of the phrase 'along with' demands this interpretation) and does not rather worship the Emmanuel with a single veneration and render him a single doxology since the Word became flesh, let him be anathema.

9. If anyone says that the One Lord Jesus Christ was glorified by the Spirit, using the power that came through him as if it were foreign to himself, and receiving from him the power to work against unclean spirits and to accomplish divine signs for men, and does not rather say that the Spirit is his very own, through whom he also worked the divine signs, let him be anathema.

10. The divine scripture says that Christ became 'the high priest and apostle of our confession' (*Heb.3.1*) and 'offered himself for our sake as a fragrant sacrifice to God the Father' (*Eph.5.2*). So if anyone says that it was not the very Word of God who became our high priest and apostle when he became flesh and man as we are, but it was someone different to him, a separate man born of a woman; or if anyone says that he made the offering also for himself and not rather for us alone (for he who knew no sin had no need of offerings), let him be anathema.

11. If anyone does not confess that the Lord's flesh is life-giving and the very-own flesh of the Word of God the Father, but says that it is the flesh of someone else, different to him, and joined to him in terms of dignity, or indeed only having a divine indwelling, rather than being life-giving, as we have said, because it has become the personal flesh of the Word who has the power to bring all things to life, let him be anathema.

12. If anyone does not confess that the Word of God suffered in the flesh, was crucified in the flesh, and tasted death in the flesh, becoming the first-born from the dead, although as God he is life and life-giving, let him be anathema.

CYRIL'S LETTER TO POPE CELESTINE[1]

Cyril to the most holy and God-beloved father Celestine. Greetings in the Lord.

1. If I had kept silent and not written to your Reverence of all that was transpiring, but instead had stayed apart from the recriminations taking care to avoid being thought of as a troublemaker, especially in matters so important as this where certain people are agitating even the orthodoxy of the faith, then I would have been able to congratulate myself on how good and safe a thing is silence, and how better it is to live the quiet life rather than one of agitation. But God himself requires our vigilance in such matters, and since the longstanding custom of the churches persuades us to communicate with your Holiness, then I write of necessity to point out that even at this moment Satan is confounding all things, raging against the churches of God, and trying to seduce people everywhere, who once were walking on the right path of faith. That all-evil wild beast is never quiet but always ready for wickedness. In the past I have kept silence. I wrote nothing at all to your Holiness about him who is now managing the affairs of the church in Constantinople, nor have I written to any other fellow minister, for it was my belief that any hasty action in such matters would itself be reprehensible. But since we have now reached the high point of evil, as it were, I considered it a matter of great urgency to speak openly and tell you of all that has happened.

2. As soon as he was ordained he was conscious that he had the duty of rousing the people to the good by his exhortations, both those who lived there and the foreign residents of whom there were many, from every city and region. But he soon began to speak outlandish things, devoid of sense, completely alien to the apostolic and evangelical faith which the Fathers had always guarded and passed on to us like

---

[1] Ep.11, PG.77.80–85; ACO 1.1.5. pp. 10–12. Written in the summer of 430 and enclosing the correspondence he had exchanged with Nestorius, together with a dossier of patristic texts collated for the controversy, and a damaging selection of Nestorius' writings.

a pearl of great price. These sermons which he preached in church, with great frequency, and did not cease from delivering, I have sent on to your Reverence so that you might have an exact understanding. I confess that although I wished to oppose him openly with a Synodical letter to the effect that we were not able to have communion with anyone who thought or preached such things, nonetheless I did not do this. I thought that one should really give a helping hand to those who had slipped, to raise them up like brothers who had fallen down, and so I exhorted him by letters to abstain from such evil opinions. It was to no avail. When he learned that we had distanced ourselves from these opinions of his to such an extent that we accused him and stood against his notions (for I will not call them teachings) then he set in motion all manner of intrigues, and even now does not cease from agitating. While we were still looking to his healing and hoping he would desist from these doctrines against Christ we realised that this was a forlorn hope when the next event transpired.

3. There was in Constantinople a bishop of the name of Dorotheus, who had the same opinions as himself, a man given to flattery, with a rash tongue, as scripture says (cf. *Prov.17.20*). In the course of the liturgy when the most Reverend Nestorius was seated on the throne of the church of Constantinople, this man rose to his feet and with a loud voice dared to say: 'If any man says that Mary was the Mother of God, let him be anathema.' At this there rose a great clamour from all the people, and many walked out. They did not want to have communion any longer with those who held such opinions. The result is that even now the people of Constantinople stay away from the liturgy, with the exception of a few of the more thoughtless, and those who fawn upon him. But all the monasteries of the vicinity and their archimandrites, and many of the Senate, will not associate with him, fearing that their faith might be harmed as long as he and those of his company he brought up with him from Antioch are all preaching perversities.

4. When his homilies were brought into Egypt, I then learned that certain thoughtless people had been carried away by them, and others were at a loss and asking one another: 'Is this correct, what he says? Is he not mistaken?' I was afraid in case this sickness might strike root in the souls of these more simple folk and so I wrote a universal epistle to the monasteries of Egypt,[2] confirming them in the correct

[2] q.v. Cyril's Letter to the Monks.

faith. Then certain people brought these same letters back to Constantinople, which were such a great help to those who read them that a great number of the officials wrote to thank me. But this served only to foment his annoyance against me, and he fought me like an enemy, having no other cause of complaint against me except that I would not suffer to think the same things as himself, and that I had set many people right by persuading them to hold the acceptable doctrines which we learned from the divine scripture, the faith which we received from the Fathers. Yet I took no regard of all his machinations against me, but left all to God who knows all and gives us the strength. Once again I wrote him another letter which contained an exposition of the true faith in digest form, at once beseeching him and summoning him to think and preach in this way.[3] But once again it was to no avail at all, for to this day he has held to what he was saying from the very outset and he does not cease from preaching perverted things.

5. Let your Reverence also know that what I have said is supported by all the bishops of the East, and all are furious and outraged, especially the most reverend bishops of Macedonia.[4] Even though he knows this he still thinks he is wiser than them all, and that he alone understands the meaning of the God-inspired scripture, and the mystery of Christ. How can it be that he does not know with an absolute certainty that when all the orthodox bishops and laity throughout the world confess that Christ is God, and that the virgin who gave birth to him is the Mother of God, then he alone who denies it must be in error? But his pride increases and in the power of his throne he treacherously plots against everybody, thinking that he will bring over us and all the others to share the same opinions as himself.

What then should we do since we cannot persuade him, and cannot make him desist from such preachings? while day by day the people in Constantinople are being corrupted or roused to anger and are looking for assistance from orthodox teachers? We are not speaking of any petty matters here, and silence would be a dangerous thing. For if Christ is blasphemed how can one be silent, especially when Paul writes: 'If I did this willingly I should have a reward, but if

[3] q.v. 2nd Letter to Nestorius.

[4] Cyril was touching on an issue he knew to be very sensitive to Rome, for the Macedonian bishops had earlier been attached to the Roman patriarchal jurisdiction but were among those territories lost when a proper patriarchal jurisdiction was created for Constantinople.

unwillingly then because this dispensation was entrusted to me' (*1 Cor.9.17*). If we have been entrusted with the dispensation of the word and the safe-keeping of the faith, then what could we say on the day of judgement if we had kept silent about such matters?

6. We did not precipitately cut off communion with him from the outset before we had communicated these things to your Reverence, so now deem fit to signify your view of the matter and whether one ought to hold communion with him, or whether one should make a bold denunciation so that none will hold communion with someone who thinks and teaches such things. There is a need for your Reverence to make known your opinion on these matters, by letters, to the most reverend and God-beloved bishops of Macedonia, and to all those in the East, for they earnestly desire that we should give them every occasion of standing with one soul and one mind to fight for the orthodox faith which is under attack.

He has anathematised, in so far as he was able, our great and glorious Fathers who said that the holy virgin was the Mother of God, and his anathema has included us too who are still living. Since he did not wish to do this in his own person he substituted another, the aforementioned Dorotheus, and he arranged for the latter to say this while he sat listening, and as soon as he descended from his throne he communicated with him by bringing the divine mysteries to their completion.

So that your Holiness may know clearly what are his statements and opinions, and what are those of our great and blessed Fathers, I have sent treatises containing excerpted sections.[5] I have arranged for them to be translated as far as was possible for those in Alexandria, and I have given the letters which I myself wrote, to the beloved Posidonius instructing him to give these also to your Holiness.

[5] cf. ACO 1.1.6. pp. 3–13 for Cyril's excerpts from the writings of Nestorius; for the biblical and patristic collection of authorities see the Ad Augustas De Fide, and the Oratio Ad Dominas, ACO 1.1.5. pp. 26–61, and ACO 1.1.5. pp. 62–118.

HOMILY GIVEN AT EPHESUS ON ST. JOHN'S DAY. IN THE CHURCH OF ST. JOHN[1]

All words fall short of the renown and glory of the saints, for, as it is written: 'They became like stars in the world, offering it the word of life' (*Phil.2.15*). When they speak about the divine mysteries how rightly we should all say to them: 'It is not you who speak but the Spirit of the Father who speaks within you' (*Mt.10.20*). They proclaimed Jesus to us, the true light, the eternal life, whom we acclaim in accordance with that saying of the blessed David: 'Let all the earth adore you and sing praise to you. Let them sing praise to your name O Most High' (*Ps.65.4*). While the comandments given through Moses were still in force and we had not yet been brought the evangelical preachings, still 'God was made known in Judaea and his name was great in Israel' (*Ps.75.2*), for Moses was 'of feeble voice' and 'slow in speech' (*Ex.4.10*) and this is why the Law was only heard in Judaea. But since the true light shone upon us and God the Word has shared in flesh and blood (*Heb.2.14*) just like us, then everything has come to be filled with him, everywhere there are temples and altars, everywhere there are choirs and worshippers, and good shepherds, and flocks of rational sheep, who by their numbers throng the sacred precincts. Before the coming of our Saviour our race was wandering on the earth; men adored the creation instead of the creator (*Rom.1.25*) and worshipped the works of their own hands, and to each of these mistaken creatures God was whatever suited him. But as I have said, the Only Begotten Word of God appeared to us, the Good Shepherd, the True Lamb, and Mary, that unwedded and holy Mother of God, for our sake gave birth to that life-giving shoot, God made man, from her own virginal womb. He is the free one in the form of a slave. For us, he was made like us; but in himself he was above all creation. He was in the abasement of our condition and also in God-befitting glory. The same one was humbled and yet enthroned beside the Father. The same one was emptied out and yet from his own fullness he

[1] Homiliae Diversae II, PG 77,985–989; ACO 1.1.2, pp. 94–96. Preached in the church and shrine of St. John at Ephesus during the Council in the summer of 431.

distributed good things to his own. As a man he worshipped along with us, but as God he is himself worshipped not only on the earth but even in the heavens. Scripture says: 'When he brought the first-born into the world he said, Let all the angels of God worship him' (*Heb.1.6*). Then who is this that is 'brought into the world'? How has he been introduced? Initiate us into this mystery evangelist, and even now explain it to us O blessed John. You were called the Son of Thunder, and you have shaken the whole earth with something great and extraordinary. Your voice is immortal; time and oblivion give way to your words. Behold what a great number of shepherds have come to you. Take away the stone for us just as the blessed Jacob did for the shepherds (*Gen.29.10*) and reveal the well of life. Grant even now that we may 'draw water from the wells of salvation' (*Is.12.3*). Rather, offer for us your own well. So, let us listen as you say: 'In the beginning was the Word, and the Word was with God, and the Word was God. He was in the beginning with God' (*Jn.1.1*). Because we have believed that the Only Begotten Word of God has an ineffable subsistence from the Father, tell us more, evangelist. Listen again as he says: 'And the Word became flesh' (*Jn.1.14*). He did not come in a man, but became flesh, that is became man. Yet, when the Only Begotten Word of God became man he did not cast aside his being as God, for he remained what he was in the assumption of flesh. The nature of the Word is unchangeable and unalterable and cannot undergo even 'the shadow of a variation' (*Jas.1.17*). This is what the blessed evangelist taught us to think, and truly he is a great and radiant star; a star of salvation, not for those who cross the seas of this world,[2] but for the merchants of righteousness, for those who long for truth, and for those who want to have a correct and faultless faith. And if anyone desires to navigate in this way let him fix the words of the God-speaking theologian in his mind like a star. This is how he shall make his passage through the bitter waves of heresies and this is how he shall arrive at a tranquil port and come to the truth itself, that is Christ, to whom be glory and power with the Father and the Holy Spirit, to the ages of ages. Amen.

---

[2] Cyril reflects the realities of life in the city of Ephesus, a major port of the ancient world. The image of the navigating star signifying correctness of path as well as being a matter of salvation for merchants traversing the seas is highly apposite to his audience.

EXPLANATION OF THE TWELVE CHAPTERS[1]

An explanation of the twelve chapters[2] which was given in Ephesus by Cyril Archbishop of Alexandria when the holy Synod asked him to provide them with a clearer interpretation of their meaning.

1. As it is written: 'All things are evident to those who have understanding, and right for those who find knowledge' (*Prov.8.9*). Those, on the one hand, who go to the sacred words of the God-inspired scripture with an acute and pure perception gather into their souls what is useful from them like a divine and heavenly treasure. Those, on the other hand, who have a mind inclined to falsity, given up to the babblings of others and avid for profane knowledge, then they will be the associates of those whom Paul writes about: 'For among them, the god of this age has blinded the minds of the unbelievers so that the radiance of the gospel of the glory of Christ will not shine on them' (*2 Cor. 4.4.*). For they are blind and are the leaders of the blind and so shall fall into the pits of destruction, just as our Saviour said somewhere: 'If the blind leads the blind both shall fall into the pit' (*Mt.15.14*). So it is that certain people have scorned the teachings of the truth and filling their own minds with demonic crookedness they strive to debase the mystery of truth knowing no bounds in the slanders they bring against the economy in the flesh of the Only Begotten. 'They do not understand what they are saying or about whom they are making their statements', as it is written (*1 Tim.1.7*).

2. Many different people have been the inventors of this kind of

---

[1] PG 76. 293–312; ACO 1.1.5. pp. 15–25; Pusey vol.6, 240–258. This explanation, the third draft of his argument, was written when Cyril was under house-arrest at Ephesus in late summer 431. The Antiochenes had found Cyril's Chapters highly objectionable, seeing in them outright proof that he was either 'Apollinarist' (argued before the Council by Andrew of Samosata, see, Against the Orientals, ACO 1.1.7.33–65) or 'Monophysitic' (argued by Theodoret of Cyr, see Letter to Euoptius, ACO,1.1.5.15–25). The issue of the theology of the Chapters, along with the canonical issue of his opening of the Council before the arrival of the Orientals, was, therefore, the chief reason for his political arrest in 431, and explains the reason for this third and succinct explanation of why the Chapters were necessary, and why they are not to be confused with either heretical position.

[2] The twelve propositions appended to Cyril's Third Letter to Nestorius.

wickedness in previous ages, but in this present time Nestorius and those with him in no way lag behind their profanity. They have risen up against Christ like those ancient Pharisees and are ceaselessly crying out: 'Why do you who are a man make yourself God' (*Jn.10.21*)? This was why it was necessary that we ourselves should strip for action against their words and anathematise their impure and profane doctrines, remembering the words the Lord spoke through the prophet: 'Listen you priests and bear witness to the house of Israel, says the Lord the Almighty' (*Amos.3.13*). And again: 'Go forth through my gates and clear the stones from the road' (*Is.62.10*). It is necessary for us who contend for the dogmas of the truth to move the stumbling stones from the highway so that the people may not fall over them, but might pass as if on level roads to the sacred and divine courts, each confessing: 'This is the gate of the Lord, and the just shall enter through it' (*Ps.117.20*).

3. Since Nestorius introduced a host of strange and profane blasphemies in his own books, it was necessary, thinking of the salvation of those who read them, that we should compose anathematisms, but not in a straightforward way as if someone had made a mental slip requiring us to write a letter of encouragement to him. No, as I have said earlier, it was necessary to demonstrate what strange things alien to piety spring from the teachings of his madness. Perhaps certain people cannot accept our words either because they really do not understand the significance of what is written, or because they have become part of the phalanx of the impure heresy of Nestorius, thereby sharing in his wickedness, and thinking the same things as him? Yet the truth can escape the notice of no one who is accustomed to think correctly. Since it is likely that certain things might not be understood by those who are laden with philosophical subtleties, I thought it necessary to interpret each anathematism briefly to show why and how they came about, and to explain their significance as best I can. In my opinion this might serve as a useful aid to the reader.

Anathematism 1.

4. If anyone does not confess the Emmanuel to be truly God, and hence the holy virgin to be Mother of God (for she gave birth in the flesh to the Word of God made flesh), let him be anathema.

Explanation 1.

5. The blessed Fathers who met of old in the city of Nicaea and set forth the definition of the orthodox and blameless faith, said that:

They believed in one God, the Father Almighty, Maker of all things visible and invisible, and in One Lord Jesus Christ, his Son, and in the Holy Spirit. They said then that he was the Word born of God, he through whom all things came to be, light from light, true God from true God, who was made flesh and was made man, who suffered and rose again. For the Only Begotten Word of the Father, since he was God by nature, took descent from Abraham as the blessed Paul says and shared in flesh and blood just like us. He was born of the holy virgin according to the flesh and became a man like us, though he did not set aside the fact that he was God (God forbid) but continues to be what he was and abides in the nature and glory of the Godhead. This is why we say that he became man, not that he underwent a change or alteration into something that he previously was not, for he is ever the same and does not admit to suffer the shadow of a change (cf. *Jas.1.17*). We declare that there was no mingling or confusion or blending of his essence with the flesh, but we say that the Word was ineffably united to flesh endowed with a rational soul in a manner which is beyond the mind's grasp, a manner such as he alone comprehends. So, he remained God even in the assumption of the flesh and he is the one Son of God the Father, Our Lord Jesus Christ. He is the same one who is before all ages and times in so far as he is understood as the Word, and the impress of God's very being (*Heb.1.3*), and it was he that in these last times became man in an economy for our sake.

6. Certain people, however, have denied his birth according to the flesh, that birth which took place from the holy virgin for the salvation of all. It was not a birth that called him into a beginning of existence but one intended to deliver us from death and corruption when he became like us. This is why the first of our anathematisms cries out against their evil faith and then confesses what is the right faith, saying that Emmanuel is God in truth, and for this reason the holy virgin is the 'Mother of God'.

Anathematism 2.

7. If anyone does not confess that the Word of God the Father was hypostatically united to the flesh so as to be One Christ with his own flesh, that is the same one at once God and man, let him be anathema.

Explanation 2.

8. The godly Paul, priest of the divine mysteries, writes: 'In truth

the mystery of piety is a great thing. God manifested in flesh, justified in the spirit, seen by angels, preached to the gentiles, believed in by the world, taken up in glory' (*1 Tim.3.16*). What then does 'manifested in flesh' mean? It means that the Word of God the Father became flesh not in the sense that his own nature was transformed into flesh through change or conversion, as we have already said, but rather that he makes that flesh taken from the holy virgin into his very own. One and the same is called Son: before the incarnation while he is without flesh he is the Word, and after the incarnation he is the self-same in the body. This is why we say that the same one is at once God and man, but do not split our conception of him into a man separate and distinct, and the Word of God equally distinct, in case we should conceive of two sons. No, we confess that there is one and the same who is Christ, and Son, and Lord.

9. As for those who think that this is not the case, or rather choose not to believe it, those who divide the One Son, and tear realities that have truly been made one apart from one another, maintaining that there was only a conjunction of man with God in terms of dignity, or authority, then we maintain that such people are alien to the orthodox and blameless faith. Even if he is called an 'apostle' or is said to have been anointed, or is designated the Son of God, still we are not ashamed of the economy. We say that he is the Word of God the Father, but when he became a man like us he was also called apostle, and anointed along with us according to the human condition. When he became like us, even though he always remained what he was, he did not deprecate our condition. No, for the sake of the economy he accepted, along with the limitations of the manhood, all those things which pertain to the human condition and he regarded nothing therein as unworthy of his personal glory or nature; for yet, and even so, he is God and Lord of all.

Anathematism 3.

10. If anyone divides the hypostases of the One Christ after the union, connecting them only by a conjunction in terms of honour or dignity or sovereignty, and not rather by a combination in terms of natural union, let him be anathema.

Explanation 3.

11. Having made a careful enquiry into the mystery of the economy with flesh of the Only Begotten, we say that the Word of God the Father was united in a wonderful and ineffable manner to a holy

body endowed with a rational soul and this is how we understand that there is One Son; although of course even in our own case it is legitimate to observe that the soul and the body are of different natures, or rather that both are composited in one living being. Certain people, however, do not think that this is the case. They divide out for us a man separate and distinct; they say that he was conjoined to the Word born of God the Father only in terms of dignity or authority but not in terms of a natural union (that is a true union) which is what we believe. In this sense the divine scripture says somewhere: 'And by nature we were the children of wrath, like all the rest' (*Eph.2.6*). And here we understand the words 'by nature' to mean 'truly'. So, those who divide the hypostases after the union and set each one aside separately, that is man and God, and those who regard them as having been conjoined only in terms of dignity are unquestionably setting up two sons, even though the God-inspired scripture says there is One Son and Lord. After the ineffable union, therefore, even if you should call the Emmanuel God, we understand him as the Word of God the Father made flesh and made man; and even if you call him man we recognise him as no less than this even though he has economically descended into the limitations of the manhood. And we maintain that he who is untouchable has become tangible, and that the invisible has become visible; for his own body which he united to himself was not an alien thing, and this is what we say was tangible and visible. As for those who do not believe in this way, and as I said divide the hypostases after the union and understand them merely to have been conjoined in terms of only dignity or authority, then this preceding anathematism shows them to be alien to those who think correctly.

Anathematism 4.

12. If anyone interprets the sayings in the Gospels and apostolic writings, or the things said about Christ by the saints, or the things he says about himself, to two prosopa or hypostases, attributing some of them to a man conceived of as separate from the Word of God, and attributing others (as divine) exclusively to the Word of God the Father, let him be anathema.

Explanation 4.

13. The Word of God is in the form of God the Father and equal to him, but did not consider that equality with God was something to be grasped, as it is written (*Phil.2.6f*), but rather humbled himself

to a voluntary self-emptying, and freely chose to lower himself into our condition, not losing what he is but remaining so as God while not despising the limitations of the manhood. So all things pertain to him: those befitting God, and those of man. Why would he empty himself out if the limitations of the manhood made him ashamed? Or if he was going to shun human characteristics who was it that compelled him by force or necessity to become as we are?

14. For this reason we apply all the sayings in the Gospels, the human ones as well as those befitting God, to one prosopon. We believe that Jesus Christ, that is the Word of God made man and made flesh, is but One Son. And so, even if he should speak in a human fashion, we relate these human things to the limitations of his manhood because, once again, that very human condition is his own. Yet, if he should discourse as God, believing him to be God made man, once again we attribute these sayings which are beyond the nature of man to one Christ and Son. But those who divide the prosopa into two, must of absolute necessity posit two sons. For just as it is not right to divide any ordinary man into two prosopa, even if he can be thought of as composed of soul and body, because he is one and the same man, it is just so in the case of the Emmanuel. Since the Word of God enfleshed and made man is One Son and Lord he has absolutely only one prosopon and we attribute to him all the human characteristics on account of his economy in the flesh, and all the divine characteristics on account of his ineffable birth from God the Father. But those who wish to make distinctions and divisions of a man set apart on one side who is a different son to the Word of God, and a God on the other side who is another different son, then they are speaking of two sons, and they rightly fall under the force of the preceding anathematism.

Anathematism 5.

15. If anyone should dare to say that Christ was a God-bearing man and not rather that he is truly God as the one natural Son, since the 'Word became flesh' (*Jn.1.14*) and 'shared in flesh and blood just like us' (*Heb.2.14*), let him be anathema.

Explanation 5.

16. The divine evangelist John said that the Word of God had become flesh, not by way of his own nature being transmuted or changed over into flesh, as we have already said (for as God he is unchangeable), but because he participated in flesh and blood just

like us, and became man. It is the custom of the God-inspired scripture to refer to man as 'flesh'. So it is written: 'All flesh will see the salvation of God' (*Lk.3.18*). But the inventors of profane doctrines, Nestorius and those with him, or those who think the same things as he does, only pretend to confess the term incarnation though in reality they do not admit that the Word of God became flesh, that is became man like us while remaining what he was. They affirm, however, that the Only Begotten Word of God dwelt in a man who was born from the holy virgin as if in one of the saints, with the result that one no longer confesses that there is One Christ and Son and Lord who is to be worshipped, but he is conceived of as a man, separate and on his own, who is held in honour because of a mere conjunction in terms of a union of dignity, and is thereby co-worshipped and co-glorified.

17. Yet the God of all dwells within us by the Holy Spirit, and even said of old through one of the holy prophets: 'For I shall dwell within them and shall walk among them, and I shall be their God and they shall be my people' (*Lev.26.12; 2 Cor.6.16*). The blessed Paul also writes: 'Do you not know that you are the temple of God and the Spirit of God dwells within you' (*1 Cor.3.16*)? And Christ himself said about his holy prophets, or rather about the saints who came before him: 'If scripture calls these 'gods' to whom the Word of God came then why do you say of one whom the Father sanctified and sent into the world, 'You are blaspheming', because I said I am the Son of God' (*Jn.10.35*)? But God does not dwell in Christ as he does in us. For he was God by nature, who became like us. He was the One and Only Son even when he became flesh. Those who dare to say that he was a God-bearing man rather than that he was God made man fall of necessity under the forementioned anathematism.

Anathematism 6.

18. If anyone says that the Word of God the Father is the God or Lord of Christ, and does not rather confess the same one is at once God and man, since according to the scriptures the Word has become flesh, let him be anathema.

Explanation 6.

19. Our Lord Jesus Christ is the One and Only true Son of God the Father, the Word who has become flesh, and together with his Father he has the dominion over all things: 'For to him every knee shall bend, in heaven, on earth, and in the underworld, and every

tongue shall confess that Jesus Christ is Lord to the glory of God the Father' (*Phil.2.10*). It is, therefore, the self-same who is lord of all in so far as he is understood to be, and actually is, God, even though he is in the flesh after the incarnation. So he is neither his own God nor his own Lord; this is a completely stupid thing to say or think, something indeed that is truly full of every wickedness. The preceding anathematism, therefore, is rightly directed against such a position.

Anathematism 7.

20. If anyone says that Jesus as a man was activated by the Word of God and invested with the glory of the Only Begotten, as being someone different to him, let him be anathema.

Explanation 7.

21. When the blessed Gabriel gave the holy virgin the good news of the birth of the Only Begotten Son of God according to the flesh he said: 'You shall give birth to a son, and you shall call him Jesus, for he shall save his people from their sins' (*Lk.1.3; Mt.1.21*). But he is also called Christ since as man he is anointed along with us as the Psalmist says: 'You have loved righteousness and hated iniquity and so God, your God, has anointed you with the oil of gladness above all your fellows' (*Ps.44.8*). Even though he himself is the dispenser of the Holy Spirit (*Jn.3.34*) and gives it in abundance to those who are worthy, since he himself is filled with it, as it is written: 'And from his fullness we have all of us received' (*Jn.1.16*), nevertheless he is said to have been anointed economically and spiritually as man when the Spirit descended upon him. This was so that the Spirit might once again abide among us whom of old he had abandoned because of Adam's transgression. And this was why the Only Begotten Word of God himself, as he becomes flesh, is called Christ, and since he has as his very own that power which pertains to God, so he performs miracles. Those who say that the good favour of the Only Begotten endowed the Christ with power honorifically, as if the Only Begotten was someone different to the Christ, thereby conceive that there are two sons, the one activating and the other activated as a man just like us; and as such they fall under the force of this anathematism.

Anathematism 8.

22. If anyone should dare to say that the assumed man ought to

be worshipped along with God the Word and co-glorified and called 'God' as if he were one alongside another (for the continual addition of the phrase 'along with' demands this interpretation) and does not rather worship the Emmanuel with a single veneration and render him a single doxology since the Word became flesh, let him be anathema.

Explanation 8.

23. We were baptised into One God, the Father Almighty, and into One Son, and indeed into One Holy Spirit. The blessed Paul says: 'Do you not know that as many of us as were baptised in Christ, were baptised into his death? And so, being buried along with him through this baptism into death, just as Christ was raised from the dead through the glory of the Father, so too shall we walk in newness of life' (*Rom.6.3–4*). So, we have believed, and we were baptised, as I have said, into our One Lord Jesus Christ, that is the Word of God the Father made flesh and made man. We were taught to worship him as one and truly God, and this applies not only to us but to the heavenly powers as well. Thus it is written: 'But when he brought the firstborn into the world he said, Let all the angels of God worship him' (*Heb.1.6*). The Only Begotten became the firstborn when he appeared as a man like us, and then he was also called a brother of them that love him. So, if anyone says that he ought to be worshipped as a man alongside but different to him who is the Word of God, or if anyone does not bring together in a true union One Christ and Son and Lord, so as to honour him with a single worship, then such a one rightly falls under the force of this anathematism.

Anathematism 9.

24. If anyone says that the One Lord Jesus Christ was glorified by the Spirit, using the power that came through him as if it were foreign to himself, and receiving from him the power to work against unclean spirits and to accomplish divine signs for men, and does not rather say that the Spirit is his very own, through whom he also worked the divine signs, let him be anathema.

Explanation 9.

25. When the Only Begotten Word of God became man, he remained, even so, God, having absolutely all that the Father has with the sole exception of being the Father. He had as his very own the Holy Spirit which is from him and within him essentially and so he brought about divine signs, and even when he became

man he remained God and accomplished miracles in his very own power through the Spirit. Those who say that he was glorified by the power of the Holy Spirit as a man like any one of us, or rather like one of the saints, but that he did not make use of his own power in a God-befitting manner, but instead used an external power and received his assumption to heaven from the Holy Spirit as a grace, then these rightly fall under the force of this anathematism.

Anathematism 10.

26. The divine scripture says that Christ became 'the high priest and apostle of our confession' (*Heb.3.1*) and 'offered himself for our sake as a fragrant sacrifice to God the Father' (*Eph.5.2*). So if anyone says that it was not the very Word of God who became our high priest and apostle when he became flesh and man as we are, but it was someone different to him, a separate man born of a woman; or if anyone says that he made the offering also for himself and not rather for us alone (for he who knew no sin had no need of offerings), let him be anathema.

Explanation 10.

27. Small indeed in the sight of the Word born from God are the human characteristics, but he did not reject them for the sake of the economy. He is by nature Lord of all, and he subjected himself to our condition, assuming the form of a slave, and was called our 'High Priest' and 'Apostle', since the limitations of the manhood summoned him even to this. He offered himself for our sake as a fragrant sacrifice to God the Father: 'For in one offering he perfected those to be sanctified for ever' (*Heb.10.14*), as it is written. I do not know how those who think otherwise are able to maintain that it was not the Word of God himself who became man so as to be called the apostle and high priest of our confession, but as it were a different man distinct from him. They say that this man was born of the holy virgin, was designated apostle and high priest, arrived at this by a promotion, and offered himself as a sacrifice to God the Father not only for our sake but for his own as well. But all of this is completely alien to the orthodox and blameless faith, for 'he committed no sin'(*1.Pet.2.22*) and he who is greater than transgression and wholly blameless of sin would have no need to offer sacrifice on his own behalf. So, because certain people who think differently reject this, and suppose instead that there are two sons, there was a great need for this anathematism to counter their wickedness clearly.

Anathematism 11.

28. If anyone does not confess that the Lord's flesh is life-giving and the very own flesh of the Word of God the Father, but says that it is the flesh of someone else, different to him, and joined to him in terms of dignity, or indeed only having a divine indwelling, rather than being life-giving, as we have said, because it has become the personal flesh of the Word who has the power to bring all things to life, let him be anathema.

Explanation 11.

29. We do not offer the holy life-giving and bloodless sacrifice in the churches as if we believed that what we offered was the body of an ordinary man like us, and the same is true with the precious blood. On the contrary, we receive it as something that has become the very own body and blood of the Word who gives life to all. For ordinary flesh cannot give life, and the Saviour himself testifies to this when he says: 'Flesh profits nothing; it is the spirit which gives life' (*Jn.6.63*). His body is understood to be, and actually is, life-giving in so far as it has become the very own [flesh and blood] of the Word. It is just as the saviour himself said; 'As the living Father sent me, and I live through the Father, so whoever eats me shall live through me' (*Jn.6.57*). Since Nestorius and those who think the same as him have foolishly dissolved the power of the mystery, this is why this anathematism has rightly been composed.

Anathematism 12.

30. If anyone does not confess that the Word of God suffered in the flesh, was crucified in the flesh, and tasted death in the flesh, becoming the first-born from the dead, although as God he is life and life-giving, let him be anathema.

Explanation 12.

31. The Word of God the Father is impassible and immortal, for the divine and ineffable nature is above all suffering, and this it is which gives life to all things and is greater than corruption or anything else that can normally cause us grief. Yet even though the Word of God the Father is so by his own being, he made his own the flesh which is capable of death so that by means of this which is accustomed to suffer he could assume sufferings for us and because of us, and so liberate us all from death and corruption by making his own body alive, as God, and by becoming the first fruits of those who have fallen asleep, and the first born from the dead (*1 Cor.15.20*).

He who endured the noble cross for our sake and tasted of death was no ordinary man conceived of as separate and distinct from the Word of God the Father but it was the Lord of Glory himself who suffered in the flesh, according to the scriptures (*1 Pet.4.1*). Because those who are trying to introduce stupid and profane teachings into the orthodox and blameless faith are saying that an ordinary man endured the cross for our sake, then this anathematism became necessary to expose the magnitude of the wickedness prevalent among them.

SCHOLIA ON THE INCARNATION OF THE ONLY BEGOTTEN.[1]

1. What Christ means.

The name Christ does not have the force of a definition, and does not denote the essence of anything. It signifies the specific quality of a thing, in the same way as 'man', or 'horse', or 'ox'. Yet it has a significance beyond this, for some of the ancients were anointed with oil in earlier times, as God saw fit, and this anointing was the symbol of the kingship. The prophets too were anointed, intellectually, by the Holy Spirit, and were thereby called Christs. This is why the blessed David sings out, in the person of God: 'Do not touch my Christs, and do no harm to my prophets' (*Ps.104.15*). And the prophet Habbakuk says: 'You came out for the salvation of your people, to save your Christs' (*Hab.3.13,LXX*).

We also say that Christ the Saviour of us all underwent an anointing. But this was neither symbolic, as if given through oil, nor was it in the manner of prophetic grace. It was not the kind that can be thought of as appointed for the improvement of some kind of work, such as we might say happened in the case of Cyrus, King of the Medes and Persians, when almighty God roused him to this; as it is said: 'Thus says the Lord to Cyrus, my Christ, whose right hand I have upheld' (*Is.45.1*). Although this man was an idolator, he was called Christ because it was as if he had been anointed for kingship by God's decree, and appointed by God to overthrow the might of Babylon.

But more on this: Since sin has had dominion over all because

[1] Composed after 431. PG 75. 1369–1412; PL 48.1005–1040 (Translation by Marius Mercator); P.E. Pusey, S. Cyrilli Alex. Epistolae Tres Oecumenicae, Oxford, 1875, pp. 498–579; E.T. P.E. Pusey, Library of Fathers of the Church, vol.47, Oxford, 1881; F.C. Conybeare, The Armenian Version of Revelation and of Cyril of Alexandria's Scholia on the Incarnation & Epistle on Easter, London, 1907, pp. 168–214; M. Richard (1952) pp. 116–128, demonstrated that the Latin version of the Scholia used by Pope Leo came from Cyril himself (prepared by Alexandria for the benefit of the Roman chancery). The whole text has not survived in the original Greek but the Latin versions are complete. The Greek exists for chs. 1, 8–11, 13, and in fragments for chs. 2,4, 25, and 34. Only the Latin text is extant elsewhere in the book. The present translation has been made from the Greek where available.

of Adam's transgression (*Rom.5.14*), the Holy Spirit departed, and all evil took place on this account. And since, through the mercy of God it was necessary for us to be made worthy of the Spirit again by being restored to our earlier condition, then the Only Begotten Word of God was made man. He appeared to those on earth with an earthly body. He was free from sin so that in his unique triumph of sinlessness the nature of mankind, now crowned once more, might be enriched with the Holy Spirit, and thus by sanctification it was refashioned for God. This was how that grace which Christ first took, as first-born among us, was passed on even to us. To teach us this, the blessed David sang about the Son: 'You have loved righteousness and hated iniquity, and so God, your God, has anointed you with the oil of gladness' (*Ps.44.8*)

The Son was thus anointed in human fashion like us, as I have said, for our sake, in the praises of innocence, and in him the nature of man was made radiant so that it now became worthy to participate in the Holy Spirit. No longer was the Spirit absent from that nature, as in former times, but now he loved to dwell within it. And so it is written: 'The Spirit came down upon Christ and rested on him' (cf *Jn.1.32*). This is why the Word of God is called Christ, since he became man like us, for our sake, in the form of a servant. As man he was anointed in the flesh, but as God he has anointed those who believe in him with his own Spirit.

2. How Emmanuel ought to be understood.

God the Word is called Emmanuel because he took descent from the line of Abraham and, like us, 'participated in flesh and blood' (*Heb.2.14*). But Emmanuel is translated as 'God is with us'. This does not mean in any localised sense, for in what place is God not present, since he fills all things? Nor does it refer to his presence in the form of his assistance to us in the way in which it is said to Joshua the son of Nave: 'And just as I was with Moses, so shall I be with you' (*Jos.1.5*). No, it applies to his coming in what was ours, in humanity, though without abandoning his own nature, since the nature of God the Word is changeless.

What is the reason that Joshua the son of Nave is still not called Emmanuel, even though it is clearly said to him: 'Just as I was with Moses, so shall I be with you?' Well, this is the reason: Although God the Word can be said to have 'been with' the saints, this is not how we say that he was 'with us', we reserve it for that time spoken of by the prophet Baruch: 'He was seen on earth and held converse with men, seeking out all manner of teaching and giving it to Jacob his son, and to Israel his beloved. For he is our God, and there is no other that can be compared with him' (*Bar.3.38*).

[Gk.] Yet in what pertains to his deity by nature he was not 'with us' because the distinction between Godhead and Manhood cannot be elided, for the great difference between the natures is vast indeed. [end of Gk.]

And so the divine David called God the Word to this most powerful union[2] even before his advent to us, when he said in the Spirit: 'Why O Lord have you stood so far off (*Ps.9.22*)?' So now he has not stood far off, but was with us. Although he remained what he was, he took descent from Abraham's line, as I have said, and assumed the form of a slave and was seen as man on earth.

But the terms Christ and Emmanuel designate the same Son to us. This is partly because he was anointed like us, by which means human nature received the Spirit in him as the first. For he was constituted the first new-beginning of the race since, as God, he anoints all those who believe in him. And it was partly because he was 'with us' in the ways I mentioned earlier. Isaiah confirmed this for us when he said of him: 'Behold a virgin has conceived and will bring forth a son, and he shall be called Emmanuel' (*Is.7.14*). Since the holy Virgin was made pregnant by the Holy Spirit she brought forth a son according to the flesh, and thus he was called Emmanuel, for the Incorporeal One was with us through a fleshly generation. This is what David told us: 'God, our God, will come openly, and will keep silence no longer' (*Ps.49.3*). And I think this is the meaning of this other saying: 'I myself who have spoken, am ready'.[3] The prophets said this even at the time the Word was still incorporeal, to indicate that he would even come corporeally.

3. What 'Jesus' means.

The name has a dynamic significance, in so far it rises from a deed, and so we ought to speak only of one Son of God, who is Christ, and Emmanuel, and Jesus. For scripture says: 'He will save his people

[2] Or in some Mss: mystical closeness.

[3] A conflated and free version, I think, of Heb. 10.6, based on Ps. 39.6–8 LXX, which is regularly used by Cyril as indicative of the incarnation, together with Jn. 9.37. The accuracy of the citation-mix has been further 'blunted' by the Latin translation.

from their sins' (*Mt.1.21*). So, just as Emmanuel signified that God the Word came 'with us' through birth from a woman, and Christ signified that as he became man so he was said to be anointed along-side us in human fashion, just so does the word Jesus signify that he saved us, his people. This is something that abundantly demonstrates him to be Lord of all in nature and in truth. The word is not spoken to indicate an ordinary man's creaturely status. It ought, properly, always to be a reference to the Only Begotten, in so far as he became man.

Perhaps it might be argued: Israel is said to be the people of Moses. And to this we might say: But Israel is so called from being the people of God. And this is true. But because it was led to rebellion, when it fashioned the calf in the desert, it was disgraced by God, and no longer did he deign to call them his own people, and now they were only assigned the name of a man. But this does not apply to us, for we are the true sons in him who is God, and 'through whom all things were made' (*Jn.1.2*). And so David says: 'For he himself made us, we did not make him, for we are the people of his pasture, the sheep under his hand' (*Ps.94.7*). And what is more, even he himself said of us: 'My sheep hear my voice, and follow after me' (*Jn.10.27*). And again: 'I have other sheep which are not of this fold, and I must gather these so there may be one flock, one shepherd' (*Jn.10.16*). And he gave this commission to the blessed Peter: 'Simon son of John do you love me? Feed my lambs, feed my sheep' (*Jn.21.17*).

4. Why God the Word should be said to be man.

[Gk.] Even though he is God by nature, the Word of God the Father is still called man in so far as he 'participated in flesh and blood just like us' (*Heb.2.14*). This was how he was revealed to those on earth, not as laying aside what he was, but as coming in the assumption of our manhood, and possessing it perfect in its own rationale [end of Gk.].

Nonetheless, even in his humanity he remained God, and Lord of all, in so far as he was born in nature and truth from God the Father. The most wise Paul shows us this most clearly when he says: 'For the first man was of the earth, and earthly, but the second man was from heaven' (*1 Cor.15.47*). But the holy Virgin gave birth to a temple united to the Word, and Emmanuel is rightly said to be from heaven, for the Word is from on high, and is born from the substance of God the Father himself. Yet, he descended to us, and then was made man, while even so he was the one from on high. John bore witness to this when he said of him: 'He who comes from above, is above all' (*Jn.3.31*). And Christ himself said to the Jewish people: 'You are from below. I am from on high' (*Jn.8.23*). And again: 'I am not of this world' (*Jn.14.16*). Even though as man he is now designated part of this world, even so, as God, he was still above the world. We can recall him saying quite clearly: 'No one has ascended into heaven except the one who came down from heaven, the Son of Man' (*Jn.3.13*). And so we say that the Son of Man descended from heaven by means of an economic union whereby the Word endowed the flesh with the radiance of his own glory and divine majesty.

5. Why God the Word is said to have been emptied out.

God the Word is 'full' in regard to his own nature, and perfect in every respect. From his own fullness he gives out his benefits to all creatures, as he said: 'I will pour out my spirit upon all flesh' (*Is.44.3*). When we say that he was 'emptied out' it has no derogatory reference to the Word's own nature nor, as might be thought, was he changed or made inferior in any respect. For he himself, just like his Begetter, is unalterable and immutable, and was never capable of any passibility. But when he became flesh, that is became man, he appropriated the poverty of humanity to himself: firstly, because even though he became man he still remained God; and secondly, because he accepted the form of a servant even though he is free in his own nature. And so, even though he is himself the Lord of Glory, he is said to receive glory. And even though he himself is Life, he is shown to be brought back to life. And even though he is the King of all, he receives dominion over all. Even though he is equal to God the Father, he obediently endured his sufferings and the cross. Because all these things were part and parcel of the human condition he adopted them as being implied along with the flesh, and so he fulfilled the economy, though always remaining what he was.

6. How Christ is one.

The divine Paul writes: 'Though there are many gods and many lords in heaven and on earth, for us there is one God and Father, from whom are all things, and we ourselves are from him; and one Lord Jesus Christ, through whom are all things, and we too are through him' (*1 Cor.8.5–6*). And the most-wise John said this about God the Word: 'All things were made through him, and apart from him nothing was made' (*Jn.1.3*). The blessed Gabriel also gave the good news to the holy Virgin saying: 'Behold you shall conceive and give birth to a son, and you will name him Jesus' (*Lk.1.31*). So, the divine Paul drew attention to the fact that all things were made through Christ Jesus, and the divine evangelist confirmed the force of the saying by speaking the truth and describing him in the Gospel as God the maker of all. What is more, the angel's word signifies that Jesus Christ was truly born from the holy Virgin. But here we are not considering God the Word as if he were apart from the humanity, no, we speak of the one effected from both things, that is God made man; the selfsame who was born in divine fashion from the Father as Word, and born in human fashion from the Virgin as man. When he is said to have been born according to the flesh, this does not connote a beginning of his existence, for he was indeed born before all the ages. Nonetheless, in this historical moment, because it was his intent to fulfil the economy, he was also born of a woman according to the flesh. And so, even though other people are also called Christs by similar appellations, there is only one Jesus Christ 'through whom all things were made', and it is not because a man was made into the maker of all things but because God the Word, 'through whom all things were made' (*1 Cor.8.5f* + *Jn.1.3*), 'participated in flesh and blood just like us' (*Heb.2.14*), and was thus called man. He did not, however, lose what he was, and for this reason even when he became flesh he is rightly understood as Maker of all.

7. How the Emmanuel is One.

In these last times God the Word is said to have been made man and, in the words of the divine Paul, 'Was manifested through his sacrifice' (*Heb.9.12*). What was this sacrifice? 'He offered his own body for us as a sweet-smelling oblation to God the Father and entered the sanctuary, once for all, not with the blood of goats or bulls, but with his own blood; and so he gained an everlasting forgiveness for those who believe in him' (*Heb.9.12.*). And so, although there were many holy people before him, none of them were ever called Emmanuel. Why was this? It was because the time had not yet arrived when he who is above every creature was to be 'with us', that is, come in our nature by means of the flesh. So, the one Emmanuel, the Only Begotten, was once and for all made man, and underwent a fleshly birth from the holy Virgin. It was said to Joshua son of Nave: 'I will be with you' (*Jos.1.5.*); but he was not Emmanuel. [God] was also 'with' Moses, but he is not called Emmanuel either. Whenever we hear the title 'God With Us' given to the Son, therefore, we should understand it in an intelligent fashion. It does not mean that he came to be with us in these last times as he is said to be with the saints, for he was with them in the manner of giving assistance. No, he was with us in the sense of being made like us, even though he did not lay aside his own nature, since, as God, he is unchangeable.

8. How we understand the Union.

A union can be accomplished in many fashions. Some people, for example, who are divided from one another in disposition, or will, or are in conflict with one another, can be said to be united in terms of a friendly reconciliation when they lay their differences aside. And we say that things are united when they are fastened to other things either by synthesis, or brought together in other ways, either by composition, or mixture, or fusion.[4] So when we say that the Word of God was united with our nature, the manner of the union is seen to be greater than human understanding. For the union was not according to one of our previously mentioned examples. No, it is altogether ineffable; known to no one at all, except God alone, who knows all things.

It is nothing extraordinary that we cannot grasp such considerations, when we sometimes investigate the constitution of things relative to us and have to confess that the comprehension of even their constitution is beyond our understanding. How, for example, should we understand man's soul to be united to his body? Who could possibly explain this? And yet, if those who are accustomed to have a slight understanding of small matters, and then even though they struggle to express them still feel it necessary to scrutinise such difficult matters which transcend our mind and speech, then in that case I should say (although the description altogether falls short of the truth) that it is fitting to understand the union of Emmanuel to be such as the soul of a man might be thought to have with its own body. For the soul appropriates[5] the things of the body even though in its proper nature it is apart from the body's natural passions, as well as those which impinge on it from without. For the body is moved to physical desires, and the soul which is within it feels these things too, because of the union, but in no way does it participate in these things, except in so far

---

[4] Parathesis, Mixis, Krasis.

[5] oikeioutai.

as it takes the fulfilment of desire as its own gratification. If the body was struck by a sword, or tortured on an iron grid, then the soul would share in its grief, because it is its own body which is suffering. But in its own nature the soul does not suffer anything of these things.

This indeed is how we attribute the union to Emmanuel. For it was necessary that the soul united to it should share in the grief of its own body, so that rising above these sufferings it could submit itself as obedient to God. But it is foolish to say that God the Word shared in feeling the sufferings. For the Godhead is impassible and is not in our condition. Yet [the Word] was united to the flesh endowed with a rational soul, and when the flesh suffered, even though he was impassible, he was aware of what was happening within it, and thus as God, even though he did away with the weakness of the flesh, still he appropriated those weaknesses of his own body. This is how he is said to have hungered, and to have been tired, and to have suffered for our sake.

Accordingly, the union of the Word with humanity can reasonably be compared with our condition. Just as the body is of a different nature to the soul, still from both we say that one man results, so too from the perfect hypostasis of God the Word and from a humanity perfect in its own right there is one Christ, and the selfsame is at once God and man. As I said earlier, the Word appropriated the affairs of his own flesh because it is his body, no one else's. And he communicates, as to his own flesh, the operation of his own divine powers. This was how he was able to give life to the dead, and to heal the sick.

9. About the Coal.

If it is necessary to demonstrate the manner of the union even from the inspired scriptures, by applying examples from typology, then we shall do so. The blessed Isaiah said: 'One of the Seraphim was sent to me holding a coal in its hand which it had taken in a pair of tongs from the altar. And it came to me and touched my lips and said: Behold this has touched your lips and taken away your transgressions, and purged your sins' (*Is.6.6–7*). We say that the coal supplies a type and image for us of the incarnation of the Word. For if he touches our lips, that is when we confess our faith in him, then he renders us purged of all our sins, and free of our ancient transgressions.

Yet we can see in this image of the coal, the Word of God as united with the manhood, and not as having cast aside what he is, but rather as having transformed what he assumed into his own glory and power. It is like fire that gains a hold on wood, penetrates, and consumes it. Although the wood does not cease to be wood, yet it is changed into the appearance and vigour of fire, and is itself reckoned as one with it. This is how you should consider it was in the case of Christ. We say that God was united to manhood in an ineffable way but preserved the manhood as it was. And he himself remained what he was; but being united once and for all he is reckoned as one with the manhood and he appropriates all that belongs to it while introducing to it the power of his own nature.

10. That the incorporeal Godhead became a body, that is flesh endowed with a rational soul; and that if we separate these things from one another then we entirely and indisputably destroy the system of the economy we understand in Christ.
In the Song of Songs the Lord introduces himself when he says: 'I am the flower of the field, the lily of the valleys (*Song of Songs 2.1 LXX*). Likewise, a perfume is something incorporeal, and yet it uses as its own the bodily form which it indwells, and thus a lily can be considered to be one thing from both elements. The absence of either one would would entirely ruin its essential rationale, for the perfume is within the particular substrate, and that substrate is something corporeal. This too is how we think about Christ, how his own transcendent and sublime nature of godhead perfumes the world in the humanity as its particular substrate. That which is incorporeal by nature becomes, as it were, embodied by means of an economic union, since he wills to be made known through a body. And in this body he works divine signs, so that we might understand that the Incorporeal One is in his very own body, just as the perfume is in the underlying flower, where both together are called the one lily.

11. That the Word comes to a true union with the humanity, wherein the things so united still remain unconfused.
The holy Tabernacle was raised up in the wilderness in accordance with God's counsel, and there in several fashions we find a figure of Emmanuel. So, for example, the God of all said to the godly Moses: 'And you shall make an Ark of Witness out of imperishable wood, two and a half cubits in length, a cubit and a half in width, and a cubit and a half in in height. And you shall gild it over with pure gold, inside and outside you shall so gild it' (*Ex.25.10–11*). This imperishable wood is a type of the incorruptible body. For cedar is

imperishable, whereas the gold as the most precious material of all is a sign for us of the sublimity of the divine nature. Note then how the Ark is entirely gilded with pure gold within and without. God the Word was united with the holy flesh, and this, I think, is the outward gilding of the Ark. The fact that he also appropriated a rational soul within the body is demonstrated by his command to gild the inside of the Ark as well. That the natures or hypostases[6] remained unconfused we know from this fact: that the gold was overlaid on the wood and remained what it was, while the wood was enriched by the glory of the gold yet did not cease to be wood on that account. The Ark can thus be taken to be a figure of Christ, as many arguments can persuade us, for it travelled ahead of the Israelites seeking out a place of rest for them, and so too did Christ say somewhere: 'I shall go on ahead and prepare a place for you' (*Jn.14.2*).

12. That God the Word, when he was made man, was not simply a man honoured by a mere conjunction, or called to a like dignity or authority with God the Word, as some people think.

The divine Paul says that the 'mystery of piety' is a great thing indeed (*1 Tim.3.16*). This is truly the case, for although he was God the Word he was 'manifested in the flesh and justified in the spirit' (*ibid*). And even though he was made man alongside us, in no way was he bounded by our infirmities; for he committed no sin, and was manifested to the angels (for they were not ignorant of his birth according to the flesh), and he preached to the nations as God made man, and so was believed on by the world. The divine Paul demonstrates this when he writes: 'Be mindful of the fact that once you were gentiles in the flesh, called the uncircumcised by those who are called the circumcision by a deed which is done in the flesh. For in that time, devoid of Christ, you were alienated from the communion of Israel, strangers to the convenant, and having no hope in the promise, being devoid of God in this world' (*Eph.2.11–12*). So, there were gentiles in this world who were devoid of God because they were apart from Christ. But because they recognised that he was truly God by nature, he too came to recognise them who confessed their faith. Then he was taken up into divine glory. The blessed David sang about this:

---

[6] Physis/ hypostasis: one of the less common applications of hypostasis as a synonym, in Cyril, for physis, signifying 'natural properties' e.g. manhood, godhead. He uses the word in this way sometimes in an apologetic context partly determined by the Antiochene practice of applying the word in this manner.

'God goes up with jubilation' (*Ps.46.6*). But he ascended with the body, not in the Godhead on its own, for he was God made flesh.

We do not believe, therefore, in someone who like us has been honoured with deity as a grace, and we do not stand betrayed as worshippers of a man. No, we believe in the Lord who appeared in the form of a slave, and who was truly like us, and yet still remained God in the humanity. God the Word did not lay aside what he was when he assumed the flesh. The selfsame is understood to be at once God and man. This is how faith understands it to be, and rightly so. But perhaps someone might say: But what is wrong with thinking that he was a man like us who attained to the godhead, rather than God who became man? To this I shall reply that a thousand objections could be set against the idea; but I shall give the essence of the argument as follows: we must resist this conception unwaveringly, and refuse to believe that it could ever be so.

Before we go on to investigate other matters to do with the economy, let us consider the defining characteristics of the flesh, and let us analyse our human condition a little more closely. Human nature is sorely tried and oppressed by great evils, damned by the curse to death, and caught in the snares of sin. It was going astray and lay in darkness. It did not know God, the true God by nature, but preferred the creation to God (*Rom.1.25*). How then could it be freed from such evils? Can we possibly say that it was right that the divine nature could be attained by a humanity which was altogether ignorant of the dignity of the heavenly nature since it was bound up in the darkness of ignorance, and corrupted by the filth of sin? How could it possibly attain the holy nature and receive glory, which no man can discover unless it is given to him? Suppose we even concede that perhaps [human nature] could recognise [the glory], and even knew how to attain to godhead. Then who taught it these things? For, 'How can they believe unless they hear' (*Rom.10.14*)? So you see, it is not capable of attaining to deity and taking that glory which befits it.

So it is more fitting, and more accurate, to hold that it was in order to save that which was being lost that God the Word, 'through whom all things came to be' (*Jn.1.3*), came down to us and entered into that which he was not, so that he might even come into the nature of man (which he did not have previously) and by this union endow it with the dignities of the divine majesty. And this, far from subjecting the unchangeable God to this nature's limits, raised it up to a transcendence of its nature. For it was fitting that incorruptible nature should attain a corruptible nature in order to free it from corruption. It was fitting that, 'He who knew no sin should be made like sinners so that he might suppress sin (*2 Cor.5.21*). For just as wherever light is present it destroys the gloom of darkness, just so in the presence of immortality all the cowardly ills [of man] take flight, and all sin fled away in the presence of him who knew no sin, and even appropriated to himself a body that was devoid of sin.

The fact that the Word, who is God, was made man, rather than it being the case that Christ should ever be thought of as a man who was deified, is clearly demonstrated from the sacred scriptures. Thus, the blessed Paul says of the Only Begotten: 'Who though he was in the form of God, did not think equality with God was something to be grasped, but emptied himself, assuming the form of a slave, made in the likeness of man, and found in fashion as a man. He humbled himself becoming obedient to death, even death on a cross. And so, God highly exalted him, and gave him the name which is above every name, that at the name of Jesus Christ every knee should bend, those in heaven, those on earth, and those in the underworld, and every tongue should confess that the Lord Jesus Christ is in the glory of God the Father' (*Phil.2.6–11 Vulg.*).

Who is this person we say was in the form of God, and in equality with God, and yet did not think the equality a thing to be grasped at but instead descended into self-emptying and into the form of a slave, humbling himself and being made in our likeness? If it was simply and solely a man born of a woman, then how did he possess such fullness so as to be understood as 'emptied out'? Or in what lofty state was he formerly positioned that he could be said to have 'humbled himself'? Or how was he made in the likeness of men if he was already that beforehand by nature? for in that case he could hardly be said to have 'been made' such. Or how can he be said to have been 'emptied out' if he was assuming the fullness of the deity? in that case since he ascended to heavenly glory is he not rather exalted to the heights?

This is why we say that it was not a man who became God, but rather God the Word, who was in the form and equality of the Father, who was emptied out for the sake of mankind. Since he was fullness, as God, this was why he was emptied out for the sake of our likeness. He was humbled on account of the flesh, but even so he did not descend from the height of divine majesty for he kept his lofty throne. He who was in the same form as the Father, and 'the very figure of his substance' (*Heb.1.3*), came in the likeness of men. And once he had become as we are, he is said to have ascended with the flesh into the glory of the deity (something which he obviously already possessed as his very own) which was done for this reason for humanity's sake.

Even with the flesh he is believed on as Lord of all, and thus 'every knee bends before him', and not to the detriment or dishonour of the Father, but rather to his glory. For the Father rejoices and is glorified when men adore the Son, even though he became like us. For again it is written: 'He did not take to himself descent from angels, but from Abraham, that he might be made like his brethren in all things' (*Heb.2.16–17*). See how the Word of God took descent from Abraham, and that it was not some man or other like us who took up the deity. He himself becomes like us (and is called our brother) as man, not in terms of the nature of deity. 'For the children participate in flesh and blood, and he himself likewise participated in them so that by death he might destroy him who had the power over death, that is the devil, and should set free those who all their lives had been held in bondage by the fear of death' (*Heb.2.14–15*).

Yet again, he himself participated in flesh and blood, just like us, for this reason which is immediately told to us in the adjoining text, where it is written: 'For what was impossible to the Law, in that it was weak through the flesh, God sent his Son in the likeness of sinful flesh, and from sin condemned sin in the flesh' (*Rom.8.3*). Note once again how a man is not shown attaining to the divine nature or rising up to its dignity, rather God the Father sending his Son in the likeness of sinful flesh, so as to destroy sin. And so, the Word who is God descended to an emptying out as he was made man, and Christ is not seen to be a simply a man attaining to the divine glory.

13. That The Word of God made man is called Christ Jesus.
Wishing to consider the mystery of the Only Begotten's economy with flesh, we say this (since we have a true opinion and hold a correct faith), that the very Word of God the Father, the true God of true God, the light of light, was himself incarnated and made man, came down, suffered, and was raised from the dead. This is how the great and holy Synod[7] defined the symbol of faith. If we wish to investigate this, and want to learn what this incarnation and becoming man really means for the Logos, then we should take note that it does not mean that he assumed a man, as if in a conjunction in terms of equality of honour or authority, or merely in terms of an attributed title of

[7] Nicaea 325.

Sonship. On the contrary, it means that he became man like us, even though the same one who economically came to assume flesh and blood, also remained unalterably and unchangeably in his own proper nature. It is one person that the god-inspired scripture (both before and after the incarnation) designates as, Only Begotten, Word, God, Image, Radiance and Impress of the Father's Very Being, Life, Glory, Light, Wisdom, Power, Strong Right Hand, Most High, Magnificence, Lord of Hosts, and other such names which are truly fitting for the deity. And similarly one person (after the incarnation) that it calls, Man, Christ Jesus, Atonement, Mediator, First Fruits of the Dead, First Born From the Dead, Second Adam, and Head of the Body that is the Church. Both sets of titles apply to him. All are his, the first series as well as those which apply in these last times of this age.

He is one, therefore, who was true God before the incarnation, and even in the manhood remained what he was, and is, and shall be. And so the one Lord Jesus Christ must not be divided up, as if there was a distinct man and a distinct deity. No, we say that Jesus Christ is one and the same, even though we recognise the difference of natures and keep them unconfused with each other.

So when sacred scripture says that all the 'fullness of the godhead dwelt bodily' (*Coloss.2.9*) in Christ we do not, for this reason, conclude that the Word simply dwelt in the man as if in a different Christ; nor do we divide things that have been united to one another so as to conclude there are two sons. We maintain that sacred scripture sometimes uses the title Christ to refer to the manhood of God the Word which he has made his very own, and which he has made in the order of a temple. For it is written somewhere about human souls: 'Those who dwell in houses of clay, of which number we too are of clay' (*Job.4.19*). Just because it calls the bodies of men 'houses of clay', should we then divide the one man into two men? Is it not entirely correct, nonetheless, to say that the human spirit dwells within the man? Even though these examples convey to us the form of our condition, and it cannot be otherwise, this still does not mean that the natures of these two things (spirit and flesh) are mutually injurious, on the contrary we should regard them rather as having advanced us along the straight road of truth.

So when we see things that happen to be dissimilar in nature brought into unity by composition, when perhaps the one is said to indwell the other, we must not divide this into two, even if we can still name each of the two united entities separately, whatever they might be. To divide them would be to dishonour the consilience into unity.

As I have said, even in the case of a man, his spirit is said to indwell him. But it is not only the spirit, but even the body which is properly called man. The most wise Paul suggested this to us when he said: 'For if our outward man is corrupted, the inner man is renewed from day to day' (*2 Cor.4.16*). So when someone says that our inner man dwells within the outer man, he is speaking the truth, but this does not indicate he has divided the one into two. The prophet Isaiah said somewhere: 'At night my spirit will keep vigil before you O God' (*Is.26.9 LXX*). Does this mean that his spirit keeps vigil before God as something different to him? Would this not surely stand exposed as nonsense? And so, even though the system of the words seems to lean to it, we should never depart from what is reasonable, but ought rather to refer the meaning of the various attributions to the sense that is appropriate in each instance.

So, if Jesus is said 'to have advanced in wisdom and grace' (*Lk.2.52*), it refers to the economy. For the Word of God allowed the humanity to exist in the manner of its own nature, but wished to provide a gradual revelation of the nature of his own deity, so that as the body grew, so also he would extend with it his own proper qualities, and then nothing alien would be seen which might terrify the onlookers because of its great strangeness. And remember how they had even said: 'But how does this man know his letters when he has never studied' (*Jn.7.15*)? This is why the 'advance' is a bodily matter and his progress in wisdom and grace befits the measures of the manhood. But we say that in his own nature he is the Word of God who has no need of any advancement, or any wisdom or grace, but on the contrary bestows wisdom and grace and every benefit on the creation.

And if Jesus is said to suffer, this passion applies to the economy too. Nonetheless it is attributed to him quite properly in so far as that which suffered was his very own. He who knew not suffering because he was impassible as God, was in the suffering body, but in so far as concerns the arrogance of his persecutors he did suffer, even though he could not suffer. It happened in so far as the Only Begotten came to be like us. So, as often as the scriptures call him man we understand the economy, even though he is God by nature, and we confess him as such.

14. Examples from the divine scripture that the Word of God made man still remained God. The Mercy Seat.

Somewhere God said to the priest Moses: 'You shall make a Mercy

Seat of pure gold two and a half cubits long, and a cubit and a half in height. You shall make two Cherubim of ornate gold, and set them on either side: one Cherubim on this side, and one Cherubim on the other side of the Mercy Seat. And thus you shall make two Cherubim over both sides, and the Cherubim will be stretching out their wings, overshadowing the Mercy Seat with their wings, and their faces will look towards one another, watching over the Mercy Seat' (*Ex.25.17–20*). This is truly a type of how God the Word remained God in his own glory and majesty even in the humanity, although because of the economy he was made like us. For Emmanuel was made our Mercy Seat through faith. The most wise John demonstrates this for us when he says: 'Children I write to you that you should not sin, but if anyone does sin he has a paraclete with the Father, Jesus Christ the Just One, and he himself is the propitiation[8] for our sins' (*1 Jn.2.1–2*). And Paul confirms it too when he says: 'Whom God proposed as a propitiation through faith in his blood' (*Rom.3.25*). Yet the Cherubim are evidently in attendance on the Mercy Seat and overshadowing it, with their wings turned towards the Propitiation, and their eyes utterly fixed on the Lord's command, for the holy host of heavenly spirits looks only to the will of God, and is never tired of gazing on God. This is why the prophet Isaiah said he saw the Son on 'a throne lifted up and exalted' (*Is.6.1*), with the Seraphim standing by and worshipping him as God.

15. Another example. The Rod of Moses.

Of old the divine Moses was sent to liberate Israel from the tyranny of the Egyptians. But because it was necessary that those who were under the yoke of a habitual slavery should first learn that God was now reconciled with them, he commanded him to perform wonders, since a wonderful miracle draws men to faith. And so Moses said to Almighty God: 'But if they do not believe me, and will not listen to my voice, but say, God did not send you, then what shall I say to them? And the Lord said, What is that in your hand? And he replied, A rod. So he said to him, Cast it onto the earth; and it became a serpent and Moses fled away from it. And the Lord said to Moses, Stretch out your hand and seize its tail. And he stretched out his hand and seized its tail and it became a rod in his hand. And God said to him, This is so that they may believe you, that

[8] Propitiation, in the Greek text, is the same as Mercy Seat.

the Lord God of their fathers appeared to you, the God of Abraham, the God of Isaac, and the God of Jacob' (Ex.4.1–5).

Note in these words the Son of God in nature and truth, who is, as it were, the rod of the Father, since the rod is the symbol of the King, and: 'To the Son he gave power over all things' (*Jn.17.2*). And this is why the divine David said: 'Your throne O God endures from age to age, a rod of equity is the rod of your dominion' (*Ps.44.7*). But he cast down the rod to the earth, that is encompassed it in an earthly body, when he sent him onto the earth through the humanity. And then he was made in the likeness of wicked men, for indeed the serpent is the symbol of wickedness. And we know that this is true from this fact, that Our Lord Jesus Christ himself, on account of the economy that took place in the flesh, assumed the bronze serpent (which Moses lifted up, as a healing of the serpent's bites) as his image and type. For he says: 'And just as Moses lifted up the serpent in the wilderness, so shall the Son of Man be lifted up, so that all who believe in him may not be lost but may have eternal life' (*Jn.3.14; Num.21.8*). Just as the serpent made of bronze was a cause of salvation to those in danger, for all who looked on it were saved, so in the same way was the Lord Jesus Christ, for all who saw him in the likeness of wicked men, in so far as he became man, came to know that he will be the cause of life, in so far as he is the life-giving God, the one to give the power of avoiding all venomous beasts, that is the evil powers. And there is another type of this here, in so far as the rod of Moses devoured the other rods which the Magi cast down on the ground (*Ex.4.2*).

And so, even though the rod was cast down upon the earth it did not remain so always, for it was taken up again, and once more became what it was. As I have said before, although the Son, that rod of the Father through whom he has the power over all things, came in our likeness, nevertheless when the economy was fulfilled he returned to heaven, and was again at the Father's right hand as 'a rod of equity and dominion' (*Ps.44.7*), for he sits at the right hand of the Father in his own majesty, possessing the highest throne, even with his flesh.

16. Another example: Moses' hand turned leprous and restored to health.

'Again the Lord God said to him, Put your hand into your bosom. And when he brought his hand back out from his bosom it had become like snow. And again he said, Put your hand into your bosom, and he put it into his bosom, and when he brought it out from his bosom it was restored once more to the colour of his flesh' (*Ex.4.6*). Now, the divine scripture calls the true Son the 'right hand' of God the Father. He himself introduces him with the words: 'I founded the heavens by my own hand' (*Is.48.13*), and the divine David also sings: 'By the Word of the Lord the heavens were made' (*Ps.32.6*). See, then, while the hand was still hidden in the bosom of Moses it was not yet made leprous, but when it was brought out it immediately became leprous. Then it was hidden again and once more brought out, when it was no longer leprous, 'for it was restored to the colour of his flesh'. And so, as long as the Word was 'in the bosom of the Father' (*Jn.1.18*), he shone with the splendour of the deity, but when he was 'brought out', as it were, through the incarnation or enmanment, then he was made 'in the likeness of sinful flesh, and was reputed among the unrighteous' (*Rom.8.3; Is.53.12*). As the divine Paul says: 'He who knew not sin, became sin for our sake, that we might become righteousness in him' (*1 Cor.5.21*). This, I think, is what the leprosy signifies, since according to the Law the leprous man is unclean (*Lev.13.2*). But because he came again into the bosom of the Father (for he was lifted up in the resurrection from the dead) then it was as if the hand was brought out again and so appeared clean. Just so will our Lord Jesus Christ appear again at the end of time in the integrity and glory of the deity, even though he did not cast off our likeness.

The blessed Paul said of Christ: 'He died once and for all to take away the sins of many. But he shall be manifested a second time, without sin, to those that look to him for salvation' (*Heb.9.28*). And so, whenever the sacred text designates Jesus Christ, you should not think of a man apart, on his own, not truly united to the Word of God himself. Rather you should consider that Jesus Christ is himself the Word of God the Father, as he has become man.

17. That Christ was not a god-bearing man, or that the Word simply indwelt a man. Rather that [the Word] was made flesh, that is perfect man, in accordance with the scriptures.

Those who have a pure faith in Christ, one that is confirmed by universally correct witness, say that it was God the Word (who is himself from God the Father) who came down in a self-emptying, assuming the form of a slave, and because he took that body which was born from the Virgin as his very own, they say that he was made like us, and was called the Son of Man. But the selfsame is God according to the Spirit and man according to the flesh. As the divine Paul said to the Jewish people: 'God once spoke to our fathers in many diverse manners through the prophets, but now in these last days, he has spoken to us in the Son' (*Heb.1.1–2*). But in what way can God the Father be thought to have spoken to us in the Son in these last days? He spoke to the ancients through the Son, in the Law, and this is why the Son says that the words spoken through the most wise Moses were his own, for he tells us: 'Do not think that I have come to destroy the Law or the Prophets. I did not come to destroy but to fulfil. For I say to you, not one jot or flourish, shall pass from the law until all shall come to pass. Heaven and earth may pass away but my word will never pass away' (*Mt.5.17*). There is also the saying of the prophet: 'I who am speaking to you, am present' (*Is.52.6. LXX*). When the Son came in the flesh, the Father then spoke to us in him, just as the blessed Paul said, 'in these last days'. But, equally, in case we did not believe that it was the same one who was Son even before the ages, he added immediately: 'Through whom he made the ages' (*Heb.1.2*), to remind us that he is the radiance of the Father's glory, and the figure of his substance.

He through whom God the Father made the world was truly made man. He did not, as some think, come in a man so that we might consider him a man who had God indwelling him. If they hold this to be the case, and rely on it as true, then surely the saying of the blessed evangelist John appears pointless: 'And the Word was made flesh' (*Jn.1.14*). If he did not become flesh what was the point of the incarnation? Or why did he say that he had become flesh? The meaning of the term 'incarnation' signifies that he became like us, though even so he remained above us, and indeed above all the creation. I think it is fitting, then, to demonstrate what I have said by persuasive examples which show that the Only Begotten was made man, yet even with his flesh is God, and not that he merely indwells a man, making him a god-bearer like others who have been participants in his own deity.

18. That God dwelt in Emmanuel in a different way than he dwells in us.

God said about us somewhere in the scriptures: 'And I will dwell in them, and walk among them, and I will be their God, and they shall be my people' (*Lev.26.12; 2 Cor.6.16*). And Our Lord Jesus Christ himself said: 'Behold I am coming, and if any shall open to me, I will enter there, and I will dine with them. I and the Father will come to him and make our dwelling with him' (*Rev.3.20; Jn.14.16*). We are even called the 'Temple of God', for scripture says: 'For you are the temple of the living God' (*1 Cor.3.17*), and again: 'Do you not know that your bodies are the temples of the Holy Spirit who is within you, whom you have from God?' (*1 Cor.6.19*).

But if they are saying that he is Emmanuel in just the same way that each of us has God dwelling within him, then let them confess it openly; and when they see him adored by us and by the angels, in heaven as much as on earth, then they will be put to shame as having held different and contrary opinions, and as having been ignorant of the purpose of the sacred scriptures, and not having in themselves that faith which was handed on to us by those who saw and ministered to the Word in the beginning (cf.*1 Tim.6.3; Lk.1.2*).

If, on the other hand, they declare him to be God, and glorified as God, simply because the Word of God the Father dwelt with him, but not because he was [the Word] made man, then let them again hear our reply: If the indwelling of God was sufficient in itself to make its recipients truly capable of becoming deities, and of being adored by men, then surely all the angels and even mankind would be deities worthy of adoration? since God indwells the holy angels, and even we have God within us by the Holy Spirit. This shows that having the Holy Spirit is not sufficient to make people into adorable deities by nature. And so, Emmanuel is God, and to be adored, not because God dwelt within him, as if in a common man (one understood as separate and distinct from God the Word) but because [the Word] became flesh, that is man, even though the selfsame remained God who is worthy of adoration.

19. Apostolic sayings in which Christ is called God.

When it speaks of the mystery of Christ scripture says: 'Which was not made known to other generations of the sons of men, as it is now revealed to the holy apostles' (*Eph.3.5*). And also: 'A mystery which was hidden for ages and generations, which has now been manifested to his saints, to whom he wished to reveal the riches of the glory of this mystery among the gentiles, which is Christ, the hope of glory in you, whom we preach' (*Coloss.1.26–28*). But if he is a god-bearer, though not truly God, how is he the riches of the glory of the mystery who is proclaimed to the gentiles? Or for that matter how is God proclaimed at all?

20. Another example.
'I want you to know what care I have for you, and for those in Laodicea, and for those who have not seen my face in the flesh, so that they might be comforted in their hearts, built up in love, and in all the riches of the fullness of understanding in the knowledge of the mystery of God, of Christ' (*Coloss.2.1*). See how here he calls the mystery of God the mystery of Christ, and wishes these people to have a full understanding of the knowledge of it. But what need was there of understanding for those who wanted to learn the mystery of Christ if they were only about to be told that God dwelt within a man? On the other hand there is need for a great deal of understanding indeed if one wants to understand how the Word, who is God, became man.

21. Another example.
'For the Word of the Lord did not only sound out from you in Macedonia and Achaia, but in every place where your faith in God has gone forth' (*1 Thess.1.8*). Note once more how he reminds us that this faith was 'in God', when even Christ says: 'He who has faith in me, has eternal life' (*Jn.6.47*). This is the doctrine he offers us about himself in his own preaching.

22. Another example.
'You yourselves know how we first came among you; how it was not in vain, but after having suffered many things beforehand in Philippi we were made bold in God to speak the gospel of God to you' (*1 Thess.2.1–2*). See how, speaking in God, he makes mention of the 'gospel of God' when it is Christ he preaches to the gentiles.

23. Another example.
'Brethren remember our labour and care. How we worked day and night so as not to be a heavy burden on you when we preached the gospel of God among you' (*1 Thess.2.9*). And again: 'And so we give thanks to God ceaselessly, because when you received the word from us you accepted it as if hearing it from God, and not as the word of men, but as the word of God who works among you who have believed' (*1 Thess.2.13*). Does he not clearly refer to his preaching of Christ as the 'gospel of God' and 'the word of God'? Indeed this is most evident to all.

[The Armenian version begins ch.24 here, and hereafter the chapters are out of sequence in varying Mss.]

'For the grace of God our Saviour has appeared to all, teaching us to live justly and soberly and religiously in this age, denying impiety and profane desires, waiting on that blessed hope, the advent of the glory of our great God and Saviour Jesus Christ' (*Tit.2.11–13*). See how Our Lord Jesus Christ is most clearly called 'Great God', for it is his advent of glory that we await, in the meantime being diligent in living soberly and blamelessly. But if he is a god-bearing man how can he be the Great God? Or how can hope in him be a blessed thing? if at least the prophet Jeremiah is true when he says: 'Cursed is he who puts his hope in a man' (*Jer.17.5*). As I said before, a god-bearer was certainly not able to make himself God.

Finally, let them tell us what is there to prevent all those others who had God within them from being God and being adored? But the blessed Paul calls Christ God, and Great, and 'having a blessed revelation', when he is clearly found speaking about Jesus and Emmanuel: 'Of whom are the fathers and the covenant and the promises, and from whom comes Christ according to the flesh, who is God, blessed above all things, to the ages of ages. Amen' (*Rom.9.4–5*). And Paul made his preaching in accordance with a divine revelation, as is clear from what he himself says: 'And then after fourteen years I again went up to Jerusalem with Barnabas, and also took up Titus. I went up on account of a revelation, and I set out for them the gospel which I preached to the gentiles. I did so privately to those who seemed to be something there, in case I ran, or had been running, in vain' (*Gal.2.1–2*). When he preaches Christ as God to the gentiles, he constantly calls his mystery a divine one. He went up, by a revelation, to Jerusalem, and set it before those who seemed to be something there (that means to the holy apostles or disciples) so that he might not be running in vain. But when he came down again from Jerusalem, and was back once more among the gentile flocks, did he change anything of what he had taught earlier? Did he not rather continue confessing Christ as God? And thus he wrote to certain people: 'I was amazed that you changed so soon from the one that called you, to another gospel, which is not another except that some are disturbing you, and wishing to pervert the gospel of Christ' (*Gal.1.6–7*). And he says again: 'But even if we, or an angel from heaven, should preach a gospel different to that which you have received, let him be anathema' (*Gal.1.18*). For this reason, therefore, he passed over all others, even though they had God dwelling within them, and preached Jesus alone as God.

24. Another example.
It is written of Christ: 'While he was in Jerusalem for the feast many people believed in his name, seeing the signs which he did. But Jesus himself did not trust himself to them, for he knew them all, and did not need anyone to give a testimony about a man, since he himself knew what was in a man' (*Jn.2.23–25*). But if he was a god-bearing man, how were the many who believed in his name at Jerusalem not deceived? Or why did he alone know the things which are in a man, when indeed no-one else knows them? for God alone is said to have made our hearts (*Ps.32.15*). Or why did he alone remit sins? For he said: 'For the Son has power to remit sins on earth' (*Mt.9.6*). Why did he alone, beyond all others, sit with God the Father's judgement? Why do the angels obey him alone? Why did he teach us to regard the Father in heaven as our common parent but spoke of him as his own particular father? Perhaps you will say that texts of this kind are to be referred to the Word who indwells? But in that case surely he too ought to say, in the manner appropriate to prophets, 'Thus says the Lord'? But when he wanted to command those things that were above the Law he assumed to himself an authority fitting to a Lawgiver, when he said: 'But I say to you' (*Mt.5.32*).

How does he say that he is a free son, and not under obligation to God? It is because he is the Son in truth. If he was a god-bearing man would he even be free in his nature? For God alone is free of this and released from obligation. He alone requires, as it were, the tribute of all, and accepts religious reverence in place of our debts. But if Christ is the end of the Law and the prophets, but yet is a god-bearing man, would it not be true to conclude that the end of all the preaching of the prophets was merely to bring us to the crime of man-worshipping?

The Law preached: 'You shall worship the Lord your God, and serve him alone' (*Deut.6.13*), and by its wisdom it led us to Christ, as to a knowledge more powerful than theirs who were in the shadows. Should we then disdain to adore the God of the Law and the prophets, and instead adore a man who had God dwelling within him? Where would it be best to conceive God's presence—in heaven or on earth? In the Seraphim or in an earthly body?

If he were a god-bearing man how is it that, 'He has participated just like us in flesh and blood' (*Heb.2.14*)? If it was said that he 'participated, just like us, in flesh and blood' as meaning that God indwelt, and that this manner of participating was the same thing as 'being made man', then since he has indwelt many saints he must also have been made man not once but a multitude of times. But why, in that case, is he said: 'To have appeared once in the consummation of the ages, for the destruction of sin by his own sacrifice' (*Heb.9.26*)? And if he was a god-bearing man then how is it that all the divine scriptures proclaim to us only one advent of the Word? If he became like a temple of God then how can Christ also be in us? As a temple within a temple? Or is it not rather as God within the temples of ourselves through the Spirit? If he was a god-bearing man why is his body alone life-giving? For if almighty God dwelt within the bodies of others was it not right that they too should be life-giving?

Somewhere, however, the divine Paul wrote: 'If someone who despised the Law of Moses was put to death without mercy on the testimony of two or three witnesses, how much worse punishment would you think someone worthy of who trod underfoot the Son of God, and regarded the blood of the covenant as something defiled (*Heb.10.28–29*)? But the Law was something divine, and the commandments were spoken through angels, so how would someone be worthy of greater punishment simply by regarding the blood of Christ as something defiled? Or how is it that faith in Christ is more powerful than the religion of the Law? Well, as we have already said, it is because Christ is not a god-bearing man like other saints, but rather is truly God, and higher than all creation. He possesses glory because the Word is God by nature, and yet became flesh, that is perfect man, since we believe that the body that was united to him was endowed with reason and soul, and that the union was entirely true.

25. How we ought to understand the phrase: 'The Word became flesh and dwelt among us.' And how the body is said to be his very own.

The blessed Paul reminds us that the Only Begotten Word of God took descent from Abraham (*Heb.2.16*), and also that 'He participated, just like us, in flesh and blood (*Heb.2.14*). We can also call to mind John who said: 'The Word was made flesh, and dwelt among us' (*Jn.1.14*). So was it the purpose of these spiritual men to teach that the Word of God suffered change, or really underwent the kind of metamorphosis that is more applicable to a creature, in order to choose of his own volition to turn into something that beforehand he was not? Or perhaps he was unwillingly forced into another nature? Far from it. He remains the same, excluding all transformation by virtue of his own nature, and not knowing how to suffer 'the shadow of a change' (*Jas.1.17*), for that heavenly nature is eternally established in its own characteristics.

It is necessary, then, to see how the Word did become flesh. In the first place divine scripture frequently calls man 'flesh', as if designating the whole of the animal from the part. Sometimes it does the same thing even by reference to the soul on its own. For it is written: 'All flesh will see the salvation of God' (*Lk.3.6*). And the divine Paul himself says: 'I did not confer with flesh and blood' (*Gal.1.16*). And the priest Moses spoke to the Israelites: 'Your fathers descended as seventy five souls into Egypt' (*Deut.10.22*). One would hardly say from this that it was naked and bodiless souls that went down into Egypt, or that God gave his salvation to soulless bodies, mere fleshy things. So, whenever we hear that 'the Word was made flesh' we understand that it means man of soul and body. For the Word, who is God, became perfect man, assuming a body that was endowed with reason and soul, which he truly united to himself. How this happened, he alone knows, for such considerations are wholly beyond the grasp of our senses. This is how he was called the Son of Man.

And yet, if it is necessary to speak of it, as if in a mirror (*2 Cor.3.18*), human sense can have some kind of notion, for the Word was united to the body which had a rational soul, in the kind of way that the soul of a man is united with its own body; for even though this is a different nature to it, the soul still has a habitual communion and union with the body to such an extent that it cannot practically be seen as a different thing to the body, in so far as through the composition of both there is one living creature formed (though as I have said earlier, the Word remained in his own proper nature). And so we say that the Word became man, not by transformation or change, and certainly not meaning that he ceased to be God. We mean that he assumed flesh from a woman and was made one with it in the womb, and in this way the selfsame came forth God and Man.

He underwent a temporal generation and accepted a beginning from the woman so that he could exist like this, but he never set aside his eternal generation from God the Father. He also allowed his flesh to be born according to the laws of its own nature, that is in the manner of a nativity. Nonetheless there was in this very deed something unlike human nature, for he was born of a virgin, and he alone had such an unwed mother. The evangelist notes how he himself made the flesh, and so dwelt among us, and this proves two points: firstly that he was made man; and secondly that he did not lose what was his own, but remained what he was.

[Gk.] He is understood entirely as one thing within another. That which indwells, that is the divine nature in the manhood, does not suffer any mixing, or confusion, or change[9] into something that formerly it was not. Something that is said to dwell within something else does not become what that thing is in which it dwells, rather it is understood to be one thing in another thing. But in respect to the nature of the Word and the nature of manhood this difference indicates to us only the distinguishing of natures, for we also understand that there is one Christ, from out of both. And so, as I have explained, even though the non-confusedness was preserved, the evangelist tells us that the Word dwelt among us, for he knows that there is only one Only Begotten Son who was incarnated and made man. [end of Gk.]

It seems to me that the divine evangelist wisely called the entire human nature 'flesh', for he says that the Word dwelt among us, and this was, I think, to note that the incarnation of the Word did not come about any other way, as for example by grace, but only for this reason that we might reap the benefit of adoption through our enriching participation in him through the Holy Spirit. This is why we believe that in Christ the highest and truest union was effected. If, on the contrary, Christ is said to dwell among us, this would make the indwelling merely a matter of relationship.[10] But since God was not said merely to have dwelt within Christ (for 'in him dwelt all the fullness of the godhead bodily' (*Coloss.2.9*)) then it did not happen by participation, or mere relationship (like the sun shining on something, or a fire giving off its heat), but rather, as I have said, by virtue of that authentic divine nature, in all that it is, making for itself an indwelling in the temple that was born from the virgin by the kind of true union I spoke of earlier. This is how he is one and how he is understood to be Christ Jesus.

I will not deny that our verbal explanations are vanquished at this key point, but this does not mean that the mystery of Christ

[9] Phyrmos; Anachysin; Metastasin.

[10] Sketiken.

is incredible, rather that it is all the more wonderful. So far as it is superior to all speech and understanding, so is it all the more worthy of every admiration.

We do not say that the Word became flesh, that is perfect man, as if constricted in the limits of the body, for that would indeed be the height of stupidity. No we believe that he still continued to fill the heaven and earth and the underworld, for in God all things are fulfilled and to him all things are small. It is difficult to comprehend or express how he could be in the particular and in the universal, indeed it is impossible to do so. But I think that he had this capacity because he is incorporeal and indivisible; and even though we say that the body of the Word was his own proprium, still it was not so in the way that laughter is the proprium of a man, or neighing the proprium of a horse. Rather the body was made his very own through a true union and thus served the function of an instrument, in order to fulfil those things which it customarily does, sin alone excepted.

If, on the other hand, the Word is said 'to have been sent', you should not anxiously ask yourselves, Where has the Incorporeal One gone? or, Where has he moved, in whom all things are fulfilled? We ought rather to understand that this 'sending' is of a different kind. It does not mean that the one sent changes from place to place, rather that he receives a sacred ministry, which we also learn was given to the disciples by Christ the Saviour of us all.

And finally, the divine Paul also says of Christ: 'Therefore, holy brethren, who share in this heavenly calling, consider Jesus the Apostle and High Priest of our confession' (*Heb.3.1*). But notice that when he depicts him as officiating in the manner of men, even though he was God by nature, he still attributes the office of apostle to him. But, as I have said before, there is nothing foolish involved in saying God the Word 'was sent'[11] by the Father, for although he most certainly fills all things and no place whatsoever lacks his presence, it is just that when we interpret divine things in human speech we are accustomed to understand the economy of an immortal nature through bodily types.

Lastly, the blessed Paul writes and tells us that the Holy Spirit fills

[11] The Latin text loses the word-play, but in Greek 'Apostolos' means 'The One Sent'. Cyril is arguing that it is not merely a term designating an inferior ministry (as Nestorius had argued, making the text a key part of his polemic), but rather a term depicting the eternal Word's entry into time.

all things: 'Since you are sons, God sent the Spirit of his Son into our hearts, in whom we cry out: Abba, Father' (*Gal.4.6*). And our Saviour himself said: 'It is good for you that I should go away, for if I do not go, the Paraclete will not come to you' (*Jn.16.7*). We must, then, attribute all such things in a religious fashion, and follow after sure knowledge. If we do so we shall profit greatly.

26. How the holy Virgin is understood to be the Mother of God. The Word of God the Father was born in an incomprehensible manner, and this generation surpasses all human understanding, and befits the incorporeal nature. Nonetheless, that which is born is understood as the very own offspring of the Begetter, and of the same essence as Him. This is why he is called the Son, a name which indicates this true and authentic parentage. Since the Father is eternally alive, it was necessary that he too should be eternally alive, for because of him God is a Father. And so: 'In the beginning was the Word, and the Word was with God, and the Word was God' (*J.1.1*), as the all-wise evangelist tells us. But in the consummation of times, for us men and for our salvation, he was made incarnate and made man. He did not lose what he was but kept his unchangeable nature, and was ever established in the highest dignity of godhead. Nonetheless, for our sake he economically underwent a self-emptying, and did not disdain that poverty which befits human nature, for: 'Though he was rich, he became poor, as it is written, that we might become rich through his poverty' (*2 Cor.8.9*). This was how he was made man and is said to have undergone a birth from a woman. And so, because he assumed from the holy Virgin a body that was truly united to himself, we say that the holy Virgin is Theotokos, for she gave birth to it humanly, or in accordance with the flesh, even though he had his generation from the Father before all ages.

But if some people think that the Word here had his beginning when he became man, this would be the height of wickedness and folly. The Saviour himself shows that such people are complete fools when he says: 'Amen I say to you, before Abraham was I am' (*Jn.8.58*). How then could he have been before Abraham if he was only born in the flesh so long afterwards? And I think the divine John also sufficiently refutes them when he says: 'This is he of whom I spoke. After me there comes a man who came before me, because he was before me' (*Jn.1.30*).

So let us leave any contention about such foolish matters and come instead to something which is profitable. Let no one be troubled when they hear that the holy Virgin is the Mother of God; let them not fill their mind with Jewish disbelief or, even worse, with pagan impiety. The Jews attacked Christ saying: 'We do not stone you for a good deed, but because you who are a man make yourself God' (*Jn.10.23*); and the sons of the pagans deride the doctrine of the church when they hear that God was born from a woman. They reap the harvest of their madness, however, when they hear our reply: 'The fool speaks like a fool, and his heart meditates on vanities' (*Is.32.6*). The meaning of our mystery is a scandal to the Jews, and foolishness to the gentiles (cf. *1 Cor.1.23*), but for us who know it, it is something truly admirable, and salvific, and worthy of belief. If there was anyone at all who dared to say that this earthly flesh had been the parent of the godhead itself, or that that nature which is above all was itself born from this creature, then it would be madness and insanity. The divine nature was not made from the earth, nor has the corruptible ever been a rootstock for incorruption, or mortality ever given birth to immortality, or the incorporeal ever been the fruit of a palpable body, or the uncreated ever born from the created, or that which has no beginning ever come from that which has a beginning.

And yet, because we maintain that the Word of God became like us, and assumed a body like our bodies, and most truly united it to himself in a secret and ineffable manner, and thus was made man after being born in a fleshly way, then what is there foolish in this, or what is there that cannot be believed? As we have often said, when the soul of man is united with the body, it is born along with it, even though it is of a different nature, and no one should ever think that the body's nature supplied the origin of the soul's substance, rather God sends it inside the body in an incomprehensible manner. But when the soul is born along with the body, we maintain that there is one being from both of them, that is man. The Word who was God, therefore, also became man and was born in accordance with the flesh, since this was necessary for humanity. So, since she gave birth to him, she is the Mother of God. On the other hand, if she did not give birth to God, then we should certainly not call the child she gave birth to 'God'. But the divine scriptures call him God, for she gave birth to God made man. He could not have been made man except through birth from a woman. And so, if she gave birth to him, how is it that she is not the Mother of God since we learn from the divine scripture that the one who is born from her is the true God?

27. Sayings about Christ.
'Behold the virgin shall conceive, and shall give birth to a son, and you shall call him Emmanuel' (*Is.7.14; Mt.1.23*). So how is the child that is born of the holy Virgin called Emmanuel when, as I have said earlier, Emmanuel signifies that the Word (true God of true God) came in our nature on account of flesh? He became Emmanuel because 'He emptied himself out' (*Phil.2.7*), and underwent a generation like our own, and had communion with us. And thus he was God in the flesh, and she who gave him a fleshly birth in accordance with the flesh was truly the Mother of God.

28. Another instance.
'For all shall set aside the vesture gathered in treachery, and the garment of changeability, happy to have them burned, for a child is born for us and a son is given to us whose dominion is on his shoulders. And he shall be called Angel of Great Counsel' (*Is.9.5–6. LXX*). Hear what the child is called, and how he underwent a generation like our own. But the heavens pointed to this child by a most radiant star, and Magi came to worship him from the farthest limits of the Earth. The angels gave the good news to the shepherds, saying that a saviour was born, and announcing the peace and even the good-will of the Father. He is an Angel of Great Counsel because he announced to us the will of the Father who 'was pleased to save the whole world in him' (*Col.1.20*), and to reconcile the world through him and in him, for being reconciled to Christ we are reconciled to God (cf. *Rom.5.10*) since the Son of God is truly God.

He himself tells us what this counsel was, of which he was the great messenger, when he says: 'For God so loved the world that he gave his Only Begotten Son, that all who believe in him should not perish but should have life eternal' (*Jn.3.16*). But this Only Begotten Son is he who was born of the holy Virgin, for it was the Word made man, God himself in the flesh, who was thus manifested to earthly creatures. And then he said: 'Whoever believes in me has life eternal' (*Jn.6.47*). He explained how it is that we believe in the Father through him and in him, when he said: 'Whoever believes in me, does not believe in me but in the one who sent me (*Jn.12.44*). And again: 'Whoever sees me has seen the one who sent me' (*Jn.12.45*).

'Hear me you islands and pay attention you nations. He shall be established after a long time, says the Lord; from the mother's womb he shall call upon my name' (*Is.49.1. LXX*). Since the Word was God, he was not unaware that he would undergo a birth, incarnated from a woman for our sake, and he also knew that God the Father would call him Christ Jesus, who proclaimed to all of us the new name of his Son, which is ever blessed on the earth. Note, then, how he calls the one who gave birth to his own body his mother. So if he knows that he is true God, then she who gave birth to him in the flesh should be called the Mother of God, and rightly so. On the other hand, if he is not God, which some people brazenly and wickedly maintain, then it follows that the holy Virgin herself ought to be deprived of this title of Theotokos.

29. That the Only Begotten is called God, even when he appears as man.

In his prayer Solomon said: 'And now Lord God of Israel fulfil that word which you spoke to your servant David. Can it be believed that God dwelt with men on earth?' (*2 Chron.6.17–18*). Note that he is amazed by the incarnation of the Word, for it seems an incredible thing that he dwelt with men on earth when he himself became man. Indeed, is it not an outstanding and truly wonderful thing that God did not turn away from what he had created, but rather cherished them, and sustained what was already in existence, and even created things that were not? Even so, it is truly an outstanding miracle that God made man should dwell on earth with men, according to the promises already made to the divine David, for it is written: 'The Lord has sworn truly to David and will not deny it' (*Ps.131.11*). And what did he swear? It was this: 'I will set the fruit of your body upon your throne' (*Ibid.*). And even though David believed that almighty God would never deny this promise, nonetheless he curiously enquired where this birth would take place. So he said: 'If I climb not upon my bed, and give no sleep to my eyes, or slumber to my eyelids, or rest to my brow, even so when shall I find a place for the Lord, a tabernacle for the God of Jacob' (*Ps.131.3–5*)? And then, since this too was revealed to him in the Spirit, and he knew the place of the fleshly generation of the Only Begotten, he proclaimed the good news saying: 'We have heard of him in Ephrata (that is Bethlehem) and we have found him in the fields of the forest' (*Ps.131.6*). By this mention of Ephrata he signified Bethlehem, as the prophet demonstrates: 'And you, Bethlehem, house of Ephrata' (*Mic.5.2*). But note how even though he believes that he was born just like us, in Ephrata, he still names him the God of Jacob whose indwelling was in a tabernacle: and thus it was that the holy Virgin gave birth to Jesus.

Elsewhere he calls him the God of Abraham, saying: 'The princes of the people are gathered with the God of Abraham' (*Ps.46.10*). He was instructed by the illumination of the Holy Spirit in the knowledge of things to come, and thus David saw with the eyes of his mind the princes of the people (that is the holy apostles)[12] gathered in the service of our Lord Jesus Christ. So, if he who was born from a woman is called the God of Abraham, and the God of Jacob, then how is the holy Virgin not the Mother of God?

30. Another instance.
The prophet Habbakuk said: 'O Lord I have heard of your renown, and have been afraid. I have considered your works and trembled. In the midst of the two living beings you shall be known and in the approach of the time you shall be made manifest. While my soul was troubled, in your anger, you shall remember mercy. God shall come from Teman, the Holy One from Mount Paran' (*Hab.3.1f LXX*). See how he is made known in the midst of two living beings, for he was born of a woman and lived up to the time of the precious cross.[13] As the blessed Paul said: 'Thanks be to God, through his body he tasted death on behalf of all' (*Heb.2.9*). But because he was God by nature, he then rose up to everlasting life. And so, he is made known here as the one who endured the precious cross in the midst of the two living beings. As he himself said somewhere to the Jewish people: 'When you have lifted up the Son of Man, then you will know that I am he' (*Jn.8.28*). See then how the text calls him very God, and tells us that he will come from Teman and Mount Paran. Teman is interpreted as meaning 'the South', and Christ appeared, not in the northern regions, but in the South of Judaea where Bethlehem is. Accordingly, since the one who came from southern Judaea, being born at Bethlehem, is called both Lord and God, how is it that the holy Virgin is not the Mother of God?

31. Another instance.
In Genesis it is written: 'And Jacob was left alone, and a man wrestled with him until morning, and when he saw that he could not overcome

---

[12] The Armenian version, following the context of the psalm, has: He saw the holy angels standing around Our Lord Jesus Christ.

[13] Cyril points to the ox and ass (from Isaiah's typology) at the nativity, and (predominantly) the two thieves hanging beside him on the cross as the fulfilment of this prophecy. Earlier tradition had read it as a sign of the Trinity.

him, he seized the side of Jacob's thigh while he was wrestling with him, and said to him, Release me, for morning has broken. But he said in reply, I will not release you unless you bless me' (*Gen.32.24–26*). And after this it says: 'And he blessed him there, and so he called the place the 'face of God' for he said, 'I have seen God face to face, and my soul is preserved.' But the sun rose and the vision of God passed, and he staggered because of his thigh' (*Gen.32.29–31*).

There is a mystical sense in this scripture, which seems to indicate the struggle which the Jews mounted against Christ, how they wrestled with him, and yet were overcome, and gained a blessing from him if they turned to him by faith, in the last times. Nonetheless it was certainly a man who was wrestling, and still Jacob called him 'the face of God'. This is not all, for he knew that the same one was God in truth, for he said: 'I have seen God face to face, and my soul is preserved.' Emmanuel is God by nature and is also called the face of God since he is 'the figure of the substance of the Father' (*Heb.1.3*). And this is how he described himself to the Jews when he spoke of God his Father: 'You have not seen his face and you do not have his word abiding in you, because you do not believe in the one he sent' (*Jn.5.38*).

The sacred scripture confirms that this man who wrestled with Jacob was the true God, for it says: 'The Lord said, Jacob arise and go up to Bethel, and dwell there, and make there an altar to the God who appeared to you when you were fleeing from the face of your brother Esau' (*Gen.35.1*). This was because when he came back from Mesopotamia, at God's command, and in fear of Esau, Jacob passed over his children and all his possessions and 'was left alone, and a man wrestled with him'.

32. Another instance.

The blessed Daniel tells us of his dreadful vision: 'I saw in a vision of the night, and behold there came one like a Son of Man on the clouds of heaven, who came up to the Ancient of Days, and they brought him into his presence, and to him was given honour and dominion, and every people, tribe, and tongue, shall serve him. His power is an everlasting power which shall not pass away, and his Kingdom shall never be destroyed' (*Dan.7.13–14*). Hear how he does not simply mention that he saw a man, so that Emmanuel might not simply be thought of as one of our number, exactly like us, but he says rather that he was 'like a Son of Man'. Since the Word was

God by nature, 'he came in the likeness of man, and was found in fashion as a man' (*Phil.2.7*). This is so that both things might be understood in the same one; that is he was neither a simple man, nor the Word apart from the humanity and the flesh. But Daniel notes how honour and dominion, which he always had, were given to him, for he says that 'every people, tribe, and tongue, shall serve him.' And so, when the Only Begotten Word of God has the whole creation serving him, and holds the dominion of the Father as his very own, even when he is in the humanity, then how is it that the holy Virgin, who gave birth to him according to the flesh, is not understood to be the Mother of God?

33. On the passion of Christ, and how it is useful to speak in two manners about one and the same person, but not to divide him into two.
Saint Paul expounds the saving passion for us when he says: 'Now, by the grace of God, he has tasted death on behalf of all' (*Heb.2.9*). And also: 'I handed on to you, in the first place, what I myself received, namely that Christ died for our sins, in accordance with the scriptures, and that he was buried, and rose again on the third day' (*1 Cor.15.3*). In addition, the all-wise Peter says: 'Christ suffered for us in the flesh' (*1 Pet.4.1*). Since we believe that Our Lord Jesus Christ is one, that is God the Word seen in human form, or made man like us, then how can we both attribute suffering to him and yet still hold him impassible as God?

It is because the suffering belongs to the economy, with God the Word reckoning those things that pertain to the flesh as his very own because of the ineffable union, and yet remaining outside suffering in so far as pertains to his own nature, since God is impassible. This is not exceptional, when we see that even the soul of man, although it remains outside suffering when the body suffers, in so far as pertains to its own nature, nonetheless is still reckoned to be involved in the suffering in so far as that which suffers is its very own body. Even though the soul is immaterial and simple, nevertheless that which suffers is not alien to it. This is how you should also understand with regard to Christ the Saviour of us all. But I will use some examples that might figuratively show for us how the Only Begotten participated in suffering in so far as pertained to his closeness to his body, and yet remained outside suffering, as God.

When almighty God ordered the most wise Moses to perform miracles so that Israel might believe that he was sent by God to deliver them from oppression, he said to him: 'You shall take water from the river and pour it upon the earth, and the water you take from the river shall be as blood upon the earth' (*Ex.4.9*). We say that the water is a certain type of life, and that the Son is Life by nature, flowing like a river from the Father, by reason of being of the same substance as he, and thus giving life to all. But it says, 'And when you pour the water on the earth it will be blood', and when the Word was made flesh of the earth, that is when he clothed himself in earthly flesh, then in that flesh he is said to have suffered a death like ours, even though he is by nature Life.

34. Another instance.
In Leviticus, God signifies that the leper is defiled and unclean, and he commanded that he ought to be cast out of the camp (*Lev.13.2f*). But if he was cured of his sickness he was to be purified in this manner: 'You shall take two undefiled birds, and cedar wood, and scarlet cloth, and hyssop, and the priest shall give the command and one bird shall be killed in an earthenware vessel in running water. And he shall take the bird that lives, and shall wash it in the blood of the bird that was slaughtered in running water, and he shall sprinkle seven times over him who is to be purified of leprosy, and he shall be cleansed' (*Lev.14.49–51*).

But the most precious blood of Christ, and the purification of sacred baptism, renders us clean and washes away the marks of defilement, repelling the mortality of fleshly desires. But take note of this, for we will pass over examination of the details of the text simply to mention, for the present, what helps to explain the mystery. Christ is compared here to two birds, not because there are two sons, but rather because there is one from both things, divinity and humanity, gathered together in unity. The birds are undefiled, and neither did our Lord Jesus Christ commit any sin, for the Word was holy in terms of both divinity and humanity. Yet he is compared to the birds in so far as he is in the heights, above the earth, and from heaven above. And Christ is the 'man from heaven' (*1 Cor.15.47*), although the holy Virgin gave birth to his flesh. And this is how he is from heaven above, for God the Word who is from the Father, and on high, took flesh from the holy Virgin, and reckoned it as his very own. As if he had brought it down from heaven above he said: 'No one has ever gone up into heaven except he who came down from heaven, the Son of Man who is in heaven' (*Jn.3.13*), for he always attributed his own characteristics to his own flesh, for once united to it he is reckoned as one with it.

But note, one bird was killed, while the other was washed in its blood, though not killed. Why is this? The Word was alive even though his own flesh was dead, and the passion was said to be common to them because of the union and the intimacy he had with the flesh. And so he himself indeed was alive, as God, but he made the body his very own, and thus intimately accepted in himself the sufferings of the body, while in his own nature he suffered nothing. It is, therefore, both useful and necessary that if we accept that in the one Christ some things are in one manner and some in another manner,[14] we still refer them all to one and the same person, and never allow him to be divided in two, even though these things might be said to be separately diverse in effect, and hardly consonant.

I am describing it as it is. We say that God the Word was born from a woman according to the flesh, although he himself commands all things to birth, and calls those which are as yet unborn to their nativity. He is born in one manner and another manner; in so far as he is man it is understood to be like our birth, and in so far as he is God by nature, he calls all things to their birth.

It is also written about him: 'The child advanced and grew strong, and was full of wisdom and grace' (*Lk.2.40/52*). But since he was perfect in nature, as God, and gave spiritual gifts to the saints from his own fullness, and since he himself was the giver of wisdom and grace, then how can the child have advanced and been filled with wisdom and grace? It is in one manner and another manner: since he himself is at once God and man, he reckons all the human characteristics as his own because of the union; but as God he is perfect, and the giver of wisdom and grace.

He is also called the First Born and the Only Begotten, and if anyone wishes to investigate the meaning of these titles then Firstborn means being the firstborn among many brethren, but Only Begotten means sole begotten; not a firstborn, nor one among many brethren. And yet he is both the one and the other. How can this be? It is in one manner, and another manner; for he is Firstborn among many brethren on account of the humanity, but the same one is the Only Begotten since, as God, he alone was born from the only Father.

---

[14] Kat' allo kai kat' allo (as in Gk. text of present section, following): i.e. occurring in two different fashions, or to be attributed in two different senses.

He is said to have been sanctified by the Spirit, and yet himself to sanctify those who approach him; to be baptised in the flesh, he who baptises in the Holy Spirit. So how can one and the same person sanctify and be sanctified? baptise and be baptised? Well it is in one manner and another manner. For he is sanctified as man and baptised as man, but he sanctifies as God and baptises in the Holy Spirit.

[Gk.] He raises the dead and is raised from the dead. He who is Life by nature is said to have been brought back to life. How can this be? It is in one manner and another manner. For he is raised from the dead and is said to be brought back to life in accordance with the flesh, but as God he gives life and raises the dead. He suffers and he does not suffer; again in one manner and another manner. For he suffers humanly in the flesh, as man, but is divinely impassible as God. [end of Gk.]

He himself has worshipped alongside us, for he says: 'You worship what you do not know, but we worship what we do know' (*Jn.4.22*). Yet he is also to be worshipped: 'For every knee shall bend to him' (*Phil.2.10*). This too is in one manner and another manner. He worships because he assumed a nature that ought to worship, but the same one is himself worshipped as being greater than that nature which worships, in so far as he is understood as God. Yet the worship is not to be divided, as if to a man set apart, and God set apart; nor indeed do we say that a man is adored 'along with him', in separate hypostases, as if conjoined to God in an equality of honour. For such a thing would be the height and extremity of wickedness. No, we must adore one incarnate Word of God, made man in such a way that we believe the body united to him was endowed, like us, with a rational soul. Almighty God did not command that we and the angels ought to worship two firstborns. There is only one who is 'brought into this world' (*Heb.1.6*). And if we investigate the manner of this 'bringing in' more closely then we will discover the mystery of the economy in the flesh. He was brought into the world when he was made man, even though in his own nature he is seen to be far removed from the world, and is believed to be truly in the heights of divinity, for he is different to all things being their creator. Thus, by nature, he is above all those things he himself made, since by nature he is God. And yet, as I said earlier, there is only one that is to be adored, even when he comes among many brethren, and for that reason is called the Firstborn.

The man who was blind from birth worshipped one son when he

was healed in that most remarkable manner. For when Jesus found him in the Temple he said: 'Do you believe in the Son of God? And he said, Who is he Lord that I may believe in him' (*Jn.9.35–36*), and Christ pointed out himself with his own body and said: 'You have seen him. It is he who is speaking with you' (*Jn.9.37*). See how he uses the singular number, not allowing God and man to be understood as separate. Indeed, if anyone should call the Emmanuel man it certainly does not mean any ordinary man, but the Word of God united to our nature. The blessed disciples worshipped him as one when they saw him walking as man in a wonderful manner on the sea, and said: 'Truly you are the Son of God' (*Mt.14.33*).

But if we say that a man ought to be worshipped along with God then we introduce a great division, for the term 'with' always compels us to think of two, except when it is applied to signify the unity formed by composition. For no one is said to live with himself, or eat with himself, or to worship with, or walk with himself; for the preposition 'with' introduces the sense of two subjects of the verb. And so, if anyone says that a man ought to be worshipped along with God, then he is clearly speaking about two sons, separate from one another; because the system of their unity, if it is understood only as an equality of honour or authority, is convicted of being untrue, and we have already demonstrated this at length.

35. Against those who say that the human characteristics apply to God the Word only relatively.

Some people babble on about the fleshly economy of the Only Begotten, and pull down this venerable and great mystery of our salvation, so beloved by the heavenly powers, into unstable interpretations. But in so doing they defile the honour and beauty of the truth. They should not try to bolster up their own opinions of orthodoxy, but should look more intently and perceptively into the sense of the sacred scriptures, and should follow the right path by agreeing with what the most holy Fathers discovered, those who were instructed by the illuminations of the Holy Spirit, and defined the symbol of faith for us when they said that God the Word, through whom all things were made, things in heaven and things on earth, was himself incomprehensibly born from the substance of the Father, and came down for us and for our salvation, was made man, suffered, ascended into heaven, and will come again at the end of time to judge the living and the dead.

But some people think that they are intelligent and learned because they are puffed up with a supercilious pride. So when they hear these words they mock them and think that these perfectly true statements are really mad ravings, especially when we believe that the knowledge of the truth was granted to the holy Fathers by the illumination of the Spirit. These people, as if they alone were able to think correctly, do not think that it was the Only Begotten Son of God, God the Word who is of the substance of the Father, who suffered for us in the flesh as man (even though he is incapable of suffering in his own nature, in so far he is understood as God). They set aside a man quite distinctly, who was born of the holy Virgin, and then they give him a degree of glory in so far as they say he was united to the Word of God the Father. When they explain the manner of the union they say an equality of dignity or authority was granted to him by God, and he was given the similar designation of Christ, and Son, and Lord. In their estimation, if the man is said to suffer anything it should be referred to God the Word only in so far as he is conjoined to the man by equality of honour, even though in the separate natures each one is what it is in itself.

But I will explain the significance of their teachings, in so far as I am able, by offering examples from the sacred scriptures. Christ was hungry, and tired from the journey. He slept, climbed in a boat, was struck by the servants' blows, was scourged by Pilate, and was spat on by the soldiers. They pierced his side with a spear, and offered him vinegar mixed with gall. He also tasted death, suffered on the cross, and suffered the other insults of the Jews. They would say that all these things are applicable to the man, even though they may be 'referred' to the person of the true Son. We believe, however, in one God the Father almighty, maker of all things visible and invisible, and also in one Lord Jesus Christ, his Son. And we refuse to separate off the man Emmanuel as distinct from the Word, for we know that the Word became man like us, and so we say that the selfsame was truly God from God, while humanly he was man from a woman, just as we are. We maintain that because of the intimacy he had with his own flesh, he even suffered its infirmities; though he retained the impassibility of his own nature, in so far as he was not only man but the selfsame was also God by nature. And in so far as the body was his very own, so too were the natural and innocent passions of the body, as well as those sufferings inflicted on him by the arrogance of others.

He suffered impassibly, because he did not humble himself in such a way as to be merely like us, rather, as I have said before, he reserved to his own nature its superiority over all these things. But if we say that he passed over into the nature of flesh by some change or transformation of his own nature, then we cannot possibly avoid confessing, even if we wanted to, that this ineffable and divine nature was passible. If, on the other hand, he remained unchanged, even though he became man like us (since it is the special characteristic of a heavenly nature to be impassible), then he could make a passible body into his very own by the union, and in that case it would be fitting that he suffers, in so far as the body suffers which is his very own. Nevertheless he himself remains impassible in so far as it is his special characteristic [as God] to be unable to suffer.

But if it is true that the Emmanuel is glorified through the Passion, just as he himself said when he was about to suffer the precious cross for our sake: 'Now is the Son of Man glorified' (*Jn.13.31*), then why is it that they are not ashamed to attribute this glory of the Passion to a man who has merely a conjunction with him in terms of equality of honour? In their opinion he merely joined a man to himself by the will and good-pleasure of the Father, and made him equal to his own glory, and granted to him that he could be called by the similar titles of Christ, and Son, and Lord, and God.

But if that were true, the Word is not really made flesh at all, and he has not become man in any real sense. So perhaps it would not be a bad thing to call all our holy teachers throughout the world false liars? But let them say, or rather come out and demonstrate, that this manner of conjunction that they introduce has the force of an incarnation, meaning that the Word was made man. If they think that this was not so, why do they avoid the truth? and invent for us this manner of a disconnected conjunction? Instead they ought to admit that the Word of God the Father was united to our humanity, and is understood to have suffered human things in his own proper flesh, while in so far as pertains to the nature of divinity he is free from all distress as God.

But by calling this a 'relation', a term they found somewhere or other, I know not where, they cast down the glory of Emmanuel so as to make him merely one of the holy prophets, setting him in the ranks of several others. I can prove that this is unquestionably what they are doing, by offering some examples from sacred scripture.

Formerly the people of Israel murmured in the desert against Moses and Aaron, saying: 'O that we had died, struck down by the Lord in Egypt when we were sitting at the flesh-pots and eating our fill' (*Ex.16.3*). Then the most wise Moses replied (for it was necessary to chastise such reckless impatience) and said; 'What are we? Your murmuring is not against us but against God' (*Ex.16.8*). For at that time almighty God ruled over the people of Israel through the holy prophets. Again how feebly they came up to Samuel and said: 'See how you are growing old, and your sons do not walk in your ways. So now appoint a king over us, such as the other nations have, who will judge over us' (*1 Sam.8.5*). The prophet felt this very deeply, and God said to him: 'Hear the voice of the people as they have spoken to you, because it is not you they have rejected, it is me they have rejected that I should not reign over them' (*1 Sam.8.7*). And Christ himself said somewhere to his holy apostles: 'Whoever receives you receives me' (*Jn.13.20*). He promises that he will say to the merciful at his judgement seat: 'Come you blessed of my Father, and receive the kingdom prepared for you from the foundation of the world' (*Mt.25.34*). He acknowledges with familiarity the righteous way they dealt with people, when he says: 'Whenever you did this to the least of these, you did it to me' (*Mt.25.40*).

In these episodes we can clearly see what the mode of 'reference' really is. The people of Israel murmured against Moses and Aaron, but the affair 'had reference' to God; yet even so, Moses and Aaron were men like us. You can understand these other episodes we mentioned above, in the same way. But, as I said earlier, all these people concerned were holy and admirable men, but men just like us. Is this how the man conjoined (as they say) to God the Word also had the reference of his sufferings? But if this is the case how is he not just an ordinary man, on his own, and nothing else? And in that case Emmanuel is not truly God, is not the Only Begotten Son, and is not God by nature.

And then why is none of the others honoured with equality of dignity and authority by the Word? (since they maintain that this man alone was made equal in all things) especially since God the Saviour of all is no respecter of persons, because he judges justly as he himself testifies (*Jn.8.15–16*). And why does he alone sit beside him on the throne? And how shall he come as judge with the angels ministering to him? Or why is he alone worshipped by us and the heavenly spirits?

But wait, he says, we find that you are doing exactly the same thing as us; for you confess that he suffered, in so far as you attribute the sufferings to the flesh, even though you keep him impassible as God. Ah, but we, my friend, have first of all united the Word and Man, and only then do we attribute the passions to the flesh while keeping him impassible as God. Although he has become like us, nevertheless we should be aware of the majesty of his heavenly dignity and his divine excellence. And so, having set out that unity as if it were constituted as the foundation of our faith, we then confess that he suffered in the flesh, while remaining outside those sufferings in so far as he had impassibility inherent in himself.

On the other hand, if we set apart man and God, separating the natures from one another, and say that the Word accepted all those things that pertained to the body as his own but only in terms of relation, then Emmanuel (a name that means God is with us), who was born from the holy Virgin, will only have that relation to God that Moses and Aaron had.

And so, even though he said through the holy prophets; 'I gave my back to the scourge, my cheeks to their blows. I did not turn away my face from the shame of their spitting' (*Is.50.6*); and again: 'They have pierced my hands and my feet, they have numbered all my bones' (*Ps.21.17–18*); and again: 'They gave me hyssop for food, and in my thirst they offered me vinegar' (*Ps.68.22*); even so we attribute all these things to the Only Begotten himself. For he suffered them economically in the flesh for our sake and in accordance with the scriptures: 'For by his wounds we have been healed, and he himself was wounded because of our sins' (*Is.53.5*). We recognise, however, that he was impassible by nature, yet if, as I have just said, the same one was at once God and man, then the sufferings certainly belonged to his humanity, while it was the proper characteristic of God to be understood to be impassible.

If we think like this, we will preserve piety, and shall come, by means of these orthodox thoughts and opinions, to arrive at 'the prize of our heavenly calling' (*Phil.3.14*) in Christ: through whom and with whom, to God the Father be glory, with the Holy Spirit, through the ages of ages. Amen.

CYRIL'S LETTER TO ACACIUS OF BEROEA[1]

Cyril, to my lord Acacius, my most beloved brother and fellow-minister. Greetings in the Lord.

1. Even now[2] your Holiness has undertaken a sollicitous involvement which befits you, for your intention is to seek the union of the churches, in accordance with the good will of God the saviour of us all; to convince us of our duty to have one mind by removing petty mindedness from our midst; to remove all causes of distress; and to re-forge the bonds of charity for what has been broken apart. It appears, however, that some [of the Orientals] while being afraid to resist your Perfection's plans openly have done so in secret, desperately trying to hide their tracks. To act in the ways they do, making impossible demands, is tantamount to declaring by their very actions that the reality of peace is not what they want.

I say these things having read the letter sent by your Perfection in which we learned that they required us to condemn and retract every writing and every letter [composed] before the council took place, and to give our assent to the creed of the orthodox faith as formerly defined by the holy fathers of the great council of Nicaea. As far as I am concerned this venerable creed is sufficient for a full and proper understanding of the faith. In itself it needs nothing more. I admit and agree with this, even if certain people do not believe this is how I think and teach.

2. Nonetheless this [demand] has greatly surprised us, for we wrote what we did because Nestorius was spitting out, all over the church, contradictory and outrageous statements against Christ the Saviour of us all. This was why we opposed him and his wicked innovations by setting up the truth against him. By God's grace many people

---

[1] Ep.33; PG.77.157–162 (Latin version); ACO 1.1.7. 147–156. The letter was written in 432 in response to the Syrian proposals for peace sent to him by Acacius, which had demanded the retraction of all his own christological writings, especially the Chapters.

[2] A sardonic touch for Cyril had appealed to Acacius to use his influence to stop Nestorius' preaching at the very outset of the controversy, and Acacius had declined involvement.

have been helped by reading these books, and coming to understand the truth of the matter they have held in honour what we said against this man.

I am at a loss to understand why those who now ought to be anathematising the foul doctrines of this man, and distancing themselves from his wickedness by turning their zeal towards everything that is opposite, are in fact trying to suppress what was written against him. What sense is there in this? Does your Holiness not realise how foolish this whole business is, if those who wrote in the defence of orthodoxy are now supposed to deny their own writings, or rather condemn their own faith? If what we have written against Nestorius and his evil teachings was not correct, then he must have been deposed without good cause. Perhaps he has even been orthodox in his thought? Was it I who was mistaken for not following him and instead writing in contradiction of what he said? for many books of Nestorius had been circulated, confusing everything, and throwing the churches into turmoil. So how can we suppress our writings against him which have, in their small way, brought profit to others?

3. In your eminent wisdom your Perfection can see that they are seeking an impossible thing. So far are they from a desire to appease the discord between us that they have taken matters back to the very beginning of this endless strife; for when they had arrived in the city of Ephesus why did they not vote in accord with the holy council against this man who had committed so many and so great blasphemies? And even if they had reserved judgement for a while, once they had read the acts of our sessions what was it that hindered them from recognising that everything had been conducted legally, and then from concurring, as I said, with that correct and blameless sentence which had been passed by everyone? No, on the contrary, they had no consideration either for God or for the zeal of those who had gathered (for this was no enquiry about some petty matter, rather about the faith through which God the Father saved the world in Christ). They showed every cruelty and every kind of enmity towards us their brethren, scornfully insulting the holy and oecumenical synod by excommunicating myself and the most reverend bishop Memnon without a trial. It was as if they stretched out their right hand against me, threatening me with the sword in wild savagery. Let us suppose that we had indeed been remiss in relation to correct doctrine, or that in some other way we had been guilty of certain transgressions—should there not have been a proper discussion? a meeting? a charge

formulated? Even though Nestorius persevered in his blasphemies for three years, on our part we all kept faith with him, as did your Holiness alongside us, as we all took counsel together how to turn him away from these blasphemies, or rather to turn him to doctrines that looked to orthodoxy and truth. But still he persisted, and in the city of Ephesus itself he even came out with much greater insults against the glory of Christ. This was why, in the end, the holy synod removed him from the priesthood as someone who had an incurable disease.

4. I would like your Holiness to recall something that has a useful bearing on present affairs. When your holy synod[3] formerly gathered in the great city of Constantinople, I myself happened to be one of the attendants. After John (Chrysostom) had been arraigned and many had submitted written charges about him, a vote was about to be taken against him. I remember then hearing your Holiness say to the holy synod: 'If I knew that John would reform his character and set aside his innate stubbornness if we pardoned him, then I would intercede on his behalf with all of you.' Once again, on that occasion, your Holiness was remarkable for having given voice to the truth. So what should the holy synod have done on finding that he[4] was unrepentant and so determined in his fight against the orthodox faith?

5. Your letter, however, has said that we should concur only with the symbol, or rather the exposition of faith, of the three hundred and eighteen.[5] On this point I would reply that it was the one intention of the holy and oecumenical synod gathered in the city of Ephesus to confirm this creed so that all might confess, believe, and teach on this basis, without addition or subtraction from it. For nothing must either be added to it, or removed from it. It was for this reason that sentence was passed against Nestorius, because he did not preserve the creed but in fact corrupted it and misinterpreted it. In no way at all did he follow it, but in the hearing of the faithful he spread the tares of different teachings, alien to the doctrine of the churches. A special rescript on this matter was, therefore, enacted at Ephesus, confirming the exposition of faith of our holy fathers who formerly

---

[3] The synod of the Oak, at Chalcedon 403, which deposed St. John Chrysostom.

[4] Cyril primarily means the synod of Ephesus, and hence Nestorius, at this point, but his lack of a definite subject reference here throws a shadow back over the memory of John too. His argument is that just as John's deposition followed legally as a result of his refusal to attend the synod of the Oak, so should that of Nestorius, who disobeyed the council of Ephesus.

[5] The Fathers of Nicaea.

gathered at Nicaea. And I sent this on to your Holiness so that you would know of it. If you read it you will know without any doubt how orthodox and blameless the rescript is. We have added to this, passages from the holy and blessed Fathers so that the readers might learn how they understood this profession of faith[6] and became our initiators in these matters. Since we have already done all these things why do [the Orientals] not concur with us? For if we all confirm the things we all agree about then peace will certainly be effected, as long as no-one contradicts the common agreement.

6. Even though they have done many terrible things against us, and set their hand to all kinds of inhumanity, yet I will be mindful of God's will, and of the wishes of the most pious and Christ-loving Emperor. We willingly forgive them, as brothers should, for what they have done to us, because we have regard for the needs of the church and the counsels of your Holiness which merit all praise. We will seek, instead, for that which seems to all to be good and correct, and which is also pleasing to our God-beloved Emperor; but they must give their assent to the condemnation of Nestorius, and anathematise his blasphemies and wicked teachings, for then there will be nothing to hinder the removal of the dissension from our midst. The churches will receive one another again, and Christ will award us the prize of peace.

7. Certain people, however, should not spew out gratuitous accusations against us, maintaining that I hold the opinions of Arius or Eunomius, as they wrote at Ephesus, for by the grace of Our Saviour I have always been orthodox and was brought up in the care of an orthodox father,[7] and have never shared the opinions of Apollinaris, God forbid, or Arius or Eunomius or of any other heretic. On the contrary I anathematise them. I do not say that the body of Christ was devoid of a soul, but confess that it was animated with a rational soul. And I certainly do not say that any confusion, or blending, or mixture took place, as some people maintain, because I know that the Word of God is by nature changeless and unalterable, and in his proper nature is altogether incapable of any suffering. That which is divine is impassible and does not admit even the 'shadow of a

[6] Cyril's argument is that although the Nicene creed is the sole criterion of orthodoxy and cannot be added to, this does not rule out the writings of the Fathers as standards of truth for these safeguard the proper interpretation of the creed. This is the reason he advances for not abandoning his own writings either.

[7] Theophilus of Alexandria.

change' (*Jas.1.17*) of suffering. On the contrary it is established with an unshakeable stability in the realities of its own goodness. I maintain, however, that it was the Only Begotten Son of God, the One Christ and Lord, who suffered in the flesh for our sake, in accordance with the scriptures, particularly with that saying of the blessed Peter (*1 Pet.4.1*).

8. My Chapters, however, were written with such force only to withstand the teachings of Nestorius[8] for he said and taught things that were not orthodox, and these are what The Chapters attack. Those who anathematise and renounce his evil opinion should stop castigating our writings and recognise, instead, that the meaning of the Chapters was directed against his blasphemies alone. Once communion has been re-established and peace has ensued between the churches, when it will be permissible for them to write to us in confidence, and us to them, if there is anything at all they do not correctly[9] understand in our writings this can easily be elucidated then. We shall, with God's help, make a fully satisfactory account as to their complete orthodoxy, not as enemies but as brothers, for in the things we have written in our war against the teachings of Nestorius there is absolutely nothing that is in disagreement with either the holy and inspired scriptures or with the exposition of faith defined by the holy Fathers, that is those who formerly gathered together in Nicaea. We wish to see peace re-established, and so are eager to obey the decrees of our most pious and God-beloved Emperor. Accordingly we will re-establish communion and come into accord with those who are willing to give a clear assent to the deposition of Nestorius, and who anathematise his evil teachings. Christ will help us to this end, for he himself is our peace, as the scriptures say (*Eph.2.14*).

9. As for those who insist that the things we wrote against the wicked teachings of Nestorius have to be renounced, then no-one will

---

[8] A difficult sentence to translate with all the ranges of implication, and doubtless intended by Cyril to be so open-ended. Lit. 'The force of the Chapters was written only against the teachings of N.' Dynamis/force can signify the power or the abruptness of the propositions in the Chapters, or perhaps merely the 'sense' of them. I think that both meanings are intended. Although he stands by the Chapters Cyril seems diplomatically to admit, as a concession, that they were very pugnacious because of their specific apologetic intent. He is signifying his readiness to settle with the Antiochenes, as in this letter or as in letter 39, on another textual basis.

[9] Orthōs: correct of orthodox. The sentence again is full of implication: If the Orientals think the Chapters are not orthodox (orthōs) it can only be because they have not read them correctly (orthōs).

agree with them. They obviously want to render us dumb in the face of his blasphemies, trying to get everyone to hush it all up. Or do they perhaps believe they can persuade us to think as he does if we are induced to deny our orthodox and blameless writings which opposed his innovations? And since some of the Orientals think fit to disparage some of my writings, twisting their meanings round in improper ways, they should know that all the most reverend bishops throughout the world have caught them in the act of doing this. For all the bishops agreed with, and continue to agree with, the orthodoxy of what I said, even though they are very exacting judges in matters concerning the divine dogmas.

10. Your Reverence ought to consider this additional fact, that peace should be established in such a way that none of the God-beloved bishops throughout the whole of the Roman dominion will dissent from it; for then it will be oecumenical and will avoid creating many other schisms in the process of healing this one. If anything unreasonable is done then they will certainly not concur with it. You ought to keep this particularly in mind. When all the bishops were gathered at Ephesus and refused to communicate with the Orientals they made it their pre-condition that [communion] could not be established until they first agreed to the deposition of Nestorius and joined with us in anathematising his doctrines. So, if this condition is not met how can communion be achieved? Which one of us would not cry out if we betrayed our own souls by denying the orthodox faith and those [decisions] which were agreed on by all, in renouncing our own writings as if they did not speak in an orthodox manner?

Is it not entirely necessary that once peace has been established I should communicate this to the most eminent of the other most reverend bishops so that they too can concur with us and also extend their fellowship to the Orientals? But who could persuade them to do this if it took place against their universal wishes, and the express determination of all that Nestorius had to be held as deposed and his absurd teachings (or rather his tomfoolery against Christ the Saviour of us all) anathematised?

11. The clergy of Alexandria and all the most reverend bishops throughout the Diocese of Egypt were greatly outraged and could scarcely contain themselves because of what the Orientals did to me, but the Most Notable Tribune Lord Aristolaus so calmed matters that he opened up for me an easy path towards peace, and consequently all have come round to the same opinion. I confess that I owe a

great debt of gratitude for what the Notable Lord has done. He has worked alongside me in everything and soothed my grief with his well-conceived ideas.

> Greet the brotherhood that is with you.
> That which is with me greets you in the Lord.

CYRIL'S LETTER TO JOHN OF ANTIOCH[1]

Epistle of the holy Cyril to John Bishop of Antioch.
Cyril to my beloved brother and fellow-minister the Lord John. Greetings in the Lord.

1. 'Let the heavens rejoice and the earth be glad' (*Ps.95.11; Eph.2.14*) for the dividing wall of partition is broken down, and sorrow has ended, and the cause of all dissension has been removed. Christ the Saviour of us all has granted to his churches the prize of peace, and the most pious and God-beloved Emperors[2] have called us to the same. For they have become most excellent and zealous imitators of the piety of their predecessors and have guarded the correct faith firm and unshakeable in their own souls. They have taken special care over the holy churches that they may have glorious renown to the ages, and make their empire most illustrious. The Lord of Hosts himself has granted them good things with a generous hand, and grants them to prevail over their enemies, gracing them with victory. For he would never prove false, and he has said: 'As I live, says the Lord, I will honour those who honour me'(*1 Sam.2.30*).

2. And so, when my God-beloved brother and fellow-minister the Lord Paul arrived in Alexandria, we were filled with joy, and rightly so, that such a man should act as mediator and had chosen to engage in such burdensome labours. It was his purpose to vanquish the envy of the devil, and bring together what had been divided; to clear away the stumbling blocks that had been thrown between us, that he might crown the churches with us and those with you with harmony and peace. It is needless to recount the manner in which they were divided;

---

[1] Ep.39, PG.77.173–182; ACO 1.1.4. pp. 15–20; Pusey vol.6, 40–52; Bindley 138–148, + 220–223; Kidd II 265–270. The letter is the reply to the Statement of belief Cyril had insisted the Orientals produce. It is dated, Spring 433. In antiquity it was called the 'Symbolum Ephesinum', and today, 'The Formula of Reunion'.

[2] Theodosius at Constantinople, and Valentinian the Western Augustus, in whose name Theodosius issued the original Sacra summoning the Bishops to the Ephesian Synod from all the imperial provinces. Cyril begins the letter with an explicit reference to imperial religious policy because the court had largely been responsible for negotiating the peace between the alienated sees.

no, we ought now to think and say things that befit the time of peace. This is why we were delighted with our happy encounter with that forementioned most religious man; who had perhaps thought he would have no small difficulties in persuading us that it was necessary to join the churches together in peace, to suppress the mockery of the heterodox and thereby blunt the sting of the devil's malice. Yet he found us so readily disposed for this, that in fact he had no difficulties at all. For we held in mind what the Saviour said: 'My peace I give to you; my peace I leave with you' (*Jn.14.27*). And we were always taught to say in our prayers: 'O Lord our God, give us peace, for you have given us all things' (*Is.26.12*). So, if anyone participates in the peace that God provides, he will be lacking in no good.

3. We are now fully convinced that the division between the churches came about altogether needlessly and groundlessly, since my lord the God-beloved bishop Paul produced a paper containing an unimpeachable confession of faith, which he affirmed had been drawn up by your Holiness and the most religious bishops of that place. The text is inserted word for word in this letter of ours. It reads as follows:

4. 'It is necessary to say briefly what we think and say about the virgin Mother of God and the manner of the incarnation of the Only Begotten Son of God. This is not our new invention but rather a full exposition of what we have received from the outset from the divine scriptures and from the tradition of the holy Fathers. We add nothing at all to the faith set out by the holy Fathers at Nicaea, for as we have just said this suffices for a complete knowledge of piety and for the denunciation of every heretical false opinion. We do not presume to speak of things that are beyond us, but we confess our own weakness and yet refute those who wish to criticise us on the grounds that we are theorising on realities beyond the scope of man.

5. And so we confess that Our Lord Jesus Christ, the Only Begotten Son of God, is perfect God and perfect Man, of a rational soul and body. He is born of the Father before the ages according to the Godhead, and the same one in these last days for us and for our salvation was born of the virgin Mary according to the manhood. The same one is consubstantial with the Father according to the Godhead, and consubstantial with us according to the manhood,[3] for there was a

[3] The stress on the 'consubstantiality' of the manhood was designed to excise any room for a Christology which harboured lingering docetic elements, such as that witnessed by Apollinaris or such as Eutyches later manifested in their unwillingness

union of the two natures, and this is why we confess One Christ, One Son, One Lord. According to this understanding of the unconfused union we confess that the holy virgin is the Mother of God, because God was made flesh and became man, and from the very moment of conception he united to himself the temple that was taken from her. As for the evangelical and apostolic sayings about the Lord, we are aware that theologians take some as common, as referring to one prosopon, but distinguish others as referring to two natures; that they interpret the God-befitting ones in accordance with the Godhead of the Christ, and the humble ones in accordance with the manhood.'[4]

6. On reading these holy words of yours and thereby finding that we too think in this way, 'for there is one Lord, one faith, one baptism' (*Eph.4.5*), we gave glory to God the saviour of all. We rejoice with one another because the churches with us, and those with you, hold a faith that concurs with the God-inspired scriptures and the tradition of our holy Fathers.

7. I have learned, however, that certain people who like to find fault have been buzzing around like fierce wasps and spitting out wicked words against me, making me out to have said that the holy body of Christ had come down from heaven, and was not from the holy virgin. So I thought it necessary to address a few words to them on this subject: O foolish people, knowing only how to slander, how were

---

to admit that in his manhood Christ was 'the same as us'. The Antiochenes have inserted this as a criticism of Cyril, whom they thought had underestimated the manhood of Christ in this way. Cyril, however, did not deny that Christ's manhood was real in the full sense of what 'real human nature' might mean. As such he was no Docetic or Apollinarist, despite what his enemies said, or despite how would-be followers such as Eutyches later misinterpreted him. Cyril, however, is anxious not to stress this truism to such a point that it resulted in a confession that Christ was a man 'like any of us'. It was Cyril's central argument that the Redeemer was certainly not like any ordinary man, but as Son of God was sinless and deifying even in his flesh. For this reason Cyril preferred to qualify the phrase 'consubstantial with us in his human nature', and reference to the relevant phrase in the Chalcedonian definition demonstrates how the Synod of 451 followed Cyril's lead in this matter, as here, where he accepts the phrase in its substantive meaning, but carefully qualifies it to secure the orthodox understanding of the uniqueness of the Saviour. His mind on this point is clearly set out in para. 11 of his Letter To the Monks.

[4] This was meant as an atack on Cyril's 4th Anathema. A proper reading of that, however, shows how Cyril can readily accept what the Antiochenes are stating here, for in the 4th anathematism he is arguing against the ascription of properties to two different subject (that is person) referents, not two nature-referents. Cyril has frequently been accused of backtracking from his earlier position in the light of this Antiochene document. Such an interpretation of his motives rests upon a careless reading of his texts.

you so led astray to such an opinion? How did you fall sick with such stupidity? You must surely know that nearly all our struggle on behalf of the faith has been engaged on the insistence that the holy virgin is the Mother of God. But if we say that the holy body of Christ, the Saviour of us all, is from heaven and not from her, then how could she possibly be understood as the Mother of God? Who was it, then, that she bore if she did not give birth after the flesh to Emmanuel?

And so, those who have talked such nonsense about me are a laughing-stock.[5]

8. The blessed prophet Isaiah did not lie when he said: 'Behold the virgin shall conceive in her womb and shall bear a son, and they shall call him Emmanuel, which being translated means God is with us' (*Is.7.14*). What the holy Gabriel said to the blessed virgin is also entirely true: 'Do not be afraid Mary, for you have found favour with God, and behold you shall conceive in your womb and give birth to a son, and you shall call him Jesus, for he shall save his people from their sins' (*Lk.1.30–31*).

So when we say that Our Lord Jesus Christ is from heaven and from above, we do not mean that his holy flesh was brought down from above and from heaven; No, we follow the divine Paul who so clearly cried out: 'The first man is of the earth, earthly, but the second man (the Lord) is from heaven' (*1 Cor.15.47*), and we also call to mind the Saviour himself who said: 'No one has ever gone up into heaven except the one who came down from heaven, the Son of Man' (*Jn.3.13*), even though he was born of the holy virgin according to the flesh, as I said before. God the Word came down from above and from heaven and emptied himself, taking the form of a slave (*Phil.2.7*), and was called Son of Man while he remained what he was, that is God, (for he is changeless and unalterable by nature) and this is why he is said to have 'come down from heaven' and is understood now to be one with his own flesh and is called the 'man from heaven' (*1 Cor.15.47*). The same one is perfect in Godhead and perfect in manhood, and we understand him to be in one prosopon, for there is One Lord Jesus Christ (*1 Cor.8.6*), even

[5] He is expressing his very low opinion of the critical merits of the works of Andrew of Samosata and Theodoret of Cyr against him, although both Antiochene theologians sometimes hit their mark and certainly stung him into a considered literary offensive from the late part of 430 onwards, which unquestionably served to clarify his thought on the Christology problem.

though we do indeed take cognisance of the difference of natures out of which we say the ineffable union was formed.

9. Those who say that there was a mixture or confusion or blending of God the Word with the flesh, let your Holiness think fit to stop their mouths,[6] for such people are probably spreading such rumours about me, as though I had thought or said this. But I am so far from thinking anything of the kind that I consider that anyone who thinks there could ever be the shadow of a change (*Jas.1.17*) in the divine nature of the Word must be completely mad. For he ever remains what he is and does not change or undergo alteration. Moreover, all of us confess that the divine Word is impassible, even if in his all-wise economy of the mystery he is seen to attribute to himself the sufferings that befall his own flesh. What is more, the all-wise Peter says: 'And so Christ has suffered for us in the flesh', and not in the nature of the ineffable deity (*1 Pet.4.1*). He bears the suffering of his own flesh in an economic appropriation to himself, as I have said, so that we may believe him to be the Saviour of all, something which is foretold by the voice of the prophet speaking in his person: 'I gave my back to the scourges, and my cheeks to the blows, and did not turn my face away from the shame of the spittings' (*Is.50.6*).

10. So, let your Holiness be assured that we follow the opinions of the holy Fathers in all things, especially our blessed and all-renowned Father Athanasius. We refuse to differ from them in any respect; let no one doubt this. I would have set down many sections from the Fathers, confirming my own words from theirs if I had not feared that the letter might become tedious because of its length. We will not allow the faith, or rather the Symbol of the faith that was defined by our holy Fathers who formerly came together in Nicaea, to be unsettled by anyone. We will not permit ourselves, or anyone else, to change one word of what is laid down there, or to go beyond even one syllable; for we remember the one who said: 'Do not remove the everlasting boundary marks which your fathers set' (*Prov.22.28*). For it was not them that was speaking but the Spirit of God the Father who proceeds from him yet is not alien to the Son in terms of his essence. The words of the holy mystagogues confirm us in this attitude, for in the Acts of the Apostles it is written: 'When they had

[6] As in his Epistle to Succensus Cyril presents here his full accord with what later constitutes the Chalcedonian Formula. Indeed, the text of the former epistle can rightly be regarded as a primary draft of the latter.

come through Mysia they tried to go on into Bithynia and the Spirit of Jesus did not allow them' (*Acts 16.7*). The divine Paul also writes in his letter: 'Those who are in the flesh cannot be pleasing to God, but you are not in the flesh but in the spirit, if the Spirit of God dwells within you. But if anyone does not have the Spirit of Christ, he does not belong to him.' (*Rom.8.8–9*).

So when certain people, who wish to pervert what is right, distort my sayings anyway they please, let this come as no surprise to your Holiness. You know that all kinds of heretics collect arguments for their own errors from the God-inspired scriptures, corrupting to their own evil opinions even the things so rightly said through the Holy Spirit, and thus calling down upon their heads the unquenchable flames.

11. Nonetheless, we have learned that certain people have published a corrupted version of that orthodox letter of our all-renowned Father Athanasius to the blessed Epictetus, and have thereby injured many. For this reason, thinking of what is useful and necessary for the brethren, we have sent your Holiness a transcript from the ancient and authentic copies which we have here.[7]

[May the Lord guard you in good health, most honoured brother. Pray for us.]

---

[7] cf. Appendix I, pp. 379–389. This important work of Athanasius, directed against earlier forms of Apollinarist and Adoptionist Christologies, was an important source in the formation of Cyril's mind.

CYRIL'S LETTER TO EULOGIUS[1]

A memorandum from the most holy Bishop Cyril to Eulogius, priest of Alexandria, residing in Constantinople.

Certain people have been attacking the exposition of faith which the Orientals have made,[2] asking why did the [bishop] of Alexandria support and even praise it since they spoke about two natures? Those who think like Nestorius are saying that even Alexandria must now think as they do, and in this way they are drawing over those who do not know the truth of the matter. It is necessary to reply to such critics that we must not feel obliged to flee from and contradict every single thing that the heretics might say. For there are many things which they confess which we do too. For example, when the Arians say that the Father is the Lord and Maker of all, we surely do not flee from such an admission on that account? It is the same in the case of Nestorius, even if he does speak of two natures to signify the difference between the flesh and God the Word. For the nature of the Word is one thing, and that of the flesh quite another. But Nestorius does not confess the union along with us. We unite these realities and confess that the self-same is one Christ, One Son, and One Lord, and we confess moreover that there is one incarnate nature of the Son;[3] just as one might say in regard to an ordinary man who results from different natures, that is body and soul. Our intellect and deductive ability recognises the difference, but we unite them and then recognise the single nature of man. This is why to acknowledge the difference of the natures is not to divide the one Christ into two.

But since every one of the Orientals imagines that we orthodox follow the opinions of Apollinaris and thinks that we teach a mixture

---

[1] Ep. 44, PG.77, 224–228; ACO 1.1.4. pp. 35–37; Wickham pp. 62–69. The letter is dated after the Formula of Reunion when Cyril was engaged on a long political and theological campaign to make the resolution of doctrine which it represented into a universally stable reality. It probably dates circa 433–435.

[2] i.e. the Formula of Reunion; Cyril's Ep.39, ACO.1.1.4. p. 17. The original format of the formula, as it came from the Easterners, is found in ACO. 1.1.7. pp. 69f. Cyril makes the significant addition of the subject reference 'the same' in its first sentence in his own reply.

[3] For the provenance of the phrase cf. Wickham (1983) fn. 3. pp. 62–63.

or confusion[4] (for they have used such terms, as if the Word of God has been changed into the nature of the flesh, or the flesh has turned into the nature of the Godhead) this is why we gave way to them: not to divide the one Son into two, God forbid, but only in so far as to confess that there occurred neither confusion nor mixing, but that the flesh was flesh assumed from a woman, whereas the Word was Word begotten from the Father, or rather that since the Word has become flesh, as John tells us, there is One Christ and Son and Lord. Try and get them all to read carefully the letter of the blessed pope Athanasius.[5] Since in his day certain people were looking for an argument and saying that God the Word made a figurative body for himself out of his own nature, he argues throughout that the body was not consubstantial with the Word. And if it was not consubstantial then there must be two different natures out of which is understood the one and only Son.

Let them take account of this. When one speaks of a union one does not signify the concurrence of a single factor, but surely of two or more which are different from one another in nature. So, if we talk of a union, we confess it to be between flesh endowed with a rational soul, and the Word, and those who speak of 'two natures' understand it in this way. However, once we have confessed the union, the things that have been united are no longer separated from one another but are thereafter one Son; and one is his nature since the Word has been made flesh. The Orientals confessed these things even if they were somewhat obscure in their terminology. For how can anyone be of the same opinions as Nestorius if they confess that the Only begotten Word of God born of the Father was the same that was born of a woman according to the flesh, and that the holy virgin was the Mother of God, and that he has one prosopon, and that there are not two Sons or two Christs but one? In his sermons Nestorius pretends to say 'One Son and Lord' but he refers the sonship and the lordship only to the Word of God, and when he comes to the economy again he speaks of the man born of the woman as a different lord conjoined [to the Word] by dignity <or equality of honour>.[6] But to say that God the Word is called Christ for this reason, simply

---

[4] synkrasis, synkhysis.

[5] To Epictetus PG.26,1049–1069, see Appendix I. For alterations of Athanasius' letter in antiquity (not otherwise known except for Cyril's complaint) see Schwartz, ACO 1.5.2. p. xv; also Lebon (1935) pp. 713–761.

[6] Schwartz in ACO regards the second phrase as an ancient dittography and brackets it off so.

because he has a conjunction with the Christ, then if Christ has a conjunction with Christ, as one to another, what difference is this from clearly stating that there are two Christs? The Orientals, however, have said nothing like this. They only tried to distinguish the terms. They make the distinction in such as way as to say that there are some terms appropriate to the Godhead, some to the manhood, and some which are referred in common as being appropriate both to the Godhead and the manhood, except that they are attributed to one and the same person. This is not what Nestorius does, for he attributes some to God the Word on his own, and others to the different son born of a woman. It is one thing to recognise a distinction in the terms, but quite another matter to divide them between two personas, one beside another.

The Letter to Acacius which begins: 'Dialogue between brothers is a pleasant and noble thing', is a rather good exposition of all these matters.[7] But you have a large number of letters in the cabinet which you ought to distribute actively. Present the Most Magnificent Chamberlain[8] with the two books which I sent; one Against The Blasphemies of Nestorius,[9] and the other which contains the Synodical Proceedings against Nestorius and those who agree with him, as well as my own replies to those who wrote against 'The Chapters', two of them being the bishops Andrew and Theodoret.[10] The same book has very good short summaries at the end about the economy of Christ, which should be helpful. Similarly present him with five letters from among those bound in leather: one of the blessed pope Athanasius to Epictetus,[11] one of ours to John,[12] and two to Nestorius, the short one and the long one,[13] and also the one to Acacius,[14] for he requested these things from us.

---

[7] Letter to Acacius of Melitene. ACO.1.1.4. 20–31; Wickham (1983), pp. 34–61.

[8] The eunuch Chryseros to whom Cyril also gave great largesse. Count Irenaeus exposed the gifts made cf. ACO. 1.4. p. 222f viz. 200lbs of gold, and many furnishings of carpets, rugs, tables, table cloths, stools, chairs in ivory and wood. See P. Battifol, 'Les présents de S. Cyrille à la cour de Constantinople', in Etudes de liturgie et d'Archaéologie Chrétienne, Paris 1919; also A H M Jones, 'The Later Roman Empire', Oxford 1986 (3rd repr) vol.1. p. 346.

[9] Contra Nestorium, ACO 1.1.6. pp. 13–106.

[10] Apologia xii Capitulorum contra Orientales, ACO 1.1.7. pp. 33–6; also Apologia xii Capitulorum contra Theodoretum ACO 1.1.6. pp. 107–146.

[11] PG.26.1049–1069.

[12] Ep.39. ACO 1.1.4. pp. 15–20: The Formula of Reunion 433.

[13] 2nd and 3rd Letters to Nestorius.

[14] ACO 1.1.4. pp. 20–31.

FIRST LETTER OF CYRIL TO SUCCENSUS[1]

Memorandum of the most holy and God-beloved archbishop Cyril to the most blessed Succensus bishop of Diocaesarea in the Eparchy of Isauria.[2]

1. I read the memorandum sent by your Holiness and was most delighted that even though you are quite capable of bringing advantage both to us and to others from your own considerable learning, you saw fit to ask us to set down in writing what is in our mind, what we stand by. Well, we think the same things about the economy of our Saviour as the holy Fathers did before us. We regulate our own minds by reading their works so as to follow in their footsteps and introduce nothing that is new into the orthodox teachings.

2. Since your Perfection enquires whether or not one ought to admit that there are two natures in Christ I thought it necessary to address this point. A certain Diodore, who had previously been a Pneumatomachian,[3] so they say, came into communion with the orthodox church. Having shook off, as he supposed, the contagion of Macedonianism, he went down straight away with another sickness. He thought and wrote that he who was born of the line of David from the holy virgin was one distinct son, and the Word of God

---

[1] Ep.45, PG. 77.228–237; ACO 1.1.6. pp. 151–157; Wickham 70–83. The letters can be dated somewhere between the period 434–438 when Cyril is engaged in combatting the continuing opposition of such Antiochenes as Theodoret.

[2] The province of Isauria had its coastline immediately north of Cyprus. Diocaesarea was the neighbouring city to Seleucia. Succensus is an intelligent theologian who serves to pass on to Cyril some genuinely difficult problems posed to his theology by the eastern theologians such as Andrew and Theodoret with whom he has communication. In the aftermath of the Ephesian council Succensus not only becomes an important sounding board against which Cyril can clarify his meaning, but a key element in the reconciliation process between Syria and Egypt. Both this text and his Second Letter to Succensus represent Cyril at his most succinct and alert.

[3] lit. Spirit-fighter.This was a 4th century heresy which denied the divinity of the Holy Spirit; a movement closely associated with Arianism, and combatted by the Cappadocian Fathers; as here it is sometimes named after its supposed founder Macedonius. Cyril's apologetic point is to blacken Diodore's reputation which ran very high in the Orient, where he was regarded as a great saint and supreme exegete. By suggesting his disreputable start (for which there is no other historical support in the tradition) Cyril suggests that heresy was his beginning and was to be his end.

the Father was again another and quite distinct son. Disguising the wolf in sheep's clothing (*Mt.7.15*) he pretended to say that Christ was one but he referred the title only to the Word and Only Begotten Son born of God the Father. Even then he attributed the title also to the one who was of the line of David, although, on his own admission, this attribution was only 'in the order of a grace'. Diodore called him a son on these terms, that is in so far as he is united to the True Son. But here he is united not in the way that we think of it, but only in terms of dignity and authority and equality of honour.

3. Nestorius became this man's pupil and being rendered dim by his books he also pretends to confess one Christ and Son and Lord, though he too has divided the One and Indivisible into two. He says that a man has been conjoined to God the Word by a shared name, by equality of honour, and by dignity. He even makes distinctions in the sayings in the evangelic and apostolic preachings which refer to Christ, and he says that some must be referred to the man (evidently the human ones) while others are only applicable to God the Word (clearly the divine ones). He makes a multitude of distinctions and sets on one side, quite separately, a man born from the holy virgin, and likewise sets apart on the other side the Son of God the Father, the Word, and for this reason he concludes that the holy virgin is not the Mother of God, merely the mother of the man.

4. We maintain, however, that this cannot be the case. We have learned from the divine scriptures and the holy Fathers to confess One Son, and Christ, and Lord. This is the Word of God the Father born from him in an ineffable and divine manner before the ages, and the same one is born from the holy virgin according to the flesh, for our sake, in the last times of this age. Since she gave birth to God made flesh and made man, for this reason we also call her the Mother of God. There is, therefore, One Son, One Lord Jesus Christ, both before the incarnation and after the incarnation. The Word of God the Father is not one distinct son, with the one born of the holy virgin being another and different son. No, it is our faith that the very one who was before the ages is the one who was born from a woman according to the flesh; not as if his Godhead took the beginnings of its existence or was called into being for the first time through the holy virgin, but rather, as I have said, that the eternal Word is said to have been born from her according to the flesh. For his flesh was his very own in just the same way as each one of us has his own body.

5. But since certain people are trying to implicate us with the opinions of Apollinaris, saying: 'If you maintain that the Word of God the Father incarnated and made man is One Son in a strict and compact union, perhaps you imagine or have come to think that some mixture or blending or confusion occurred between the Word and the body, even a transformation of the body into the nature of Godhead? We are fully aware of such implications and we refute such a slander when we say that the Word of God, in an incomprehensible manner, beyond description, united to himself a body animated with a rational soul, and came forth as man from a woman, not becoming what we are by any transformation of nature but rather by a gracious economy. For he wished to become man without casting off his natural being as God, and even when he descended into our limitations, and put on the form of the slave, even so he remained in the transcendent condition of the Godhead and in his natural state as Lord.

6. And so, we unite the Word of God the Father to the holy flesh endowed with a rational soul, in an ineffable way that transcends understanding, without confusion, without change, and without alteration,[4] and we thereby confess One Son, and Christ, and Lord; the same one[5] God and man, not someone alongside someone different, but one and the same who is and is known to be both things. For this reason he sometimes speaks economically as man, in human fashion; and at other times, as God, he makes statements with divine authority. It is our contention that if we carefully examine the manner of the economy in the flesh and attentively investigate the mystery, we shall see that the Word of God the Father was made man and made flesh but did not fashion that sacred body from his own divine nature, but rather took it from the virgin. How else could he become man except by putting on the human body? As I have said, if we understand the manner of the incarnation we shall see that two natures come

[4] Note the relationship with this and the Chalcedonian settlement of 451 (see Bindley, 1950 p. 235) Cyril can be seen to supply three quarters of the final settlement making the case all the more pressing that a genuinely objective reassessment of Chalcedon ought to view it more and more as taking a thoroughly Cyrilline line, rather than seeking an active 'compromise' (as has often been suggested) between Alexandrian and Antiochene traditions. In the light of the former interpretation the separation between the christological policies of The Council of Chalcedon and the Council of Constantinople II (553) is by no means as great as many western commentators have described it.

[5] The recurring stress on the subject referent 'the same one' is again taken up into the Chalcedonian symbol.

together with one another, without confusion or change, in an indivisible union. The flesh is flesh and not Godhead, even though it became the flesh of God; and similarly the Word is God and not flesh even if he made the flesh his very own in the economy. Given that we understand this, we do no harm to that concurrence into union when we say that it took place out of[6] two natures. After the union has occurred, however, we do not divide the natures from one another, nor do we sever the one and indivisible into two sons, but we say that there is One Son, and as the holy Fathers have stated: One Incarnate Nature of The Word.

7. As to the manner of the incarnation of the Only Begotten, then theoretically speaking (but only in so far as it appears to the eyes of the soul) we would admit that there are two united natures but only One Christ and Son and Lord, the Word of God made man and made flesh. If you like we can take as our example that very composition which makes us men. For we are composed of body and soul and we perceive two natures; there is one nature of the body, and a different nature of the soul, and yet one man from both of them in terms of the union. This composition from two natures does not turn the one man into two, but as I have said there is one man by the composition of body and soul. If we deny that there is one single Christ from two different natures, being indivisible after the

[6] The point here marks a crucial difference with the line that Chalcedon subsequently takes, for Cyril is happy to accept the notion of 'two natures' but feels that this needs qualification if it is to avoid a tendency towards the kind of separatism that has been advocated by Nestorius. He wishes to speak of a concurrence to unity 'from two natures' but does not posit a union that abides 'in two natures'. For Cyril, to abide in two natures means to abide in an 'un-united' condition that can only be theoretically applied before the incarnation takes place; the incarnation itself is the resolution to union of the two natures. He is genuinely puzzled why anyone should continue to insist on the phrase 'in two natures'. The qualification applied by Chalcedon 'abiding inseparably in two natures' secures Cyril's essential point—although many Cyrillines after 451 found the 'two natures' language unacceptable (or unnecessarily paradoxical) which caused the Monophysite schism. The following paragraph in the text demonstrates Cyril's intent quite clearly and marks him off from later 'monophysite' thought, for he is clearly thinking of the notion of composition to unity from disparates (such as the analogy of the single man composed of body and soul). In the second Letter to Succensus he says, quite explicitly that only the term 'inseparably' makes two natures language orthodox—but that he suspects his opponents of not using the word honestly. The concept of two natures as a primary vehicle for language about the incarnation, therefore, strikes him as too static and too weak to carry the sense of the dynamic economy which for him constitutes the incarnation. Even in Chalcedon the primary stress of the incarnational scheme is not supplied by the two natures language.

union, then the enemies of orthodoxy will ask: 'If the entirety amounts to one nature then how was he incarnated or what kind of flesh did he make his own?'

8. But I found in your memorandum a certain suggestion of the idea that after the resurrection the holy body of Christ the Saviour of us all was changed into the nature of Godhead so that the whole is henceforth only Godhead, and so I thought it necessary to address this point as well. The blessed Paul explains for us the reasons of the incarnation of the Only Begotten Son of God when he writes: 'In so far as the law was powerless, since it was weakened by the flesh, God sent his own Son in the likeness of sinful flesh and for sin. He condemned sin in the flesh in order that the requirement of the law might be fulfilled in us who no longer walk according to the flesh, but according to the spirit' (*Rom.8.3–4*). And again: 'Since the children have a fellowship of flesh and blood, he too shared in flesh and blood so that by death he might destroy the one who has the power of death, that is the devil, and might liberate all those who throughout their lives were held in bondage by the fear of death. He did not take to himself descent from angels but from the line of Abraham, which is why it was necessary for him to be made like his brethren in all things' (*Heb.2.14–17*).

9. We maintain, therefore, that since human nature was suffering corruption because of Adam's transgression, and since our intellect was being tyrannised by the pleasures or rather the innate impulses of the flesh, then it was necessary that the Word of God should be incarnated for the salvation of us who are on this earth. This was so he could make his own that human flesh which was subject to corruption and sick with its desires, and destroy corruption within it since he is Life and Life-giver, bringing its innate sensual impulses to order. This was how the sin that lay within it was to be put to death, for we remember how the blessed Paul called our innate impulses the law of sin (*Rom.7.23*). From the time that human flesh became the personal flesh of the Word it has ceased to be subject to corruption, and since he who dwelt within it, and revealed it as his very own, knew no sin being God, as I have already said, it has also ceased to be sick with its desires. The Only Begotten Word of God did not bring this about for his own benefit, for he is ever what he is, but evidently he did it for ours. And if we were subject to the evils following from Adam's transgression then Christ's benefit also must come to us, that is incorruption and the putting to death

of sin. This is why he became man. He did not assume a man as Nestorius thinks. The scripture says that he was wearied from the journey, experienced sleepiness, anxiety, pain, and all the blameless human passions (cf. *Jn.4.6; Mt.8.24; Mt.26.38* et passim) for this very reason that we might believe that he did become man, even though he remained what he was, that is God by nature. On the other hand, to assure those who saw him that he was truly God as well as being man, he worked divine signs, rebuking the sea (*Mt.8.26*), raising the dead (*Jn.11.43*), and performing other wonderful works. He even endured the cross so that by suffering death in the flesh (though not in the nature of the Godhead) he might become the first-born from the dead (*Col.1.18*). He opened up the way for human nature to incorruption and despoiled Hell, taking pity on the souls who were imprisoned there.

10. Even after the resurrection the same body which had suffered continued to exist, although it no longer contained any human weakness. We maintain that it was no longer susceptible to hunger or weariness or anything like this, but was thereafter incorruptible, and not only that but life-giving as well since it is the body of Life, that is the body of the Only Begotten. Now it is radiant with divine glory and is seen to be the body of God. So, even if someone should call it 'divine' just as one might call a man's body 'human', such a fitting thought would not be mistaken. In my opinion this is what the most-wise Paul said: 'Even if we have known Christ according to the flesh, nonetheless we know him so no longer' (*2 Cor.5.16*). As I have said, because it was God's own body it transcended all human things, yet the earthly body itself did not undergo a transformation into the nature of Godhead, for this is impossible, otherwise we would be accusing the Godhead of being created and of receiving into itself something which was not part of its own nature. It would be just as foolish an idea to talk of the body being transformed into the nature of Godhead as it would to say the Word was transformed into the nature of flesh. For just as the latter is impossible (for he is unchangeable and unalterable) so too is the former. It is not possible that any creature could be converted into the essence or nature of Godhead, and the flesh is a created thing. We maintain, therefore, that Christ's body is divine in so far as it is the body of God, adorned with unspeakable glory, incorruptible, holy, and life-giving; but none of the holy Fathers has ever thought or said that it was transformed into the nature of Godhead, and we have no intention of doing so either.

11. Your Holiness ought to be aware of this fact too, that our father Athanasius of blessed memory, formerly the bishop of Alexandria, wrote a letter to Epictetus the bishop of Corinth when certain people raised these issues in his time, and this is full of all orthodoxy. But because Nestorius was refuted by it, and because the defenders of the orthodox faith read it, and were able to discredit those who wanted to share Nestorius' opinions, then his party could not endure its charges against them and so they did an evil deed, something worthy of their profane heresy, they corrupted the letter and published it with omissions and interpolations to make it seem that the famous man shared the opinions of Nestorius and his party. This was why it was necessary to take a transcript from the copies we have here, and send it on to your Reverence in case certain people there show you a corrupted version. The most holy and reverend bishop Paul of Emesa raised this matter when he came to Alexandria, and we found that his copy of the letter had been corrupted and falsified by the heretics, and so he asked for a transcript from copies we have here to be sent off to the Antiochenes. And indeed we did send one.

12. In complete accord with the orthodox doctrine of the holy Fathers we have composed a book against the teachings of Nestorius and another against certain people who have criticised the meaning of the Chapters.[7] I have also sent on these texts to your Reverence so that if there are any other of our brethren who share our faith and are of the same mind as us but are carried away by the vain babblings of certain people, and begin to think that we have changed our mind on what we have said against Nestorius, they can be proven wrong by reading them, and can learn that we brought him to order quite rightly and properly as one who was in error. They can see that even now we are just as actively engaged in fighting his blasphemies on every side. Your Holiness, whose mental powers are even greater, will be able to help us by writing and by prayer.

[7] viz. Contra Nest. ACO.1.1.6 pp. 13–106; also the defence of the Anathematisms as directed either against Theodoret of Cyr (ACO 1.1.6.pp. 107–146) or against the Orientals (ACO 1.1.7.pp. 33–65). The anathematisms, or 'Chapters', are found appended to the 3rd letter to Nestorius. Cyril's Explanation of the meaning of the Chapters is included in the present translations.

SECOND LETTER OF CYRIL TO SUCCENSUS[1]

Another memorandum written in reply to our[2] questions by the same, to the same Succensus.

1. Truth makes herself plain to those who love her, but hides, I think, and tries to escape the notice of complicated minds, for they show that they are not worthy to look on her with radiant eyes. And those who love the blameless faith seek the Lord, as it is written, 'in simplicity of heart' (*WS.1.1*), but those who walk down twisting alleys and have a 'crooked heart' as it is said in the psalms (*Ps.100.4*) gather for themselves complicated pretexts for their distorted thoughts in order to pervert the straight ways of the Lord and seduce the souls of the simpler folk into believing they ought to hold what is not right. I say this after having read your Holiness' memorandum and having found in it certain unsound propositions which were advanced by those with an unaccountable love for the perversity of so-called knowledge (cf. *1 Tim.6.20*). They were as follows:

2. 'If Emmanuel was composed from two natures', they say, 'and after the union one conceives of only one incarnate nature of the Word, then it necessarily follows that we must admit he suffered in his own nature.' The blessed Fathers who defined for us the venerable creed of the orthodox faith said that it was the Word of God himself, the Only begotten from God's own essence, through whom are all things, who became incarnate and was made man. Evidently we would not say that these holy ones were unaware of the fact that the body that was united to the Word was animated by a rational soul, and so, if anyone says that the Word was made flesh he is not thereby confessing that the flesh united to him was devoid of a rational soul. It was this, I think, (no, I'm quite sure of it) that the all-wise evangelist John meant when he said that the Word became flesh (*Jn.1.14*), not as if he were united to a soulless flesh, God forbid, and not as if he underwent any change or alteration, for he remained what he

[1] Ep.46, PG.77.237–245; ACO 1.1.6. pp. 157–162; Wickham 84–93.

[2] Evidently Succensus was the one responsible for publishing the documents.

was, that is God by nature. He took it on himself to become man and was made like us in the flesh, from out of a woman, and yet he remained a single Son, though indeed no longer without the flesh as he was of old before the time of his incarnation, but now clothed as it were in our nature. And even though the flesh endowed with a rational soul was not consubstantial with the Word born from God the Father, with whom it was united (for we can mentally envisage the difference of natures in the things united), nonetheless we confess One Son and Christ and Lord, since the Word has become flesh. When we say 'flesh', therefore, we mean 'man'. If we confess that after the union there is one enfleshed nature of the Son how does that imply by necessity that he suffered in his own nature? Certainly, if there was nothing in the system of the economy that was capable of suffering, they would have been right to conclude that since there was nothing there that was passible then the suffering must of necessity have fallen upon the nature of the Word. On the other hand, if the word 'incarnate' implies the whole system of the economy with flesh [for he was made flesh precisely by taking descent from Abraham and being made like his brethren in all things (*Heb.2.16*) and assuming the form of a slave (*Phil.2.7*)] then in that case those who argue that it is an absolutely necessary implication of his assumption of flesh that he has to undergo suffering in his own nature are talking utter nonsense. It is the flesh which has to be seen as undergoing suffering while the Word remains impassible. Nonetheless we do not rule out the legitimacy of saying that he suffered, for just as the body became his very own, just so can all the characteristics of the body be attributed to him, with the sole exception of sin, in terms of the economy by which he made them his own.

3. They also said the following: 'If there is one incarnate nature of the Word then it absolutely follows that there must have been a mixture and confusion, with the human nature in him being diminished or 'stolen away' as it were.' Once again those who twist the truth are unaware that in fact there is but one incarnate nature of the Word. The Word was ineffably born from God the Father and then came forth as man from a woman after having assumed flesh, not soulless but rationally animated flesh; and if it is the case that he is in nature and in truth one single Son, then he cannot be divided into two personas or two sons, but has remained one, though he is no longer fleshless or outside the body but now possesses his very own body in an indissoluble union. How could saying this

possibly imply that there was any consequent necessity of mixture or confusion or anything else like this? For if we say that the Only Begotten Son of God, who was incarnate and became man, is One, then this does not mean as they would suppose that he has been 'mixed' or that the nature of the Word has been transformed into the nature of flesh, or that of the flesh into the Word's. No, each nature is understood to remain in all its natural characteristics for the reasons we have just given, though they are ineffably and inexpressibly united, and this is how he demonstrated to us the one nature of the Son; though of course, as I have said, it is the 'incarnate nature' I mean. The term 'one' can be properly applied not just to those things which are naturally simple, but also to things which are compounded in a synthesis. Such is the case with a human being who comprises soul and body. These are quite different things and they are not consubstantial with each other, yet when they are united they constitute the single nature of man, even though the difference in nature of the things that are brought into unity is still present within the system of the composition. So, those who say that if there is one incarnate nature of God the Word, then it necessarily follows that there must have been a mixture or confusion with the human nature being diminished or 'stolen away', are talking rubbish. It has neither been reduced nor stolen away, as they say. To say that he is incarnate is sufficient for a perfectly clear indication of the fact that he became man. And if we had kept silent on this point there might have been some ground for their calumny, but since we add of necessity the fact that he has been incarnated then how can there be any form of 'diminution' or 'stealing away'?

4. They have also said: 'If the same one is understood to be perfect God and perfect man, and consubstantial with the Father in the deity, and consubstantial with us in the manhood, then how can there be a perfection if the nature of man no longer endures? and how can there be consubstantiality with us if our essence, that is our nature, no longer subsists?' The explanation or response contained in the preceding section adequately answers these points. For if we had said that there was one nature of the Word and had kept silent and not added that it was 'incarnate', as if we were excluding the economy, they might perhaps have had a point when they pretended to ask where was the perfection in the humanity or how did our human essence endure. But since both the perfection in the humanity and the assertion of our human essence is implied by the word 'incarnate'

then let them stop leaning on this broken staff (*Is.36.6*). For if anyone took away from the Son his perfect humanity he could rightly be accused of throwing the economy overboard, and of denying the incarnation. But if, as I have said, when we say that he was incarnated this is a clear and unambiguous confession of the fact that he became man, then there is nothing at all to prevent us from thinking that the same Christ, the One and Only Son, is both God and man, as perfect in humanity as he is in deity. Your Perfection expounds the rationale of the salvific Passion most correctly and very learnedly when you assert that the Only Begotten Son of God, in so far as he is understood to be, and actually is, God, did not himself suffer [bodily things] in his own nature, but suffered rather in his earthly nature. Both points must be maintained in relation to the one true Son: that he did not suffer as God, and that he did suffer as man, since his flesh suffered. However, these people think that here we are introducing what they call 'Theopaschitism'. They do not understand the economy and make wicked attempts to displace the sufferings to the man on his own, foolishly seeking a piety that does them harm. They try to avoid confessing that the Word of God is the Saviour who gave his own blood for us, and say instead that it was the man Jesus understood as separate and distinct who can be said to have achieved this. To think like this shakes the whole rationale of the fleshly economy, and quite clearly turns our divine mystery into a matter of man-worshipping. They do not understand that blessed Paul said that he who is of the Jews according to the flesh, that is of the line of Jesse and David, is also the Christ, the Lord of Glory (*1 Cor.2.8*), and is 'God ever blessed and over all' (*Rom.9.5*). In this way Paul declared that it was the very own body of the Word which was fixed to the cross, and therefore he attributed the crucifixion to him.

5. I understand that another query has been raised in regard to these matters, as follows: 'So, anyone who says that the Lord suffered only at the level of the flesh, makes that suffering mindless and involuntary. But if anyone says that he suffered with a rational soul, so that the suffering might be voluntary, then there is nothing to prevent one from saying that he suffered in the nature of the manhood, and if this is the case then how can we deny that the two natures endured after the union? So, even if one says: 'Christ, therefore, having suffered for us in the flesh' (*1 Pet.4.1*), this is no different from saying: 'Christ having suffered for us in our nature'.

This objection is yet another attack on those who say that there is one incarnate nature of the Son. They want to show that the idea is foolish and so they keep on arguing at every turn that two natures endured. They have forgotten, however, that it is only those things that are usually distinguished at more than a merely theoretical level which split apart from one another in differentiated separateness and radical distinction. Let us once more take the example of an ordinary man. We recognise two natures in him; for there is one nature of the soul and another of the body, but we divide them only at a theoretical level, and by subtle speculation, or rather we accept the distinction only in our mental intuitions, and we do not set the natures apart nor do we grant that they have a radical separateness, but we understand them to belong to one man. This is why the two are no longer two, but through both of them the one living creature is rendered complete. And so, even if one attributes the nature of manhood and Godhead to the Emmanuel, still the manhood has become the personal property of the Word and we understand there is One Son together with it. The God-inspired scripture tells us that he suffered in the flesh (*1 Pet.4.1*) and it would be better for us to speak this way rather than [say he suffered] in the nature of the manhood, even though such a statement (unless it is said uncompromisingly by certain people) does not damage the sense of the mystery. For what else is the nature of manhood except the flesh with a rational soul? We maintain, therefore, that the Lord suffered in the flesh. And so they are simply splitting hairs when they talk about him suffering in the nature of the manhood, which serves only to separate it from the Word and set it apart on its own so that one is led to think of him as two and no longer the one Word of God the Father now incarnated and made man. To add the qualification 'inseparably' seems to indicate that they share the orthodox opinion along with us, but this is not how they really think, for they understand the word 'inseparable' in the same empty sense as Nestorius. They say that the man in whom the Word took his dwelling was inseparable from him in terms of equality of honour, identity of will, and authority, all of which means that they do not use the words straightforwardly but with a certain amount of trickery and deceit.

NESTORIUS' REPLY TO CYRIL'S SECOND LETTER[1]

Nestorius to the most reverend and God-beloved fellow-minister Cyril. Greetings in the Lord.

1. I will pass over the insults against me contained in your extraordinary letter, as meriting only the patience of a doctor. It will have its reply, in actions, soon enough.[2] There is something, however, that will not allow silence because if it is hushed up it has the potential of being very dangerous indeed. So, in so far as I am able I will try to make a concise exposition of it for you, cutting out all long-windedness, to spare you any nausea in the face of an over-long, obscure, and indigestible tract.[3] I will begin with Your Charity's own very wise words, and will cite them exactly. What, then, are these words of wondrous teaching contained in your letter? 'The great and holy synod[4] said that it was the Only Begotten Son himself, naturally born from God the Father, true God from true God, light from light, through whom the Father made all things, who was the one who came down, was made flesh, was made man, suffered, and rose again on the third day.'

2. These are the words of Your Reverence and you surely recognise them as your own. But now hear ours, a fraternal exhortation on piety, and one which the great Paul gave as a testimony to his beloved Timothy: 'Apply yourself to reading, to encouragement, to teaching, for if you do this you will save yourself and those who hear you' (*1 Tim.4.13,16*). Why is this phrase 'apply yourself' relevant? because in your letter you have misunderstood the tradition contained in those holy texts you have read, and so have fallen into ignorance (understandable enough)[5] by thinking that they said the Word of God, coeternal with the Father, was passible. But look over these words

---

[1] ACO. 1.1.29–32; PG. 77.49; Loofs, Nestoriana 173–180.

[2] A threat to Cyril that Nestorius would pursue the charges that had been raised in Constantinople against Cyril's administration by some dissidents.

[3] Heavy irony directed against Cyril's literary reputation. Both Nestorius and Theodoret mocked Cyril's style as well as his theology.

[4] Of Nicaea.

[5] Again heavily ironic, and suggesting that Cyril was ill-educated.

a little more carefully if you please, and you will find that this divine chorus of fathers did not say that the consubstantial Godhead was passible, or that it underwent a recent birth (since it is coeternal with the Father), or that it was raised to life (since it raised up the destroyed temple). And if you lend me your ears so that I can supply some fraternal healing, then I will cite the very words of the holy Fathers in order to free you from the calumnies you have raised against them and against the holy scriptures.

3. They said: 'I believe in our Lord Jesus Christ, his Only Begotten Son.' Note how they set out at the beginning, as foundations, these terms of 'Lord' and 'Jesus' and 'Christ' and 'Only Begotten', as common names for both the Godhead and the manhood. And then they go on to build the tradition of his incarnation and passion and resurrection on this [foundation]. First they set out certain terms as indicative of, and common to, both natures, for then there is no danger of bringing division between things that apply to the Sonship and the Lordship, and no danger of making things that apply to both natures disappear in an indiscriminate reference to the Sonship alone.

4. Paul has been their teacher in this, for when he made mention of the divine incarnation and was about to add a reference to the passion, he first posited Christ as a common term for both natures, as I have just said previously, and then went on to speak in a way that applies to both natures. What does he say? 'Have this mind among you which was in Christ Jesus. Though he was in the form of God he did not count equality with God a thing to be grasped but (to give the general sense) became obedient to death, death on a cross' (*Phil 2.5,6,8*). Since he was going to mention the death, he posited the title Christ so that no one might imagine that God the Word was passible, for Christ is a term that applies to both the impassible and the passible natures in a single persona.[6] This is how Christ can be said, without danger, to be both passible and impassible; impassible in the Godhead, but passible in the nature of his body.

5. I could say many things on this subject. In the first place, when referring to the economy, the holy Fathers never speak of a 'generation' but an 'incarnation'. I am conscious, however, how the promise of brevity I made in my introduction reins in my discourse. This makes me pass on to the second point Your Charity raises.

[6] Here, and elsewhere throughout this letter, 'prosopon'.

6. I applaud the fact you make a division between the natures according to Godhead and manhood, admitting their conjunction in one persona; and also that you deny that God the Word had need of a second generation from a woman; and that you confess that the deity cannot undergo any suffering. All this is truly orthodox and contrary to all the evil opinions the heretics have entertained about the dominical natures. But as for the rest [of your letter] if it contains some hidden wisdom, incomprehensible to the ears of those who hear it read, then you alone have the wit to know. As far as I am concerned it seems to contradict your earlier statements. For the one you first proclaimed as impassible and not needing a second generation, you subsequently introduce (how I know not) as passible and newly created. It is as if those attributes naturally inherent in God the Word were destroyed by this conjunction with the temple; or as if men regarded it as an insignificance that this sinless temple had undergone birth and death on behalf of sinners; or as if we ought not to believe the voice of Our Lord himself when he cried out to the Jews: 'Destroy this temple and in three days I will raise it up' (*Jn.2.19*)—not 'Destroy my Godhead and in three days it shall be raised up.' Once again, although I would like to expand on this, I am mindful of my promise and must, therefore, speak with all brevity.

7. All throughout the sacred scriptures, wherever mention is made of the Lord's economy, the birth and the sufferings are not passed down to us as if they applied to the Godhead, but to the manhood. This means that the holy virgin should be described, in a more exact designation, not as 'Mother of God' but 'Mother of Christ'. Listen to the Gospel crying out these facts when it says: 'The Book of the generation of Jesus Christ, the Son of David, Son of Abraham' (*Mt.1.1*). Obviously God the Word was not the Son of David. If you like take this other witness: 'And Jacob begot Joseph, the husband of Mary, from whom was born Jesus who is called Christ' (*Mt.1.16*). Again, examine another text that bears witness for us: 'This was how the birth of Jesus Christ came to pass. His mother Mary was betrothed to Joseph when she was found to have conceived of the Holy Spirit' (*Mt.1.18*). But who would ever take this to mean that the Godhead of the Only Begotten was a creation of the Holy Spirit? And what should we say of the text: 'And the Mother of Jesus was there' (*Jn.2.1*), or again, 'And with Mary the Mother of Jesus' (*Acts 1.14*), or 'For that which is conceived in her is of the Holy Spirit' (*Mt.1.20*), or 'Take the child and its mother and flee to Egypt' (*Mt.2.13*), or

'Concerning his Son who was born of the line of David according to the flesh' (*Rom.1.3*), or again (in relation to his sufferings) 'God, by sending his own Son in the likeness of sinful flesh, and on sin's account, condemned sin in the flesh' (*Rom.8.3*), or again 'Christ died for our sins' (*1 Cor.15.3*), or 'Christ suffered in the flesh' (*1 Pet.4.1*), or 'This is my body (not my Godhead note) which is broken for you' (*1 Cor.11.24*). There are a thousand other texts which all testify to humankind that it is not the deity of the Son that should be regarded as something recent or capable of bodily suffering, but the flesh which is associated with the nature of the Godhead. Why does Christ refer to himself as both Lord of David, and David's son, when he says: 'What is your opinion of the Christ? Whose son is he? And they said to him, David's son. But in reply Jesus said to them, Then why does David, in the Spirit, call him Lord when he says, The Lord said to my Lord, sit on my right'? (*Mt.22.42–44*). It is because he is entirely David's son according to the flesh, but David's Lord according to the Godhead. It is entirely right and fitting to the Gospel traditions to confess that the body is the temple of the Godhead of the Son, and a temple that is united in a sublime and divine conjunction, in such a way that the nature of the Godhead appropriates the characteristics of this [temple]. But to attribute to the Godhead, in the name of this appropriation, the properties of the flesh that is associated with it (and I mean generation, suffering, and death)—then this is either the error of a pagan mentality, brother, or a spirit sick with the madness of Apollinaris and Arius and the other heresies, or even something far worse. For those who allow themselves to be carried away by this notion of 'appropriation' must of necessity admit that because of this appropriation God the Word was involved in sucking at the breast, and in a gradual growth, and in trepidation at the time of the passion, needing the assistance of an angel. I will make no mention of circumcision, sacrifice, sweating, hunger; all those things which, joined with the flesh, are actually adorable because they were done for our sake, but which, if they are attributed to the Godhead, are merely lies and become the grounds for our rightful condemnation as blasphemers.

8. These are the traditions of the holy Fathers. These are the precepts of the divine scriptures. This is how one theoretically should understand both the philanthropy and the authority of God. As Paul said, addressing everyone: 'Reflect on these things, immerse yourself in them, so that your progress will be obvious to all' (*1 Tim.4.15*).

On the other hand, you do well to concern yourself about those who are scandalised.[7] So my thanks for the fact that your spirit is always thinking about divine affairs, and thank you for your interest in me. But you should know that you have been deceived by those who have been deposed here by the holy synod[8] for holding Manichean opinions, or by clerics who perhaps hold to your opinions. In fact the affairs of the church improve day by day, by the grace of Christ. The people flourish so much that those who see their number cry out in the words of the prophet: 'The earth will be filled with the knowledge of the Lord as the sea is covered by great waters' (*Is.11.9*). The Royal Court is overjoyed at the way the doctrines have been illuminated. In short, as anyone can discover, in terms of all the God-fighting heresies or the orthodoxy of all the churches, then that text has been fulfilled among us: 'The house of Saul goes to ruination, but the house of David goes from strength to strength' (*2 Sam.3.1*).[9]

9. We send you these words as brothers conferring with a brother.[10] 'But if anyone still loves to dispute,' then Paul himself can cry out to him through us that, 'Neither we, nor the churches of God, have such a custom' (*1 Cor.11.16*).

I, and those with me, heartily salute your whole brotherhood in Christ. Keep well and do not cease praying for us most venerable and reverend lord.

---

[7] An ironic reference to Cyril's earlier letters alerting him to his anxiety over the reports he had heard about the scandal Nestorius' sermons had caused in the city.

[8] The Home Synod of Constantinople.

[9] Behind the text one might suspect that there is another allusion intended here: that Nestorius feels secure in his proximity to the Emperor and is characterising Cyril's Alexandria as the house of Saul waning before the rising star of the church of Constantinople.

[10] There is a clear suggestion in the use of the plural here, following the mention of the Home Synod in the previous paragraph, that Nestorius intended his letter to carry a suggestion (and threat) of synodical weight. The reference earlier to 'certain clerics who perhaps hold to your opinions' was a clear signal to Cyril that Nestorius intended to proceed against him, if allowed the opportunity, just as he had deposed leading archimandrites in the capital who had disagreed with his theology.

THE SYNODICAL DEPOSITION OF NESTORIUS[1]

The priest Peter of Alexandria, senior notary, said: 'We also have [in our hands] the books of the blasphemies of the Very Reverend Nestorius. From one of them we have selected excerpts. If [the holy synod] so desires we shall read them.'
Bishop Flavian of Philippi answered: 'Let this be read and inserted in the Acts.'

From The Book of the Same Nestorius. Quaternion 17 On Dogma.[2]
So when the divine scripture wishes to speak about the birth of Christ from the blesed virgin, or his death, nowhere does it apply the word 'God'. It uses either 'Christ', or 'Son', or 'Lord', for these terms are the semantic indicators of the two natures, and signify either the one or the other, or both of them together. For example, when scripture describes for us the birth from a virgin what does it say? 'God sent us his son' (*Gal.4.4.*). It did not say 'God sent us God the Word', no, it adopts a term that signifies the two natures. But since the Son is man and God it says: 'He sent his son, born of a woman.' (*Gal.4.4.*) so that when you hear 'born of a woman', and then see that the preceding title signifies the two natures, you will admit that this birth from the blessed virgin is that of the Son. For she gave birth to the Son of God and is thus the Christ-mother. Yet, since the Son of God is two-fold in regard to his natures, she did not so much give birth to the Son of God as give birth to the manhood, and the latter is Son because of the Son conjoined to it.

Similarly from the same Book, Quaternion 21.[3]
Look at the implication here, you heretic. I do not refuse the title 'Christ-mother' to the virgin, for I know what a noble thing it was for her to receive God,[4] and that through her the Lord of all came

---

[1] The process of deposition as held at the First Session of the Council of Ephesus, June 22nd 431. Texts: ACO 1.2.45–64.

[2] Loofs, Nestoriana (Halle, 1905) 273.18–274.17.

[3] Loofs, Nestoriana, 277.19–278.2.

[4] A word-play: As a receiver of God Mary is Theodochos, but not Theotokos (pronounced almost the same in Byzantine Greek).

forth, and that the Sun of Righteousness shone forth through her. On the other hand I think the enthusiasm for this title a little suspect.[5] In what sense have you understood this 'coming forth'? I do not mean 'coming forth' as a simple synonym for 'was born', for I am not so ready to forget the distinctions. I was taught by the divine scriptures that God 'came forth' from the virgin Christ-mother, but nowhere at all am I taught that God was born from her.

And In another place:[6]

And so, nowhere does the divine scripture say that God was born of the virgin Christ-mother, but rather that it was Jesus, the Christ, the Son, or the Lord [who was so born]. All of us confess these things, for this is what the divine scripture has taught, and wretched is the man who does not accept this straightforwardly. 'Rise, take up the child and his mother' (*Mt.2.13*), this is what the angels say. Perhaps the archangels knew the meaning of his birth better than you do? 'Rise, take up the child and his mother.' Note that they did not say: 'Rise, take up God and his mother.'

Similarly from the same Book, Quaternion 24.[7]

And so, as we were saying [in regard to the text]: 'Do not be afraid to take Mary as your wife, for that which has been begotten in her . . .' (*Mt.1.20*). How exactly should we transcribe the verb in this instance; as 'begotten' or 'born'?[8] Either way would not be an outrage on the sense of the passage (for that which is conceived in her is of the Holy Spirit). On the other hand, if we were to say that God the Word had been conceived in her womb [then this would be an outrage] for it is one thing to be conjoined to the one who is conceived, but another thing altogether to be actually conceived. For scripture says: 'That which is in her has been begotten in her by the Holy Spirit'; that is, the Holy Spirit has created the one inside her. The Fathers knew, then, since they understood the divine scriptures, that if we

[5] Perhaps more than a merely rhetorical device: Nestorius preached the original draft of his books in the cathedral, and there the congregation applauded points it wished to emphasise. The implication seems to be that he would not allow his congregation to hold to a Marian devotion they obviously wished to preserve, and is here actually correcting those who heckled him at this point of his discourse by applauding the general point he was intent on attacking.

[6] Loofs, Nestoriana 278. 5–13.

[7] Loofs, Nestoriana 285.24–287.21.

[8] Lit. 'with two n's or one?' referring to the variant introduced if one were to read genethen instead of gennethen.

imposed the sense of 'being engendered' instead of 'being incarnated' then the result would be either to make God the Word into the son of the Holy Spirit, or to give him two fathers; for if we attribute generation to him then we will find that God the Word is a creature of the Holy Spirit. So, fleeing from this term 'generation' they set out the phrase 'came down for us men and for our salvation, and was made flesh'.[9] What does 'made flesh' mean? It does not mean changing from Godhead into flesh. In this phrase 'and was made flesh of the Holy Spirit' they were following the evangelist. When the evangelist dealt with his incarnation he avoided attributing the term 'generation' to the Word, but instead used 'incarnation'. Where was this? Let us hear: 'And the Word became flesh' (*Jn.1.14*). He did not say, 'And the Word was born by means of the flesh.' For whenever the apostles or evangelists have referred to the Son they have said that he was born of a woman. So please, I beg you, pay attention to what you read. Where they use the titles of the Son and speak of him as being born from a woman, then they use the term 'begotten', but where they are referring to the Word himself none of them has ever dared to talk about a birth through the manhood. Listen to what the blessed evangelist John said when he dealt with the Word and his incarnation: 'The Word was made flesh' (that is, assumed flesh) 'and dwelt among us' (that is clothed himself in our nature and lived among us) 'and we beheld his glory' as the Son. He did not say: 'We beheld the birth of the Word.'

Similarly from the same Book, Quaternion. 15 On Dogma.[10]
In this way we must also designate Christ in the flesh as God because of his conjunction with God the Word, even though we know that the one who appears to us is a man. Listen how Paul proclaims both realities when he says: 'Christ, in the flesh of the Jews, he who is God above all' (*Rom.9.5*). First of all he confesses the man, and then he describes the one who appears to us as God by virtue of his conjunction with God. This is so that no one might ever imagine that Christianity is involved with man-worshipping.

Similarly from the same Book, Quaternion 27.[11]
But, as we have said, the word 'God' refers to the maker of all things,

---

[9] The Nicene Creed.
[10] Loofs, Nestoriana. 248.10–249.1.
[11] Loofs, Nestoriana 289. 6–15.

and it also means Moses (for scripture says 'I have set you as god over Pharoah' (*Ex.7.1*)). Israel too is the Son of God (for scripture says 'Israel is my first-born son' (*Ex.4.22*)). We have also seen how Saul was Christ (for scripture says 'I will not lay my hand upon him for he is the Christ of the Lord' (*1 Sam.24.7*)), and Cyrus is likewise Christ (for scripture says 'Thus says the Lord to Cyrus my Christ' (*Is.45.1*)). Babylon too is holy (for scripture says 'I will instruct them for they are sanctified and I direct them' (*Is.13.3*)). Well, in the same way, we also speak of Christ as Lord, and God, and Son, and Holy One, and Anointed; but although the sharing of names is similar, it does not mean the same dignity.

Similarly from the same Book, Quaternion 15.[12]
'Have this mind among you which was in Christ Jesus. Though he was in the form of God he emptied himself, assuming the form of a slave' (*Phil.2.5,7*). Scripture did not say 'Have this mind among you which was in God the Word. Though he was in the form of God he assumed the form of a slave.' No, it adopted the term 'Christ' as the semantic indicator of the two natures, and then it was able to affirm without danger that he assumed the form of a slave, and could call him God, dividing out these affirmations unattributably into the duality of natures.

Similarly from the same Book, Quaternion 16.[13]
It continues: 'So that in the name of Jesus, every knee shall bow, in heaven, on earth, and under the earth, and every tongue shall confess that Jesus Christ is Lord' (*Phil.2.10–11*). I venerate the one who is borne on account of the one who bears him. I worship the one who is visible on account of the one who lies hidden. God is inseparable from the one who is visible, and because they are not divided so I do not divide the reverence [given]. I divide the natures but I unite the worship.

Similarly from the same Book, Quaternion 17 On Dogma.[14]
Even before the incarnation God the Word was Son and God, and united with the Father, but in these latter days he assumed the form of a slave. But since he was Son and was called such in advance,

[12] Loofs, Nestoriana 254. 5–12.
[13] Loofs, Nestoriana 261.20–262.6.
[14] Loofs, Nestoriana 275. 1–11.

then after the assumption of the flesh he can no longer be called a son separately and on his own, in case we should teach that there are two sons. Yet in so far as he is conjoined to the one who was Son in the beginning, that is to the one who conjoins himself to him, then one cannot admit any division in terms of the dignity of sonship—and I am speaking precisely about the dignity of sonship, not the natures. For this reason, the Word of God is also called Christ, in so far as he has a continuous association with the Christ.

Similarly from the same Book, Quaternion 15 on Dogma.[15]
We, therefore, preserve an unconfused conjunction of the natures, and we confess God in a man. We worship a man in common veneration through the divine conjunction with almighty God.

Similarly from the same Book, Quaternion 6.[16]
Consider what is added on here immediately afterwards, as it says: 'that he might become a faithful and compassionate High Priest in our dealings before God. For in so far as he himself suffered temptation he is able to bring aid to those who are being tempted' (*Heb.2.17,18.*). So, the suffering High Priest is compassionate, but it is the temple which is passible, not the deity who brings to life the one who suffered.

Similarly from the same Book, Quaternion 27.[17]
He says: This is so that you might learn how intimate was the conjunction between the Godhead and the Lord's flesh, witnessed in that newborn child. For the same one was newborn child, and also Lord of the newborn child. We should praise this concept, but do not applaud it without examination for what I have said is that the same one was a newborn child and dwelt within the newborn child.

Similarly from the same Book, Quaternion 1.[18]
The activities of the Trinity are common, and can only be distinguished in terms of the hypostases. So, the glory of the Only Begotten is sometimes referred to the Father (for scripture says 'It is my Father who glorifies me' (*Jn.8.54*)), sometimes to the Spirit (for scripture says 'The Spirit of truth shall glorify me' (*Jn.16.13,14.*)), and sometimes to the majesty of Christ.

---

[15] Loofs, Nestoriana 249. 1–4.
[16] Loofs, Nestoriana, 234.10–16.
[17] Loofs, Nestoriana, 292.1–6.
[18] Loofs, Nestoriana 225.13–18.

Similarly from the same Book, Quaternion 16.[19]
Speaking of the Son: It is He who says: 'My God, my God, why have you forsaken me?' (*Mt.27.46*). It is he who submitted to death for three days. Nonetheless I worship him along with the deity in so far as he is a co-operator with the divine majesty.
And in another place:[20]
I venerate the one that is borne on account of the one who bears him. I worship the one who is visible on account of the one who lies hidden. God is inseparable from the one who is visible, and because they are not divided I do not divide the reverence [given]. I divide the natures but I unite the worship. For it was not God in himself who was fashioned within a mother, neither was it God in himself who was created by the Holy Spirit, nor God in himself who was buried in a tomb; otherwise we would evidently be worshippers of a man, worshippers of a corpse. But, since God was in that one who was assumed, then because the assumed man was thereby conjoined to the one who assumed, him he is called God alongside him.

Similarly from the same Book, Quaternion 3 Against the Heretics.[21]
Speaking of the Holy Spirit he says: How could he be a slave when he works along with the Son and the Father? If you look into the activities of the Holy Spirit you will find them in no way inferior to those of the Son and the Father—not as if the one Godhead is divided up, but in the sense that the divine scripture (in order to show the equality of the Trinity) respectively attributes to each hypostasis things which pertain to the single power. It seems to me that this equality begins in the works that occur within Time. God 'the Word became flesh and dwelt among us' (*Jn.1.14*). The Father has made the assumed humanity sit alongside him (for scripture says 'The Lord said to my Lord—Sit at my right hand' (*Ps.109.1*)). The Spirit, descending, confirmed the glory of the assumed man (for scripture says 'When the Spirit of truth comes he shall glorify me'(*Jn.16. 13,14*)).

Similarly from the same Book, Quaternion 6.[22]
Speaking of Christ: For he was sent to preach forgiveness to the captives as the apostle notes when he tells us that this is the one who has

---

[19] Loofs, Nestoriana, 260.4–7
[20] Loofs, Nestoriana 262.3–12.
[21] Loofs, Nestoriana 226.14–227.3.
[22] Loofs, Nestoriana, 235.6–236.6.

been made a faithful High Priest for God (*Heb.2.17*), for he became such, and was not so from all eternity. This is he, you heretic, who progressed little by little to the dignity of the High Priesthood. Listen to the voice of the one who proclaims this to you so clearly. As scripture says: 'For in the days of his flesh he offered prayers and supplications with tears and loud crying, to the one who had the power to save him from death. And he was heard because of his reverence. Although he was Son, he learned obedience through his sufferings, and having been made perfect he became, for all those who obey him, the cause of eternal salvation' (*Heb.5.7–9*). But he was made perfect in a gradual progress, you heretic. And John cries out about this in the Gospel:[23] 'For Jesus advanced in age and wisdom and grace' (*Lk.2.52*). Paul's testimony accords with this when he says: 'Having been made perfect he became, for all those who obey him, the cause of eternal salvation, and was acclaimed by God with the title of High Priest in the order of Melchisedek' (*Heb.5.9–10*).

And further on:[24]

Since he is called 'High Priest', why do you misinterpret Paul by mixing up the impassible God the Word with an earthly image, thus making the High Priest passible?

Similarly from the same Book, Quaternion 7.[25]

'And so, [holy] brethren, who have shared in this heavenly calling, consider Jesus the Apostle and High Priest of our confession, who was faithful to the one who constituted him' (*Heb.3.1,2*).

And then, further on:[26]

Since he is our sole High Priest, compassionate, of our race, and trustworthy, then do not pervert our faith in him. He has been sent to us from Abraham's race as the [High Priest] of the blessing in so far as he brought with him the sacrificial offering of his own body which he offered up for himself and for the race. Take note, that having made the point that it was not necessary for Christ to do so, he still says that he did offer sacrifice for himself as well as for the race.

---

23 A mistaken reference to Luke's Gospel which follows.
24 Loofs, Nestoriana 236. 12–14.
25 Loofs, Nestoriana 240. 1–4.
26 Loofs, Nestoriana 240. 4–9.

Similarly from the same Book, Quaternion 4.[27]

Listen, then, and pay attention to the words, for scripture says: 'He who eats my flesh' (*Jn.6.56*). Remember that this is said about the flesh, and that this word 'flesh' is not added by me—so then I cannot be accused by them of misinterpreting. He says: 'He who eats my flesh and drinks my blood.' He did not say, 'He who eats my Godhead and drinks my Godhead,' but 'He who eats my flesh and drinks my blood abides in me and I in him.'

And in another place:[28]

But to sum up, 'He who eats my flesh and drinks my blood abides in me and I in him.' Remember that this is said about the flesh. 'Just as the living Father has sent me' (*Jn.6.57*), me whom you see. But in case I am misinterpreting let us listen to what follows: 'Just as the living Father has sent me'—well, my opponent says that this refers to the Godhead. I say it refers to the manhood. Let us see who is misinterpreting here. 'Just as the living Father has sent me'—the heretic says that here it is talking about the Godhead, meaning that he has sent God the Word. So, 'Just as the living Father has sent me, so I live (and according to them that means the divine Word) through the Father'. But after this there follows: 'And whoever eats me shall live' (*Jn.6.58*). In that case what is it we are eating? the Godhead or the flesh?

Similarly from the same Book, Quaternion 16.[29]

He says: In general terms if you study the whole scope of the New [Testament] you will never find death ever attributed to the Godhead, but rather to Christ, or the Son, or the Lord. For throughout scripture the terms 'Christ, and 'Son', and 'Lord', are the specific terms used to connote the two natures of the Only Begotten. Sometimes they refer to the deity, sometimes to the manhood, and sometimes to both. For example when Paul in his epistles proclaims: 'Though we were enemies we have been reconciled to God through the death of his Son' (*Rom.5.10*), he is speaking about the manhood of the Son. But when he says, in his Letter to the Hebrews, 'God has spoken to us in his Son, through whom he made the Ages' (*Heb.1.2*), he is clearly referring to the deity of the Son. For the flesh is not the Maker of

27 Loofs, Nestoriana 227.20–228.3.
28 Loofs, Nestoriana 228. 4–16.
29 Loofs, Nestoriana 269.14–27.

the Ages, since it was only made itself after many ages.
And in another place:[30]
It is not the Godhead which has James for a brother, and it is not the death of God the Word which we proclaim when we are nourished by the Lord's body and blood.

Similarly from the same Book, Quaternion 23.[31]
He says: I see among our people a great piety and a very fervent sense of religion, but when it comes to the knowledge of God they have slipped into ignorance of the doctrines. This is not the fault of the laity, but (how shall I say this becomingly?) because your teachers have not had the occasion to present the doctrines to you in a properly exact fashion.
Peter the priest of Alexandria, and senior notary, then said: See how here he openly admits that none of the teachers before him had ever spoken to the people such things as he has spoken.
Flavian Bishop of Philippi said: Since these dreadful things Nestorius has said are blasphemous, and our ears can no longer bear to be sullied by them, let each of these blasphemies of his be inserted into the synodical Acts, for the condemnation of him who has taught such things.[32]
The holy synod said:[33] Apart from other matters, since the Most Reverend Nestorius refused to obey our summons, and would not receive the most holy and reverend bishops whom we sent, then of necessity we have had to proceed to the examination of the impieties he has uttered and written in his epistles and in those writings which have been read out to us; [impieties] even in those things he has recently been speaking even in this very city in front of witnesses. All of this convicts him of thinking and preaching wickedly. We are compelled, therefore, by the canons and by the letter of our most holy father and fellow-minister Celestine, the bishop of the church

---

[30] Loofs, Nestoriana 271.1–3.
[31] Loofs, Nestoriana 283. 2–8.
[32] The Letter of Bishop Capreolus of Carthage was then read to the Synod. In it the Bishop gave news of the death of St. Augustine, and urged that the Synod should tolerate no innovation in any matters concerning the Faith. This final point was acclaimed by the Bishops present (as having a prophetic reference to Nestorius as an innovator). ACO.1.2.52–54. Then there followed the official sentence against Nestorius as in the text.
[33] ACO 1.2.52–64.

of Rome, albeit with many tears, to come to this terrible sentence against him.

Our Lord Jesus Christ, who has been blasphemed by this man, has decreed through this present most holy synod that the same Nestorius is excluded from the dignity of the episcopate and the whole assembly of hierarchs.[34]

On the day following the deposition of the same Nestorius, this document was sent to him by the holy synod:

The Holy Synod, gathered together in Ephesus, by the grace of God, in accordance with the decree of our most righteous and Christ-loving Emperors, to Nestorius, the new Judas.

Know that because of your wicked preaching and your disobedience of the canons, on this 22nd day of the present month of June in accordance with the ecclesiastical prescripts you have been deposed by the holy synod and excluded from all ecclesiastical dignity.

---

[34] The list of 197 episcopal endorsements follows on this, headed by the signatures of: Cyril of Alexandria, Juvenal of Jerusalem, Flavian of Philippi, Firmus of Cappadocian Caesarea, Memnon of Ephesus, Acacius of Melitene, and Theodotus of Ancyra.

APPENDIX 1

The Letter of St. Athanasius to Epictetus Bishop of Corinth[1]

Athanasius, to my lord Epictetus, beloved brother, and longed-for fellow minister. Greetings in the Lord.

1. For my part I had hoped that all the empty talk of all the heretics in existence had been ended by the council held at Nicaea, for the faith which the Fathers confessed there, in accordance with the holy scriptures, is enough in itself to overthrow all impiety and to establish orthodox faith in Christ. Accordingly, when various councils were subsequently convoked in Gaul and Spain and Great Rome, it was as if all those who assembled were moved by the same spirit and by a unanimous vote condemned those still secretly holding to Arianism; I mean Auxentius at Milan, Ursacius, Valens, and Caius of Pannonia. Because [the Arians] were pretending that they too had conciliar authorities, it was announced universally that no council should be recognised in the catholic church except that which was held at Nicaea, that victorious trophy over every heresy, and especially over Arianism on whose account it was assembled. How is it then that even after this some people are still trying to stir up doubts and raise questions? If, in fact, they belong to the Arian party it is not surprising that they disparage the creed drawn up against them. They are like the Greeks who, when they hear it said that 'the idols of the pagans are silver and gold, the work of men's hands' (*Ps.113.12 LXX*), regard the doctrine of the divine cross as 'foolishness' (*1 Cor.1.18*). On the other hand if these people who wish to unsettle matters by their questions come from those who seem to be orthodox believers, those who agree with and uphold what was proclaimed by the Fathers, then (as scripture says) they are simply 'giving their neighbours brackish and bitter waters to drink' (*Hab.2.15 LXX*) and 'stirring words about for no purpose except to subvert the simple' (*2 Tim.2.14*).

[1] A revised and modernised version of the translation in, Library of Fathers of the Church, vol.45, Later Treatises of St. Athanasius, Oxford, 1881, pp. 45–60. Athanasius wrote the letter circa 372.

2. I am writing this after having read the [synodical] minutes sent to me by Your Piety.[2] I wish they had never been written so that not even a remembrance of such things might be transmitted to posterity. For who ever heard the like? Who was it that taught, or learned such things? For, 'Out of Sion shall go forth God's Law, and the word of the Lord from Jerusalem' (*Is.2.3.*), but where did such things as this come from? Which Hades belched forth such a saying as that the body derived from Mary was co-essential with the Godhead of the Word? or that the Word was changed into flesh, and bones, and hair, and a whole body, and was altered from his own nature? And whoever heard in the church, or ever from any christian lips, that it was only as a figure of speech,[3] not by nature, that the Lord bore a body? Who has ever been so wicked as to say or think that the Godhead itself, which is co-essential with the Father, was circumcised, or reduced from perfection to imperfection, or that it was not the body that was fastened to the Word but the very essence of Creative Wisdom? If someone maintained that the Word framed for himself a passible body by alteration of his own essence, rather than taking it from Mary, who would call this man a christian? Who was it[4] that devised this godless impiety, even to the point of thinking and proposing that if anyone affirms the Lord's body was taken from Mary they must thereby affirm that the flesh which the Saviour took and put on from Mary was of the essence of the Trinity? From what source did these people vent the equally wicked doctrine that the body did not originate later than the Godhead of the Word, but has been continuously co-eternal with it, since it was composed from the

[2] Epictetus, as metropolitan of the province of Achaia, had presided over a discussion held between two opposing parties circa. 372. Both sides ostensibly professed agreement with the Nicene creed, but whereas one regarded Christ as the greatest of the saints, a personal instrument of the Logos, who indwelt the man Jesus, the other party stressed the 'divine status' of Christ to such an extent they believed his body was not earthly but heavenly, even consubstantial with his deity. The clash of these opposing opinions represented a first draft, as it were, of the argument that was later to be exemplified in the extremes of Diodore and Nestorius on the one hand, and Apollinaris and Eutyches on the other. Athanasius sets out a doctrine which corrects both positions. Leo the Great, in 452 (Ep.109.), said of the letter: 'He asserted the incarnation so lucidly and carefully that in the heretics of his own time he had already defeated Nestorius and Eutyches.'

[3] lit. Thesei.

[4] It was a doctrine that was later credited to Apollinaris, and indeed this letter became a standard patristic anti-Apollinarist treatise, although the main element of Apollinarist doctrine (the lack of mind or soul in Christ) is noticeably missing from the exposition.

essence of Wisdom? And how is it that so-called christians[5] have dared even to doubt whether the Lord who came forth from Mary is Son of God in essence and nature, and according to the flesh is of the seed of David and the flesh of Saint Mary? Who are they who have become so reckless as to say that the Christ who suffered in flesh and was crucified is not Lord, and Saviour, and God, and Son of the Father? How can people still want to be called christians when they say that the Word came into a holy man as into one of the prophets, but that he was not himself made man[6] as if he took his body from Mary, and [teach] instead that the Christ was one, but the Word of God (Son of the Father before all ages, and before Mary) was another?

3. These opinions were stated in your minutes; differently expressed, it is true, but with one intent, and having the same meaning, impious in its tendency. On account of these opinions, dispute and discussion were going on between men who take pride in the confession that the Fathers made at Nicaea. I am surprised that Your Piety endured it, and did not silence the people who said these things, and propound to them the true religious faith; so that they might either listen and be quiet, or contradict it and be deemed heretics. For christians would never utter or listen to such opinions as these, for they are altogether alien to apostolic doctrine. This is why I have caused the statements of these men, as they have already been quoted, to be inserted in my letter, simply as they stand, so that anyone who merely hears them will see their disgraceful and wicked character. Although, perhaps, I should have refuted them at greater length, and thoroughly exposed the folly of those who have entertained such notions, yet now my letter has reached this point it might be better to write no more; for one should not elaborate and scrutinise opinions which have so clearly been shown to be bad, in case contentious people still regard them as open to question. I will give such views no other reply than this: It is enough that this is not the language of the catholic church, nor were the Fathers of this mind. Nonetheless, in case the inventors of evil things should take advantage of such an absolute silence as a warrant for further audacity, it might be a good thing to mention a few points taken from the divine scriptures. Perhaps in this way

[5] This passage was read out in the First Session of the Council of Ephesus. Cyril quotes it in his Apology Against the Orientals, Pusey LFC 47,(1881) p. 274

[6] cf. Cyril, De Recta Fide, 6. Pusey (1877) p. 16; ibid. 23, p. 74; ibid. 26, p. 84.

they can be confounded and might cease holding these vile notions.

4. How did it ever cross your minds, you people, to say that the body was co-essential with the Godhead of the Word? This is the best place to start, for when this point is proved false, so will all the others. Well, it is impossible to discover any foundation for such a statement in the divine scriptures, for they say that God became present in a human body. Furthermore, the Fathers who met at Nicaea said that the Son himself, not the body, was co-essential with the Father, and they confessed that he was 'of the essence of the Father', but that the body, on the other hand, was from Mary, in accordance with the scriptures. In that case either disown the Nicene Council and assert the things you do in the manner of the heretics, or if you mean to be children of the fathers do not hold opinions contrary to the statements they wrote down. You can also perceive the absurdity of your position from the following argument: if the Word is co-essential with the body, a thing that has its nature from the earth, and the Word is also co-essential with the Father himself, as the Fathers tell us, then the Father himself must be co-essential with the body which was derived from the earth. But then why do you go on censuring the Arians for calling the Son a creature, when you yourselves have called the Father co-essential with the creatures? and passing on to a different form of wickedness have argued that the Word has been converted into flesh, and bone, and hair, and sinews, and an entire body, and has been altered from his own nature? It is time for you to admit plainly that he was born from earth; for from earth comes the nature of the bones and of the whole body. So what is the point of this wild extravagance which even drives you into self-contradiction? for while you call the Word co-essential with the body you indicate a comparison of the one with the other; but when you say that the Word was converted into flesh, you imagine a change of the Word himself.[7] Who will bear to listen to you any longer, even when you only talk of such things? For you have gone astray into impiety more thoroughly than any other heresy has done. If the Word was co-essential with the body then it is superfluous to make mention of Mary or of [God's] use of her as an instrument; because such an eternal body would be able to exist even before Mary, according to you, like the Word himself since he is co-essential with the body. But then what need was there for the Word to dwell among us, either

[7] cf. Cyril's 2nd Letter to Nestorius; De Recta Fide, 10.9, Pusey (1877) p. 28.

to put on what is co-essential with himself, or to be changed from his own nature and become body? For the Godhead does not 'take hold' of itself (*Heb.2.16*), so that it should put on what is co-essential with itself; neither did the Word who redeems the sins of others commit sin, so that, being changed into body, he might offer up himself for himself as a sacrifice, and redeem himself.

5. It is not like this at all. God forbid. No, 'He took to himself the seed of Abraham,' as the Apostle said, 'and thus was made like his brethren in all things' (*Heb.2.17*), and received a body like our own. This was why Mary was necessary, that he might receive this body from her, and offer it up as his own for us. Isaiah prophetically pointed her out when he said: 'Behold the Virgin' (*Is.7.14*), and Gabriel was sent to her not simply as a virgin, but as a 'virgin betrothed to a man' (*Lk.1.27*), so that by the mention of the man who betrothed her he might demonstrate that Mary was a real human being. This is why scripture mentions her giving birth, and says 'She wrapped him in swaddling bands' (*Lk.2.7*), and that the breasts which he sucked were called blessed (*Lk.11.27*), and that a sacrifice was offered because he who was born had 'opened the womb' (*Lk.2.23*). Now all these things were indications of a virgin giving birth to a child. Gabriel announced the good news to her in very careful language, saying not simply 'that which shall be born in you', but 'born from you', so that there might be no hint of a body introduced into her from outside, rather that men might believe the body was naturally born from her. Nature itself plainly indicates to us that it was impossible for a virgin to have milk unless she had given birth to a child, and impossible for a body to be nourished by milk and wrapped in swaddling bands, unless it had been naturally born. This is the body that was circumcised on the eighth day, the one which Symeon took into his arms, the one that became a boy, and grew up, and reached its thirtieth year. For it was not the case, as some have imagined, that the very essence of the Word was changed so as to be circumcised, for it is immutable and unchangeable, as the Saviour himself says: 'Behold I am and I change not',[8] and as Paul writes, 'Jesus Christ, the same yesterday, and today, and forever' (*Heb.13.8*). No, it was the impassible and incorporeal Word of God who dwelt within that body which was circumcised, carried about, which ate and drank, and laboured,

[8] A mixed allusion to Mal.3.6 and Lk.24.39. For Athanasius it was the Logos who spoke in the prophets even before the incarnation.

and was nailed to the cross, and suffered. It was this body which was laid in the tomb when he 'went to preach to the spirits in prison' (*1 Pet.3.19*), as Peter said, [even though he was not separated from it].[9]

6. Moreover this will give a complete proof of the folly of those who say that the Word was changed into bones and flesh. For if such were the case, there would have been no need of any tomb; for the body would have gone by its own power to preach to the spirits in Hades. As it was, while he himself went to preach, the body was wrapped by Joseph in linen and laid in Golgotha. This makes it clear to all that the body was not the Word, but rather the Word's body. And it was this body which, after it had risen from the dead, Thomas handled[10] and saw in it the marks of the nails which the Word himself endured when he saw them fixed into his own body, and did not prevent them even though he could have done so, but appropriated[11] to himself what belonged to the body, as belonging to himself, the incorporeal Word. So, when the body was struck by the guard he said, 'Why did you strike me?' (*Jn.18.22*), as himself the one who suffered; and even though the Word was by nature intangible, still he said, 'I gave my back to the scourges, and my cheeks to the blows, and I did not turn my face away from shameful spitting' (*Is.50.6*). For the Word was present with the human body, and what it suffered he referred to himself so that we might be made able to partake of the Godhead of the Word. It was a marvel that he was the one suffering, yet not suffering:[12] suffering in so far as the body which was his very own suffered, yet not suffering in so far as the Word, being God by nature, is impassible. The Incorporeal One himself was present in the passible body, and the body had in itself the impassible Word, who all the time was abolishing the infirmities of the body itself. This he was doing, and this is how it came about, so that he might take what was ours[13] and offer it up in sacrifice so as to abolish it and in return clothe us with what was his. This is why the Apostle said, 'This corruptibility must put on incorruption,

---

[9] The last phrase is probably a later gloss.

[10] Cyril, De Recta Fide, 42, Pusey (1877) p. 144.

[11] A favourite word of both Athanasius and Cyril after him to describe the manner of the incarnation: idiopoieito. Cf. Athanasius, Con. Arianos 3.33; Cyril, 2nd Letter to Nestorius, paras. 4,7; Apol. Adv. Orientales,12.

[12] The source of Cyril's, 'He suffered impassibly': apathōs epathen.

[13] i.e. mortality and corruptibility.

and this mortality must put on immortality' (*1 Cor.15.53*).

7. This did not take place merely notionally as some have thought, God forbid! For when the Saviour really and in truth became man, salvation was effected for the whole of man. If, as they say, the Word was only in the body notionally, and this 'notion' is said to be a phantasm, then the so-called salvation and resurrection of men will also be found to have taken place merely in semblance, something the wicked Manicheans[14] thought to be the case. But our salvation is no imaginary thing; nor is it the body only, but in reality the whole man, both body and soul, which has attained to salvation in the Word himself. So then, that which was derived from Mary was by nature human, according to the divine scriptures, and the body of the Lord was real, and was real because it was the same as our own, for Mary was our sister, since we are all from Adam. No one can doubt this who keeps in mind what Luke wrote. For after he rose again from the dead some thought that they were not seeing the Lord in the body derived from Mary, but were looking at a spirit instead, and so he said to them, 'See from my hands and my feet, and the marks of the nails, that it is I myself. Touch me and see, for a spirit does not have flesh and bones as you see that I have. And when he had said this he showed them his hands and feet' (*Lk.24.39–40*). This also refutes those who have dared to say that the Lord was changed into flesh and bones, for he did not say, 'See me who am flesh and bones' but, 'See me who has flesh and bones'; this was so we would not think the Word himself was converted into such things, but might believe that he possessed them, both before his death and after his resurrection.

8. Having demonstrated these points, it is superfluous to touch on the other matters or mention them at all; since the body the Word indwelt was not co-essential with the Godhead but truly born of Mary, and the Word himself was not converted into flesh and bones. This is what John meant by his saying, 'The Word became flesh' (*Jn.1.14*), as can be ascertained from similar statements, such as that written by Paul: 'Christ became a curse for us' (*Gal.3.13*). He did not himself become a curse, but he is said to have become a curse because he took the curse on himself for our sakes. Likewise he became flesh not by being changed into flesh, but because he assumed living flesh

---

[14] The Manicheans stand here for all forms of Docetism: the mere appearance of bodily reality in the incarnation.

for our sake, and so became man. To say,'The Word became flesh' is just the same as saying, 'The Word became man', as in the text of Joel, 'I will pour out my spirit upon all flesh' (*Joel.2.28*). This promise did not extend to the irrational animals, but was addressed to men, for whose sake also the Lord became man. Since this is the meaning of the expression, then all those who have thought that the flesh which came from Mary pre-existed her, or that before her the Word had a kind of human soul, and had always existed in it before he came to dwell in the world, are rightly condemned. And those who have said that the flesh was incapable of death and had an immortal nature will also be silenced. For if he did not die how was it that Paul passed on to the Corinthians what he also received namely, 'that Christ died for our sins, in accordance with the scriptures' (*1 Cor.15.3*). How could he possibly rise again unless he had died? Even those who have entertained the thought that if the body is said to be from Mary then a Quaternity replaces the Trinity, will be put to confusion. Such people have argued that 'if we call the body co-essential with the Word then the Trinity remains a trinity because the Word does not introduce anything foreign into it; but if we say that the body which came from Mary was human, then a quaternity is necessarily substituted for a trinity on account of the addition of the body, since the body is essentially foreign to the Word who is within it.'

9. They do not realise how they contradict themselves by saying this. For even if they say that the body was not from Mary, but was itself co-essential with the Word, even so they would be convicted, on their own terms, of holding a quaternity, the very point over which they make such a hypocritical fuss to avoid being thought to have held such an opinion. The Fathers teach that the Son is not the Father himself, but is co-essential with the Father, and is called co-essential Son in relation to the Father. In just the same way a co-essential body would not be the Word himself, but distinct from the Word, and since it is distinct then even on their terms the Trinity would be a quaternity; although, of course, it is not the true and really perfect and undivided Trinity which receives an addition, only the trinity as they conceive it. But how can they still be christians if they conceive of a different God to the real God? And even in that other sophism of theirs one can discern the greatness of their folly. If they deduce that a quaternity is asserted instead of a trinity, because it is written in the scriptures that the Saviour's body was from Mary and was human (on the grounds that an addition of the body has taken place),

then they have made a serious mistake by placing a created thing on the same level as the Creator, imagining that the Godhead could ever receive addition. They obviously do not understand that the Word became flesh, not for the sake of any addition to the Godhead, but so that the flesh might rise again. Just so, it was not for the Word's own improvement that he came forth from Mary, but that he might redeem the race of men.[15] So how can they think that the body which is redeemed and vivified through the Word can make any addition to the Godhead of the Word who redeemed it? On the contrary, it was the human body which received a great addition by the Word's union and communion with it; for instead of its mortality, it has become immortal; and whereas it was animal, it has become spiritual; and whereas it came from the earth, it has passed through the doors of heaven. But the Trinity, even now that the Word has received a body from Mary, is still a trinity, receiving no addition or diminution since it is ever perfect, and in Trinity is acknowledged one Godhead, and so in the church is proclaimed one God, the Father of the Word.

10. Considering this, even those who have said that the one who came forth from Mary was not himself the Christ and Lord and God, will also be silenced from now on. For if he was not God in a body how was it that as soon as he had come forth from Mary he was called 'Emmanuel, which being translated means God-With-Us' (*Mt.1.23*)? If it was not the Word in the flesh then how did Paul write to the Romans: 'Of whom is Christ according to the flesh, who is God over all, blessed for ever, Amen' (*Rom.9.5*)? So let those who have denied that the Crucified One is God, acknowledge their error, and yield to the divine scriptures, and especially to Thomas who cried out, 'My Lord and my God' (*Jn.20.28*), after seeing the marks of the nails in him. The Son who is God, and Lord of Glory (*1 Cor.2.8*), was in that body which was ignominiously pierced with nails and treated with dishonour; and the body truly suffered when it was pierced on the cross, and from its side flowed blood and water; yet since it was the Temple of the Word it continued to be filled with the Godhead. This was why the Sun withdrew its radiance and darkened the earth when it saw its creator enduring this in the body which was being outraged; and the body itself, although it had a mortal nature, transcended its own nature by rising again, because of the Word present

[15] Cyril sustains this point that everything within the incarnation was done 'as an economy' of salvation: (kat' oikonomian).

in it; and its natural tendency to corruptibility was arrested for once it had put on the super-human Word it became incorruptible.

11. As for those who imagine that the Word came to a certain man born of Mary in the way he came to each of the prophets, it is pointless examining this, for their wild notion carries its own refutation on its face. For if this was the way he came why was this man born of a virgin rather than being born from a man and a woman as all the other saints have been born? If this was the way the Word came then why is the death of every saint not said to have taken place 'for us', but only the death of this man? And if the Word dwelt with all the prophets why is it said in regard to Mary's son alone that he dwelt 'once only at the completion of the ages' (*Heb.9.26*)? If he came as he did in the saints of former times why was it that all those others did not rise again after death? Why was it Mary's son alone that rose again on the third day? If the Word came just as he did in all the rest why is it that Mary's son alone is called Emmanuel, in so far as she gave birth to a body filled with Godhead? For Emmanuel signifies 'God-with-us'. If this was how he came why is he spoken of as eating, and drinking, and labouring, and dying only in the case of Mary's son, and not in every saint who ate, and drank, and laboured, and died? All that his body suffered is spoken of as if he himself suffered it.[16] In the case of all the others it is said simply that they were born and died, but of Mary's son only is it said that, 'The Word became flesh' (*Jn.1.14*).

12. And so, it appears that to all the others the Word came in order that they should prophesy; but from Mary the Word himself took flesh and came forth as man, being in his nature and essence the Word of God, but according to the flesh made man, as Paul said, from the seed of David and the flesh of Mary (*Rom.1.3*). This is the one the Father made manifest when he said at the Jordan and on the mountain, 'This is my beloved Son, in whom I am well-pleased' (*Mt.3.17; 17.5*). This is the one the Arians have denied, but we recognise and worship, not dividing the Son and the Word, but knowing that the Word himself is the Son, through whom all things were made, and we were redeemed. This was why it surprised us how any controversy could have arisen among you over things so obvious. But thanks to the Lord, just as we had been pained by reading through your minutes, so were we delighted when we came to their conclusion.

---

[16] The doctrine of the exchange of properties (antidosis idiomatum).

For the parties separated in agreement with each other, and were at peace in the confession of the pious and orthodox faith. It is this fact which has persuaded me, having pondered the matter at length, to write this short letter; for I took into account that possibly my silence might cause pain instead of joy to those who by their agreement had given us cause for rejoicing.

And so, I beg Your Piety in the first instance, and the hearers in the second, to accept this letter in good part, and if there is anything in it which is defective as to true religion, to correct it and to inform me. And if what I have written is not apposite to the subject, or is imperfect as from a man 'unskilled in speech' (*2 Cor.11.6*), I pray that all will excuse my clumsiness in the forms of discourse.

Salute all the brethren who are with you. All those who are with us salute you. May you live in health in the Lord, beloved and truly longed-for.

APPENDIX 2

St. Gregory Nazianzen's Letter To Cledonius[1]

Gregory, to our most reverend and God-beloved brother and fellow-presbyter Cledonius.[2] Greetings in the Lord.

I would like to know what is this fashion of innovation in things concerning the church which allows anyone who likes, even the passer-by, to 'tear apart the flock' (*Ps.79.14.*) that has been well led, and to plunder it by larcenous attacks, or rather by piratical and fallacious teachings. For if our present assailants had any ground for condemning us in regard to the faith, even so it would not have been right for them to have ventured on such a course without giving us notice. They should rather have first persuaded us, or have been willing to be persuaded by us (if at least any account is to be taken of us as God-fearers, who have laboured for the faith, and brought advantage to the church), and only then (if at all) to have made innovations; for then perhaps there would be an excuse for their outrageous conduct. But since our faith has been proclaimed, both in writing and apart from writing, here and in distant parts, in times of danger and in times of safety, then how is it that some people are making such attempts, while others keep silence?

The worst of it is not that these men instil their own heresy into simpler souls by means of those who do even worse things (although this too is shocking), but that they also tell lies about us and say that we share their opinions and sentiments. This is how they bait their

---

[1] Ep. 101. PG 37. 176–193. This version is, with a few stylistic amendments, replacement of omitted or paraphrased passages, and corrections where recourse to the Greek text clarified the obscurities of the Victorian language, substantially the translation of Browne and Swallow (St. Gregory Nazianzen: Select Orations and Letters. Nicene and Post Nicene Fathers, series II, vol.7, London, 1894).

[2] Cledonius was the priest in charge of the church at Nazianzus after Gregory had given up the charge, and before the consecration of Bishop Eulalius. The letter is dated 383–384. Gregory had left the area to seek a Spa cure and heard from Cledonius that Apollinarist dissidents had targeted his church in his absence. This local problem stimulated him to write what subsequently became (along with Athanasius' Letter to Epictetus) a classic patristic refutation of the Apollinarist christology. Cyril's use of the text is quite evident at several key points.

hooks, and by this subterfuge maliciously achieve their desired ends; for they have made our simplicity (which looked on them as brothers not as foes) into a support of their wickedness. Not only this, but they also assert, as I am told, that they have been received by the Western Synod, at which they were formerly condemned, as is well known to everyone. If, however, those who hold the views of Apollinaris have either now or formerly been received back, then let them prove it and we will be content. For it is evident that they can only have been received if they gave their assent to the orthodox faith; it would be impossible on any other terms. They could surely be able to prove such a thing by the minutes of the synod, or by letters of communion, for this is the regular synodical procedure. But if this is all talk, their own invention, devised for the sake of appearances, and to give them credibility with the masses by advancing such references, then tell them to hold their tongues, and refute them; for we believe that such a task is well suited to someone of your personal ability and orthodoxy.

Do not let them deceive themselves or other people with the assertion that the 'Lordly Man', as they call him (who is rather our Lord and God), is devoid of a human mind. For we do not sever the man from the Godhead, but we teach that He is one and the same who formerly was not man, but God and only Son, eternal, unmingled with body or anything corporeal, who in these last days has even assumed manhood for our salvation; passible in His flesh, impassible in His Godhead; circumscribed in the body, uncircumscribed in the Spirit; the selfsame earthly and heavenly, tangible and intangible, comprehensible and incomprehensible, to this end that in the selfsame who was entire man and also God, entire humanity which had fallen through sin might be created anew.

If anyone does not believe that Saint Mary is the Mother of God (Theotokos) he is severed from the Godhead. If anyone should assert that He only passed through the Virgin as through a channel, and was not at once divinely and humanly formed in her (divinely because without the intervention of a man; humanly because in accordance with the laws of gestation), then he is equally godless. If anyone should assert that the manhood was formed and was afterwards clothed with the Godhead, then he too is to be condemned. For this would not be a generation of God but a flight from generation. If anyone introduces the notion of Two Sons, one of God the Father, the other of the mother, and discredits the unity and identity, may he lose his part in the adoption promised to those who believe aright. For God and

Man are two natures, as also soul and body are; but there are not two sons or two gods; nor are there two men here, even though Paul talks this way about the 'inner man' and the 'outer man'. If I must state it briefly: there is one thing and another thing from out of which is the Saviour (for the invisible is not the same as the visible, and the timeless is not the same as the time-bound), but there is not one [person] alongside another [person].[3] God forbid! For both things are made one by the mixture,[4] for God is made man, and man is made god; or however else one can put it.[5] And when I speak of 'one thing and another thing' it is the reverse of what is the case in the Trinity; for there we acknowledge different [persons] so as not to confuse the hypostases, although there are not different things here, for the three are one and the same in Godhead.[6]

If anyone should say that [the divine power] was operative in Him by grace as in the case of a prophet, but was not and is not united to Him essentially, then let such a one be empty of the higher powers, or rather full of the opposite.[7] If anyone will not worship the crucified one let him be anathema, and be numbered with the deicides. If anyone asserts that He was made perfect by works, or that after His baptism, or after His resurrection from the dead, He was counted worthy of an adoptive sonship, like those whom the Greeks reckon as added to the ranks of the gods, then let him be anathema. For that which has a beginning or progress or is made perfect is not God, although the expression may be used of His gradual manifestation.[8] If anyone should assert that He has now divested himself of His holy flesh and that the Godhead is stripped of the body, or should deny that He is now with His body and will come again with it, then let such a man not see the glory of His coming. For where is His body

[3] (Allo kai allo ouk allos kai allos): two elements one subject in Christ.

[4] Synkrasis.

[5] The incarnation of God is the deification of man: in particular in Christ, but by implication generically for the race; thus incarnational theology, for Gregory, is soteriological throughout. This is his fundamental argument against the Apollinarists.

[6] In trinitarian theology there is plurality of person and singularity of nature; in christology there is the reverse—singularity of person and plurality of nature.

[7] i.e. If anyone maintains a christology based on grace (Christ as a specially graced man) rather than on nature (Christ as God himself) then such a person not only has no grace (to inform his theology) but has proved himself demonic in intent. Gregory is radically attacking the Antiochene tradition.

[8] i.e. It is not permissible to speak of the advancement of a man to heavenly glory; orthodox theology uses 'advancement language' (as manifested in the scriptures for example) only in reference to the earthly economy of the saviour where he gradually revealed his divine power in the unfolding stages of his human life.

now, except with the one who assumed it? For it was not laid by in the Sun, according to the babble of the Manicheans, as if it would be honoured by dishonour;[9] nor was it poured forth into the air and dissolved, as is the nature of a voice or the flow of an odour, or the course of a lightning flash that never endures. If such were the case how could He have been be touched after the resurrection, or afterwards seen by those that pierced Him, since Godhead is invisible by nature? On the contrary, He will come again with His body, as I have learned, in such form as He was seen by His disciples on the mountain,[10] as He showed Himself for that moment when His deity overpowered His carnality. And just as we say this to disarm suspicion, so we write this other point so as to correct a novel teaching. If anyone should assert that His flesh came down from heaven instead of being from here, or that it is not of us even though above us, then let him be anathema. For the words, 'The second man is the Lord from heaven and, as is the heavenly, such are they that are heavenly'; and also, 'No man has ever ascended into heaven except He who came down from heaven, the Son of Man who is in heaven',[11] and other such texts, are to be understood as referring to the union with the heavenly. In the same way the texts, 'All things were made by Christ', and 'Christ dwells in your hearts',[12] do not refer to that nature of God which can be perceived but to that which can be intuited, for their names are mingled like the natures,[13] and flow into[14] one another by virtue of their natural union.[15]

Anyone who has put his trust in Him as a man without a human mind, must be mindless himself, and quite unworthy of salvation. For what He has not assumed He has not healed; but that which is united to His Godhead is also saved. If only half of Adam had fallen then that which Christ assumes and heals might only be half as well; but if the whole of Adam's nature fell then it must be united to the whole nature of the Begotten One, and so be saved as a whole. So let them

---

[9] i.e. Misguided attempts to honour the divine status of Christ by an embarrassed and negative attitude to the body he assumed (trying to 'get rid of' the body as soon as possible) do no honour at all to the Godhead who himself wished to assume that body for the cause of salvation.

[10] Of Transfiguration.

[11] 1 Cor. 15.47–48; Jn.3.13.

[12] Jn.1.3; Eph. 3.17.

[13] The doctrine which later was designated as the exchange of properties.

[14] lit. Have a [mutual] perichoresis.

[15] lit. by the system of their organic growth together: symphyia.

not begrudge our complete salvation, or clothe the Saviour only with bones and nerves and the mere depiction of humanity. Even the Arians would say that His manhood was devoid of soul in order to attribute passion to the Godhead, since that which moves the body is also the principle of suffering. But if He has a soul and yet is without a mind—then how can He be a man at all, since man is not a mindless animal? Such an opinion would necessarily imply that while His form and tabernacle were human, His soul would have been that of a horse or an ox or some other of the mindless creation. In that case, it would have been this that He saved, and I would have been deceived by Truth Himself. It would be a case of one person being honoured, and someone else boasting about it. But if His manhood was a spiritual intellect endowed with mind then let them stop being so mindless.

One might say, moreover, that if the Godhead took the place of the human intellect then how does it affect me? For Godhead joined to flesh alone is not man, nor to soul alone, nor to both of them apart from intellect, for this is the most essential part of man. So keep the whole man and mingle[16] Godhead with it, so that you may benefit me in my completeness. And yet they argue that He could not contain two perfect [natures]. This is true if you only look at Him in a material fashion. For a bushel measure will not hold two bushels, nor will the space of one body hold two or more bodies. But if you look instead at what is intellectual and incorporeal, remember that I, in my single personality, can contain soul, reason, mind, and the Holy Spirit; and before me, this world (by which I mean the system of things visible and invisible) contained Father, Son and Holy Spirit. For such is the nature of intellectual existences that they can mingle[17] with one another and with bodies, incorporeally and invisibly. For many sounds are comprehended by one ear; and the eyes of many are occupied by the same visible objects, and the sense of smell by several odours; nor are the senses narrowed by each other, or crowded out, nor are the objects of sense diminished by the multitude of the perceptions. But where is there a mind of man or angel so perfect in comparison with the Godhead that the presence of the greater must crowd out the other?[18]

---

[16] lit. Mix in: (mixis).

[17] lit. mignysthai.

[18] In other words Apollinaris' argument that Christ cannot unite two complete realities (humanity and divinity) fails to convince because it presupposes that the

A single sunbeam seems nothing in the face of the Sun, and dampness seems a very little thing in comparison to a river; but why should we have to remove the smaller thing before we can give room to the greater and more perfect—as if we had to take away radiance from our house, or moisture from the earth [before we could appreciate the sun or a river]? But how can one thing contain two complete realities, whether it is a matter of a house containing both the sunbeam and the sun, or the earth containing both dampness and rivers? This is a matter for investigation for the question is indeed worth considering. Do they not know that what is perfect by comparison with one thing, may be imperfect by comparison with another, as a hill compared with a mountain, or a grain of mustard seed compared with a bean or any other of the larger seeds, even though it may be called larger than any of its own kind? Or, if you like, take the case of an angel compared with God, or a man compared with an angel. In the same way our mind is perfect and commanding, but only in respect to our soul and body, not absolutely perfect. It is a servant and subject of God, not a sharer of his princedom and honour. So was Moses a god to Pharoah, yet a servant of God, as it is written (*Ex.7.1; Num.12.7*); and the stars which illumine the night are hidden by the sun so much that you would not even know of their existence by daylight; and a little torch brought close to a great blaze is neither destroyed, nor is it seen, nor is it extinguished; but it is all one blaze, the greater prevailing over the other.

But, perhaps someone might argue, our mind is subject to condemnation.[19] What then of our flesh? Is that not subject to condemnation as well? You must, therefore, either set aside the latter on account of sin, or admit the former on account of salvation. If He assumed the worse part that He might sanctify it by His incarnation, is He not able to assume the better part that it might be sanctified by His becoming man? If the clay was leavened and has become a new lump,[20] you wise men, shall not the image be leavened and mingled with God, being deified by His Godhead? I will add this also: if it was the case that the mind was utterly rejected as being prone to sin and subject to damnation, and for this reason He assumed a body

two things are comparable material objects. Gregory refuses to describe divinity in these terms.

[19] And thus the Word of God would not adopt a defiled reality.

[20] A strangely mixed metaphor induced by Gregory's combination of 1 Cor.5.7 and Mt.13.33/Lk. 13.21.

but left out the mind, then there is an excuse given for those who sin with the mind; for according to you even God has acknowledged the impossibility of healing the mind. Let me state the implications of all this. You, my good sir, dishonour my mind. If you call me a 'man-worshipper', then I call you a 'flesh-worshipper'.[21] You do so in order to tie God down to the flesh having no other way to do so, and thus you take away the wall of partition (*Eph.2.14*). Now, what is my theory, though I am an ignorant man and no philosopher? I say that mind is mingled with mind, as being nearer and more closely related, and through this medium [mingled] with the flesh too, since it is a mediator between God and carnality.

What is more, let us see how they account for the assumption of manhood, or the assumption of flesh as they call it. If it was in order that God, who is otherwise incomprehensible, might be comprehended and might converse with men through his flesh, as through a veil, then this theatrical presentation and drama they have staged is pretty enough; not to say that it was open to Him to converse with us in other ways, as of old in the burning bush or in the appearance of a man (*Ex.3.2; Gen 18.2*). But if it was in order that he should destroy the condemnation by sanctifying like by like, then just as he needed flesh for the sake of the flesh which had incurred condemnation, and soul for the sake of our soul, so He needed mind for the sake of mind, for not only had it fallen in Adam, but it was the first to be affected, as the doctors say of illnesses. For that which received the commandment was that which failed to keep the commandment, and that which failed to keep it was that also which dared to transgress; and that which transgressed was that which stood most in need of salvation; and that which needed salvation was that which He took upon Himself. Thus a mind was assumed.

This has now been demonstrated, whether they like it or not, by 'geometrical' and 'necessary' proofs, to use their own jargon. What is happening here is like a man who has injured his eye, and because of this has then hurt his foot; you cannot attend to the foot and neglect the eye. Or it is like a painter who has made a bad drawing; you cannot alter the picture while pretending to the artist that he has

[21] The Apollinarists argued that if the flesh of Christ was ensouled then it had to have a separate personality—a man alongside God the Word; and thus their opponents were illegitimately worshipping a man (the human Jesus) as God. Gregory denies the syllogism by reversing it.

done well. If these arguments overwhelm them so that they take refuge in the proposition that it is possible for God to save man even apart from the mind, then I suppose that it would be possible for him to do so, even apart from the flesh, by a mere act of will, just as he works all other things, and has achieved them without a body. But on those grounds take away the flesh and the mind together so that your monstrous folly may be complete. But they have been deceived by the letter, and therefore they run to the flesh because they do not know the custom of scripture.[22] We will teach them this too. For what need is there even to mention, to those who know it, the fact that everywhere in scripture He is called 'man' and 'the Son of Man'?

If, however, they rely on the passage, 'The Word was made flesh and dwelt among us' (*Jn.1.14*), and because of this they erase the noblest part of man (as cobblers do the thicker part of skins), in order to fasten together God and the flesh, then it is time for them to admit that God is God only of the flesh and not of souls, because it is written, 'As you have given him power over all flesh' (*Jn.17.2*), and, 'To you all flesh shall come' (*Ps.64.3.*), and, 'Let all flesh bless your holy name' (*Ps.144.21*), which means 'every man'. Or again, they must suppose that our fathers went down into Egypt invisible and without bodies, and that only the soul of Joseph was imprisoned by the Pharoah because it is written, 'They went down into Egypt as seventy five souls' (*Acts 7.14*), and, 'His soul was put in irons' (*Ps. 104.18*), a thing which could never actually be manacled. People who argue in this way do not realise that such expressions are used by synecdoche, that is declaring the whole by the part, as when scripture says that young ravens call upon God, to indicate the whole of the feathered race; or when Pleiades, Hesperus, and Arcturus are mentioned, instead of all the stars and His providence over them (*Ps.148.3; Job 9.9*).

Indeed, in no other way could the love of God towards us be so manifested than by the way he remembered our flesh, and for our sake descended even to our lowest part. For everyone who has a spark of sense will acknowledge that flesh is less precious than soul. This is why the passage, 'The Word was made flesh', seems to me to be equivalent to that in which it is said that he was made sin, or made a curse for us (*2 Cor. 5.21; Gal.3.13*); not that the Lord was transformed

---

[22] The following biblical examples in Gregory's text are a systematic mockery of his opponents excessive literalism in biblical interpretation. He argues that it is the wrong theological method of the Apollinarists which has led them to their wrong conclusions about Christ.

into either of these things (how could he be?) but because by taking them upon Himself He took away our sins and bore our iniquities (*Is.53.4–5 LXX*). This, then, is enough to say at the present time for the sake of clearness, and of being understood by the multitude. I write this with no desire to compose a treatise, but only to check the progress of deceit; and if it is thought a good idea, I will give a fuller and more substantial account of these matters later.

But there is a matter which is more serious still, a special point which I ought not to pass over. I wish they were 'cut off' (*Gal.5.12*) who trouble you by introducing another circumcision, a second Judaism, and a renewed system of sacrifices.[23] For if this were to happen what would hinder Christ being born again to set them all aside once more, and again being betrayed by Judas, and crucified and buried, and rising again, that all may be fulfilled in the same order, like the Greek system of cycles in which the same revolutions of the stars bring round the same events? Let these sophists, who glory in the multitude of their books, tell us how they decide which events are to reoccur and which are to be omitted.

They have even been so inflated with their opinion on the Trinity, as to have falsely accused us of being unsound in the faith, and have led astray the crowds, so it is necessary that people should know that although Apollinaris granted the name of Godhead to the Holy Spirit, he did not preserve the power of the Godhead. For to make the Trinity consist of great, greater, and greatest, as of light, ray, and sun, that is the Spirit, the Son, and the Father (as is clearly stated in his writings), is a ladder of Godhead that does not lead us up into heaven, but carries us down away from heaven. We recognise God the Father and the Son and the Holy Spirit, and these not as mere titles dividing inequalities of rank or of power, but as there is one and the same title, so there is one nature and one substance and one power in the Godhead.

But if anyone who thinks we have spoken rightly on this subject reproaches us with holding communion with heretics, then let him prove that we are open to this charge, and we will either convince him or retire. But it is not safe to make any innovation before judgement is given, especially in a matter of such importance, and connected with issues so great. We have protested, and continue to protest this

[23] Apollinaris apparently taught that the Millenium would include the material restoration of Jerusalem (Basil, Epp.263, 265).

before God and men. And know this, that we would not have written even this letter if we had not seen the church being torn asunder and divided, among their other tricks, by their present synagogue of vanity (*Ps.25.5 LXX*). In response to us saying and maintaining these things, if anyone should reject us as unworthy of credit, either because he might thus gain some personal advantage, or through fear of men, or monstrous littleness of mind, or through some neglect of pastors and governors, or through love of novelty and proneness to innovations, and should attach himself to these people, so dividing the noble body of the church, then such a man will bear his judgement, whoever he may be, and shall give account to God in the Day of Judgement. But if their long books and their new psalters (contrary to that of David), and the grace of their poetry, are taken for a third Testament, then we too will compose psalms, and will write much in verse. For we also think we have the Spirit of God, if indeed this is a gift of the Spirit, and not a human novelty.

I would like you to declare publicly that I will not be responsible for overlooking such an evil, as if this wicked doctrine were receiving sustenance and strength from our indifference.

STUDY BIBLIOGRAPHIES

EDITIONS AND TRANSLATIONS OF ST. CYRIL

A fully detailed account of Cyril's writings can be found in Clavis Patrum Graecorum vol. III. ed. M. Geerard. Turnhout. 1979. nos. 5200–5438.

Explanations of the contents of Cyril's treatises and bibliographical data (valid up to the mid-seventies) is provided in an excellent survey by Johannes Quasten, Patrology, vol.3. The Golden Age of Greek Patristic Literature, Utrecht/Antwerp, 1975, pp. 116–142.

Primary Sources

The best critical text for most of the Cyrilline literature relating to the christological controversy is that of:

E. Schwartz. Acta Conciliorum Oecumenicorum. Concilium universale Ephesinum Bk. I. vols. 1–5. Berlin/Leipzig. 1927–1930.

The collected works of Cyril were gathered together in the 17th century by J. Aubert, and in the 19th century A. Mai completed the omissions. These editions formed the basis of the collection published by:

J.P. Migne in Patrologiae Cursus Completus: Series Graeca. (PG) vols. 68–77. 1st Edn. Paris 1859 (reprint Turnhout 1991).

Subsequently P.E. Pusey published seven volumes of critical editions (and several translations) of important treatises and biblical commentaries of Cyril. These critical texts are still the best editions for many of the exegetical works. Pusey's translations, however, were often excessively literalist (following the prescripts of his father E.B. Pusey who presided over the publishing project of 'Library of Fathers of the Church.') and are of diminished usefulness today. The editions comprise:

P.E. Pusey. Sancti Patris Nostri Cyrilli archiepiscopi Alexandrini in XII Prophetas. 2 vols. Oxford. 1868.

——, S.P.N. Cyrilli arch. Al. In d. Johannis Evangelium. Accedunt fragmenta varia necnon tractatus ad Tiberium diaconum duo. 3 vols. Oxford 1872.

——, S.P.N. Cyrilli arch. Al. XII Capitum Explanatio, XII Capitum Defensio utraque, Scholia de Incarnatione Unigeniti. Oxford. 1875.

——, S.P.N. Cyrilli arch. Al. De Recta Fide ad Imperatorem, De Incarnatione Unigeniti Dialogus, De Recta Fide ad Principissas, De Recta Fide ad Augustas, Quod Unus sit Christus Dialogus, Apologeticus ad Imperatorem, Oxford. 1877.

Syriac Fragments:

The Syriac version of Cyril's Commentary on Luke was published by:

J.B. Chabot. Corpus Scriptorum Christianorum Orientalium. vol. 70. Paris, 1912. (Latin Translation by R. Tonneau, CSCO 140, Louvain, 1953).

Other Syriac fragments can be found in the collected works of Severus of Antioch by:

J. Lebon. CSCO. 93–94, 101–102, 111–112, & 119–120.

More recently R.Y. Ebied and Lionel Wickham have edited and published new Syriac discoveries:

R.Y. Ebied & L.R. Wickham: A Collection of Unpublished Syriac Letters of Cyril of Alexandria. CSCO. vols. 359–360. Louvain. 1975.

——, The Letter of Cyril of Alexandria to Tiberius the Deacon. Syriac Version. Le Museon. 83. pp. 433–482.

——, An Unknown Letter of Cyril of Alexandria in Syriac. JTS (NS) 22, 1971, 420–443.

The most recent critical editions of Cyril's dogmatic works are those in the Sources Chrétiennes series (with a French translation and excellent introductory studies) by:

G.M. De Durand. Cyrille d'Alexandrie. Deux Dialogues Christologiques. SC, vol.97, Paris, 1964.

——, Cyrille d'Alexandrie: Dialogues sur la Trinité. SC, vols. 231,237, & 246, Paris. 1976, 1977, 1978.

P. Burguière & P. Evieux.

——, Cyrille D'Alexandrie: Contre Julien. SC, vol.322, Paris. 1985.

Some of the Ethiopic sources relating to the council of Ephesus have been edited by:

B.M. Weischer. Homilien und Briefe zum Konzil von Ephesos. Wiesbaden, 1979. (Qerellos, 4.1).

English Translations of Works by Cyril:

R Payne-Smith. A Commentary Upon the Gospel According to S. Luke by Cyril, Patriarch of Alexandria. 2 vols. Oxford, 1859.

P.E. Pusey. The Three Epistles of St. Cyril. (The Dogmatic Letters to Nestorius). Oxford. 1872.

——, The Commentary on St. John. vol.1. Library of Fathers of the Church, vol.43, Oxford, 1874.

——, That The Christ is One. Library of Fathers of the Church, vol.46, Oxford, 1881.

——, Five Books Against Nestorius; Against Diodore and Theodore; Scholia on The Incarnation. Library of Fathers of the Church, vol. 47, Oxford, 1881.

T. Randell. Commentary on John. vol.2. Library of Fathers of the Church, vol. 48, Oxford, 1885.

C.A. Heurtley. On the Faith and The Creed. Dogmatic Teaching of the Church of the Fourth and Fifth Centuries. (incl. Cyril's dogmatic letters to Nestorius). Oxford. 1886.

T.H. Bindley. The Oecumenical Documents of the Faith. (dogmatic letters to Nestorius; Ep. 39 to John of Antioch). 1st Edn. London 1899. (repr. 1906 & 1950).

F.C. Conybeare. The Armenian Version of Revelation and Cyril of Alexandria's Scholia on the Incarnation, and Epistle on Easter. (from Armenian texts). London. 1907.

J.B. Kidd. Documents Illustrative of the History of the Church. vol.2, London 1938 (reproducing Heurtley for the dogmatic letters). The 3 letters and the Letter to John of Antioch turn up in several other florilegia volumes subsequently, e.g. E.R. Hardy, The Christology of the Later Fathers. London. 1954).

A more imaginative and varied collection of Cyrilline translations (with critical Greek text) has been prepared by L.R. Wickham. This is prefaced by an excellent historical and theological introduction:

L.R. Wickham. Cyril of Alexandria: Select Letters. Oxford. 1983.

The complete Letters of Cyril (including some only extant in Coptic) have also been rendered (with varying degrees of accuracy) by:

J.I. McEnerney. St. Cyril of Alexandria: Letters. Fathers of the Church. vols. 76–77, Washington 1987.

The important treatise: 'That The Christ Is One,' one of Cyril's last and most mature christological works, is now available in modern translation from the Greek critical text:

J.A. McGuckin. St. Cyril of Alexandria: That The Christ Is One. New York, 1994.

BIBLIOGRAPHY A

GENERAL HISTORICAL AND THEOLOGICAL STUDIES

D'ÀLES A. Le Dogme d'Ephèse. Paris, 1931.

BAYNES N.H. 'Alexandria and Constantinople: A study in ecclesiastical diplomacy.' Journal of Egyptian Archaeology, 12, 1926, 145–156; reprinted in: Byzantine Studies and Other Essays, London, 1955, 97–115.

BETHUNE-BAKER. J. Introduction to the Early History of Christian Doctrine. London, 1903.

CAMELOT T. 'De Nestorius à Eutyches. L'opposition de deux christologies.' in Grillmeier-Bacht [Chalkedon] vol.1, Würzburg, 1951, 213–242.

Ephèse et Chalcédoine. Paris, 1961.

DAGRON G. 'Les moines et la ville. Le Monachisme à Constantinople jusqu'au concile de Chalcédoine 451.' Travaux et Memoires 4, 1970, 230–275. Naissance d'une Capitale. Constantinople et ses Institutions de 330 à 451. Paris. 1974.

DAVIS L.D. The First Seven Ecumenical Councils (325–787). Wilmington, Delaware. 1987.

DUCHÈSNE L. The Early History of the Christian Church. vol.3, London, 1924.

DVORNIK F. 'The Authority of the State in Oecumenical Councils.' The Christian East, 14, 1934, 95–108. Early Christian and Byzantine Political Philosophy. 2 vols. Washington D.C. 1966.

FERGUSON E. (with McHUGH M.P. & NORRIS F.W.) Encyclopedia of Early Christianity. New York & London, 1990.

FESTUGIÈRE A.J. Ephèse et Chalcédoine: Actes des Conciles. (French Translation of select texts from Schwartz), Paris, 1982.

FICKER G. Eutherius von Tyana. Ein Beitrag zur Geschichte des Epheseinischen Konzils vom Jahre 431. Leipzig. 1908.

FOSS C. Ephesus after Antiquity. A Late Antique, Byzantine, and Turkish City. Cambridge. 1979.

FREND W.H.C. 'Popular religion and christological controversy in the Fifth Century.' SCH vol.8, Cambridge 1972, 19–29. The Rise of the Monophysite Movement. Cambridge, 1979. The Rise of Christianity. Philadelphia, 1984.

GRILLMEIER A. & BACHT H. Das Konzil von Chalkedon. Geschichte und Gegenwart. 3 vols. Würzburg. 1951–1952. (Ephesus' doctrine: cf. vol.1, 160–164).

GREGORY T.E. Vox Populi. Popular opinion and violence in the religious controversies of the fifth century AD. Columbus, 1979.

HALL S.G. Doctrine and Practice in the Early Church. London, 1991. (211–222).

HEFELE C.J. Histoire des Conciles. Vol.2, pt.1. Paris, 1908.
HOLUM K.G. Theodosian Empresses: Women and Imperial Dominion in Late Antiquity. London, 1982.
JOANNOU P.P. 'La legislation imperiale et la christianisation de l'empire romain 311–476.' OCA 192, Rome, 1972.
JONES A.H.M. The Later Roman Empire. (3rd reprint) vols. 1–2, Oxford, 1986.
KELLY J.N.D. Early Christian Doctrines. (5th edn.) London-New York, 1978.
KRAATZ W. (tr.) Koptische Akten zum ephesinischen Konzil vom Jahre 431. Berlin, (T.U. 26.2).
LIÉBAERT J. L'Incarnation. vol.1, Des Origines au Concile de Chalcédoine. Paris, 1966.
LUIBHEID C. 'Theodosius II and Heresy.' JEH, 16, 1965, 13–38.
MEYENDORFF J. Christ in Eastern Christian Thought. Washington, 1969.
ORTIZ DE URBINA I. 'Il dogma di Efeso.' REB, 11, 1953, 233–240.
OTTLEY R.L. The Doctrine of the Incarnation. vol.2, London. 1896.
PELIKAN J. The Christian Tradition. vol.1. The Emergence of the Catholic Tradition (100–600). Chicago-London, 1971.
PRESTIGE G.L. God in Patristic Thought. London 1936. Fathers and Heretics. London, 1940.
QUASTEN J. Patrology. Vol.3, Utrecht-Antwerp 1975.
SAGI-BUNIC T. 'Documentatio doctrinalis Ephesino-Chalcedonensis.' Laurentianum 3, 1962, 499–514. 'Duo perfecta et duae naturae in definitione dogmatica Chalcedonensi.' Laurentianum 5, 1964 (extract). Deus perfectus et homo perfectus a concilio Ephesino ad Chalcedonense. Rome, 1965.
SCHWARTZ E. Acta Conciliorum Oecumenicorum. Berlin 1914–1940. (repr. 1959–1974).
SELLERS R.V. Two Ancient Christologies: A study in the Christological Thought of the Schools of Alexandria and Antioch in the early history of Christian Doctrine. London, 1940. The Council of Chalcedon. London, 1953.
THOMPSON E.A. 'The Foreign Policies of Theodosius II and Marcian.' Hermathena, 76, 1950, 58–75.
TIXERONT J. Histoire des Dogmes dans l'Antiquité chrétienne. vol.3, (3rd edn.) Paris, 1912.
TURNER H.E.W. Jesus The Christ. London 1976.
YOUNG F. From Nicaea to Chalcedon. London 1983.
WOLFSON H.A. The Philosophy of the Church Fathers. vol.1, Cambridge, Mass. 1956.

BIBLIOGRAPHY B

CYRILLINE STUDIES

ABD'AL-MASSIH Y. 'S. Cyrille dans la Liturgie de l'Église Copte.' in Kyrilliana, Cairo, 1947, 303–318.

ABEL F.M. 'Parallelisme exégétique entre S. Jerome et S. Cyrille d'Alexandrie.' Vivre et Penser (Paris) 1, 1941, 94–119 & 212–230. 'Cyril d'Alexandrie dans ses rapports avec la Palestine,' in Kyrilliana', Cairo, 1947, 203–230.

D'ÀLES A. 'Le symbole d'union de 433.' RSR 3, 1931, 257–268.

AUBINEAU M. 'Deux Homelies de S. Cyrille d'Alexandrie.' AB 90, 1972, 100.

BACHT H. 'Die Rolle des orientalischen Mönchtums in den kirchenpolitischen Auseinandersetzungen um Chalkedon (431–519).' pp. 193–314 in, Grillmeier-Bacht (Edd), Das Konzil vom Chalkedon, vol.2, Würzburg, 1953.

BARDY G. 'Acace de Berée et son rôle dans la controverse nestorienne.' Rev. SR 18, 1938, 20–44. 'Atticus de Constantinople et Cyrille d'Alexandrie.' Histoire de l'Église depuis les origines jusqu'à nos jours. (Ed.) A. Fliche & V. Martin, vol.4, Paris, 1937, 149–162.

BASETTI-SANI G. 'Il primato di Cristo in S. Cirillo.' in Kyrilliana, Cairo, 1947, 137–196.

BATTIFOL P. 'Les présents de Saint Cyrille à la Cour de Constantinople.' Ètudes de Liturgie et d'Archaéologie Chrétienne. Paris 1919. 'Un épisode du concile d'Ephèse (juillet 431) d'après les actes coptes de Bouriant.' in Mélanges offèrts a G. Schlümberger, vol.1, Paris, 1924, 28–39.

BAUER F.X. Proklos von Konstantinopel: Ein Beitrag zur Kirchen und Dogmengeschichte des 5 Jahrhunderts. München, 1919.

BELL H.I. 'Anti-semitism in Alexandria.' JRS 31, 1941, 1–18.

BERTHOLD G.C. 'Cyril of Alexandria and the Filioque.' Stud Pat. 19,2, Louvain 1989, 143–147.

BOLLANDUS J. Acta Sanctorum. January, vol.2. Antwerp, 1643, pp. 843–854.

BRIGHT W. 'Saint Cyril of Alexandria.' DCB, vol.1, 763–773.

BURGHARDT W.J. The Image of God in Man according to Cyril of Alexandria. Washington. 1957. 'St. Cyril of Alexandria.' New Catholic Encyclopedia, 4, 571–576, New York, 1967.

VON CAMPENHAUSEN H. The Fathers of the Greek Church (E.T.) New York 1959, London 1963, ch.12.

CAPMANI J. 'La communicacion del Espiritu Santo en la Iglesia—Cuerpo Mistico como principio de sua unidad segun San Cirilo de Alejandria.' RES 17, 1957, 173–204.

CHADWICK H. 'Eucharist and Christology in the Nestorian Controversy. JTS (NS) 2,1951, 145–164.

CHARLIER N. 'Le Thesaurus de Trinitate de S. Cyrille d'Alexandrie. RHE 45, 1950, 25–81. 'La doctrine sur le Saint Esprit dans le 'Thesaurus' de S. Cyrille d'Alexandrie. Stud Pat. II (TU. 64), Berlin, 1957, 187–193.

DEVREESSE R. 'Les actes du concile d'Ephèse.' RSPT, 18, 1929, 223–242, 408–431.

DIEPEN H.M. 'Les Douze Anathématismes au Concile d'Ephèse et jusqu'en 519.' Rev Thom. 55, 1955, 300–338. 'La christologie de S. Cyrille d'Alexandrie et l'anthropologie néo-platonicienne.' Euntes Docete 9, 1956, 20–63. 'Stratagèmes contre la théologie de l'Emmanuel. À propos d'une nouvelle comparaison entre S. Cyrille et Apollinaire.' Divinitas 1, 1957, 444–478.

DORRIE H. Hypostasis: Wort und Bedeutungsgeschichte. Göttingen, 1955.

DRAGAS G.D. St. Athanasius Contra Apollinarem. (Church and Theology vol.6) Athens, 1985.

DRATSELLAS C. Questions of the Soteriological Teaching of the Greek Fathers with special reference to St. Cyril of Alexandria. Athens 1968. Man in his Original State and in the State of Sin According to S. Cyril of Alexandria. Athens. 1971. 'Questions on Christology of St. Cyril of Alexandria.' Abba Salama, 6, 1975, 203–232.

VAN DEN DRIES J. The Formula of St. Cyril of Alexandria: Mia Physis tou Theou Logou Sesarkomene. Rome, 1939.

DRIOTON E. 'Cyrille d'Alexandrie et l'ancienne religion Égyptienne.' in Kyrilliana, Cairo, 1947, 231–246.

DUBARLE A.M. 'L'ignorance du Christ dans S. Cyrille d'Alexandrie.' Eph Th Louv. Jan-Mar, 1939, 111–120. 'Les conditions du salut avant la venue du Sauveur chez S. Cyrille d'Alexandrie.' RSPT 32, 1948, 359–362.

DUPRÉ LA TOUR A. 'La "Doxa" du Christ dans les oeuvres exégétiques de S. Cyrille d'Alexandrie.' RSR 48, 1960, 521–543; 49, 1961, 68–94.

DE DURAND G.M. Deux Dialogues Christologiques. SC. 97, Paris 1964. Dialogues sur la Trinité I–III. SC.vols. 231,237,246, Paris, 1976–1978. 'Une Lettre méconnue de S. Cyrille d'Alexandrie.' in Alexandria: Mélanges offèrts a C. Mondésert. Paris 1987, 351–363.

EBERLE A. 'Die Mariologie des hl. Cyrillus von Alexandrien.' Freiburg, 1921.

EBIED R.Y. & WICKHAM L.R. 'The Letter of Cyril of Alexandria to Tiberius the Deacon: Syriac Version.' Mus. 83, 433–482. 'An Unknown Letter of Cyril of Alexandria in Syriac.' JTS (NS) 22, 1971, 420–443. 'A Collection of Unpublished Syriac Letters of Cyril of Alexandria.' CSCO 360, Louvain, 1975.

FATICA L. I Commentari a Giovanni di Teodoro di Mopsuestia e di Cirillo d'Alessandria. Rome 1988.

FRAIGNEAU-JULIEN B. 'L'efficacité de l'humanité du Christ selon S. Cyrille d'Alexandrie.' Rev Thom. 55, 1955, 615–628. 'L'inhabitation de la sainte Trinité dans l'âme selon S. Cyrille d'Alexandrie. RSR 30, 1956, 135–156. 'Un traité anonyme de la S. Trinité attribué à S. Cyrille d'Alexandrie.' RSR 49, 1961, 188–211, 386–405.

FRANSES D. 'Cyrille au Concile d'Ephèse.' St C 7, 1931, 369–398.

GALTIER P. 'Le Centenaire d'Ephèse.' RSR 21, 1931, 169–199. 'Les anathématismes de S. Cyrille et le Concile de Chalcédoine.' RSR 23, 1933,

45–57. L'Unité du Christ. Paris 1939. 'Unité ontologique et unité psychologique dans le Christ.' BLE 41–42, 1940–41, 161–175, 216–232. 'S. Cyrille d'Alexandrie et S. Leon le Grand à Chalcédoine.' in Grillmeier/Bacht (Edd), Das Konzil von Chalkedon 1, Würzburg, 1951, 345–387. 'L'Unio secundum hypostasim chez S. Cyrille.' Gregorianum 33, 1952, 351–398. 'S. Cyrille et Apollinaire.' Gregorianum 37, 1956, 584–609.

GAUDEL A. 'Kenose.' in DTC 8, 1925,2339–2349.

GEBREMEDHIN E. Life-Giving Blessing. An Inquiry into the Eucharistic Doctrine of Cyril of Alexandria. Uppsala, 1977.

GIUDICI G. 'La dottrina della grazia nel commento ai Romani di S. Cirillo d'Alessandria.' Diss. Gregorianum, Rome, 1951.

GNOLFO G. 'Il problem pedagogico in S. Cirillo.' in Kyrilliana, Cairo, 1947, 273–294.

GRANT R.M. 'Greek Literature in the Treatise De Trinitate and Cyril's Contra Julianum.' JTS (NS) 15, 1964, 265–299.

GRILLMEIER A. Christ in Christian Tradition. vol.1, (2nd Edn.) London, 1975. 473–487.

DE GROOT J.F. 'De leer van den hl. Cyrillus van Alexandrie over de heiligmakende genade.' Theolog. Studien 31, 1913, 343–358, 501–515.

HARDY E.R. Christian Egypt: Church and People. New York, 1952. 'The further education of Cyril of Alexandria, 412–444: Questions and Problems.' Stud Pat. 17,1, 1982, 116–122.

HARING N.M. 'The character and range of influence of St. Cyril of Alexandria on Latin theology, 430–1260.' Medieval Studies, 12, 1950, 1–19.

HEBENSPERGER J.N. Die Denkwelt des hl. Cyrill von Alexandrien. Ein analyse ihres philosophischen Ertrags. Augsburg, 1927.

HEFELE C.J. (Annotated by Dom. Leclercq). Histoire des Conciles. Vol.2, Part 1. Paris, 1908, pp. 248–422.

HULSBOSCH A. 'De hypostatische vereniging volgens den Hl. Cyrillus van Alexandrie.' StC 24, 1929, 65–94.

IMHOF P. & LORENZ B. Maria Theotokos bei Cyrill von Alexandrien. München, 1981.

JANSSENS L. 'Notre filiation divine d'après S. Cyrille d'Alexandrie.' Eph Th Louv. 15, 1938, 233–278.

JOUASSARD G. 'L'activité littéraire de S. Cyrille d'Alexandrie jusqu'à 428.' in Mélanges E. Podechard, Lyons 1945, 159–174. 'Cyrill von Alexandrien.' RAC vol.3, 499–516. 'Marie à travers la Patristique: maternité divine, virginité, saintété.' in Maria: Études sur la S. Vierge (Ed. H. du Manoir) vol. 1, Paris, 1949, 69–157. 'Une intuition fondamentale de S. Cyrille d'Alexandrie en christologie dans les premières années de son episcopat. REB 11, 1953, 175–186. 'Un problème d'anthropologie et de christologie chez S. Cyrille d'Alexandrie.' RSR 43, 1955, 361–378. 'S. Cyrille d'Alexandrie et le schema de l'incarnation Verbe-Chair.' RSR 44, 1956, 234–242. 'Impassibilité du Logos et impassibilité de l'âme humaine chez Cyrille d'Alexandrie.' RSR, 45, 1957, 209–244. 'S. Cyrille d'Alexandrie aux prises avec la 'communication des idiomes' avant 428 dans ses ouvrages anti-ariens.' Stud. Pat. 6, 1962, 112–121.

JUGIE M. 'La terminologie christologique de S. Cyrille d'Alexandrie.' EO 15, 1912, 12–27.

KANNENGIESSER C. 'Athanasius of Alexandria and the foundation of traditional Christology.' Theological Studies 34, 1973, 103–113.

KERRIGAN A. S. Cyril of Alexandria: Interpreter of the Old Testament. Analecta Biblica 2, Rome, 1952. 'The Objects of the Literal and Spiritual Senses of the New Testament according to St. Cyril of Alexandria.' Stud Pat. 1 (TU 63) Berlin, 1957, 354–374.

KOEN L. The Saving Passion. Incarnational and Soteriological Thought in Cyril of Alexandria's Commentary on the Gospel According to St. John. Uppsala, 1991.

KOPALLIK J. Cyrillus von Alexandrien: eine Biographie nach den Quellen gearbeteit. Mayence 1881.

LABELLE J.M. 'S. Cyrille d'Alexandrie.' Rev SR 52, 1978, 135–158; ibid.53, 1979, 23–42.

LANGGARTNER G. 'Der descensus ad inferos in den Osterbriefen des Cyrill von Alexandrien.' in Wegzeichen: Festgabe. H. Budermann, Würzburg, 1971, 95–100.

LAVAUD B. (with H.M. Diepen). 'S. Cyrille d'Alexandrie: court traité contre ceux qui ne veulent pas reconnaitre Marie Mère de Dieu.' Rev Thom. 56, 1956, 688–712.

LEBON J. 'Alteration doctrinale de la Lettre à Epictète de S. Athanase.' RHE 31, 1935, 713–761.

LEBOURLIER J. 'Union selon hypostase: ébauche de la formule dans le premier livre pseudoathanasien Contre Apollinaire.' RSPT 44, 1960, 470–476.

LIÉBAERT J. S. Cyrille d'Alexandrie et l'Arianisme: Les sources et la doctrine Christologique du Thesaurus et des Dialogues sur La Trinité. Lille, 1948. La Doctrine Christologique de S. Cyrille d'Alexandrie avant la querelle Nestorienne. Lille, 1951. 'S. Cyrille d'Alexandrie et la culture antique.' MSR 12, 1955, 5–26. L'Incarnation: vol.1. Des Origines au Concile de Chalcédoine. Paris 1966. 'L'évolution de la christologie de S. Cyrille d'Alexandrie à partir de la controverse nestorienne. La lettre Paschale xvii et la lettre aux moines (428–429).' MSR 27, 1970, 27–48. 'Concile d'Ephèse.' DHGE vol.1, cols. 561–574.

LIETZMANN H. (Ed.) Apollinaris von Laodicea und seine Schule. Tübingen, 1904.

LOUTH A. 'Reason and Revelation in S. Athanasius.' SJT 23, 1970,385–396. 'The concept of the Soul in Athanasius CG-De Inc.' Stud Pat. 13, 1975, 227–231. 'The use of the term 'idios' in Alexandrian theology from Alexander to Cyril.' Stud Pat. 19,2, Louvain, 1989,198–202.

LYONNET S. 'S. Cyrille d'Alexandrie et 2 Cor. 3,17.' Biblica 32, (Rome) 1951, 25–33

McCOY J.D. 'Philosophical Influences on the Doctrine of the Incarnation in Athanasius and Cyril of Alexandria.' Encounter (Indianapolis) 38, 1977, 362–391.

McENERNEY J.I. St. Cyril of Alexandria: Letters. (E.T. 'Fathers of the Church', vols. 76–77), Washington 1987.

McINERNEY J.L. 'Soteriological Commonplaces in Cyril of Alexandria's Commentary on John.' in Disciplina Nostra, (Ed.) D.F. Winslow, Philadelphia, 1979, 179–185.

McGUCKIN J.A. 'Christian Asceticism and the Early School of Alexandria.' Studies in Church History, vol.22, pp. 25–39, Cambridge, 1985. The Transfiguration of Christ in Scripture and Tradition. New York, 1987. 'The Concept of Orthodoxy in Ancient Christianity.' PBR 8,1, 1989, 5–23. 'The Influence of the Isis cult on St. Cyril of Alexandria's Christology.' Studia Patristica. vol.24, Louvain, 1992, 191–199. 'Origen on the Jews.' Studies in Church History, vol.29, Cambridge, 1992, pp. 1–13. 'St. Cyril of Alexandria: That The Christ Is One.' SVS Press, New York, 1994.

MAHÉ J. 'Les Anathématismes de S. Cyrille d'Alexandrie et les évêques orientaux du patriarchat d'Antioche.' RHE 7, 1906, 505–543. 'La date du Commentaire de S. Cyrille d'Alexandrie sur l'Évangile selon S. Jean.' BLE, 8, 1907, 41–45. 'L'Eucharistie d'après S. Cyrille d'Alexandrie.' RHE 8,1907,677–696. 'La sanctification d'après S. Cyrille d'Alexandrie.' RHE 10, 1909, 30–40, 469–492. 'Cyrille d'Alexandrie.' DTC vol.3, 1911, 2476–2527.

MALLEY W.J. Hellenism and Christianity: The conflict between Hellenic and Christian Wisdom in the Contra Galilaeos of Julian the Apostate and the Contra Julianum of St. Cyril of Alexandria. Rome 1978.

DU MANOIR H. 'L'argumentation patristique dans la controverse nestorienne.' RSR 25, 1935, 441–461, 531–560. 'Le problème de Dieu chez Cyrille d'Alexandrie.' RSR 27, 1937, 385–407. 'L'Église Corps du Christ chez S. Cyrille d'Alexandrie.' Gregorianum, 19, 1939, 537–603, 83–100, 161–188. Dogme et Spiritualité chez S. Cyrille d'Alexandrie. Paris 1944.

DE MARGERIE B. 'L'exégèse christologique de S. Cyrille d'Alexandrie.' NRT 102, 1980, 400–425.

MEIJERING E.P. 'Some reflections on Cyril of Alexandria's rejection of Anthropomorphism.' in (Ibid.) God Being History. Amsterdam, Oxford, 1975, 128–132. 'Cyril of Alexandria on the Platonists and the Trinity.' in (Ibid.) God Being History, Amsterdam, Oxford, 1975, 114–127.

MELONI P. 'Il digiuno quaresimale e S. Cirillo Alessandrino.' in Kyrilliana, Cairo, 1947, 247–272.

MEYENDORFF J. ' "Eph ho" (Rom.5.12) chez Cyrille d'Alexandrie et Théodoret.' Stud Pat. 4, 1961, 157–161.

MICHAUD E. 'S. Cyrille d'Alexandrie et l'Eucharistie.' RIT 10, 1902, 599–614, 675–692.

DE M.V. MONSEGU B. 'La teologia del Espiritu Santo segun San Cirilo de Alejandria.' RES 7, 1947, 161–220. 'Unidad y Trinidad, propriedad y apropriacion en las manifestaciones trinitarias, segun la dotrina de San Cirilo Alejandrino.' RES 8, 1948, 1–57.

MUHLENBERG E. Apollinaris von Laodicea. Göttingen, 1969.

MUNIER H. 'Le lieu de la naissance de St. Cyrille d'Alexandrie.' in Kyrilliana, Cairo, 1947, 197–202.

NACKE E. Das Zeugnis der Väter in der theologischen Beweisführung Cyrills von Alexandrien nach seiner Briefen und anti-nestorianischen Schriften. Münster, 1964.

NAU F. 'St. Cyril and Nestorius.' ROC 15, 1910, 365–391; 16, 1911, 1–54.

NÉDONCELLE M. 'Prosopon et persona dans l'antiquité classique.' Rev SR 22, 1948, 277–299. (see also Richard M.)

NEYRON G. 'S. Cyrille et le Concile d'Ephèse.' in Kyrilliana, Cairo, 1947, 203–230.

NEWMAN J.H. 'On St. Cyril's formula: Mia Physis Sesarkomene.' in Tracts Theological and Ecclesiastical. London, 1874, 283–336.

NILUS A.S.B. De Maternitate divina Beatae Mariae Virginis. Nestorii et Cyrilli sententiae. Rome, 1944.

NORRIS R.A. 'Christological models in Cyril of Alexandria.' Stud Pat. 13,1975, 255–268.

PAPADOPOULOS C. 'The Festal Letters of St. Cyril of Alexandria.' (Greek Text). E Ph. 31, 1932, 25–45. St. Cyril of Alexandria (Greek text). Alexandria, 1933.

PARVIS P.M. 'The Commentary on Hebrews and the Contra Theodorum of Cyril of Alexandria.' JTS (NS) 26, 1975, 415–419.

PAYNE-SMITH R. Commentary on the Gospel of St. Luke by St. Cyril Patriarch of Alexandria. (2 vols. E.T.) Oxford, 1859.

PHILIPSBORN A. 'La compagnie d'ambulanciers 'parabalani' d'Alexandrie.' Byzantion, 20, 1950, 185–190.

PUIG DE LA BELLACASA J. 'Los doce anatematismos de S. Cirilo. Fueron aprobados por el Concilio de Efeso?' EE 11, 1932, 5–25.

RAVEN C.E. Apollinarism. Cambridge, 1923.

REGAZZONI P. 'Il Contra Galilaeos dell'Imperatore Giuliano e il Contra Julianum di S. Cirillo Alessandrino.' Didaskaleion 6, 1928, 1–114.

REHRMANN A. Die Christologie des hl. Cyrillus von Alexandrien. Hildesheim. 1902.

RICHARD M. 'Proclus de Constantinople et la théopaschisme.' RHE 38, 1942, 303–331. ' L'introduction du mot 'hypostase' dans la théologie de l'incarnation.' MSR 2,1945,5–32, 243–270. (see also M. Nédoncelle). 'Les traités de Cyrille 'Alexandrie Contre Diodore et Theodore et les fragments dogmatiques de Diodore de Tarse.' in Mélanges F. Grat, Paris, 1946, vol. 1, 99–116. 'S. Athanase et la psychologie du Christ selon les Ariens.' MSR 4, 1947, 5–54. 'Acace de Mélitène, Proclus de Constantinople et la Grande Arménie.' in Memorial L. Petit: Mélanges d'histoire et d'archéologie byzantines. Bucharest 1948. 393–412. 'Le pape Leon le Grande et les Scholia de incarnatione Unigeniti de S. Cyrille d'Alexandrie.' RSR 40, 1952, 116–128. 'Deux lettres perdues de S. Cyrille d'Alexandrie.' Stud. Pat.7, 1966, 274–277.

RIDOLFI A. 'S. Cirillo nella luce del Pontificato Romano.' in Kyrilliana, Cairo, 1947, 17–36.

DE RIEDMATTEN H. 'Some neglected aspects of Apollinarist Christology.' Dom Stud. 1, 1948, 239–260. Apollinarism and Fourth Century Christology. (Diss. Oxford) 1951. 'La christologie d'Apollinaire de Laodicée.' Stud Pat 2 (TU 64) Berlin 1957, 208–234.

ROLDANUS J. Le Christ et l'homme dans la théologie d'Athanase d'Alexandrie. Leiden 1968.

ROMANIDES J.S. 'St. Cyril's "One physis or hypostasis of God the Logos incarnate" and Chalcedon.' GOTR 10, 1964–65, 82–107.

ROUGÉ J. 'Les debuts de l'épiscopat de Cyrille d'Alexandrie et le Code Théodosien.' in Alexandria: Mélanges offerts à C. Mondésert. Paris, 1987, 339–349.

RUCKER I. Das Dogma von der Persönlichkeit Christ und das Problem der Häresie. (Studien zum Concilium Ephesinum IV), Oxenbronn, 1934. Cyrill und Nestorius im Lichte der Ephesus-Enzyklika. Oxenbronn, 1934.

SAGUES J. 'El Espiritu Santo en la sanctificacion del hombre segun la dotrina de San Cirilo de Alejandria.' EE 21, 1947, 35–83.

SALAVERRI J. 'El argumento de tradicion patristica en la antigua Iglesia.' RES 5, 1945, 107–119.

SANTER M. 'Ek Pneumatos Agiou kai Marias tes Parthenou.' JTS (NS) 22, 1971, 162–171. 'The authorship and occasion of Cyril of Alexandria's Sermon on the Virgin (Hom. Diversae iv).' Stud Pat. 12, 1975, 144–150.

SAUER J. Die Exegese des Cyrill von Alexandrien nach seinem Kommentar zum Johannesevangelium. Freiburg. 1965.

SCHAFER A. 'Die christologie des hl. Cyrill von Alexandrien in der römischen Kirche (432–534).' Theologische Quartalschrift, 77, 1895, 421–447.

SCHWARTZ E. 'Cyrill und die Mönch Victor.' Sitzungsberichte der Wiener Akademie der Wissenschaften, (Phil. Hist. Klasse), 208, 4, Vienna, 1928.

SIDDALS R.M. 'Oneness and difference in the Christology of Cyril of Alexandria.' Stud Pat. 18,1, Oxford, 1983, 207f. 'Logic and Christology in Cyril of Alexandria.' JTS (NS) 38, 1987, 341–367.

SIMONETTI M. 'Alcune osservazioni sul monofisimo di Cirillo d'Alessandria.' Augustinianum 22, 1982, 493–511.

SOUVAY C.L. 'The Twelve Anathematizations of St. Cyril.' CHR 5, 1926, 627–635.

STAROWIEYSKI M. 'Le titre Theotokos avant le concile d'Ephèse.' Stud Pat. 19,2. Louvain 1989, 166–172.

STRUCKMANN A. Die Eucharistielehre des hl. Cyrill von Alexandrien. Paderborn, 1910.

TAWIL J. 'S. Cyrille dans la Liturgie Grecque Byzantine.' in Kyrilliana, Cairo, 1947, 295–302.

TROOSTER S. 'De hl. Geest en de Menswording bij Cyrillus van Alexandrie.' BiNJ, 18, 1957, 375–397.

TSIRPANLIS C. 'Christological aspects of the thought of St. Cyril of Alexandria.' chs. 1–3 in (Ibid.) Greek Patristic Theology, New York, 1979.

VACCARI A. 'La grecità di S. Cirillo d'Alessandria.' Studi P. Ubaldi, Milan, 1937, 27–39.

VOÖBUS A. Discoveries of great import on the Commentary on Luke by Cyril of Alexandria. Stockholm, 1973.

WEIGL E. Die Heilslehre des hl. Cyrill von Alexandrien. Mainz, 1905. Christologie vom Tode des Athanasius bis zum Ausbruch des Nestorianischen Streites. München 1925.

WEISCHER B.M. 'Der Dialog dass 'Christus einer ist' des Cyrill von Alexandrien.' Or Chr 51, 1967, 130–185.

WICKHAM L.R. Cyril of Alexandria: Select Letters. (E.T.), Oxford, 1983.

'Symbols of the Incarnation in Cyril of Alexandria.' in Typos, Symbol, Allegorie bei den östlichen Vatern und ihren Parallelen im Mittelalter. Edd. M Schmidt & C.F. Geyer, Regensburg, 1982, 41–53. 'Cyril of Alexandria.' Encyclopedia of Early Christianity, New York, 1990, 249–250.

WILES M.F. 'The nature of the early debate about Christ's human soul.' JEH 16, 1965, 139–151.

WILKEN R.L. 'Tradition, Exegesis, and the Christological Controversies.' Church History 34, 1965, 123–145. 'Exegesis and the History of Theology: Some reflections on the Adam-Christ typology in Cyril of Alexandria.' Church History 35, 1966, 139–156. Judaism and the Early Christian Mind: A study of Cyril of Alexandria's Exegesis and Theology. London 1971.

WOLF J.B. Commentationes in S. Cyrilli Alexandrini de Spiritu Sancto doctrinam. Wurzburg, 1934.

WOLFSON H.A. 'Philosophical implications of Arianism and Apollinarism.' DOP, 12, 1958, 3–28.

YOUNG F.M. 'Christological ideas in the Greek Commentaries on the Epistle to the Hebrews.' JTS (NS) 20, 1969, 150–163. 'A re-consideration of Alexandrian Christology.' JEH 22,1971, 103–114. From Nicaea to Chalcedon, pp. 213–229,240–265, London, 1983. 'Exegetical Method and Scriptural Proof—The Bible in Doctrinal Debate.' Stud Pat. 19, 1989, 291–304.

BIBLIOGRAPHY C

STUDIES ON ANTIOCHENE CHRISTOLOGY

ABRAMOWSKI L. 'Der Streit um Diodore und Theodor zwischen ben beiden ephesinischen Konzilien.' ZKG 67, 1955–56, 252–282. 'Zur Theologie Theodors von Mopsuestia.' ZKG 72, 1961, 263–293. Untersuchungen zum Liber Heraclidis des Nestorius. CSCO 242, Subsidia 22, Louvain, 1963.

ABRAMOWSKI L. & GOODMAN A.E. (Eds.) A Nestorian Collection of Christological Texts. Vol. 1 (Syriac); vol.2. Introduction, E.T., and Indices. Cambridge, 1972.

ABRAMOWSKI R. 'Untersuchungen zu Diodor von Tarsus.' ZNW 30, 1931, 234–261. 'Der theologische Nachlass des Diodor von Tarsus.' ZNW 42, 1949, 19–69.

AMANN E. Théodore de Mopsueste. DTC 15, 235–279. 'La doctrine christologique de Théodore de Mopsueste.' Rev SR 14, 1934, 160–190. 'L'affaire Nestorius vue de Rome.' Rev SR 23, 1949, 5–37, 207–244; ibid. 24,1950, 28–52, 235–265.

ANASTOS M.V. 'Nestorius was orthodox.' DOP 16, 1962, 119–140.

BARDY G. 'Les débuts du Nestorianisme. 428–433.' in, Histoire de l'Église (Eds.) A. Fliche & V. Martin, vol.4, Paris, 1937, 163–196.

BEBIS G.S. Converging Trends in Nestorian Research From the Perspective of Orthodoxy. (Greek Text), Athens, 1964. 'The Apology of Nestorius: A new evaluation.' Stud Pat. 11, 1972, 107–112.

BERTRAM A. Theodoreti episcopi Cyrensis doctrina christologica. Hildesheim, 1883.

BETHUNE-BAKER J.F. Nestorius and His Teaching. Cambridge, 1908.

BRAATEN C.E. 'Modern Interpretations of Nestorius.' Church History 32, 1963, 251–267.

BRIÈRE M. 'La légende Syriaque de Nestorius.' ROC, 15, 1910. 17f.

CHABOT J.M. Synodicon Orientale ou receuil de Synodes Nestoriens. Paris. 1902.

CHESNUT R.C. 'The Two Prosopa in Nestorius' Bazaar of Heraclides.' JTS (NS) 29, 1978, 392–408.

DEVRÉESSE. R. Essai sur Théodore de Mopsueste. (ST 141), Rome 1948.

DEWART J. The Theology of Grace of Theodore of Mopsuestia. Washington, 1971. 'The notion of "Person" underlying the Christology of Theodore Mopsuestia.' Stud Pat. 12, 1975, 199–207.

DIEPEN H.M. 'L'assumptus Homo à Chalcedoine.' Rev Thom. 51, 1951, 573–608. Douze Dialogues de Christologie Ancienne. Rome. 1960. 'L'assumptus Homo patristique.' Rev Thom. 63, 1963, 225–245, 363–388; ibid. 64, 1964, 32–52.

DRIVER G.R. & HODGSON L. The Bazaar of Heraclides. Oxford, 1925.

EHRHARD A. Die Cyrill von Alexandrien zugeschriebene Schrift: Peri tes tou Kyriou enanthropeseos—ein Werk Theodorets von Cyrus. Tübingen, 1888.

GALTIER P. 'Théodore de Mopsueste: sa vrai pensée sur l'incarnation.' RSR 45, 1957, 161–186, 338–360.

GREER R.A. Theodore of Mopsuestia. Exegete and Theologian. London, 1961. 'The Image of God and the Prosopic Union in Nestorius' Bazaar of Heraclides.' in Lux in Lumine, (Ed.) R.A. Norris, Essays to Honour W.N. Pittenger, New York, 1966, 46–61. 'The Antiochene Christology of Diodore of Tarsus.' JTS 17, 1966, 327–341. The Captain of Our Salvation. Tubingen, 1973.

GRILLMEIER A. 'Das Scandalum Oecumenicum des Nestorius in Kirchlich-dogmatischer und theologiegeschichtlicher Sicht.' Schol. 36, 1961, 321–356. Christ in Christian Tradition. vol.1, (2nd Edn.) London 1975. 414–472, 488–519, 559–568.

GUINOT J.N. 'Présence d'Apollinaire dans l'oeuvre exégétique de Théodoret.' Stud Pat. 19,2, Louvain, 1989, 166–172.

HEFELE C.J. Histoire des Conciles. vol. 2, pt.1. Paris, 1908, 219–247.

HODGSON L. 'The Metaphysic of Nestorius.' JTS 19, 1918, 46–55.

JOUSSARD G. 'Le cas de Nestorius.' RHE 74, 1979, 346–348.

JUGIE M. Nestorius et la controverse nestorienne. Paris, 1912.

KOCH G. Die Heilsverwirklichung bei Theodor von Mopsuestia. München, 1965. Strukturen und Geschichte des Heils in der Theologie des Theodoret von Kyros. Frankfurter Theologische Studien 17, Frankfurt, 1974.

LOOFS F. Nestoriana. Halle 1905. Nestorius and his place in the History of Christian Doctrine. Cambridge, 1914.

McGUCKIN J.A. 'The Christology of Nestorius of Constantinople.' PBR 7, 2–3, 1988, 93–129. 'Did Augustine's Christology depend on Theodore Mopsuestia?' Heythrop Journal, 31, 1990, 39–52.

McKENZIE J.L. 'Annotations on the Christology of Theodore Mopsuestia.' Theological Studies 19, 1958, 354–373.

McNAMARA J. 'Theodore of Mopsuestia and the Nestorian Heresy.' ITQ 19, 1952, 254–268; ibid. 20, 1953, 172–191. 'Theodoret of Cyrus and the unity of Person in Christ.' ITQ 22, 1955, 313–328.

MANDAC M. 'L'Union christologique dans les oeuvres de Théodoret anterieures au Concile d'Ephèse. Eph Th Louv. 47, 1971, 64–96.

MONTALVERNE J. Theodoreti Cyrenensis doctrina antiquior de Verbo inhumanato.' Studia Antoniana 1, Rome 1948.

NAU F. Le Livre de Héraclide de Damas. Paris 1910.

NORRIS R.A. Manhood and Christ. A Study of the Christology of Theodore of Mopsuestia. Oxford, 1963.

PATTERSON L. Theodore Mopsuestia and Modern Thought. London 1926.

PERICOLI-RIDOLFINI F. 'La controversia tra Cirillo d'Alessandria e Giovanni d'Antiochia nell'epistolario di Andrea da Samosata.' Rivista degli Studi Orientali 29, 1954, 187–217.

REINE F.J. The Eucharistic Doctrine of the Mystagogical Catecheses of Theodore Mopsuestia. Washington, 1942.

RICHARD M. 'Un écrit de Theodoret sur l'unité du Christ après l'incarnation.'

Rev SR 14, 1934, 34–61. 'L'activité littéraire de Théodoret avant le Concile d'Ephèse.' RSPT 24, 1935, 83–106. 'Notes sur l'évolution doctrinale de Théodoret.' RSPT 25, 1936, 459–481. 'Théodoret, Jean d'Antioche et les moines d'Orient.' MSR 3, 1946, 147–156. 'Les traités de Cyrille d'Alexandrie contre Diodore et Théodore et les fragments dogmatiques de Diodore de Tarse.' in Mélanges F. Grat, Paris, 1946, 99–116.

VAN ROEY A. 'Two new documents of the Nestorian controversy.' Stud Pat. 7, 1966, 308–313.

ROMANIDES J.S. 'Highlights in the debate over Theodore of Mopsuestia's Christology and some suggestions for a fresh approach.' GOTR, 5, 1959–1960, 140–185.

SCIPIONI L.I. Richerche sulla christologia del Libro di Eraclido di Nestorio: La formulazione teologica e il suo contesto filosofico. Paradosis II, Freiburg, 1956. Nestorio e il Concilio di Efeso: storia, dogma, critica. Studia Patristica Mediolanensia, 1. Milan, 1974.

SELLERS R.V. Two Ancient Christologies. London, 1940.

SULLIVAN F.A. The Christology of Theodore of Mopsuestia. Rome, 1956. 'Further notes on Theodore Mopsuestia: A reply to Fr. McKenzie.' Theological Studies 20, 1959, 264–279.

SWETE H.B. Theodori Episcopi Mopsuesteni in Epp. Beati Pauli Commentarii. (Introduction) vol.1, Cambridge, 1880; Farnborough 1969.

TONNEAU R. & DEVRÉESSE R. (Eds.) Les Homelies Catéchétiques de Théodore de Mopsueste. ST 145, Rome, 1949.

TURNER H.E.W. 'Nestorius reconsidered.' Stud Pat. 13, 1975, 306–321.

VINE A.R. An Approach to Christology: An interpretation and development of some elements in the metaphysic and christology of Nestorius as a way of approach to an orthodox christology compatible with modern thought. London. 1948.

VOGHT H.J. 'Papst Coelestin und Nestorius.' in Konzil und Papst: fur H Tuchle. München 1975, 85–102.

WILES M.F. 'Theodore Mopsuestia as Representative of the Antiochene School.' in, Cambridge History of the Bible, vol.1, 1970, 489–510.

YOUNG F.M. From Nicaea to Chalcedon. London 1983, 182–240.

ZIEGENHAUS A. 'Die Genesis des Nestorianismus.' MTZ 23, 1972, 335–353.

BIBLIOGRAPHY D

FURTHER CYRILLINE STUDIES

BLANCHETTE, O. 'St. Cyril of Alexandria's Idea of Redemption.' Sciences Ecclésiastiques 16, 1964, 455–480.

BOULNOIS, M. O. 'Le souffle et l'Esprit: Exégèses patristiques de l'insufflation originelle de Gen.2.7 en lien avec celle de Jn. 20.22.' Recherches Augustiniennes 24, 1989, 3–37.

——. 'Le paradoxe trinitaire chez S. Cyrille d'Alexandrie.' Paris, (Institut des Etudes Augustiniennes), 1994.

——. 'L'Eucharistie, mystère d'union chez Cyrille d'Alexandria: les modèles d'union trinitaire et christologique.' Revue des Sciences Religieuses 74, 2000, 147–172.

——. 'Liberté, origine du mal, et prescience divine selon Cyrille d'Alexandrie.' Revue des Etudes Augustiniennes 46, 2000, 61–82.

GOULD G. 'Cyril of Alexandria and the Formula of Reunion.' Downside Review 106, 1988, 235– 252.

HALLMAN J.M. 'The Seed of Divine Fire: Divine Sufferings in the Christology of Cyril of Alexandria and Nestorius of Constantinople.' Journal of Early Christian Studies 5, 1997, 369–391.

KEATING, D.A. 'The Baptism of Jesus in Cyril of Alexandria: The Re-Creation of the Human Race.' Pro Ecclesia 8, 1999, 201– 222.

——.'The Two-Fold Manner of Divine Indwelling in Cyril of Alexandria: Redressing an Imbalance.' Studia Patristica 37, 2001, 543–549.

——.'The Appropriation of Divine Life in Cyril of Alexandria.' DPhil. Diss. Oxford University, 2000. (Forthcoming in OUP Theological Monographs Series).

MCGUCKIN, J.A. 'St. Cyril of Alexandria: Homily on the Feast of St. John the Theologian.' Sourozh (Journal of the Russian Orthodox Church in England) 51, Autumn 1993, 34–35.

——. 'Moses and the Mystery of Christ in St. Cyril of Alexandria's Exegesis.' Coptic Church Review 21.1 , 2000, 24–32.

——. 'Moses and the Mystery of Christ in St. Cyril of Alexandria's Exegesis.' Coptic Church Review 21.2 , 2000, 98–114.

——. 'St. Cyril of Alexandria.' in The Dictionary of Historical Theology, T. A. Hart (Ed.). Exeter (and Eerdmans), 2000.

——. 'The Paradox of the Virgin–Theotokos: Evangelism and Imperial Politics in the Fifth Century Byzantine World.' in Maria (A Journal of Marian Theology) 3, Autumn 2001, 5–23.

——. 'Cyril of Alexandria: Bishop and Pastor.' in The Theology of Cyril of Alexandria; A Critical Appreciation, T. Weinandy, and D.A. Keating (Eds.).

London and New York, 2003, 205–236.
——. 'Il Lungo Cammino Verso Calcedonia.' (The Long Road to Chalcedon: The unfolding nexus of Christological definition from Origen to Dioscorus). in Il Concilio di Calcedonia 1550 Anni Dopo, A. Ducay (Ed.). Rome, 2002, 13–41.
——. 'Cyril of Alexandria.' in The Westminster Handbook to Patristic Theology, J. A. McGuckin. Louisville, Kentucky, 2004.
MCKINION, S.A. Words, Imagery, and the Mystery of Christ; A Reconstruction of Cyril of Alexandria's Christology. Leiden, 2000.
MEUNIER, B. Le Christ de Cyrille d'Alexandrie: L'humanité, le salut, et la question monophysite. Paris, 1997.
O'KEEFE, J. J. 'Interpreting the Angel: Cyril of Alexandria and Theodoret of Cyrus, Commentators on the Book of Malachi.' PhD. Diss. Catholic University of America, 1993.
——. 'Christianizing Malachi: Fifth Century Insights from Cyril of Alexandria.' Vigiliae Christianae 50, 1996, 136–158.
——. 'Kenosis or Impassibility? Cyril of Alexandria and Theodoret of Cyrus on the Problem of Divine Pathos.' Studia Patristica 32, 1997, 358–365.
——. 'Impassable Suffering? Divine Passion and Fifth Century Christology.' Theological Studies 58, 1997, 39–60.
RUSSELL, N., (Trs.). Cyril of Alexandria. London, 2000.
UNGER, D. 'Christ Jesus: The Secure Foundation according to St. Cyril of Alexandria.' Franciscan Studies 7, 1947, 1–25.
WEINANDY, T.G. 'The Soul–Body Analogy and the Incarnation: Cyril of Alexandria.' Coptic Church Review 17, 1996, 59–66.
——. 'The Incarnation–The Impassable Suffers.' in Does God Suffer?, T.G. Weinandy. London and New York, 2000, 172–213.
WEINANDY, T.G., AND D. A. KEATING (Eds.). The Theology of St. Cyril of Alexandria: A Critical Appreciation. London and New York, 2003.
WELCH, L.J. Christology and Eucharist in the Early Thought of Cyril of Alexandria. San Francisco, 1994.
——. 'Logos–Sarx? Sarx and the Soul of Christ in the Early Thought of Cyril of Alexandria.' St. Vladimir's Theological Quarterly 38, 1994, 271–292.
WILKEN, R.L. 'St. Cyril of Alexandria: The Mystery of Christ in the Bible.' Pro Ecclesia 4, 1995, 454–478.
——. 'St. Cyril of Alexandria: Biblical Expositor.' Coptic Church Review 19, 1998, 30–41.

INDEX OF ANCIENT NAMES

(Excluding Cyril and Nestorius)

INDEX OF THEMES

SCRIPTURAL INDEX

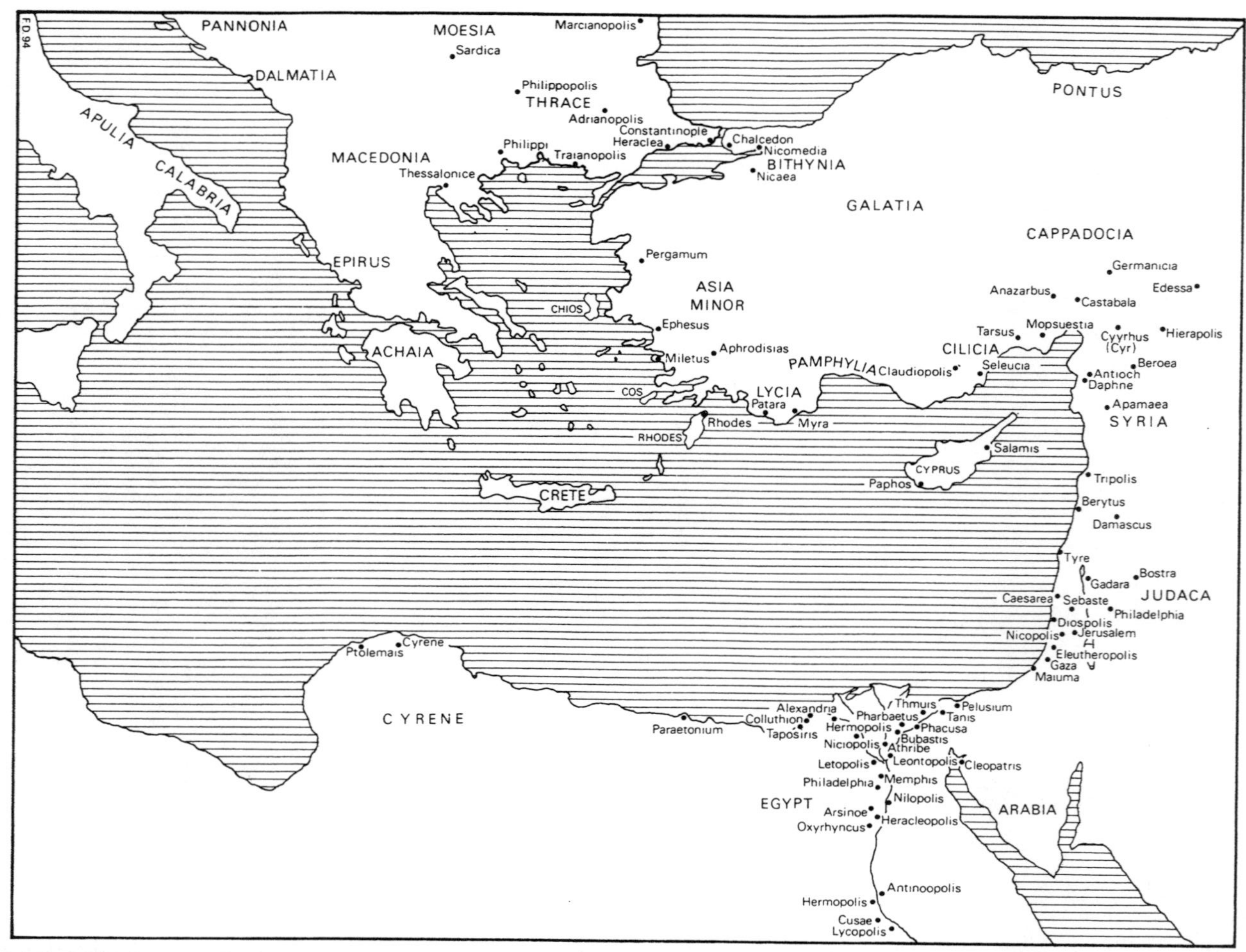

PANNONIA
DALMATIA
MOESIA
Sardica
Marcianopolis
Philippopolis
THRACE
Adrianopolis
Constantinople
Heraclea
Chalcedon
Nicomedia
BITHYNIA
Nicaea
PONTUS
APULIA
CALABRIA
MACEDONIA
Philippi
Traianopolis
Thessalonice
GALATIA
CAPPADOCIA
EPIRUS
Pergamum
ASIA
MINOR
Germanicia
Edessa
Anazarbus
Castabala
CHIOS
Ephesus
Tarsus
Mopsuestia
Cyyrhus
(Cyr)
Hierapolis
ACHAIA
Miletus
Aphrodisias
PAMPHYLIA
Claudiopolis
CILICIA
Seleucia
Beroea
Antioch
Daphne
COS
LYCIA
Patara
Apamaea
SYRIA
Rhodes
Myra
RHODES
Salamis
CYPRUS
Tripolis
Paphos
CRETE
Berytus
Damascus
Tyre
Gadara
Bostra
JUDACA
Caesarea
Sebaste
Philadelphia
Diospolis
Nicopolis
Jerusalem
Eleutheropolis
Gaza
Maiuma
Ptolemais
Cyrene
C Y R E N E
Alexandria
Thmuis
Pelusium
Pharbaetus
Tanis
Colluthion
Hermopolis
Phacusa
Paraetonium
Taposiris
Bubastis
Niciopolis
Athribe
Letopolis
Leontopolis
Cleopatris
Philadelphia
Memphis
EGYPT
Nilopolis
ARABIA
Arsinoe
Heracleopolis
Oxyrhyncus
Antinoopolis
Hermopolis
Cusae
Lycopolis
F.D. 94

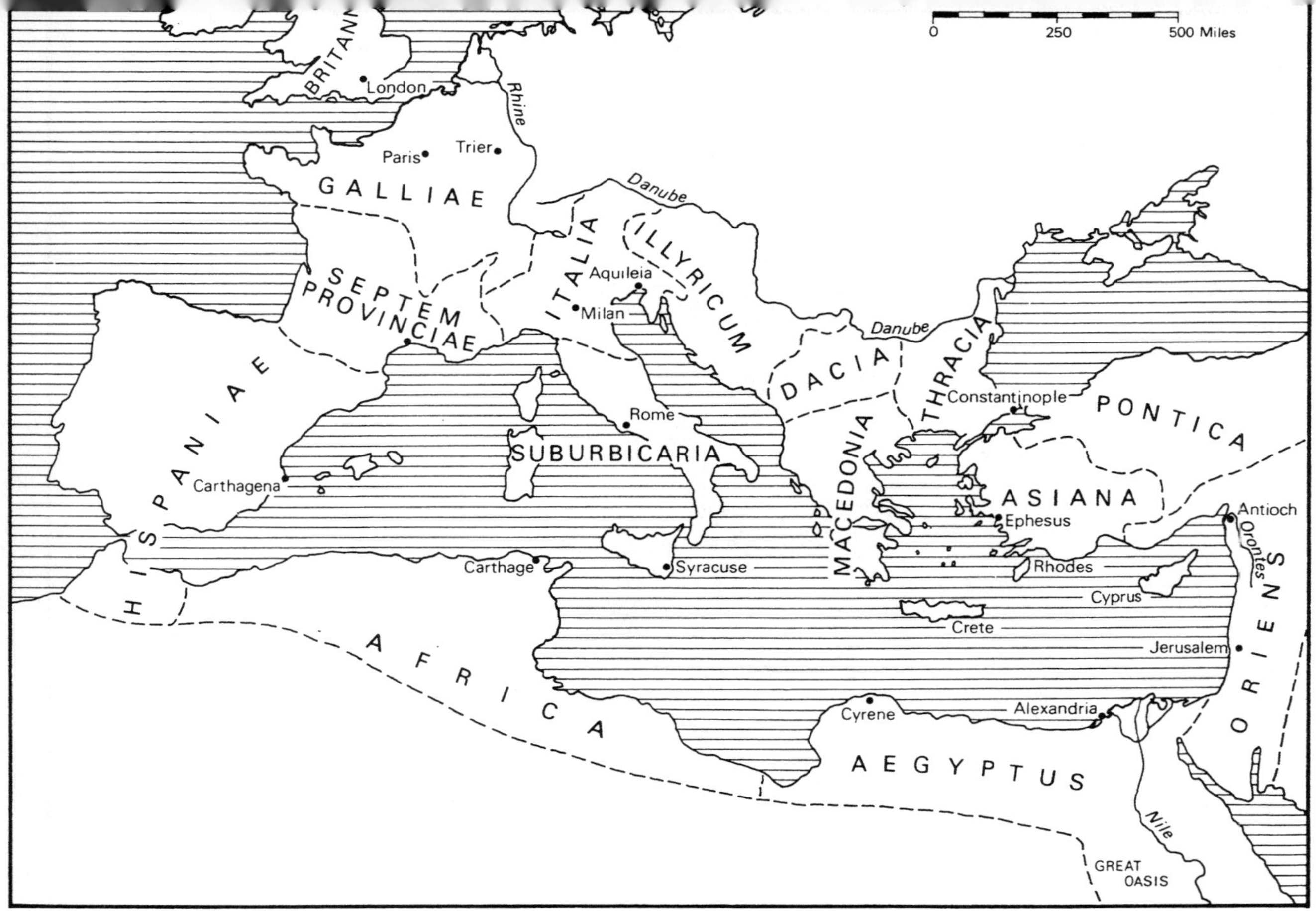

The Roman Empire

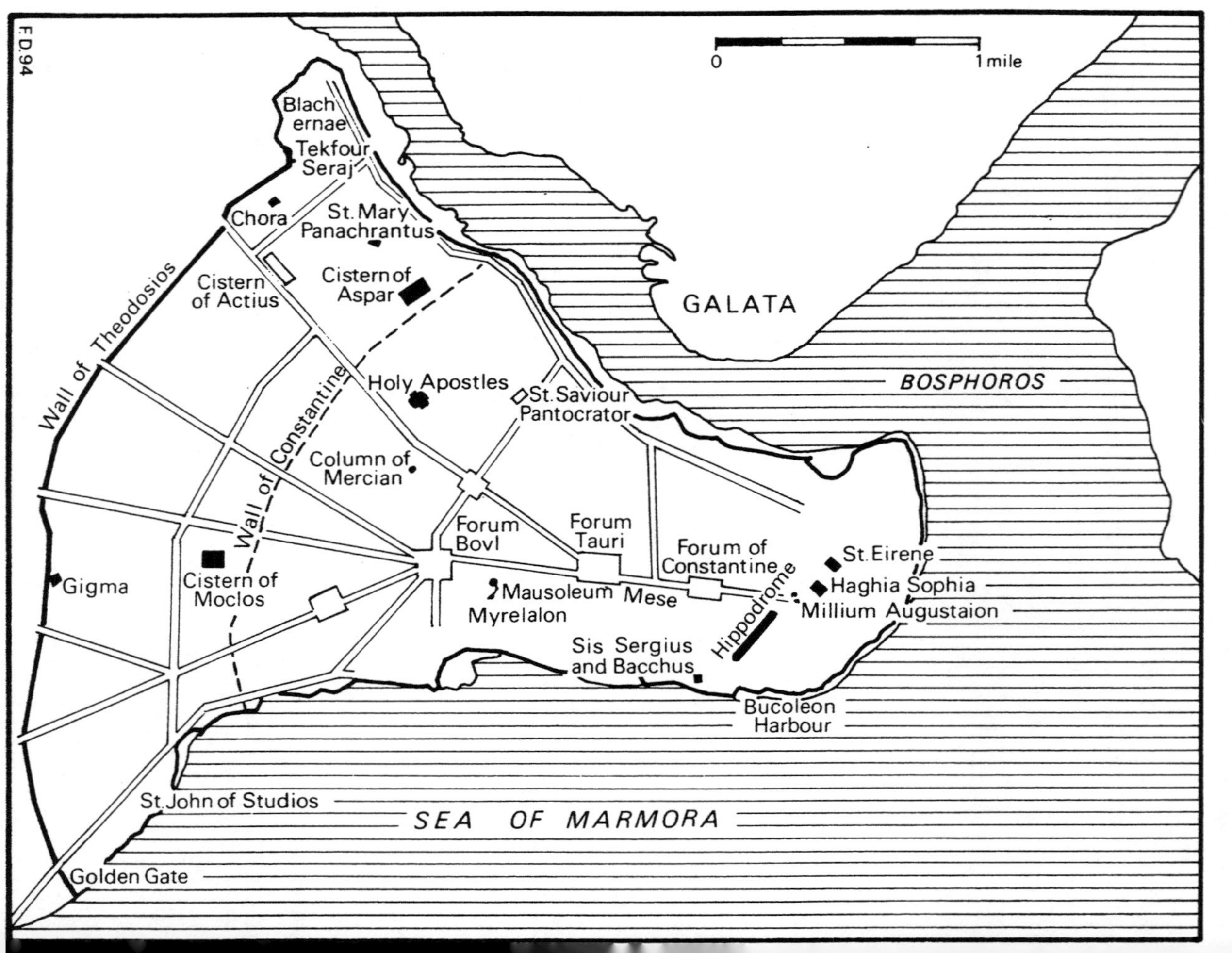

F.D.94
0
1 mile
GALATA
BOSPHOROS
SEA OF MARMORA
Blachernae
Tekfour Seraj
Chora
St. Mary Panachrantus
Cistern of Aspar
Cistern of Actius
Wall of Theodosios
Wall of Constantine
Holy Apostles
St. Saviour Pantocrator
Column of Mercian
Forum Bovl
Forum Tauri
Forum of Constantine
St. Eirene
Haghia Sophia
Millium Augustaion
Hippodrome
Mausoleum
Myrelalon
Mese
Sis Sergius and Bacchus
Bucoleon Harbour
Gigma
Cistern of Moclos
St. John of Studios
Golden Gate

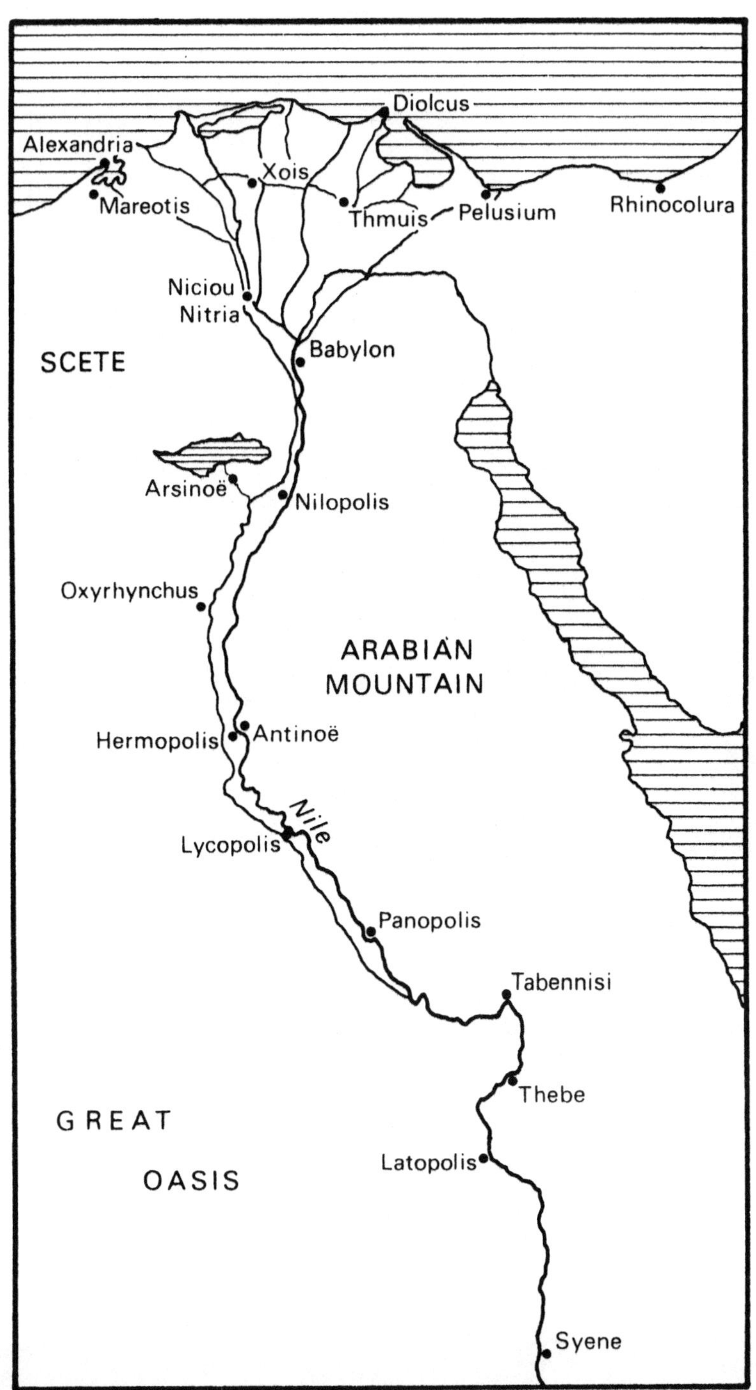

Christian Egypt

MEDITERRANEAN SEA
Myrmex
Pier
Pharos (Lighthouse)
Pier
Temple of Isis Iochias
Macedonian Acropolis
GREAT HARBOR
PHAROS I
Temple of Isis Phariae
Fort
Matouma
Posidium
Timonium
Antirrhodos
Arsenal
Palace
Broucheion
Heptastadion
Present Shoreline
EUNOSTOS HARBOR
Emporium Caesarium
Temple of Bendis
Obelisks
Theater
Public gardens
Aspendia
Navalia
Kibotos
Fort
Tycheum Agora
St. Athanasius
Hadrian's Palace
Temple of Isis Plusia
Tetrapylon
Temple of Saturn
Dromus
Paneum
Sema
Temple of Serapis
Fort
Gymnasium
Sungate
Palestra
Dicosterium
Transversal Ave.
Moon Gate
Dromos
Theonas Ch.
Mosque of Amrou
Byzantine and Arab Walls
Macedonian camp
Jewish Quarter
Delta Quarter
Sepulchers
Copriae
Canopic Street
Copriae
Sepulchers
Hyppodrome
Canopian Gate
Eleusis on Sea
Jewish Christian Sepulchers
Hypogea
Roman Camp
Roman military Cemetery
Temple
Vallis Juxtus Sepulcra
Temple of Ceres and Proserpina
ELEUSIS PLAIN
Temple
Hypogea
Eleusis
St. Peter Martyr Cemetery
Suburb of the Necropolis
Catacombs
Western Necropolis
Hypogea
Catacombs
Christian Catacombs
Rhakotis
Column of Diocletian
Great Serapeum
Copriae
Harbor the of river
Mole
Phiale
Underground Chapel
Fluvius Novus
(Canal of Alexandria)
Port of the Lake
Great Mole
Lake Canal
LAKE MAREOTIS
0
1 mile
FD 94

Plan of Alexandria